Merchandise Buying

Merchandise Buying

Third
Edition

Maryanne Smith Bohlinger

Professor, Marketing Management
Coordinator, Retail Management/Fashion Buying Programs
Community College at Philadelphia

Allyn and Bacon

Boston   London   Sydney   Toronto

Copyright © 1990, 1983 by Allyn and Bacon
A Division of Simon & Schuster, Inc.
160 Gould Street
Needham Heights, MA 02194

© 1977 Wm. C. Brown Publishers

Series Editor: Henry Reece
Series Editorial Assistant: Katherine Grubbs
Production Administrator: Marjorie Payne
Text Designer: Suzanne Harbison
Cover Administrator: Linda Dickinson
Manufacturing Buyer: William Alberti
Composition Buyer: Linda Cox

Library of Congress Cataloging-in-Publication Data

Bohlinger, Maryanne Smith.
  Merchandise buying.
  Includes bibliographical references.
  1. Purchasing.   I. Title
HF5437.B535   1990   658.7′2   89-18104
ISBN 0-205-12196-9

Printed in the United States of America
10 9 8 7 6 5 4 3 2 1   94 93 92 91 90

Printed in the United States of America
10 9 8 7 6 5 4 3 2 1   94 93 92 91 90

To my husband, Jerry

Contents

11 ■ THE RESOURCES OF MERCHANDISE: DOMESTIC AND FOREIGN   375

12 ■ SERVICES OFFERED BY MERCHANDISE RESOURCES   411

Preface

This text has been written for those students who may someday enter the retail marketplace as well as for the retailing practitioner who desires a review of basic buying and merchandising principles. This text has been written also for those who are already in business for themselves and who want to strengthen their entrepreneurial and managerial skills.

The major goals of this text, *Merchandise Buying, Third Edition,* is to enable the reader—whether college student, retailing practitioner, or new entrepreneur—the opportunity to become a good merchandise planner and decision maker and to be able to adjust successfully to ever-changing conditions in the retailing environment.

As in the first and second editions, *Merchandise Buying, Third Edition,* provides information that is teachable and readable, rich in content, stimulating, yet practical. Thanks to the suggestions of reviewers and of professors who used the second edition, a number of practical elements were retained and a number of revisions were made in the third edition.

Merchandise Buying, Third Edition, continues to retain these practical elements:
- A one-semester format
- Examples of nationally known stores illustrating merchandising principles
- A list of merchandising categories in fashion and home furnishings to make students aware of the many career possibilities open to them
- A table of trade organizations and publications to direct students toward their specific career objectives
- An entire section in chapter 3 devoted to getting a job in the retail business
- Small business management tips that will assist new entrepreneurs
- The most current information from all major academic and professional/trade publications
- Hundreds of real-life examples to capture and hold the student's interest.

Merchandise Buying, Third Edition, provides improved pedagogical aids including updated statistics and references to help students increase their knowledge of merchandising.

■ Performance Objectives
■ Study guides and review boxes
■ Tables, sample store forms, and illustrations
■ Trade terminology highlighted in italics and listed at the end of each chapter
■ Questions for Discussion and Review
■ Mini-cases presenting typical retail situations
■ Retailing Activities to Stimulate Interest and Participation
■ The Retail Student's Reference Library

Merchandise Buying, Third Edition, continues to provide appendices as valuable retailing guides:

■ Appendix A: Glossary of Trade Terms
■ Appendix B: Merchandise Mathematical Formulas
■ Appendix C: Selected Firms Seeking Qualified People
■ Appendix D: Small Business Management Aids to Assist the New Entrepreneur
■ Appendix E: Selected Manufacturers of Men's, Women's, Children's, and Infants' Wear Seeking Qualified Merchandising Graduates

Merchandise Buying, Third Edition, has been substantially revised and updated in order to provide an in-depth coverage of merchandising principles that will both challenge students and ensure a working knowledge of the retail trade.

■ Chapters are restructured to flow more logically through the merchandising/buying process.
■ Up-to-date computer applications to merchandising covering such diverse topics as electronic retailing (chapter 1), technological advancements (chapter 2), dollar planning (chapter 7), unit planning (chapter 8), the merchandise control process (chapter 9), and electronic marking systems (chapter 12).
■ Organization charts in chapter 4 further illustrate the merchandising function and its relationship to other store functions for the small business, the department and specialty store, and the chain operation.
■ Merchandise math formulas and examples are illustrated in chapters 7, 8, 9, 14.
■ Expanded coverage of merchandise resources—domestic and foreign—(chapter 11) discusses trade-market centers, problems when

purchasing goods in foreign markets, a listing of major foreign producers, the importance of the import order form, and the role of the
customs broker.

- Chapter 13 highlights techniques that a buyer may use when determining the selection of manufacturer's brands, private labels, and
designer labels.

- The following revisions in chapters 1, 2, 3, 4, 5, 7, 8, 9 are significant:

Chapter 1 has been expanded to include information on marketing, marketing channels of distribution, and the role of retailing in
the marketing system. A description of various types of retail stores
and their evolution into the merchandising giants of the 1990s—for
example, hypermarkets, warehouse retailers, and home centers. Off-
price retailers have also been included. Identification of trends in
non-store retailing such as the explosion of electronic retailing—
video catalogs/cable shopping—has been highlighted. Department
store retailing, the high growth-rate of specialty stores, and the tremendous growth in shopping malls throughout the country and in
Canada have been emphasized.

Chapter 2 has been updated to include discussions on the buyer's
role in merchandising in the 1990s and how he/she must keep pace.
Specific topics include: economic and market trends, technological
advancements in the computer field and their application to retailing, and competitive strategies used. The use of diversifications and
mergers by large retailers to sustain and enhance sales, and the
implications of federal regulations are discussed.

Chapter 3 has been updated and reorganized to include discussions on the buyer's responsibility in merchandising and how the
degree of responsibility may be affected by the organizational structure of the retail store (discussed in further detail in chapter 4),
types of goods offered, store's dollar volume, and location of store
branches or units.

Chapter 4 has been reorganized to include an in-depth discussion
of how a store's organizational structure will affect buying responsibilities. Similarities and differences that exist among the department store, chain operation, and the small business are stressed
with detailed coverage on central buying.

Chapter 5 includes a section on the consumer decision-making
process and elements that make up the process. In addition, information regarding the buying roles of family members and the family
life cycle, definition, and stages has been included.

Chapter 7 has been rewritten and it discusses the planning process—the logical first step when developing a merchandise assortment whether for a fashion department or departments carrying
hard goods. The planning process includes both dollar planning (in

terms of merchandise budgets) and unit planning (in terms of merchandise lists). Unit planning will be discussed further in chapter 8.

Chapter 8 continues the discussion on the merchandise planning process—unit planning. Features include a discussion on how unit plans are developed, how to plan a basic stock list, how to plan a model stock, and how to plan fill-ins for the model stock plan and home furnishings.

Chapter 9 has been updated and deals with the control function of management and its application to merchandising.

■ CONTENTS

The text is divided into five parts. The first four chapters provide an overview of the retailing environment and include discussions on such topics as: the role of retailing in the marketing system; the evolution of retailing; external forces affecting the buyer's environment such as technological advancements, competition, diversifications, and mergers; the buyer's responsibilities in merchandising; and similarities and differences in buying responsibilities.

The next two chapters discuss the role of the buyer in forecasting consumer needs, wants, and desires, and such topics as understanding consumer behavior and the importance and application of fashion information.

The following three chapters deal with the buyer's role in merchandise management—the planning and controlling process—and such topics as dollar planning, unit planning, and the merchandise control process, that is, systems and applications.

The next four chapters discuss merchandise resources (both domestic and foreign) and the types and importance of resident buying offices, resources of merchandise (both domestic and foreign), services offered by merchandise resources, and the importance of developing good buyer/vendor relations.

The remaining two chapters deal with the buyer's role in preparing merchandise for sale, pricing merchandise for profit, and the role of the buyer in the selling process.

Five appendices are provided: Appendix A: Glossary of Trade Terms Used in Merchandise Buying; Appendix B: Merchandise Math Formulas Used by Buying Specialists and Their Assistants; Appendix C:

Selected Firms Seeking Qualified People for Merchandising Positions; Appendix D: Small Business Management Aids (to assist the new entrepreneur in decision making); and Appendix E: Selected Manufacturers of Men's, Women's, Children's, and Infant's Wear Seeking Qualified Merchandising Graduates.

■ INSTRUCTOR'S MANUAL

The Instructor's Manual includes chapter outlines, lecture notes, chapter summaries, teaching objectives, answers to end-of-chapter questions, answers to section-ending mini-cases, suggested projects to stimulate students' interest and participation, and a listing of transparencies.

Acknowledgments

There are a number of people to whom I owe a debt of gratitude in the preparation of this third edition. This textbook would not have been possible without the encouragement and advice of many dedicated individuals in the field of retailing. I am most grateful to Ms JoAnne Disanto of the John Wanamaker Department Store and Mr. Richard Dallas of the Strawbridge & Clothier Department Store, both in Philadelphia, for their generous assistance and cooperation. I would also like to express special thanks to the National Retail Merchants Association, O'Shea's Department Store, Sears, K-Mart Corp, Bailey Banks & Biddle, Lord & Taylor, The Gift Gallery, La Bella Moda, Vanity Fair, Saks Fifth Avenue, L.S. Ayres, QVC Network, Inc., Mitsubishi Electronics America, Inc., Filene's Basement, Rouse Co., Hechinger, International Fashion Boutique Show, Retail News Bureau, Macy's, Mr. Paul M. Mazur, and to the many other retail executives who have made significant contributions.

I am most grateful to my colleagues at Community College of Philadelphia for their helpful suggestions and comments, and especially to my students, whose desire for knowledge of and enthusiasm for the retail fashion industry has inspired me to prepare the third edition.

Finally, I wish to thank Peter Gordon, Southeast Missouri State University; David Netherton, Old Dominion University; Ray Tewell, American River College; Morton Klein, Fashion Institute of Technology; Ellen Goldsberry, University of Arizona, who patiently reviewed this manuscript.

Merchandise Buying

SECTION

1

The Buyer's Role in the Retailing Environment

Courtesy of The Rouse Co., Columbia, Maryland.

Elements of Buying and Merchandising

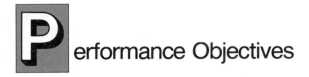erformance Objectives

After reading this chapter, the student should be able to accomplish the following:

1. Define marketing and discuss how the various definitions of marketing differ.

2. Discuss various marketing functions.

3. Define marketing channel of distribution and discuss activities of various channel members.

4. Define retailing, retailer, and retail store.

5. Learn what distinguishes retailers from other members of the channel of distribution.

6. Explain the role of retailing in the marketing system.

7. Discuss the evolution of different types of retail stores and relate how these stores have adapted to different conditions in the marketplace.

8. Outline and explain the various forms of nonstore retailing.

Elements of Buying and Merchandising

Marketing is defined as human activity directed at satisfying needs and wants through exchange processes. (Courtesy of Hechinger, Landover, Md.)

INTRODUCTION

Before we can begin a discussion of retail buying and the various activities the retail buyer is concerned with in merchandising, it is important to understand the place of retailing in the competitive business environment.

We have all had the experience of shopping at different types of stores—specialty, department, variety, discount, or boutique. In addition, we have visited a fast-food franchise, made retail purchases over the telephone, traveled to factory outlets, watched the "shopper channel" on television, and perused catalogs. Although personal experiences such as these provide some insight into various retailing activities, we need to go beyond personal experiences in order to fully comprehend the job of buying specialist. We need to examine organizational, operational, and competitive strategies of the types of retail stores as well as their place in the marketing system as a whole. We will begin our discussion with a definition of marketing, learn the place of retailing in the marketing system, and review how various types of retail stores have evolved. We will examine recent trends in retail store development as well as the effect of nonstore retailing on buying decisions used by retailers, entrepreneurs, and storebuyers alike.

PART 1—The Buying Activity: An Introduction

MARKETING: DEFINITION AND FUNCTIONS

According to the American Marketing Association, *"Marketing may be defined as the performance of business activities that direct the flow of goods and services from producer to consumer or user."*[1] This definition, however, excludes the operations of private and public nonprofit organizations that are also involved in marketing.

A more contemporary definition of marketing applies to all organizations that perform marketing-like activities. With this in mind, *marketing is defined as human activity directed at satisfying needs and wants through exchange processes.*[2]

As the term implies, *marketing* is focused on the marketplace and, for many generations of shoppers, the word *marketing* meant going to a store or marketplace to make purchases. For this reason most people mistakenly think the primary function of marketing is to advertise and sell goods. In the broadest sense, then, the function of marketing is to bring buyer and seller together. The buyer and seller, however, are only part of a larger "marketing mix" that includes many activities such as research, product development, pricing, distribution, storage, credit, and risk taking. It is interesting to note that about one-third of the 95 million working people in the United States are engaged in marketing or a related activity.

Functions Performed by Marketing

1. Advertising and Selling Goods
2. Market Research
3. Product Development
4. Pricing
5. Distribution
6. Storage
7. Arranging Credit
8. Risk Taking

Marketing professionals help create and bring about exchanges by performing certain functions. Some may stress one function over another. For example, manufacturers take responsibility for transporting goods to convenient locations. Wholesalers alert retailers to the product's availability. Retailers provide a convenient exchange place for the ultimate consumer. Some functions, such as providing product information, setting market price, and risk taking, may be shared by a number of marketing specialists. What is important to remember, however, is that an individual or organization must perform these functions in order for an exchange to occur.

However, how are these various marketing specialists organized in the marketing system in order for the exchange process to occur?

MARKETING CHANNELS OF DISTRIBUTION: DEFINITION

Various marketing specialists are organized in the marketing system through a *channel of distribution that may be defined as the sequence of marketing specialists or activities involved in bringing a product from the producer to the ultimate consumer.* Figure 1–1 illustrates a basic channel of distribution consisting of the manufacturer, the wholesaler, the retailer and the ultimate consumer.

As you can see, the marketing channel of distribution can be characterized by a number of different channel members or activities ranging from the complex to the simple.

One distribution method (and the most complex) is the purchase of goods through both wholesalers and retailers. In this case, manufacturers rely on wholesalers to reach retailers who in turn will stock their products and sell them to final consumers.

A second distribution method is for manufacturers to go directly to retailers, eliminating the wholesaler. Usually, producers of appliances, furniture, and designer clothing use this method.

A third distribution method is for the manufacturer to go directly to the final consumer, eliminating both the wholesaler and the retailer. These

Figure 1–1　A Basic Channel of Distribution

```
Method 1   Manufacturer → Wholesaler → Retailer → UC
Method 2   Manufacturer ──────────────→Retailer → UC
Method 3   Manufacturer ────────────────────→ UC
Method 4   Manufacturer → Wholesaler        → UC
```

producers use direct marketing techniques such as direct mail, catalogs, door-to-door selling, or television. Examples are Avon cosmetics, Spiegel mail order, and Tupperware.

A fourth distribution method, the factory store, is for the manufacturer to sell to the wholesaler who in turn goes directly to the final consumer. In this case the wholesaler becomes a "wholesale outlet"—or the wholesaler may be a sidewalk stand or street vendor.

What is important to remember, however, is that, even though a manufacturer or wholesaler may choose to eliminate a retailer when attempting to reach the final consumer, it *cannot eliminate the retailing function.* Thus, manufacturers or wholesalers who sell directly to consumers have taken over, not eliminated, the retailing function in the channel of distribution.

Specifically, however, what is retailing and what distinguishes retailing from other market specialists and activities?

RETAILING: DEFINITION AND DISTINGUISHING CHARACTERISTICS

Retailing may be defined as the summation of all activities involved in the sale of goods or services directly to the ultimate consumer for personal, non-business use. A retailer is a merchant whose primary business is selling goods or services directly to the ultimate consumer. The retail institution or store is the place where the actual sales activity or exchange takes place.

However, what distinguishes retailers from other members of the channel of distribution, that is manufacturers and wholesalers?

1. Retailers sell in small quantities.

Retailers sell in smaller, individual units more frequently than do manufacturers or wholesalers who usually sell in larger quantities such as cases or lots.

2. Retailers sell to the general public in a convenient location.

Retailers provide a pleasant shopping environment with business hours and atmospherics (lighting, displays, music, etc.) that are targeted to the shopping tastes of the consumer. Manufacturers and wholesalers are less concerned with the physical appearance of the business, are usually open nine to five, five days a week, and gear their marketing strategies to other middlemen such as rack jobbers, distributors, wholesalers, and retailers. Factory and wholesale outlets are an exception.

3. Retailers charge a higher price per unit of merchandise.

The consumer usually purchases only a few units at a time from a retailer while manufacturers and wholesalers purchase quantities of goods such as cases or lots. As a result of purchasing large amounts of goods, wholesalers and manufacturers are given discounts that lower the unit price per item.

4. Retailers use a one-price policy.

Consumers usually accept the price of items set by the retailer. Wholesalers and manufacturers will bargain the price of goods based on quantity purchase, type of credit, shipping terms, services provided, etc.

5. Retailers rely on the general public to visit the store.

Retailers rely on the general public to make the initial contact by visiting the store. Wholesalers and manufacturers make the initial sales contact, usually by employing sales representatives to call on various accounts.

THE ROLE OF RETAILING IN THE MARKETING SYSTEM

The role of retailing in the marketing system involves several activities.

1. Retailing brings retailers (sellers) and customers (buyers) together.

By advertising and promoting products or services, retailers draw customers into the store thereby encouraging them to buy.

2. Retailing gives the product or service place utility.

By having the product or service available (in stock) the retailer provides merchandise at a convenient time and place for the customer.

3. Retailing provides feedback.

By carefully watching consumer buying habits, retailers pass information on to manufacturers and wholesalers who in turn can provide consumers with what they want.

4. Retailing breaks bulk.

By buying large quantities of merchandise, retailers can break goods into smaller, more convenient packages or units as well as have more goods available at any one time.

5. Retailing assumes storage function.

By receiving goods in advance of the season, retailers assist the distribution system by assuming the storage function, facilitating the movement of goods along the distribution channel.

6. Retailing assumes risk.

By purchasing goods from manufacturers or wholesalers in advance of the season or before goods are sold, the retailer runs the risk of being stuck with unsold merchandise, which could lead to little or no profits. However, this practice gives other middlemen a more stable financial environment.

RETAIL INSTITUTIONS: AN EVOLUTION

If you had the opportunity to trace retailing transactions throughout the course of history, you would find that such activities occurred as early as prehistoric times. Records show that the caveman would trade goods for other goods that would provide the basic necessities of a very primitive lifestyle. The business transaction was a very simple one, since producer met face to face with consumer to accomplish an exchange. That meeting was the beginning of what is known today as retail trade.

References to retail trade and the many business transactions involved have been found in the numerous writings of the ancient Egyptians, about 3000 B.C. They are said to be the first people to have a well-developed system of trade. It would be interesting to visualize the Egyptian trader in the marketplace drawing up business contracts, negotiating for a loan, formalizing a trade agreement, and extending credit to customers.

During the Middle Ages (which historians place between the fall of Rome in A.D. 476 and the fall of Constantinople in 1453), populations expanded and provided more opportunities to sell goods. The town became the center of distribution for craftspeople and traders alike. Here the skilled worker organized a business in a small dwelling and began producing goods by hand and manufacturing them to order. This worker was called a handcraft manufacturer.

Business expansion continued through what is often referred to as the Age of Exploration (1295–1620). The Florentines, the Spaniards, and the Portuguese turned their attention to exploration. New trade routes to India, Africa, and the Americas were discovered. The explorers could not have left their harbors if it had not been for the merchant capitalists, who lent money on the promise that goods found in the New World would be received as payment. Preparing the ship for its long voyage, as well as the search for goods throughout the world, lent itself to large-scale wholesaling by the merchants.

Populations continued to expand, and more goods were in demand. It soon became apparent that the handcraft manufacturer was unable to produce enough goods to meet this demand, while continuing to sell and advertise products. Farmers were also affected by the growth in population. Since agricultural products were necessary for basic subsistence, farmers had to expand production and, consequently, had to spend most of their time on the farm and less time traveling to and from the market square. It was becoming increasingly difficult for both the handcraft manufacturer and the farmer to produce or manufacture goods as well as to transport and sell such commodities to the consumer.[3]

RETAILING IN THE UNITED STATES

It was not until the late 1700s and the Industrial Revolution that enough goods were produced to satisfy the ever-increasing demand. This revolution within industry was very important to the development of retail trade, since, for the first time, a commodity surplus was provided. Due to technological innovations, such as the steam engine, the telegraph, and the cotton gin, employment was provided to men and women that raised the level of economic output. Handcraft manufacturers, who sold the goods produced in their own shops, gave way to mass production in the factory. Merchants and moneylenders continued to accumulate the necessary capital to finance the equipment, machinery, land, and buildings required. Mass production led to standardization and simplification of production.

During this period of industrial expansion, retail merchants discovered that a division and greater specialization of labor was needed. The buying activity, which had been performed by the store owner, soon was delegated to a particular individual within the store. This individual was made responsible for deciding what to buy, where to buy, how much to buy, and what price to ask. Such a person was called a *buyer*. He or she became the specialist within the retail institution who was responsible for getting the merchandise into the hands of the ultimate consumer.

DEVELOPMENT OF DIFFERENT TYPES OF STORES

Trading Post and Wagon Peddler

As the population of the eastern United States continued to grow, the frontier was extended further west. Two very popular forms of retailing were found in the frontier settlements: the trading post and the wagon peddler. The trading post was usually located on a main route of travel and was eagerly sought by wagon trains as they crossed the frontier. It provided an opportunity for trade and exchange of information. The peddler's wagon was often a trading post on wheels. The existence of roads made it possible for the peddler to carry a variety of merchandise and travel greater distances to supply the needs of the sparsely populated frontier. Thus, the wagon peddler or trader became the forerunner of the traveling salesperson.

General Store

The general store of the eighteenth century became a popular form of retailing in small communities and rural areas. The general store provided a greater selection of products and better service than did the trading post. The merchandise of the general store was not separated according to type of goods, particular style, or size but was placed in a haphazard manner throughout the store. These stores provided a variety of staple goods, such as sugar, flour, coffee, salt, dried meat, tools, cloth, gunpowder, whiskey, hides, and clothing, which was purchased from traveling salesmen or peddlers. The general store was conveniently located between the nearest city and the farmlands; the farmer who patronized it accepted the merchandise selection and usually did not question the prices. Credit was often extended, with payment for goods due "when the crops came in."

Specialty Store

By the middle of the nineteenth century, such a variety of goods were being produced in the United States that the general store concept, which placed merchandise haphazardly throughout the store, was no longer tolerable. The unlimited offerings of the manufacturers necessitated the specialization of goods by retailers; thus we have the beginning of the specialty store. This retail establishment carried only one or a few lines of closely related items. Millinery shops, fashion-accessory shops, and leather-goods stores are examples of specialty retail businesses. As a result of industrialization and the increased purchasing power of the consumer, these specialty stores became more and more common.

Today, specialty-store retailing has become a high-growth sector in a competitive consumer market. Specialty-store retailers attempt to meet the needs of a limited but homogeneous consumer market. Large numbers of specialty stores, such as Banana Republic (featuring natural fiber clothing with safari themes), Gap Inc. (featuring color-coordinated sportswear), The Limited Inc. (featuring apparel for the young career woman), and Victoria's Secret (a Limited Inc. subsidiary featuring chic, lacy lingerie), comprise most large shopping centers. In 1986, The Limited Inc. and its subsidiaries was the largest seller of womens' apparel with sales over $3 billion and profits totalling $227.8 million, a 57% increase from 1985 (Figure 1–2).

Limited-Line Store

The limited-line store also became popular during the mid-nineteenth century. The limited-line store narrowed its merchandise offerings even more than the specialty store. The limited-line store carried goods within a single merchandise line ("children's shoes" rather than "shoes"), within a partic-

Figure 1–2 Specialty store retailers are cashing in. What are general merchandisers doing about it? *Source: USA Today,* March 9, 1987, "Retailers See Big Profits in Small Shops," by Jesus Sanchez.

Some Reasons Why Specialty Store Retailers Are Successful

- Instead of trying to sell everything to everyone, as is the case with general merchandisers, specialty retailers cater to smaller segments of the market.
- Specialty retailers can respond more quickly to changing consumer tastes since their operations provide substantial freedom for innovation.
- Since there are more two-worker families, there is less time to shop. It is easier to shop in a specialty store where merchandise is conveniently located rather than spending time wandering through a department store looking for a particular item.
- The shopping mall, where a number of different types of specialty stores can be found, has become one large department store. The one-stop shopping concept, long the drawing card of the department or chain store, has become the drawing card of the shopping mall.

How Are General Merchandisers Meeting the Challenge?

- Sears, rather than going through the expense of opening its own specialty stores, has entered specialty retailing by creating a Sears Special Merchandise Unit whereby it purchased a specialty retailing chain.
- Montgomery Ward has changed its "warehouse store image" by changing selling areas into specialty departments offering women's fashion apparel, children's shoes, and electronics.
- K Mart, the discount giant, purchased such specialty stores as Waldenbooks, Builders Square and Pay Less Drug Stores.

ular price range ("better" rather than "moderate"), or according to size ("tall and big" rather than "average"). This type of business is dominated by small stores or "mom and pop stores" and is also readily apparent in shopping centers and malls. For example, O'Shea's of Laconia, New Hampshire (Figure 1–3) began as a limited-line store and later expanded its operation by adding ready-made clothing.

Chain Store

The chain store had its beginnings during the latter part of the nineteenth century. The owner of the specialty store or the limited-line store now purchased two or more stores that were similar in merchandise offerings and were controlled by one individual. Among early chain-store operations were

Figure 1-3 On April 25, 1875, Dennis and John O'Shea began a dry goods operation. In December of that year, the brothers expanded their operation adding ready-made clothing. By 1978, O'Shea's had become the largest retailer in the state of New Hampshire. (Courtesy of O'Shea's, Laconia, New Hampshire.)

the Great Atlantic and Pacific Tea Company, Incorporated (A & P, 1859), the food giant; the J. C. Penney Company, Incorporated (1902), dry goods; and F. W. Woolworth Company (1879), variety stores. The chain-store organization is credited with being the first to venture into large-scale retailing in the United States.

Today, the chain-store operation has become complex. By definition, *any retail organization that operates more than one unit can be classified as a chain.* However, the *Census of Business* identifies a small chain operation as one that operates 2 to 10 units and a large chain operation as 11 or more units. Small chains are usually local and regional operations while large chains operate on a regional or national level.

Department Store

By the beginning of the twentieth century, a departmentalized type of retailing emerged. Interestingly, however, the department store began as early as the sixteenth century. The early colonists imitated their English ancestors by providing small booths or stands, all under the same roof and each carrying a line of merchandise. During the 1880s, however, the department technique of merchandising took on a more sophisticated appearance and became more complicated as a result of increased competition. The typical offerings of the department store in the hard-goods lines were furniture, large and small appliances, and tools, while in the soft-goods area, fashion accessories and articles of clothing were typical. The department store also provided services for the customer, such as custom tailoring, alterations, delivery service, and credit arrangements. The consumer was provided with luxury items as well as necessities.

Many of the retail stores of the nineteenth century are still in existence today. John Wanamaker of Philadelphia (Figure 1–4) opened a men's and

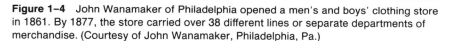

Figure 1–4 John Wanamaker of Philadelphia opened a men's and boys' clothing store in 1861. By 1877, the store carried over 38 different lines or separate departments of merchandise. (Courtesy of John Wanamaker, Philadelphia, Pa.)

boys' clothing store in 1861. By 1877, the store carried more than thirty-eight different lines or separate departments of merchandise, ranging from carpeting to ladies' hair ribbons. Wanamaker's was one of the first retail stores to adopt a one-price policy, which set the example for others in the field. This retail policy discontinued consumer bargaining and reduced credit; thus, many retail outlets began to operate on a cash-only basis. Other early department stores were R. H. Macy and Company, Incorporated (1858), in New York (Figure 1–5), and Marshall Field & Company (1881) in Chicago.

Figure 1–5   R. H. Macy and Company, Incorporated opened its doors in New York City in 1858. Today, Macy's at Herald Square is the world's largest retail store. (Courtesy of R. H. Macy and Co., Inc., New York City, N.Y.)

The department-store method of retailing spread rapidly after 1900. Many department stores expanded or followed population growth into particular areas and opened "branch stores." These branch stores were smaller units carrying a representative selection of the goods offered in the "mother store," or main store.

Today, even though most department stores share the common characteristic of departmentalization, they differ in terms of ownership and operational characteristics. The independent branch department store (one that has no ownership affiliation with other department stores or retail organizations) are almost an endangered species. However, other large branch department stores have become members of ownership groups whereby the branch department store becomes part of the central buying activity of the ownership group. However, each acquired store maintains its own identity. The years 1987 to 1988 saw more changes in department store retailing than in any other period in history. For example, Campeau Corporation, a Canadian-based retail-shopping-center developer, acquired Allied Stores Corporation. Later, Campeau Corporation acquired Federated Department Stores (Figure 1–6).

Figure 1–6   Major Acquisitions and Mergers. *Sources: Philadelphia Daily News*, Business, Wednesday, November 30, 1988; *Women's Wear Daily*, Thursday, June 16, 1988; and *Stores*, July 1988, pp. 34–6.

1985	R. H. Macy merges its Midwest and Atlanta divisions
1986	May Department Stores Co. acquires Associated Dry Goods Corp.
	Federated Department Stores merges Shillito Rikes into Lazarus and Richway into Gold Circle
	Dillards purchases 27 of Allied Stores' Joskes units in Texas and Phoenix
	Dillards purchases the four-store Cain Sloan Division from Allied Stores
	Dillards and developer Ed. J. DeBartold acquire the 12 Higbee Department stores
1987	Campeau Corporation acquires Allied Stores Corporation
1988	A & S sells its two Pennsylvania stores to Philadelphia-based Strawbridge and Clothier Department Store
	Campeau Corporation acquires Federated Department Stores (Bloomingdales, A & S, Burdines, Lazarus, Rich's/Gold-Smiths, and the Children's Place, which it later sold)
	May Co. acquires Foley's
	Macy's acquires Bullocks and I. Magnin from Federated Department Stores
1989	Campeau Corporation sells Ann Taylor specialty retail chain, Foley's, and Filene's to May Department Stores

Supermarket

The supermarket had its beginnings during the depression era of the 1930s. Up to that period food was sold in small neighborhood stores that offered a limited selection and charged high prices. During the depression, incomes were extremely low, and promoters of the supermarket concept used low prices to appeal to the consumer. The supermarket was primarily a self-service store; it was departmentalized and carried a full line of food products, including fresh meats, vegetable produce, and dairy products. The supermarket, like the department store, provided the one-stop concept for the con-

Figure 1–7 Today, supermarkets have broadened their merchandise lines to include nonfood items such as health and beauty aids, underwear and socks, housewares, and so forth. If this trend continues, supermarkets could well become the ''general store'' of the future. (Courtesy of Food Fair Stores, Inc.)

sumer, who now had the opportunity of purchasing all needed foodstuffs at one location instead of making separate trips to various food markets.

The early supermarket was located in low-rent areas, had a minimum of displays and decor, and offered limited personal service. It provided a means for independent retailers to meet the competition of the chain store. However, large food chains such as A & P also turned to this innovative method of food service to reach new consumer markets. The supermarket concept had a tremendous impact on the distribution methods of the retail trade. The impact was felt not only in the food trade but in the whole area of retailing.

Today, supermarkets have broadened their merchandise lines to include nonfood items such as health and beauty aids, underwear and socks, housewares, magazines, greeting cards and stationery supplies, small appliances, auto accessories, and whatever else will appeal to the consumer. If this trend continues, supermarkets could well become the "general store" of the future (Figure 1–7).

Discount House

The discount house is an innovation in retailing that became popular during the 1940s. The principal retailing philosophy of the discount house has been low overhead, low prices, and rapid turnover. The mass-merchandise buyer offers limited service in return for lower prices. This method of selling has found its way into all types of retail establishments, for example, the department store, the supermarket, and the specialty shop. The early discount-house buyer purchased primarily hard goods, such as furniture and kitchen appliances. These cut-rate retailers expanded their operations on a large scale into the soft-goods or fashion-apparel line. One of the largest discount houses was E. J. Korvette, founded in New York City in 1948.

Problems faced by the discounter are primarily a result of an increase in first-rate competition in the discount field, consumer resistance to crowded store conditions, and sloppy presentation of soft-goods lines; in healthy economies customers tend to be drawn to retail stores with better decor.

Today, most discounters are aggressive advertisers. Discount store ads appeal to a large segment of society using a broad message appeal highlighting brand names, convenience (service, store hours, location, parking), merchandise selection, and especially, price. Newspapers, television, and radio ads are the principal media used to reach the economy-minded consumer.

Franchise

The franchise, which dates back to the 1890s, became a popular method of retailing during the 1950s. In franchising, a business firm or sponsor, called a *franchisor,* grants operating rights to a given business, called a *franchisee.* A key ingredient in franchising is the working relationship between the franchisor and the franchisee.

Five types of franchises can be identified. In the first type, wholesalers offer franchise contracts to independent retailers in such trades as hardware, grocery, drugs, and auto supply. This type of franchise provides small retailers with the benefits of volume buying as well as other operating assistance. A second type of franchise involves manufacturers and wholesalers. The soft-drink industry is perhaps the best example, since syrup manufacturing companies such as Pepsi-Cola, Seven-Up, and Coca-Cola will franchise local bottlers, who in turn sell the bottled drinks to retail outlets. A third type is the manufacturer-retailer franchise, in which manufacturers, for example, appliance and television producers, will grant franchises to dealers to cover their line of products. Individual dealers can have several manufacturers' franchises; for instance, they can carry Whirlpool, Magnavox, and other products. A manufacturer-retail franchise that covers the entire business outlet is the fourth type. In this type the manufacturer franchises the total business operation. For example, General Motors and other auto makers, as well as Mobil and Shell petroleum refiners, will determine the retailer's marketing strategy and business operations. The franchisee will manage the business operation on a daily basis in return for a salary and a share of the profits. The fifth type of franchise is the service franchise, in which the major component is a service arrangement. Examples may include food (McDonald's, Dairy Queen); employment (Kelly Girl); income-tax preparation (H & R Block, Inc.); automobile rental (Hertz, Avis); and motel/hotel accommodations (Howard Johnson, Holiday Inn). The service franchise is the most common type of franchise today.

Retail-Sponsored Cooperative Chain

This type of retail operation was originally formed to combat competition from large chain operations. The cooperative chain store is owned by a group of independent retailers who have organized their own wholesale company with its own warehouse and offices. The wholesaling activity is owned on a cooperative basis, thus providing its member stores with an opportunity to partake in group buying activities to meet competition from large chain stores. However, unlike the chain-store operation, cooperative chain stores are still independently operated and owned. Individual cooperative members may or may not identify themselves as part of the cooperative, and they may or may not use common advertising and marketing programs.

The cooperative chain store is most common in the food industry. Examples are Associated Grocers and Certified Grocers.

Wholesale-Sponsored Voluntary Chain

The wholesale-sponsored voluntary chain, in contrast, is owned by a wholesaler who develops a merchandising plan that independent retailers join voluntarily. Individual stores will remain independent in ownership; however, they surrender most of their operating control to the wholesaler. They will agree to operate under the name of the chain and offer the wholesaler private brands of merchandise. In return, the stores will receive assistance such as lower wholesale prices, store displays, advertising copy, and marketing information. Examples of voluntary chain stores are Independent Grocers Alliance (IGA), Super Value, Rexall, Walgreen, and Ace Hardware.

Shopping Center

The shopping center has been the most influential retailing innovation since World War II (Figure 1–8). With the movement of people from the city to the suburbs, the deterioration of urban shopping districts, availability of transportation, the habit of leisurely family shopping, and traffic congestion in the city, the shopping center has become popular. It offers the advantages of convenient location and parking.

Shopping centers vary in size and type. There are large regional shopping centers with 500,000 to 1,000,000 square feet of building area on 50 to 100 acres of land in the larger metropolitan areas. These contain branches of one to three major department stores, women's and men's clothing stores, shoe stores, a variety store, restaurants, a bank, a supermarket, a drugstore, and other specialty stores. Usually 100,000 families are required in the immediate trade area to support this type of shopping center. In 1985, for example, 78 percent of Americans—some 185 million—shopped in a large enclosed mall at least once a month and 93 percent had been to a mall within a six-month period. Surveys have demonstrated that American teenagers and Americans in general spend more time in the mall than anywhere else except home, school, or workplace.[4]

Next down the scale is the community shopping center, which usually contains a branch department store, specialty stores, a supermarket, and a drugstore. The community shopping center serves the needs of smaller cities, as well as drawing customers from isolated neighborhoods. Oftentimes, however, the community shopping center will suffer from the competition of large regional centers, since the larger stores can offer a greater merchandise assortment.

The neighborhood center or "baby shopping center" is the smallest type. It usually contains a supermarket, a drugstore, some specialty shops,

Figure 1-8 During the past decade and throughout the 1990s there has been and continues to be a tremendous growth in shopping malls throughout the country and in Canada. (Courtesy of Rouse Company, Columbia, Md.)

A. Bayside Marketplace, Miami, Fl., 235,000 square feet.

B. Harborplace, Baltimore, Md., 141,000 square feet.

C. The Gallery at Market East, Philadelphia, Pa., 1,319,000 square feet.

beauty and barber shops, and a variety of "mom-and-pop" stores. Neighborhood shopping centers draw their customers from a neighborhood of 5,000 to 10,000 families.

During the past decade and throughout the 1990s there has been and continues to be tremendous growth in shopping malls throughout the United States and Canada. For example, the 1986 Guinness Book of World Records called the West Edmonton Mall, West Edmonton, Canada, the "largest shopping mall in the world." The mall, which is the size of 108 football fields, contains the world's largest indoor amusement park and the largest indoor water park. It contains 11 major department stores, over 110 eating places, 200 women's apparel stores, 35 men's stores, and 50 shoe stores. The mall also has several theme areas, for example, an ice skating rink, a Spanish galleon on its own lake, four submarines, 37 animal displays, and a petting zoo.[5]

Figure 1–9 illustrates the growth of shopping centers throughout the country.

Figure 1–9 Major Mall Development Throughout the Country

ALMEDA MALL
Houston, Texas
810,000 Sq. Ft.
Department stores:
Foley's; JC Penney; Palais Royal;
  Bealls

AUGUSTA MALL
Augusta, Georgia
493,000 Sq. Ft.
Department stores:
Rich's; Macy's; JC Penney

BAYSIDE MARKETPLACE
Miami, Florida
235,000 Sq. Ft.

BEACHWOOD PLACE
Cleveland, Ohio
455,000 Sq. Ft.
Department stores:
Saks Fifth Avenue; Higbee's

BURLINGTON CENTER
Burlington Township, New Jersey
570,000 Sq. Ft.
Department stores:
Strawbridge & Clothier; Sears

CAPEL SQUARE
New Haven, Connecticut
405,000 Sq. Ft.
Department stores:
Macy's

CARILLON
Houston, Texas
183,000 Sq. Ft.

CENTRAL PARK
San Antonio, Texas
604,000 Sq. Ft.
Department stores:
Dillards; Sears; Bealls

CHERRY HILL
Cherry Hill, New Jersey
1,192,000 Sq. Ft.
Department stores:
Strawbridge & Clothier; Macy's; JC
  Penney

THE CITADEL
Colorado Springs, Colorado
1,000,000 Sq. Ft.
Department stores:
JC Penney; Merryn's; May D & F

COLLEGE SQUARE
Cedar Falls, Iowa
566,000 Sq. Ft.
Department stores:
Younkers; Petersen Harned Von
  Maur; Donaldson's; Wal-Mart

THE MALL IN COLUMBIA
Columbia, Maryland
882,000 Sq. Ft.
Department stores:
Woodward & Lothrop; Hecht's;
  Sears

EASTFIELD MALL
Springfield, Massachusetts
668,000 Sq. Ft.
Department stores:
Sears; JC Penney; Steiger's

ECHELON MALL
Echelon, New Jersey
1,076,000 Sq. Ft.
Department stores:
Strawbridge & Clothier; JC Penney;
  Stern's

EXTON SQUARE
Exton, Pennsylvania
436,000 Sq. Ft.
Department store:
Strawbridge & Clothier

FANEUIL HALL MARKETPLACE
Boston, Massachusetts
219,000 Sq. Ft.

FRANKLIN PARK
Toledo, Ohio
810,000 Sq. Ft.
Department stores:
J. L. Hudson; JC Penney; Jacobson's

THE GALLERY AT HARBORPLACE
Baltimore, Maryland
135,000 Sq. Ft.

THE GALLERY AT MARKET EAST
Philadelphia, Pennsylvania
1,319,000 Sq. Ft.
Department stores:
Strawbridge & Clothier; Stern's;
  JC Penney

GALVEZ MALL
Galveston, Texas
389,000 Sq. Ft.
Department stores:
Sears; Eiband's

GOVERNOR'S SQUARE
Tallahassee, Florida
691,000 Sq. Ft.
Department stores:
Sears; JC Penney; Maas Bros.

THE GRAND AVENUE
Milwaukee, Wisconsin
845,000 Sq. Ft.
Department stores:
The Boston Store; Marshall Field's

GREENGATE MALL
Greensburg, Pennsylvania
619,000 Sq. Ft.
Department stores:
Joseph Horne; Montgomery Ward;
  JC Penney

HARBORPLACE
Baltimore, Maryland
141,000 Sq. Ft.

HARUNDALE MALL
Glen Burnie, Maryland
368,000 Sq. Ft.
Department store:
Hutzler's

HIGHLAND MALL
Austin, Texas
1,080,000 Sq. Ft.
Department stores:
Joske's; Scarbroughs; JC Penney;
  Foley's

HULEN MALL
Fort Worth, Texas
541,000 Sq. Ft.
Department stores:
Foley's; Montgomery Ward

THE JACKSONVILLE LANDING
Jacksonville, Florida
126,000 Sq. Ft.

KENDALL TOWN & COUNTRY
Miami, Florida
525,000 Sq. Ft.

KEOIPPI MALL
Keokuk, Iowa
178,000 Sq. Ft.
Department stores:
JC Penney; Spurgeons

THE MALL IN ST. MATTHEWS
Louisville, Kentucky
554,000 Sq. Ft.
Department stores:
JC Penney; Bacon's

MARSHALLTOWN MALL
Marshalltown, Iowa
342,000 Sq. Ft.
Department stores:
JC Penney; Sears; Younkers; Wal-
  Mart

MIDTOWN SQUARE
Charlotte, North Carolina
259,000 Sq. Ft.
Department stores:
Burlington Coat Factory; Burlington
Shoes & Accessories

MILITARY CIRCLE
Norfolk, Virginia
837,000 Sq. Ft.
Department stores:
Thalhimers; JC Penney; Smith &
  Welton; Leggets

MONDAWMIN/METRO PLAZA
Baltimore, Maryland
584,000 Sq. Ft.

MUSCATINE MALL
Muscatine, Iowa
355,000 Sq. Ft.

Department stores:
JC Penney; Petersen Harmed Von
   Maur; Wal-Mart

NORTH GRAND MALL
Ames, Iowa
356,000 Sq. Ft.
Department stores:
JC Penney; Sears; Younkers

NORTH STAR
San Antonio, Texas
1,300,000 Sq. Ft.
Department stores:
Dillard's; Frost Bros.; Foley's; Saks
   Fifth Avenue; Marshall Field

NORTHWEST ARKANSAS
Fayetteville, Arkansas
527,000 Sq. Ft.
Department stores:
JC Penney; Sears; Dillards

NORTHWEST MALL
Houston, Texas
807,000 Sq. Ft.
Department stores:
Foley's; JC Penney

OAKWOOD
Gretna, Louisiana
714,000 Sq. Ft.
Department stores:
Sears; D. H. Holmes; Mervyn's

OUTLET SQUARE
Atlanta, Georgia
550,000 Sq. Ft.
Department stores:
Burlington Coat Factory; Marshalls

OWINGS MILLS
Baltimore, Maryland
800,000 Sq. Ft.
Department stores:
Saks Fifth Ave.; Macy's; Hecht's

PARAMUS PARK
Paramus, New Jersey
750,000 Sq. Ft.
Department stores:
Abraham & Straus; Sears

PERIMETER MALL
Atlanta, Georgia
1,200,000 Sq. Ft.
Department stores:
Rich's; JC Penney; Macy's

PLYMOUTH MEETING
Montgomery County, Pennsylvania
792,000 Sq. Ft.
Department stores:
Strawbridge & Clothier; Hess; Ikea

RANDHURST
Mount Prospect, Illinois
1,173,000 Sq. Ft.
Department stores:
Carson, Pirie, Scott; Montgomery
   Ward; Berger's, Spiess Main
   Street

RIVERWALK
New Orleans, Louisiana
180,000 Sq. Ft.

SALEM MALL
Dayton, Ohio
836,000 Sq. Ft.
Department stores:
Sears; JC Penney; Lazarus

SANTA MONICA PLACE
Santa Monica, California
567,000 Sq. Ft.
Department stores:
The Broadway; Robinson's

SHERWAY GARDENS
Toronto, Ontario
905,000 Sq. Ft.
Department stores:
Eaton's; Simpsons; Holt Renfred

THE SHOPS AT NATIONAL PLACE
and NATIONAL PRESS BUILDING
Washington, D.C.
125,000 Sq. Ft.

THE SHOPS AT TABOR CENTER
Denver, Colorado
115,000 Sq. Ft.

SOUTH DeKALB
Decatur, Georgia
663,000 Sq. Ft.

Department stores:
Rich's; JC Penney

SOUTH STREET SEAPORT
New York, New York
258,000 Sq. Ft.

STATEN ISLAND MALL
Staten Island, New York
922,000 Sq. Ft.
Department stores:
Sears; Macy's

ST. LOUIS UNION STATION
St. Louis, Missouri
160,000 Sq. Ft.

MALL ST. VINCENT
Shreveport, Louisiana
438,000 Sq. Ft.
Department stores:
Sears; Vellan's

TALBOTTOWN
Easton, Maryland
88,000 Sq. Ft.
Department store:
JC Penney

TAMPA BAY CENTER
Tampa, Florida
882,000 Sq. Ft.
Department stores:
Burdine's; Sears; Montgomery
   Ward

VILLAGE OF CROSS KEYS
Baltimore, Maryland
66,000 Sq. Ft.
Village Square Retail; Village
   Square Office; Quandrange Office
   Building; Cross Keys Inn

WESTLAND MALL
West Burlington, Iowa
345,000 Sq. Ft.

Department stores:
JC Penney; Younkers

WHITE MARSH
Baltimore, Maryland
1,147,000 Sq. Ft.
Department stores:
Macy's; Sears; Woodward &
   Lothrop; Hutzler's; JC Penney

WILLOWBROOK
Wayne, New Jersey
1,520,000 Sq. Ft.
Department stores:
Macy's; Stern's; Steinbach; Sears

WOODBRIDGE CENTER
Woodbridge, New Jersey
1,539,000 Sq. Ft.
Department stores:
Abraham & Straus; Stern's;
   Steinbach; Hahne's; JC Penney

FUTURE MALL DEVELOPMENT

AUGUSTA MALL EXPANSION
Augusta, Georgia
120,000 square feet of new retail
   space
Opening, Spring, 1990.

PIONEER PLACE
Portland, Oregon
155,000 square feet of retail space
Opening, Spring, 1990

ARIZONA CENTER
Phoenix, Arizona
150,000 square feet of retail space
Opening, Fall, 1990

OAKLAND CITY CENTER
Oakland, California
350,000 square feet of retail space
Opening, 1992

(Courtesy of Rouse Company, Columbia, Md.)

> **Explain the Development of Each of the Following Types of Retailers.**
>
> **How was the buying-selling activity performed?**
>
> Trading post; Wagon peddler
> Specialty store
> Chain-store operation
> Supermarket
> Franchise
>
> Limited-line store
> Department store
> Discount house
> Cooperative chain; Voluntary chain
>
> General store
> Regional shopping center
> Community shopping center
> Neighborhood shopping center
> Discount shopping center

PART 2—The Buying Activity Today

RETAIL STORES

The Hypermarket

The hypermarket is usually a combination discount store, supermarket, and drugstore selling a wide variety of both hard and soft goods, operating out of a warehouse-type of building, offering only self-service, and undercutting traditional retailers by 15 to 20 percent. Today, there are approximately 25 hypermarkets scattered across the United States.

The hypermarket was first introduced into the United States by a European retailer, Carrefour. This type of retailing operation may have as many as 30 to 50 checkout counters, be close to 200,000 square feet in size, provide parking for 4,000 cars, and do a sales volume in excess of $40 million dollars per year.

Euromarche, the second-largest hypermarket operator in France, operates Bigg's, a Cincinnati-based retailer that is both a supermarket and discount department store covering over 200,000 square feet. Involved in the Bigg's operation is Super Valu Stores Inc. of Minneapolis, the largest food wholesaler in the United States. In 1986, Wal-Mart's opened Hypermarket

USA followed in 1987 by Auchan, also a French-based hypermarket retailer. Auchan has 130,000 square feet of selling space, 55 checkout registers, and wide aisles from 8 feet to 20 feet. Shoes and domestics occupy half the 23,000-square-foot apparel area.[6]

Off-Price Retail Stores

The off-price retailer, as the name suggests, are specialty-store retailers who sell primarily fashion apparel and accessories to brand-conscious consumers at discount prices, usually 20 to 60 percent below regular retail prices. The store's buying and merchandising policies such as prompt payments, little advertising allowances, little or no return privileges, and markdown adjustments permit the off-price retailer to buy for less thus passing the savings on to the consumer. Off-price retailers are usually located in modest facilities, advertise on a limited basis, and provide self-service selling, thereby limiting expenses. T. J. Maxx and Marshalls are examples of off-price retailers.

Distressed Discount Stores

Unlike the more conventional discount store that sells national or manufacturers' name brands at below market price, the distressed discount store sells merchandise that may be classified as damaged, discontinued, seconds, or irregulars. Low-quality foreign goods and surplus merchandise may also make up the merchandise mix. The distressed discount store caters primarily to the low-income consumer.

Warehouse Retail Store

A popular retailing development that began during the 1980s, warehouse retailing is a combination warehouse facility (usually free standing, no frills environment, limited sales assistance) and showroom (sometimes including catalog sales) displaying sample merchandise. Once again, buying policies dictate low operating expenses so that prices remain less than traditional store offerings. However, since the warehouse showroom is usually a single-line hard-goods retailer of furniture, appliances, or carpeting, consumer services such as credit, delivery, and installation are necessary. Examples are Levitz Furniture and Wicks.

Home Centers

In the past decade, the growth in the number of "do-it-yourselfers" has fostered the development of the home-center type of retail store (Figure 1–10).

Figure 1–10 In the past decade, the growth in the number of "do-it-yourselfers" has fostered the development of the home-center type of retail store. (Courtesy of Hechinger, Landover, Md.)

It is a combination hardware store, lumber yard, and self-service home-improvement center. Home centers usually have showroom displays and stock building materials, hardware, paints, plumbing and heating equipment, electrical supplies, garden and yard equipment, household appliances, and home furnishings. Examples are Mr. Good Buy, Handy Man and Hechinger.

Factory Outlet Store

Factory outlet stores are direct-selling outlets for manufacturers, usually in the clothing trade. Manufacturers use these outlets to sell quality merchandise made for this purpose along with seconds, irregulars, production overruns, and surplus merchandise. Many of these outlets are located together in outlet malls. Examples are Vanity Fair, Black and Decker, and Corning.

The Outdoor Market

Another popular form of retailing, the outdoor market (farmers' or flea market) offers consumers a wide variety of goods that are usually self-made, handcrafted, or used. The consumer assumes that the goods are offered at bargain prices. The seller usually pays the sponsor or business operator for the use of the market's physical facilities.

Street Vendors

A very popular type of retailing since the 1970s, street vendors are usually found on congested city streets offering food (hot dogs, sodas, hamburgers, Italian ice), fashion apparel, and accessories (Figure 1–11). Street vendors are usually entrepreneurs who are required to secure a mercantile license, operate from a stand or table, and do their own buying from local manufacturers or wholesalers—street vendors may offer handcrafted or specialty imported items. Once again an early form of retailing has managed to take its place among the contemporary giants of the retail industry.

Figure 1–11   A very popular type of retailing since the 1970s, street vendoring is usually found on busy city streets offering a variety of items, from hot dogs and sodas to women's fashion accessories. (Photograph by Steve Hawkins)

NONSTORE RETAILING

A retailing transaction may occur without a customer actually visiting a store. In this case, retailers do not operate from conventional facilities such as a store front, use displays, or provide in-store selling or atmospherics. Over the last decade we have experienced rapid changes in technology, demographics and lifestyles, and institutional trends. As a result, various forms of nonstore retailing promise to become even more popular by the year 2000. Examples are mail order retailing, catalog retailing, automated retailing, door-to-door selling, telephone sales, and electronic retailing.

Mail Order Retailing

As the term implies, mail order retailing is a form of direct marketing that attempts to reach prospective customers by mail, receive orders by mail, and make deliveries by mail. For example, if you see a magazine ad for a "do-it-yourself" book, you the consumer will fill out a form (mailing piece) and, along with a check, mail the form and wait approximately 4 to 5 weeks for delivery. Today, however, the mail-order operation varies from the original mail-order concept due to changes in product offerings, business operations,

Figure 1–12 Catalog sales have proved to be a popular form of nonstore retailing. Some chain stores, for example, Sears Roebuck and Company, provide store areas where customers can select merchandise from catalogs and place orders. (Courtesy of Sears Roebuck and Co.)

consumer contact, and method of order placement (the telephone has become increasingly popular).

Catalog Retailing

Catalog retailing, which is a variation of mail order retailing, dates back to the nineteenth century and the period of the general store when Montgomery Ward and Sears began to offer a variety of merchandise by catalog (Figure 1–12). General-store owners were rather unconcerned about the activities of the catalog house since they were convinced that people would not purchase merchandise they had never seen or inspected. However, with the development of the postal service and newer methods of mail delivery, these goods could be delivered inexpensively and efficiently. Today, traditional nonstore retailers such as Spiegel, Avon, and Lillian Vernon have experienced significant growth in the catalog business. Many traditional retailers such as Neiman-Marcus, Bloomingdale's, and Macy's use catalogs to stimulate sales, especially during the Christmas season and during major sales promotions.

Automated Retailing

Automated retailing (vending machines) dates back to the 1940s and has since become an important form of retailing, especially when in-store selling is not possible. Vending machines are used primarily to sell cigarettes, candies, soft drinks, hot beverages, and accessory items. As a result of improved technology, vending machines have been extended to meet the leisure needs of consumers through electronic games, pinball machines, and jukeboxes. Accounting for approximately 1 percent of total retail sales, vending machines have found their way into cafeterias (or vendeterias as they are sometimes called), college dormitories, hospital waiting rooms, and other areas where people want fast, convenient service.

As stated, the greatest advantage of vending machines is their convenience; however, they are high-cost operations requiring accurate and efficient stocking. Equipment repairs are frequent. Also, the prices charged for goods sold in this way are often 20 to 25 percent higher than the same products sold elsewhere. On a much smaller scale, vending machines are similar to convenience stores in that they may be used by consumers to meet emergency or after-hour needs.

Door-to-Door Selling

Door-to-door selling, also called *home retailing,* had its beginning with the wagon peddler of frontier days. It is still a popular form of retailing, especially in the cosmetics, toiletries, housewares, and home furnishings lines. Companies that have successfully used door-to-door selling are Avon, a cosmetics company; Tupperware, a company selling kitchenwares; and Fuller Brush, a company selling housewares.

A popular technique used to encourage sales is party selling or the party plan. In this approach, the sales person makes a sales presentation in the home of the host or hostess who has invited friends and relatives (potential customers) to a "party." Products are demonstrated, and orders are taken. Merchandise ranging from jewelry to household goods have found their way into the consumer's lifestyle as a result of door-to-door selling.

Telephone Retailing

Over the years this form of nonstore retailing has taken on a variety of forms. For example, a customer may call a retailer to place an order for a "pizza to go," flowers on Mother's Day, prescription drugs, place an order from a catalog, or call a toll-free number on television. Today, however, many of us perceive telephone retailing as "nuisance calls," whereby a computerized-dialing system calls a list of prospective customers in a particular target market during specific time periods (usually around dinnertime), and a robot-type voice makes a sales pitch for everything from waterproofing a basement to investing in the stock market.

Electronic Retailing

The past decade has brought us a most innovative form of nonstore retailing—electronic retailing that utilizes electronics and video systems. A form of electronic retailing, Videotex, uses "data and graphics which are transmitted from a computer network over telephone or cable lines and displayed on a subscribers' TV or computer-terminal screen."[7] With the demand for more leisure time and with it the desire for more convenience, it is predicted that by the mid-1990s, Videotex will account for approximately 15 percent of the home sales market.[8]

The use of video catalogs also has great potential for nonstore retailing. For example, Sears has test marketed a video catalog called the *Tele-Shop Catalog*. A catalog is transferred onto video discs, and the shopper may view the catalog at home on television and then telephone orders to Sears—or in-store shoppers may view the catalog on display terminals and then place an order.

Another form of electronic retailing, cable shopping, also affords potential customers a variety of product choices. Shopper channels or fashion channels provide detailed product information, a toll-free number, return privileges, and fast delivery. Cable shopping also has the potential for becoming a popular form of nonstore retailing in the near future.

Explain How the Following are Examples of Nonstore Retailing

1. Mail-order retailing
2. Catalog retailing
3. Automated retailing
4. Door-to-door selling
5. Telephone sales
6. Electronic retailing

Chapter Summary

Marketing may be defined as the performance of business activities that direct the flow of goods and services from producer to consumer or user. However, a more contemporary definition defines marketing as human activity directed at satisfying needs and wants through exchange processes. Most people mistakenly think the primary function of marketing is to advertise and sell goods. However, marketing is also concerned with research, product development, pricing, distribution, storage, credit, and risk taking.

Marketing specialists are organized in the marketing system through a channel of distribution that is a sequence of marketing specialists or activities involved in bringing a product from the producer to the ultimate consumer. The marketing channel of distribution can be characterized by a number of different channel members or activities ranging from the simple to the complex. It is important to remember that even though a manufacturer or wholesaler may choose to eliminate a retailer when attempting to reach the final consumer, it cannot eliminate the retailing function.

Retailing is the summation of all activities involved in the sale of goods or services directly to the ultimate consumer for personal, nonbusiness use. A retailer is a merchant whose primary business is selling goods or services directly to the ultimate consumer. The retail institution or store is the place where the actual sales activity or exchange takes place. Retailing possesses characteristics that distinguish it from other members of the distribution channel such as manufacturers and wholesalers. The role of retailing in the marketing system involves several activities.

Retailing transactions have existed since the beginning of time, evolving from the trading post and the wagon peddler to the giant hypermarkets of today. However, a retailing transaction may occur without a customer actually visiting a store. This is called nonstore retailing.

Trade Terminology

DIRECTIONS: Briefly explain or discuss each of the following trade terms:

1. Marketing
2. Marketing channel of distribution
3. Retailing
4. Retailer
5. Retail institution or store

Questions for Discussion and Review

1. Define marketing. How do the various definitions of marketing differ?

2. Discuss the functions performed by marketing. Why do most people mistakenly think the primary function of marketing is to advertise and sell goods? What do you think is the primary function of marketing?

3. What is a marketing channel of distribution?

4. The marketing channel of distribution can be characterized by a number of different channel members or activities ranging from the complex to the simple. Discuss.

5. Discuss this statement: "Even though a manufacturer or wholesaler may choose to eliminate a retailer when attempting to reach the final consumer, it cannot eliminate the retailing function."

6. Define retailing. What distinguishes retailers from other members of the channel of distribution?

7. Define retailer and retail institution.

8. Discuss the role of retailing in the marketing system.

9. What types of retail stores are still in existence today? How have these stores adapted to different conditions in the marketplace?

10. Why is retailing considered the last stage in the marketing system?

11. What is meant by the term *nonstore retailing?* Give examples.

References

THE RETAIL
STUDENT'S REFERENCE LIBRARY

Bennett, Peter D. *Marketing.* New York: McGraw Hill Book Co., 1988.

Bittel, Lester R. and Burke, Ronald S. *Business in Action: An Introduction to Business.* New York: McGraw Hill Book Co., 1988.

Boone, Louis E. and Kurtz, David L. *Contemporary Marketing.* Chicago: Dryden Press, 1989.

Buskirk, Bruce. *Readings and Cases in Direct Marketing.* Lincolnwood, Illinois: NTC Publishing Group, 1989.

Ezell, Mason Mayer. *Retailing.* Plano, Texas: Business Publications, Inc., 1988.

Fischer, Stanley. *Economics.* New York: McGraw Hill Book Co., 1988.

Justic, Robert and Judd, Richard J. *Franchising.* Cincinnati: South Western Publishing Co., 1989.

Goodman, Jacob and Kaminski, Denis. *Kaman's Fashions for Less.* New York: McGraw Hill Book Co., 1988.

Kobs, Jim. *Profitable Direct Marketing.* Lincolnwood, Illinois: NTC Publishing Group, 1989.

Kurloff, Arthur and Hemphill, John M. *Starting and Managing the Small Business.* New York: McGraw Hill Book Co., 1988.

Lewis, Philip C. and Lewis, Chad T. *The Donut Franchise: A Microcomputer Simulation.* New York: McGraw Hill Book Co., 1986.

————. *Enterprise Sandwich Shops: A Market Simulation.* New York: McGraw Hill Book Co., 1985.

————. *Marketing Peanut Butter: A Microcomputer Simulation.* New York: McGraw Hill Book Co., 1986.

Rathbun, Robert Davis. *Shopping Centers and Malls.* New York: Retail Reporting Bureau, 1989.

Roth, Robert. *International Marketing Communications.* Lincolnwood, Illinois: NTC Publishing Group, 1989.

Stone, Elaine and Samples, Jean. *Fashion Merchandising: An Introduction.* New York: McGraw Hill Book Co., 1985.

Sroge, Maxwell. *How to Create Successful Catalogs.* Lincolnwood, Illinois: NTC Publishing Group, 1989.

————. *Inside the Leading Mail Order Houses.* Lincolnwood, Illinois: NTC Publishing Group, 1989.

Wingate, Isabel B.; Gillespie, Karen R.; and Barry, Mary E. *Know Your Merchandise: For Retailers and Consumers.* New York: McGraw Hill Book Co., 1985.

Witek, John. *Response Television: Combat Advertising of the 1980s.* Lincolnwood, Illinois: NTC Publishing Group, 1989.

Wyman, John. *Successful Telemarketing.* Lincolnwood, Illinois: NTC Publishing Group, 1989.

REFERENCES

1. Committee on Definitions, *Marketing Definitions: A Glossary of Marketing Terms* (American Marketing Association, 1960), New York, N.Y., p. 15.
2. Philip Kotler, *Marketing Management,* 6th ed (Englewood Cliffs, N.J.: Prentice Hall, Inc. 1986), p. 19.
3. Miriam Beard, *A History of Business* (Ann Arbor: University of Michigan Press, 1938), pp. 1–52.
4. William S. Kourinski, *The Malling of America* (New York: Morrow, 1985), pp. 24–29.
5. Ibid.
6. "Auchan Opens U.S. Hypermarket," *Discount Store News,* October 24, 1988.
7. "Videotex: What It's all About," *Marketing News,* November 25, 1983, p. 16.
8. "Videotex to Curtain Canada In-Store Retailing: Study Predicts 15% Home Penetration by 1990," *Marketing News,* November 25, 1983, p. 20.

External Forces Affecting the Buyer's Environment

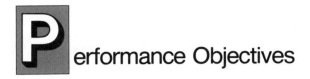

Performance Objectives

After reading this chapter, the student should be able to accomplish the following:

1. Discuss market trends and their implications for the retail buyer.

2. Relate how economic conditions have an impact on the merchandising methods used by retailers.

3. Review technological advancements and their applications to retailing.

4. Explain how the following trends will affect the retailer's competitive environment: discounting, merchandise scrambling, franchising, catalog presentations, new store images, retail-store trends, diversifications, and mergers.

5. Become aware of the advantages as well as the risks involved in international retailing.

6. Outline and discuss federal legislation in the areas of competition and customer relations.

External Forces Affecting the Buyer's Environment

Figure 2–1 The Mitsubishi T2100 POS Terminal keeps track of all transactions. On demand, it reports accumulated totals by sales associate, terminal, hour, department, and item. Timely information of this kind helps the retailer plan ahead. (Courtesy of Mitsubishi Electronics America, Inc., Torrance, Calif.)

INTRODUCTION

As you read in the previous chapter, marketing is primarily focused on the marketplace and for this reason most people mistakenly think the primary function of marketing is to advertise and sell goods. However, marketing includes many activities such as research, product development, pricing, distribution, storage, credit, and risk taking.

Marketing professionals help create and bring about exchanges by performing certain functions. These marketing specialists are organized in the marketing system through a channel of distribution in which retailing is the last stage.

Retailing transactions have occurred throughout the course of history. For example, in the United States different types of stores have developed from the trading post and wagon peddler to the department store with branches to large chain store operations. Many of these stores have merged their merchandising philosophies to become the hypermarket, off-price retailer, or factory outlet of today. Nonstore retailing has also seen tremendous growth.

In this chapter, we are concerned with the buyer of the 1990s. Since merchandising is always in a state of change, persons involved in the operations of a retail business must keep pace by meeting the challenge of competition, keeping abreast of innovations in distribution, being constantly aware of federal legislation, and developing an awareness of the socioeconomic forces that are inherent in the retailer's environment in both domestic and foreign markets.

PART 1—Role of the Buyer of the 1990s

FACTORS AFFECTING
CHANGES IN THE ENVIRONMENT

The merchant is constantly dealing with large numbers of people with different desires, changing economic status, changing tastes, and different lifestyles. The far-sighted buyer must be prepared to accept and anticipate change and respond to these changes. There are six factors affecting change. They are:

1. Market trends
2. Economic conditions
3. Technological advancements
4. Competition
5. International retailing
6. Federal regulation

MARKET TRENDS

According to the Bureau of the Census, population trends for the future are:

- Population Size.
  There will be 268 million people in the United States by the year 2000, up from 253 million in 1990.

- Median Age.
  In 1990 the median age of the population will be 33. By the year 2000 the median age will be 36.
- Average Household Size.
  In 1985 the average household size was 2.69 people. It will fall to 2.48 people per household by the year 2000.
- People Living Alone.
  Over one-fourth of all households will consist of people living alone or with nonrelatives.
- Total Number of Households.
  In 1985, the total number of households was 87 million. By the year 2000, total number of households is expected to reach approximately 110 million.
- Older Population.
  Today, almost 32 million people are 65 years of age or older. By the year 2000 the number will exceed 35 million.
- Minority Growth.
  Projected percentage of total population of African-American, Asian, Hispanic, and other minorities is 16.9 percent by the year 2000 compared with 14.1 percent of the total population in 1980.

Other factors in market trend forecasting include mobility of people and the shifting of populations from the cities to the suburbs and the emergence of a better-educated and well-informed consumer who will demand better quality merchandise, more conveniences, and more service. In recent years, there has been more emphasis on leisure living, more women working outside the home, and a shorter work week.

Implications for the Retail Buyer

The buyer must cater to the needs and wants of consumers. For the youth market there are merchandise assortments of contemporary styles with bright colors and patterns. The merchant continues to cater to the middle-aged market since established money is more predictable. For the over-65 age group, however, the factor of the fixed income must be considered. Store buyers use promotional senior-citizen discounts in combination with existing senior-citizen discounts on transportation. This type of "icing-on-the-cake" sale can add valuable sales dollars to the overall profit.

With an increase in the number of people living alone, supermarkets will provide smaller portions and package sizes. The two-income household provides opportunities for the purchase of luxury items. With the growth in minorities, retailers need to provide food, music, menus, and clothing that has appeal to specific minority groups.

When populations shift from urban areas to the suburbs, the retailer follows, building branch stores and locating in shopping centers. This trend will force department-store and chain-store buyers to review buying methods in order to more efficiently meet the demands of the surburban shopper. Since people are more mobile and will drive from one shopping center to another, the retailer has to provide a wider assortment of goods, pleasant and clean surroundings, and knowledgeable sales help to draw the customer away from the competition. Also, people have a tendency to discard clothing, furniture, etc. when moving, especially long distances.

The increase in the number of two-worker households and single parents has significant implications for the retailer. Large amounts of money are spent on time-saving devices such as major appliances and household equipment. Since most working people cannot shop during regular store hours, stores will provide the convenience of a catalog for home shopping. Fast-food restaurants, convenience foods, and prepared foods cater to the needs of those who do not have time for food preparation.

Leisure living, characterized by shorter working hours and more time for recreation, has encouraged the retailer to lengthen the business day by two or more night openings a week. Some stores are open seven days a week, unless prohibited by blue laws (laws that prohibit Sunday sales), while food stores may stay open twenty-four hours a day. Additional store space is designed to fill leisure time—tea gardens, snack bars, and even babysitting services. The merchandise assortment also reflects leisure living. Sportswear, particularly tennis, jogging and cycling wear, has dominated the recreational-clothing market. Sporting goods such as golf clubs, bowling balls, and snorkling equipment are widely used throughout store displays. Some stores have added travel bureaus and ticket offices to appeal to the consumer's leisure-living style.

ECONOMIC CONDITIONS

Since the Industrial Revolution of the eighteenth century, mass production has raised the level of employment, increased consumer purchasing power, and improved the standard of living. An increase in the personal income level, particularly in the middle class, has led to a greater spending capacity for many consumers, which in turn affects total retail sales.

The economic recession of the early 1980s had a tremendous impact on retail buyers and their merchandising methods. Due to high unemployment, the increase of small business failures, the energy crisis, high food prices, and a high rate of inflation, consumers became cautious about the way they spent their money. Retailers encountered many problems, since they found themselves catering to a price-conscious consumer trade that became more selective when making purchases. Also, more demands were placed on retailers to provide a variety of merchandise as a result of the easy availability of consumer credit afforded by retailers and financial institutions alike.

Implications for the Retail Buyer

Since the consumer has the potential to increase spending power, the retailer is constantly working to bring the consumer into the retail store. Advertising campaigns on television, radio, and newspaper; special events; additional store promotions; and emphasis on service and uniqueness of imports are but a few of the techniques employed by the buyer. Easy credit terms, coupons and trading stamps, and special charge accounts are promotional methods utilized by the merchandise buyer to attract the customer to the particular store or department.

During the early 1980s, however, the buyer had an especially difficult business period. As a result, merchants had to deplete inventories, reduce sales personnel, take heavy markdowns, offer a better selection of merchandise, and become more discriminating when making purchases. Advertising and promotional methods were re-evaluated in relation to costs and sales. Some department-store and chain-store operations had to consolidate their operations by closing marginal-profit stores as well as abandoning expansion activities. Retail buyers had to make adjustments. Some merchandise, especially fashion goods, became more difficult than usual to obtain because manufacturers were not producing without firm orders; however, the lower inventories planned by many buyers created more reorders and in the long run minimized the shortage problems. The merchandising practice of buyers during that period was to hold on, avoid overextending, and keep a careful watch on receivables.

Trading-stamp giveaways are no longer at big supermarket chains and gas stations, but they are beginning to make a comeback with employee-incentive plans and small-town retailers. Trading-stamp industry experts say incentive plans among companies like General Motors, Dow Chemical, International Telephone & Telegraph, Coca-Cola, and Holiday Inns now represent $50 million annually in sales in this category, and that figure is expected to double during the 1990s.

There are other elements within the economic structure that affect the retail buyer's success. The presence of labor unions may force the employees of a store to strike, which leads to a loss of thousands of dollars in sales as well as a loss in store patronage. Retailers may also be affected by business conditions in other firms. For example, if a source of supply were to go out of business, change its product line, raise prices, or relocate, the retailer would have to seek comparable alternatives.

TECHNOLOGICAL ADVANCEMENTS

Over the past several decades tremendous strides have been made in technology, particularly in the field of electronic data processing (EDP). This has many implications for the progressive retailer. For example, the computer has provided speedy, reliable, and accurate information that facilitates managerial decision making. It is used by buyers for internal store operations such as inventory control, payroll, credit and collections, and order processing.

Electronic point of sale (POS) systems (electronic cash registers) provide prices for untagged merchandise, automatically take markdowns, print future sales promotional information on sales tickets, and approve (provide bank code) credit cards and bank checks (Figure 2–1). By the end of 1990, for example, all K Mart stores will have a POS system that will give each store the capability of recording the sale of every SKU (stock keeping unit) in the store on a daily basis and then transmitting the information via satellite to corporate headquarters. In addition to POS and the satellite network, K Mart's automation package includes layaway systems, instant credit authorization, employee scheduling, basic accounting systems, and full centralization, that is, all merchandise will be assigned from central headquarters.[1]

K Mart has also implemented an electronic check and credit card authorization system that allows the store to quickly obtain credit-card approval for purchases with daily settlement of charges. The new system also can debit customer checking accounts. Within an electronic banking network, the system allows the purchase price of a product to be deducted from the shopper's bank account and at the same time transfers payment to the retailer's account. It is estimated that by the mid-1990s, 40% of K Mart stores will use the new POS system.[2]

Another example of technology is ADP (automatic data processing). This is an accounts-receivable system that enables a merchandise supplier (manufacturer, vendor, or wholesaler) to make collections from retailers, as well as making accurate credit decisions. The ADP accounts-receivable system includes a customer ledger card that shows the complete life-span of a transaction, from the creation of an invoice to the receipt of the payment and all that has occurred in between. A separate aging schedule provides the names and addresses of the accounts, the amount owed, and the amount past due. This information is useful in following up delinquent accounts and helps to speed up the collection of the money.

Electronic data processing and its application to various phases of retailing will be stressed throughout this book.

Implications for the Retail Buyer

Despite the developments of technology, there seems to be a gap between the advantages of EDP and its use by retail buyers. Often a great deal of technical training is required on the part of retail management to change over efficiently to the use of EDP equipment. Time and money are also required. A great deal of experience goes into training of store personnel to use the equipment efficiently and capitalize on the investment. However, EDP has been used successfully for such activities as merchandise planning, pricing, credit and collections, accounting statements, and inventory control. Electronic equipment still poses a host of questions in terms of cost, obsolescence, and consumer acceptance.

COMPETITION

Competition is an ever-present element in retailing. Characteristics of the competitive environment are the numerous types and sizes of retail stores, urban redevelopment, the overlapping or scrambling of merchandise, and the wide range of services being offered to consumers. During the early 1990s retailers will develop new merchandising techniques, more innovative methods of distribution, and more intensified sales promotions to coax consumers into stores and shopping centers.

Implications for the Retail Buyer

Retail institutions must adapt to changes in the environment if they are to survive.

Department Stores—Change of Image. Department stores will receive greater competition from specialty stores. For example, Nordstrom, a women's specialty store, opened a 336,000 square foot store on San Francisco's Market Street. Considered a secondary location, the Market Street area is three blocks from fashionable Union Square (and Macy's) and is not considered a prime retail area because of crime and dilapidated buildings. Furthermore, the store is not on ground level but occupies the top five floors of the eight-story San Francisco Centre. In order to offset the problem of location, however, Nordstrom offers special services and exclusive merchandise. Special services include a 3000 square foot spa, located on the fifth floor that offers facials and massages, special water therapy administered in specially designed tubs, and Spa Nordstrom, a private label line. Other special services include valet parking, and enlarged dressing rooms in the designer apparel areas where refreshments are served.

The specialty retailer offers approximately 150,000 pairs of shoes (a Nordstrom trademark), exclusive cosmetic lines, designer and better-priced apparel, a designer collector's department, and hot-sellers in designer sportswear.[3]

Off-Price Retailers—Stock Major Brands. Off-price retailers will continue to dominate the fashion apparel markets thereby emerging as strong competitors to both department and specialty stores. For example, Nordstrom

Figure 2–2   When Edward A. Filene opened the doors to his original "bargain basement" store in Boston in 1908, he was quite clear about what conditions constitute a bargain: (1) A price offering a substantial saving compared with its normal value; and (2) Reliable quality. With those simple principles, Edward Filene, his associates and successors, built one of the world's great retailing institutions. (Courtesy of Filene's Basement, Inc., Wellesley, Mass.)

opened Nordstrom Rack, an off-price operation consisting of 11 units in 1987, and Neiman Marcus opened a 30,000 square foot, off-price unit called Last Call. A key strategy of most off-price retailers has been a continued emphasis on stocking major brand names. For example, Burlington Coat Factory continues to upscale its brand name apparel offerings by using department-store-like fixtures and displays (Figures 2–2 and 2–3).

Conventional Discounter—New Store Design. The conventional discounter faces competitive challenges from the distressed discounter. For example, K Mart has experimented with new floor plans and store design for its medium- and small-sized stores. Experiments include a racetrack traffic pattern with soft lines grouped in the interior, accessories grouped near checkout counters, and hard lines distributed around the perimeter.

From Hypermarkets to Flea Markets—More Competition. Hypermarkets capitalize on the one-stop concept thereby creating competitive havoc for discounters and supermarkets alike. The open-air market (flea markets and farmers' markets) along with street vendors have managed to interest a significant number of consumers, drawing them away from discounters and factory outlets.

Nonstore Retailing—Major Dimension in the 1990s. Nonstore retailing with sales of 78 billion predicted by the mid-1990s represents a major dimension of retailing (Figure 2–4). Rapidly improving technology, changes in demographics and lifestyles, and retail store trends—all in one way or another will contribute to the overall expansion of nonstore retailing. Technological advances in computers, telephones, cable television, order process-

Figure 2–3 Ten Top Off-Price Retailers in 1988

1. T.J. MAXX, Framingham, Mass.
2. Marshalls, Wakefield, Mass.
3. Ross Stores, Newark, Calif.
4. Burlington Coat, Burlington, N.H.
5. Loehmann's, Bronx, N.Y.
6. Filene's Basement, Wellesley, Mass.
7. Sym's, Lundhurst, N.J.
8. Kids 'R' Us, Rochelle Park, N.J.
9. Clothes Time, Anaheim, Calif.
10. Dress Barn, Stamford, Conn.

Source: *Discount Store News,* May 9, 1988, p. 32

Figure 2-4   A Sampling of Catalog Firms Selling Apparel and Housewares

Ambassador, Phoenix, Ariz.	Luggage, inexpensive, jewelry, housewares, gifts
Austad's, Sioux Falls, S.D.	Golf clubs, clothing, accessories
Banana Republic, San Francisco, Calif.	Travel, outdoor sportswear
Brookstone, Peterborough, N.H.	Tools, housewares
Eddie Bauer, Seattle, Wash.	Outdoor clothing, sportswear
J.C. Penney, New York, N.Y.	General merchandise
L.L. Bean, Freeport, Me.	Classic and outdoor clothing, sporting goods
Land's End, Dodgeville, Wisc.	Classic and outdoor clothing, luggage
Lillian Vernon, Mt. Vernon, N.Y.	Inexpensive gifts, housewares, toys
Sears, Roebuck & Co., Chicago, Ill.	General merchandise
The Sharper Image, San Francisco, Calif.	Electronics, gifts, jewelry
Spiegel, Chicago, Ill.	General merchandise
Yield House, North Conway, N.H.	Furniture and furniture kits

ing, merchandise presentations, video equipment, and the like will allow businesses to reduce costs, speed up deliveries, and appeal to the lifestyles of the 1990s. For example, a catalog division of Bloomingdale's, Bloomingdale's By Mail, Ltd. (BBM) did an estimated $100 million in sales in 1987. BBM accounted for more business than any of the 17 store units except for the flagship store.[4]

With the popularity of cable television throughout the 1980s, cable shopping networks have become big business and, thus, competition for traditional retailers. For example, in 1988, QVC Network, Inc. in West Chester, Pa. reached more than 13 million cable homes, of which approximately 9 million received the program 24 hours a day. The shopper cable program has gained rapid consumer acceptance for its emphasis on quality and customer service. Products offered include home furnishings, jewelry, collectibles, consumer electronics, and many other items. Well-known brand names are presented as well as outstanding values from Sears, Roebuck and Co. (Figure 2-5).

Diversifications and Mergers

As stated in Chapter 1, the decade of the 1980s saw large retailers attempting to sustain or enhance sales growth through diversifications and mergers.

Figure 2–5 With the popularity of cable television, cable shopping networks have become big business. QVC Network, Inc., in West Chester, Pa., reached more than 13 million cable homes. Products offered include home furnishings, jewelry, collectibles, consumer electronics, and many other items. (Courtesy of QVC Network, Inc., West Chester, Pa.)

Diversification allows retailers to become active in businesses outside their particular trade. For example, Sears in 1981 acquired Dean Witter Reynolds, the fifth-largest stock brokerage firm in the United States and Coldwell,

How Have the Following Trends in Retailing Helped the Buyer Respond to Competitive Changes?

Department Stores—Change of Image
Off-Price Retailers—Stocking Major Brands
Conventional Discounters—New Store Design
From Hypermarkets to Flea Markets—The Competition Continues
Diversifications and Mergers—A Way to Sustain Sales

Banker and Co., the largest real-estate broker. Mergers occur between similar types of retailers. By merging, retailers attempt to maximize their resources, thereby gaining a competitive advantage.

PART 2—Role of the Buyer in the 1990s: A Continuation

INTERNATIONAL RETAILING

During the 1980s more and more U.S. retailers looked to expansion into foreign markets as domestic markets became saturated. For example, Jewel, a Chicago-based supermarket chain, owns 41 percent of Aurrera, Mexico's largest retailer. Kentucky Fried Chicken expanded to European markets. 7-Eleven stores may be found in Japan. McDonald's has entered markets throughout the world including Japan, Canada, and Europe. Today, approximately 50 percent of McDonalds sales comes from foreign markets.

A large number of foreign retailers have entered U.S. markets, especially in the food industry. For example, Wienerwald of Switzerland owns Lums Restaurants, International House of Pancakes (IHOP), and Ranch House Restaurants. Tengelmann of Germany owns A&P and Imasco of Canada owns Hardee's fast-food restaurants. Foreign firms having 10 percent or more ownership interest in companies accounted for 15 percent of total U.S. supermarket sales in 1990.

Implications for the Retail Buyer

As previously stated domestic markets may become saturated or stagnant so retailers will look to international markets for retailing opportunities. Foreign markets may represent better growth opportunities, offer products or services not yet available, be less competitive, or offer tax or investment opportunities. For example, by 1993, European markets will merge to become one major market center, thereby expanding the marketplace. The overall implications of this expansion are not totally known as yet. However, it is expected that European exports to the United States will increase by 4 to 5%.

However, retailers must be aware of the risks involved. There are cultural differences, a common currency exchange is yet to be determined, management styles may not be easily adaptable, foreign governments may place heavy restrictions on operations, or distribution systems may be inadequate.

In developing international marketing strategies, retailers must pay particular attention to the concept of standardization. In other words, can product lines, methods of operation, and advertising strategies followed in domestic markets be directly applied to foreign markets?

Chapter 11 will provide a more in-depth discussion on this topic.

FEDERAL REGULATIONS

Over the years increased attention has been given to legislation governing the retailer's locations, methods of distribution, the hours during which the store may operate, and methods of advertising merchandise. More than ever before the consumer is demanding guarantees of product quality, product safety, protection, and satisfaction in products purchased. The old saying "buyer beware" has been reversed to the point where retailers have become very defensive and the saying "seller beware" has become more applicable.

As you will learn in Chapter 14, "Pricing Merchandise for Profit," federal legislation affecting retailers began with the Sherman Antitrust Act of 1890, the Clayton Act of 1914, and the Federal Trade Commission Act of 1914. These antitrust laws, which have an indirect effect upon consumers, were designed to protect against monopoly in business and unfair methods of competition. The Robinson-Patman Act, a landmark law that has been on the books since 1935, primarily prohibits price discrimination among competing customers except for certain limited situations. This act was originally designed to protect small retail firms from the cutthroat competition of big business.

Implications for the Retail Buyer

Today the federal government is increasing its efforts to provide fuller protection for consumers. More recent federal legislation has been directed specifically to the relationship between retailers and consumers. The Federal Trade Commission (FTC), the Food and Drug Administration (FDA), the Federal Communications Commission (FCC), and the Consumer Products Safety Commission (CPSC) are some government agencies that have become active in protecting consumers in regard to advertising claims, price discrimination, fabric quality, guarantees and warranties, consumer credit, flammable products, poisons, and allergenic ingredients (see Fig. 2–6). It is imperative that retail buyers have an understanding of federal legislation, since the decision on the part of governmental agencies to continue this consumer-protection movement will depend in part on the willingness of merchants to regulate their own trade activities and to operate with integrity.

Figure 2–6 Today, the federal government is making increased effort to provide fuller protection for consumers. More recent federal legislation has been directed specifically to the relationship between retailers and consumers.

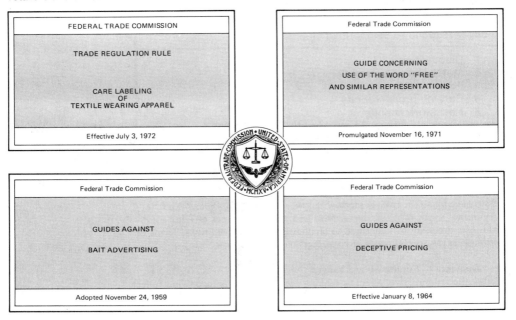

Laws Regulating Competition

The government tries to ensure that no one group gains too much economic power and that consumers continue to have a wide variety of choice. There are three categories of laws used by the government to regulate competition: (1) antitrust laws, (2) unfair trade practice laws, and (3) price-competition laws.[5] Some of these laws will be discussed in detail in Chapter 14, "Pricing for Profit."

Antitrust Laws

The Sherman Antitrust Act, 1890. The first important legislation designed to combat monopolies.

The Clayton Act, 1914. The Clayton Act amended the Sherman Antitrust Act, which proved too vague to be effective. This act supplemented existing laws against unlawful restraints and monopolies.

Unfair Trade Practice Laws

Federal Trade Commission Act, 1914; amended 1938. This act was passed to create a Federal Trade Commission (FTC), and to define its powers and duties. The Wheeler-Lea Act of 1938 amended the Federal Trade Commission Act. It stated that unfair methods of competition in commerce are illegal.

Export Trade Act, 1918. The FTC has the power to enforce the provisions of the Export Trade Act, which was passed to promote export trade. The meaning of "export trade" was defined, as well as the meaning of "trade within the United States." This act also prohibited unfair methods of competition in export trade.

Lanham Trademark Act, 1946; amended 1962. This act was passed to provide for the registration and protection of trademarks used in commerce. The FTC may apply to cancel a trademark on certain grounds, as specified by the law.

Price-Competition Laws

The Robinson-Patman Act, 1936. The act amended Section 2 of the Clayton Act. It was passed to supplement existing laws against unlawful restraints and monopolies. This law will be discussed in detail in Chapter 14, Pricing Merchandise for Resale.

Miller-Tydings Act, 1937. The act amended Section 1 of the Sherman Act and legalized the practice of resale price maintenance in interstate commerce.

Laws Affecting Customer Relations

The government is making increased efforts to provide fuller protection of consumers. Legislation has been passed to protect consumers in the following areas: (1) extension of credit, (2) product safety, (3) consumer protection, and (4) packaging, labeling, and advertising.[6]

Extension of Credit

Truth in Lending Act, 1968 (Consumer Credit Protection Act). This law was passed to protect the consumer in the use of credit. The law requires a full disclosure of the terms and conditions of finance charges in credit transactions. The Consumer Credit Protection Act created the National Commission on Consumer Finance to study and make recommendations on the need for further regulation of the consumer finance industry.

Fair Credit Billing Act, 1974. The act amended Section 102 of the Truth in Lending Act and increased consumer credit protection by adding provisions against inaccurate and unfair credit billing and credit-card practices.

Equal Credit Opportunity Act, 1974. The act amended the Truth in Lending Act by probiting discrimination on the basis of sex or marital status. The purpose of this law is to require that financial institutions and other firms engaged in the extension of credit make that credit equally available to all credit-worthy customers without regard to sex or marital status.

Product Safety

Wool Products Labeling Act, 1939. This law was passed to protect producers, manufacturers, distributors, and consumers from the unrevealed presence of substitutes and mixtures in spun, woven, knitted, felted, and other manufactured wool products. The FTC has the responsibility for enforcing the law.

Fur Products Labeling Act, 1951. The act was passed to protect consumers and retailers against misbranding, false advertising, and false invoicing of fur products and furs.

Flammable Fabrics Act, 1953; amended 1967. This law was passed to regulate the manufacture of highly flammable clothing. The act prohibits the introduction or movement in interstate commerce of articles of wearing apparel and fabrics that are highly flammable. In 1967 this act was amended to cover a wider range of clothing and interior furnishings.

Consumer Products Safety Act, 1972. This law established a new independent federal regulatory agency, the Consumer Product Safety Commission (CPSC). The Commission's primary goal is substantially to reduce injuries associated with consumer products. The responsibilities held by the Flammable Fabrics Act were transferred to the Consumer Product Safety Commission. Federal standards may be applied to the following areas:

General wearing apparel, effective 1954
Large carpets and rugs, effective 1971
Small carpets and rugs, effective 1971
Mattresses and mattress pads, effective 1973
Children's sleepwear, sizes 0–6X, effective 1972
Children's sleepwear, sizes 7–14, effective 1975

Textile Fiber Products Identification Act, 1958; amended 1965. The act was passed to protect producers and consumers against misbranding and false advertising of the fiber content of textile fiber products. The FTC has the responsibility for the enforcement and the policing of this law.

Consumer Protection

Magnuson-Moss Warranty—Federal Trade Commission Improvement Act, 1975. The act provided minimum disclosure standards for written consumer product warranties. It also defines minimum federal content standards for such warranties and amended the Federal Trade Commission Act to improve its consumer-protection activities.

Postal Reorganization Act, 1960. This act prohibited the mailing of unordered merchandise except for free samples that are clearly and conspicuously marked, as well as merchandise mailed by a charitable organization soliciting contributions.

Guide Concerning the Use of the Word "Free" and Similar Representations, 1971. The FTC has adopted a guide to encourage those merchants who make "free" and similar offers in connection with the sale of a product or service to comply voluntarily with the Federal Trade Commission Act. The guide defines the meaning of the word "free," establishes conditions for the use of the term, and identifies the supplier's responsibilities.

Packaging, Labeling, and Advertising

Fair Packaging and Labeling Act, 1966; amended 1968. The intent of this act is to regulate interstate and foreign commerce by preventing the use of unfair or deceptive methods of packaging or labeling of certain consumer products distributed in commerce.

Federal Cigarette Labeling and Advertising Act, 1965. This act was passed to regulate the advertising of cigarettes as well as to regulate packages of cigarettes that are manufactured, imported, or packaged for export from the United States.

Food, Drug, and Cosmetic Act, 1938. This law requires that a cosmetic be labeled without false or misleading representation and with information regarding the product, its manufacturer or distributor, and the quality of its contents. Four regulations have been issued by the Food and Drug Administration (FDA) in 1972 and 1973 that will afford consumers greater protection.

Regulation 1: A voluntary registration with FDA by cosmetic firms. As of 1974 a total of 771 manufacturing establishments out of an estimated 1,000 had registered. The cosmetics marketed by those companies represent approximately 85 percent of the cosmetic products now on the market.
Regulation 2: A call to cosmetic companies to submit formula information. As of 1974, only 50 percent out of 486 firms had submitted this information.
Regulation 3: The industry is asked to report to FDA any product experiences it learns about from consumers.
Regulation 4: This regulation requires cosmetic ingredients to be listed on the label, effective January 1, 1976.

Care Labeling of Textile Wearing Apparel, 1972. The FTC has ruled that it is an unfair method of competition and an unfair or deceptive act or practice to sell in commerce any textile product in the form of a finished article of wearing apparel that does not have a label or tag permanently

Explain How the Retail Buyer Will Meet the Challenge of Federal Legislation. How Will the Acts Listed Affect the Business Environment?

Laws Regulating Competition

The Sherman Antitrust Act, 1890
The Clayton Act, 1914
Federal Trade Commission Act, 1914, Amended 1938
Export Trade Act, 1918
Lanham Trademark Act, 1946, Amended 1962
The Robinson-Patman Act, 1936
The Miller-Tydings Act, 1937

Laws Affecting Customer Relations

Truth in Lending Act (Consumer Credit Protection Act), 1968
Fair Credit Billing Act, 1974
Equal Credit Opportunity Act, 1974
Wool Products Labeling Act, 1939
Fur Products Labeling Act, 1951
Flammable Fabrics Act 1953, Amended 1967
Consumer Products Safety Act, 1972
Textile Fiber Products Identification Act, 1958, Amended 1965
Magnuson-Moss Warranty—Federal Trade Commission Improvement Act, 1975
Postal Reorganization Act, 1960
Guide Concerning the Use of the Word "Free" and Similar Representations, 1971
Fair Packaging and Labeling Act, 1966, Amended 1968
Federal Cigarette Labeling and Advertising Act, 1965
Food, Drug, and Cosmetic Act, 1938
Care Labeling of Textile Wearing Apparel, 1972
Guides Against Bait Advertising, 1959
Guides Against Deceptive Pricing, 1964
Guides Against Deceptive Advertising of Guarantees, 1960

affixed or attached by the manufacturer of the finished article. The label or tag must clearly inform the consumer on instructions for the care and maintenance of the article.

Guides Against Bait Advertising, 1959. The FTC has adopted guides to protect consumers against bait advertising and related switch practices.

Such practices are declared unlawful and unfair methods of competition in commerce.

Guides Against Deceptive Pricing, 1964. The FTC has adopted guides to aid businesspersons who seek to conform to business practices that meet the requirements of fair and legitimate merchandising. The basic objective of these guides is to enable the retail buyer to advertise goods honestly and to avoid offering the consumer nonexistent bargains that will be misunderstood.

Guides Against Deceptive Advertising of Guarantees, 1960. The FTC has adopted guides to be used in the evaluation of the advertising of guarantees. In general, any guarantee in advertising must clearly inform the consumer of the nature and extent of the guarantee, the way in which the guarantor will perform, and the identity of the guarantor.

One Thing the Far-Sighted Buyer Must Be Prepared for Is to Accept and Anticipate Change. How Have the Following Affected the Buyer's Retailing Environment? How Has the Buyer Responded?

(1) Market Trends
(2) Economic Conditions
(3) Technological Advancements
(4) Competition
(5) International Retailing
(6) Federal Regulations

Chapter Summary

The buyer of the 1990s must keep pace by meeting the challenge of competition, keeping abreast of innovations in distribution, being constantly aware of federal legislation affecting retailers and consumers, and developing an awareness of the socioeconomic forces that are inherent in the retailer's environment in both domestic and foreign markets. Factors such as (1) market trends, (2) economic conditions, (3) technological advancements, (4) competition, (5) international retailing, and (6) federal regulations and their implications for the retail buyer are important.

Competition is an ever-present element in retailing. The buyer must be aware of trends in retailing such as (1) discounting, (2) merchandise scrambling, (3) franchising, (4) catalog presentation, (5) new store images, (6) retail store trends, and (7) diversification and mergers.

Discounting has changed from its original philosophy of low overhead and little service. Today it has become a major method of retailing in all types of stores.

More and more U.S. retailers have expanded into foreign markets as domestic markets became saturated. Foreign markets may represent better growth opportunities; however, retailers must be aware of the risks involved.

Over the years increased attention has been given to legislation governing the retailer's business activities. Laws regulating competition include: antitrust, unfair trade practice, and price competition. Laws affecting customer relations include: the extension of credit, product safety, consumer protection, and packaging, labeling, and advertising.

The past decade saw large retailers who attempted to sustain or enhance sales growth through diversification and mergers. Diversification allows retailers to become active in businesses outside their particular trade. Mergers occur between similar types of retailers.

Trade Terminology

1. Diversification
2. Mergers

Questions for Discussion and Review

1. Refer to the information on market trends. Discuss how this information may be used by the retail buyer of designer clothing, men's sportswear, and infant and toddler clothing.

2. How has the increase in the number of two-income households and single-parent households affected the retailer's business environment?

3. How will the retail buyer meet the challenge presented by increased federal legislation? Name and explain five examples of federal legislation of which the buyer should be aware.

4. Discuss various examples of technological advancements and their application to retailing. What technological advancements are affecting retail store operations today?

5. Compare the discount house of the past with the discounter of today? What changes have taken place? What are the reasons for such changes?

6. Explain five retailing trends the buyer should be aware of when attempting to respond to competitive changes?

7. Discuss the advantages as well as risks involved for the retailer who expands into foreign markets.

8. Define diversification and merger. Give examples of each.

9. Give examples of how retail institutions have adapted to changes in the environment in order to maintain a competitive edge.

10. Discuss present trends in the economy and the way economic conditions influence business strategies used by the retail buyer.

References

THE RETAIL
STUDENT'S REFERENCE LIBRARY

Barry, Thomas E. *Marketing.* New York: Dryden Press, 1987.

Compliance with Simplified Truth-in-Lending. New York: NRMA, 1985.

Directory of Retail Software. New York: NRMA, 1985.

Essential Strategies to Improve Productivity in a Maturing Marketplace. New York: NRMA, 1985.

Fair Credit Billing Act, New York: NRMA, 1985.

The Federal Trade Commission's Credit Practice Rule: Its Evolution and Impact on Retailing. New York: NRMA, 1985.

Harwell, Edward. *Management Development for Discount Stores.* New York: Lebhar Friedman, Inc., 1985.

How to Select an Advanced Communications System. New York: NRMA, 1985.

NRMA Standard Merchandise Classifications (Revised). New York: NRMA, 1985.

NRMA Voluntary Retail Identification Standards. New York: NRMA, 1985.

OCR—An Implementation Handbook. New York: NRMA, 1985.

OCT—A Cost Benefit Study. New York: NRMA, 1985.

Perspectives on Retail Strategic Decision Making. New York: NRMA, 1985.

Productivity in General Merchandise Retailing. New York: NRMA, 1985.

The Profit Maker, New York: NRMA, 1985.

A Retailer's Guide to Controlling Communications Expenses. New York: NRMA, 1985.

Rising Telecommunications Costs: Sources and Solutions. New York: NRMA, 1985.

Smart, Albert. *The How To's of Retail Franchising.* New York: Lebhar Friedman, Inc. 1985.

REFERENCES

1. "New Look at K Mart: Technology, Special Key," *Stores,* July, 1988, p. 39–40.
2. Electronic POS Debit System Draws Near At K Mart," by Dean Evans. *Discount Store News,* September 16, 1988, p. 84.
3. *Women's Wear Daily,* Nordstrom-SF: "A Blockbuster of An Opening," Steve Ginsberg. October 12, 1988, p. 32.
4. *Women's Wear Daily,* November 11, 1988, p. 33.
5. *Federal Trade Commission: The Statutes* (Washington D.C.: The Commission, December, 1981).
6. Ibid.

The Buyer's Responsibilities in Merchandising

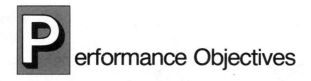

Performance Objectives

After reading this chapter, the student should be able to accomplish the following:

1. Define retail buyer and buying.

2. Discuss four factors affecting the scope of the buyer's job.

3. Learn three major classifications of organizational structure used by most retail stores.

4. Become aware of the five major categories of buying responsibilities.

5. Identify basic qualities that make a buyer a good manager.

6. Define assistant buyer.

7. Become aware of the responsibilities of the assistant buyer.

8. Explain the personal qualifications representative of many fields of management.

9. Prepare a chart listing the numerous merchandise categories that require buyer responsibilities.

10. Review steps in the retailing selection process.

The Buyer's Responsibilities in Merchandising

Figure 3-1 The buyer is the key individual in the retail store responsible for providing merchandise that will meet the needs of consumers. (Courtesy of La Bella Mods, Conshohocken, Pa.)

INTRODUCTION

In the previous chapter you read that retail merchandising is always in a state of change and those persons involved in the operations of a retail business are active and continually on the go. The buyer of the 1990s is no exception. He or she must keep pace by meeting the challenge of competition, keeping abreast of innovations in distribution, being constantly aware of federal legislation affecting retailers and consumers, and developing an awareness of the socioeconomic forces that are inherent in retailing in both domestic and foreign markets.

In this chapter we are concerned specifically with the buyer's responsibilities in merchandising. We will discuss the scope of the buyer's job and how the degree of responsibility may be affected by the organizational structure of the retail store, types of goods offered, the store's dollar volume, and location of store branches or units.

There are similarities in buying responsibilities. The buyer has a job as a manager, market forecaster, and merchandise planner.

You will learn about the challenge of retail buying and what it takes to go into merchandising. Types of available buying positions and opportunities for retail training will be discussed.

PART 1—Scope of the Buyer's Job

Although oftentimes called *department manager* in some types of retail stores, a *retail buyer* (Figure 3–1) may be identified as the key individual in the retail institution who is responsible for providing merchandise that will meet the needs of consumers. The action or activity performed by the buyer is called buying and may be defined as the purchase of consumer goods in relatively large or wholesale quantities for subsequent resale in smaller (retail) lots to the ultimate consumer.[1]

Many activities fall within the job responsibilities of a retail buyer. Although the buyer is often identified as one who travels to Hong Kong or Taiwan, views the latest fashions from Paris or London, or visits trade centers in Atlanta, Chicago, or Miami, the job of the buyer encompasses much, much more. The buyer's job requires an energetic, multi-talented person whose responsibilities range from housecleaning the department to making major merchandising decisions.

FACTORS AFFECTING THE SCOPE OF THE BUYERS JOB

Factors affecting the scope of the buyer's job are: (1) the organizational structure of the retail store, (2) the types of goods offered, (3) the store's dollar volume, and (4) the location of store branches or units.

The Organizational Structure of the Retail Store

There are three major classifications of organizational structure used by most retail stores (this topic will be covered in detail in Chapter 4).

Department and Specialty Stores with Branches. In department and specialty stores several individuals along with the buyer (for example, merchandise managers and assistant buyers) are assigned the responsibility of buying merchandise for one or more departments in the parent store or flagship store as well as for the branches. The buyer who works out of the main store also has the responsibility for the managerial functions of both the main store and branches. The buyer is responsible for department sales, selecting merchandise, making merchandise plans, budgeting, being sensitive to changes in customer demand, and being familiar with the peculiarities of the wholesale market. In recent years, with department stores and specialty stores expanding into markets that may be several miles away from the parent store, it has become increasingly difficult for store buyers to supervise selling activities. As a result this trend toward separation of buying and selling (a method that has proven to be successfully used by chain stores) places the selling activity under the supervision of the branch store manager. There are arguments for maintaining the present system of combining the buying and selling activities, and there are arguments for separating the buying and selling activities.

Centralized Management of Chain Stores. Since chain-store operations consist of many units that are similar in merchandise offerings and widespread over a particular geographical region, managerial and buying activities are centralized. Each unit in the chain offers similar types of goods, therefore it is more practical and more economical for one buyer to purchase goods for all the units of the chain rather than to have separate buyers for each member store. Since the buyer is primarily concerned with purchasing, the job of training sales people, inventory reordering, and so forth are the responsibilities of store managers.

The chain-store buyer or central buyer is located at a main headquarters, which is found in the major market center. For example, if the buyer is responsible for buying fashion apparel and accessories, he or she may be located in New York City; if responsible for purchasing sportswear, in Los Angeles; or, if responsible for purchasing home furnishings, in Atlanta or Chicago.

The chain-store buyer becomes an expert in the area of specialization because he or she is centrally located in the major market. The buyer must give close attention to market changes, take advantage of quantity and off-season purchases, make special arrangements with manufacturers for private labeling or branding, locate new manufacturers and vendors, and make accurate forecasts concerning supply conditions, production, and distribution. Being responsible for the movement of large quantities of merchandise, he or she must be constantly alert to changes in consumer demand and market trends, must effectively communicate with store managers about local consumer buying trends, and, if a buyer of fashion goods, must keep abreast of changes in fashion. These responsibilities can be overwhelming, and for this reason the chain-store buyer is usually a seasoned merchandiser who possesses a wealth of background and experience in a particular area of specialization.[2]

Independent Stores. In a small retail store the owner-manager is usually responsible for all the merchandise sold. He or she is, therefore, not only responsible for the management activities of the entire business but the buying-selling activity as well. As the buyer, the owner-manager visits the local markets and arranges to visit major market centers, with the number of buying trips dependent upon his or her time, energy, and finances. While visiting manufacturers, he or she is responsible for the selection of the merchandise assortment, the breadth and depth of the selection, and the placement of orders with vendors.

Next time you visit your nearest shopping center, take note of the number of small businesses selling everything from pet supplies to Indian jewelry to silk flower arrangements.

Types of Goods Offered

Types of goods carried by the retail store will affect the scope of the buyer's job.

Discount House Buyer. The mass merchandise buyer or discounter is primarily concerned with price. The buyer will continuously comb the market for the best prices, the best deals, convenient service, and merchandise lines that will appeal to the majority of customers. The buyer will concentrate on vendors and manufacturers who will offer "special buys," even though this may cause an imbalance in already existing lines of merchandise.

Most discount houses concentrate on selling home furnishings and related types of hard goods, with limited offerings in soft goods such as clothing and accessories. The discount-house buyer will usually purchase only those soft goods that have proved to be successful. Being responsible for the movement of low-priced merchandise in large quantities, the discount-house buyer must be constantly aware of supply and distribution conditions, changes in consumer demand, the state of the economy, and the amount of competition in the marketplace. He or she will work closely with market and trade specialists and remain in constant contact with store managers.

Variety-Store Buyer. Today, although the small five-and-dime or variety store still exists, most variety stores have grown into large chain operations (for example, F. W. Woolworth Company). The buyer for a variety store is located at a central headquarters and provides merchandise that appeals to the basic needs of the customers and lends itself to a self-service type of operation. Since the usual variety store provides hard goods (for example, pots and pans, kitchen utensils, hammers and nails), as well as soft goods (children's wear, linens and towels, curtains and drapes), buyers are appointed to cover specific markets to procure the best buys at the best prices. The variety-store buyer also assumes many of the responsibilities characteristic of the chain-store buyer.

Specialty-Shop Buyer. The specialty-shop buyer must adjust buying activities to meet the needs of the immediate trade area, since business depends to a great degree on the patronage of local customers. Since a specialty shop usually deals with single types of merchandise such as women's apparel and fashion accessories, its buyers will specialize in those particular markets when planning the store's merchandise assortment. The specialty-store buyer will visit local as well as central markets and, if the budget permits, foreign trade centers. He or she will work with the manager of each store in determining the merchandise assortment; assist in the formulation of effective buying policies; locate and negotiate with vendors and manufacturers who offer the best prices, service, and quality goods; forecast future trends that may affect sales; and keep current and accurate records. Since the entire store operation is oriented towards a particular line of goods, the specialty-store buyer is an expert in that particular area and does not necessarily have the vast market coverage usually required of the chain-store buyer.

Dollar Volume

A buyer who is responsible for purchasing large volumes of merchandise will spend the most time in the pursuit and purchase of goods, while the small volume buyer must pursue purchasing opportunities and attend to other managerial functions, such as training sales people.

By way of example, the large discount-chain buyer (who is responsible for purchasing goods for perhaps 2,000 to 3,000 stores) spends a great deal of time in the trade markets looking for the best prices, best deals, and lines of goods that will appeal to the majority of customers across the country. On the other hand, the department- or specialty-store buyer (who may be responsible for purchasing goods for, perhaps, 12 to 16 branch stores) concentrates not only on the procurement of goods but also assumes managerial responsibilities. The independent retailer (who may own more than one store) concentrates his or her efforts not only on the procurement of goods but on the management activity of the entire business.

Location of Store Branches or Units

As you have previously read, retail stores—large chain operations or department and specialty stores with branches—that have a significant number of branches or store units geographically located great distances from the parent store or central office virtually find it impossible for their buyers to engage in "on-the-floor" activities. By contrast, in retail organizations—smaller department stores and independent operations—where branch stores or units are located in close proximity, the buyer has the opportunity to become involved with "on-the-floor" activities.

Review How the Following Will Affect the Scope of the Buyer's Job

The Organizational Structure of the Retail Store
    Department and Specialty Stores with Branches
    Centralized Management of Chain Stores
    Independent Stores
The Types of Goods Offered
    Discount-House Buyer
    Variety-Store Buyer
    Specialty-Store Buyer
The Store's Dollar Volume
    Discount-Chain Buyer
    Department- or Specialty-Store Buyer
    Independent Retailer
The Location of Store Branches or Units
    Large Chain Operation
    Department and Specialty Store with Branches
    Independent Store

BUYING RESPONSIBILITIES

The scope of the buyer's job is dependent upon the organizational structure of the retail store, the types of goods offered, the store's dollar volume, and the location of store branches or units. For these reasons, therefore, it is important to keep in mind that the duties and responsibilities discussed may not necessarily be performed by all buyers. For purposes of discussion, however, buying responsibilities may be categorized as follows: (1) management responsibilities, (2) market forecasting, (3) merchandise planning and selection, (4) working with resources, and (5) preparing merchandise for sale.

Management Responsibilities

Successful buying depends a great deal on team play—the ability of people to work together for a common objective or goal. The buyer may have constant contact with salespeople, merchandise managers, staff personnel, other store buyers, and customers. He or she has the responsibility of running a good department, attracting consumers to the store, and, of course, maximizing profit. To fulfill these basic responsibilities, the buyer must have the ability to function as a manager. He or she must accept and discharge executive responsibility for carrying out company policy in and out of the store and must be able to get people to work together.[4]

With so many activities and responsibilities, the buyer is an important link in management's communication network. For example, in a department store the divisional merchandise manager communicates store policies down to the buyer. In turn, the buyer communicates with the assistant buyer, sales personnel, vendors, manufacturers, and customers. The buyer must also be alert to changes in personnel attitudes and values, market and supply conditions, and consumer buying habits. Such changes should be communicated upwards to top management through the divisional merchandise manager.[5]

What makes a buyer a good manager? What qualities must a buyer possess to foster team spirit and enthusiasm?

Basic Qualities for Management

Communicating with others
Fostering team spirit
Securing action
Delegating work

Communicating with Others. The most important quality for an individual considering a management position in any type of organization is the ability to communicate. This is especially true in an organization as complex as the retail store, which may have as few as two or as many as a thousand employees, and which has contacts with middlemen and consumers on a daily basis.

Communication is a daily job for the retail buyer. Some policies are formulated by top management and may remain as long as the store is in business, while other policies may last only briefly. The buyer must be aware of changes in policy and must communicate store philosophy to customers, to employees, and to new personnel.

Fostering Team Spirit. The buyer is responsible for getting people to work together as a team (Figure 3–2), and so must communicate enthusiasm and spirit to others. To accomplish this, the buyer must communicate his or her own enthusiasm for the store, the merchandise, and the customers. Since nothing is quite so contagious as enthusiasm and love for the job, individuals, whether they be the sales force, the vendors in the marketplace, or the

Figure 3-2 Successful buying depends on team play—on the ability of people to work together for a common goal. (Courtesy of The Gift Gallery, Havertown, Pa.)

store's customers, will be influenced and exert themselves willingly in the buyer's behalf. Remember: *buyers are selected for their managerial ability; however, the difference between a strong buyer and a weak buyer is the ability to build a team and foster enthusiasm!*

Securing Action. Since good management begins with the individual, the buyer who wants to secure action from others should first consider his or her own personality. A buyer who is indifferent and lacks purpose and direction can expect the same lack of interest in subordinates. The buyer must, therefore, delegate work that is planned in advance and well organized, and must consider the feelings of others. Then he or she can be assured that subordinates will take pride in their work and do their jobs competently and enthusiastically.

Delegating Work. Deciding who will do what job is an important phase of management. Today, so many buyers are responsible for more than one selling location (for example, the branch store), that proper delegation of work must be carefully and thoughtfully planned. The proper delegation of work responsibility involves three steps: (1) selecting the right person for the job, (2) assigning duties and responsibilities that are exact, and (3) following up to see that the job is executed properly.

1. Selecting the right person for the job. When selecting an individual for a particular job assignment, care must be taken that each person is placed in a position that will develop his or her talents and provide worthwhile experience. In selecting individuals as mid-management trainees, heads of stock, or assistants, their work habits, abilities, and experience must be considered. A person who is very successful doing one kind of job may be totally unsuccessful in another. Special care and consideration should be given to those individuals who will be responsible for the department in the absence of the buyer. A thoughtful executive will select the strongest possible subordinates and then continue to train them for increasing responsibility.

2. Assigning duties and responsibilities that are exact. An individual who is to work properly and efficiently must completely understand what is expected of him or her. The buyer must communicate directions in such a way that they are completely understood by subordinates. Direct and explicit instructions will decrease the likelihood of error and wasted time and energy. Subordinates should be encouraged to ask questions if they do not understand their assignments, and the buyer must have the patience and understanding to teach proper store methods and techniques.

3. Following up to see that the job is executed properly. When the buyer follows up, he or she must be careful not to embark upon a faultfinding mission or to discourage people's incentive and initiative. Follow-up, when accomplished properly, will encourage the worker to continue progress and provide satisfaction in a job well done. If fault is found, the buyer should be constructive in criticism and should attempt to determine the reason for the error, should offer suggestions for improvement, and assist the person in accomplishing it. This, however, may only be done through good human relations and a thorough understanding of individual differences.

Explain How the Following Are Important in the Delegation of Work Responsibility

1. Selecting the right person for the job
2. Assigning duties and responsibilities that are exact
3. Follow-up

Market Forecasting

The retail buyer also works in the capacity of a market specialist. The buying executive must be aware of external forces (market trends, economic conditions, technological advancements, and so forth) that will affect consumer attitude. The buyer needs to be knowledgeable about computer application(s) in merchandising, understand consumer behavior and what affects consumer buying decisions in the market place, and understand the importance and application of fashion information not only to fashion apparel but to all categories of merchandise. (More detailed discussion on these topics will be covered in later chapters.

Merchandise Planning and Selection

The buyer is a *planner*. He or she must know the essentials of good planning and the importance of record keeping since the buyer is instrumental in preparing the merchandise budget. Store buyers must know how assortment plans are developed. The buyer is also vital in the application of control system to merchandising. Knowing what merchandise to buy as well as how much to buy is an important buying responsibility.

TABLE 3–1.   A summary of buying responsibilities.

1. Formulating effective buying policies
2. Understanding the retail consumer; determination of the goods that consumers need and want
3. Effectively communicating with market and trade specialists
4. Continuously visiting local markets as well as central trade markets
5. Keeping abreast of market trends, economic conditions, competition, supply conditions, and methods of distribution
6. Developing an awareness of fashion trends and their influence on fashion merchandise as well as on other merchandise lines
7. Planning for effective merchandise control
8. Planning and selecting the merchandise assortment
9. Working with merchandise resources (vendors, manufacturers, suppliers)
10. Pricing merchandise for a profit
11. Advertising, displaying, and selling merchandise for resale
12. Employing good management techniques when working with trade specialists as well as store executives and personnel
13. Working as a liaison between the parent store and branch stores; between store managers and department managers

Working With Resources

The buyer must visit domestic and foreign trade centers. He or she may use the services of a resident buying office. The retail buyer must be aware of techniques used in making buying contacts, as well as in developing good buyer-vendor relations.

Preparing Merchandise for Sale

The store buyer must be aware of the legal aspects of pricing. Determining wholesale price, taking markdowns, and determining the retail price are all part of the buyer's job. The buyer must be an effective communicator. He or she should be aware of the psychological aspects of advertising, and determine how advertising is planned and the importance of ethics in advertising. As stated earlier, the buyer is a manager. Therefore, he or she manages retail salespeople and trains sales personnel. (More detailed discussion on these topics will be covered in Chapter 15). Table 3–1 contains a summary of buying responsibilities.

THE BUYER'S ASSISTANT

A retail buyer, whether a buyer for a department store, a chain operation, or a discount house, is basically in business for himself or herself. The buyer is responsible for the operation of the entire department and for making a profit for the department or store. Duties and responsibilities are far-reaching and often complex. With such broad responsibilities, the buyer must have the ability to delegate authority to subordinates, thus gaining needed time and energy to go about the business of buying.

In the department-store operation the buyer is out of the store much of the time; therefore, responsibilities are delegated to an assistant or understudy. The *assistant buyer* is an individual who has been selected for managerial potential and is capable of assuming the managerial functions of the department in the absence of the buyer. Table 3–2 lists the responsibilities of the assistant buyer.

The position of assistant buyer is of interest to many college graduates. This is usually the first position in mid-management in the retail store, particularly in the department store; it provides the graduate with the experience and training necessary for upper-management positions, especially the position of retail buyer. Part 2 of this chapter will discuss assistant buyer training in the retail department store.

TABLE 3-2. Responsibilities of the assistant buyer.

1. Managerial functions of the department when the buyer is out of the store
2. Paperwork involved with the movement of merchandise onto and off of the floor
3. Receiving, marking, and stock-keeping activities, and invoice and order checking problems
4. Presentation of new merchandise for display, coordinating promotion ads with the merchandise, and department housekeeping
5. Store communications; supervising salespeople; knowledge of merchandise trends and promotions; establishment of good communications among the merchandise staff and with management; visits to branch stores or other stores in the unit and maintenance of good telephone contacts

PART 2—Buying as a Career

THE CHALLENGE OF RETAIL BUYING

Usually, when retailing students are asked about their future plans and aspirations, a great number respond that they would like to be retail buyers. The merchandising function seems to be the most glamorous aspect of the retail operation, since it is directly involved with the public. Also, it affords opportunities for advancement in many areas of merchandising and in a variety of types of retail organizations.

The student who is interested in pursuing a career in retail buying will discover a great personal challenge (Figure 3–3). As a result of changes in consumer demand and changes brought about by the computer, the buyer's role is increasingly demanding. Retailers are extremely dependent on all kinds of changes. They must be both imaginative and analytical if they are to meet the challenges brought about by change and must take advantage of the opportunities it presents if they are to serve the consumer well.

For the most part, a career in retailing demands *a keen interest in merchandise, an equally keen interest in people, and an understanding of the world of fashion.* A unique element of retailing is that there is scarcely a career goal that cannot be reached through a retail organization.

WHAT IT TAKES

When attempting to discuss personal qualifications for a position in any profession, it is important to remember that each person is a unique individual

Figure 3-3 The merchandising function affords many opportunities for advancement in retailing. The student who is interested in pursuing a career in retailing will discover a great personal challenge.

with unique characteristics. Guidelines may be developed to assist students in the choice of a career or field of endeavor; however, it is the responsibility of the individual to determine what best meets his or her goals and aspirations. The following presents a listing of those personal qualifications that are needed not only in retailing but also in many of the fields of management. Special skills required depend on the responsibilities of the particular position. The responsibilities and qualifications of a buyer and those of the assistant will be discussed throughout this book. Generally, the following characteristics may be considered: (1) educational background, (2) attitude,

Figure 3-4 Attitude, dedication to hard work, long hours, knowledge of the trade, and enthusiasm add up to a successful retailer. (Courtesy of L. S. Ayers, Indianapolis, Ind.)

(3) dedication to hard work, (4) dedication to long hours, (5) knowledge of the trade, (6) enthusiasm, and (7) managerial ability[6] (Figure 3-4).

Educational Background

Today a great deal of emphasis is placed upon the college degree, whether from the four-year college or the two-year college. What is the reason for this emphasis? Generally, the educational system develops discipline in learning, sharpens intellectual abilities, and provides a frame of reference that may guide the student in the choice of a career. For students interested in pursuing careers as a buyer, the following core business subjects should be considered.

Retailing Math. A knowledge of the basic mathematical process required for business calculations is essential. The fundamentals of arithmetical operations and business problem-solving techniques are basic mathematical skills needed in retailing. The student will be surprised at the extent to which business judgments depend upon accurate figures.

Management. An introductory course in the field of management will present an organized body of knowledge applicable to various management situations. As stated previously, the buyer and the assistant buyer are responsible for communicating company policy both in and out of the store and, therefore, are vital links in management's communications network.

Marketing. Marketing is the process by which trading relationships are established and maintained in a complex and specialized economy. Learning the role of the marketing function as a social institution and understanding consumer characteristics and buying habits and the relationship of various marketing systems to the American economic system will assist the retail buyer in the decision-making process.

Advertising. Communications within the marketplace will provide the consumer with the necessary information to find the right goods at the right place and for the best price. Advertising is the basic persuasion tool utilized by retail firms to sell their products. An understanding of advertising will familiarize the student with the social, psychological, economic, and governmental constraints involved in the development of such a communications system.

Retail Management. The functions of management as specifically related to the retailing industry are of paramount importance to a student pursuing a career in the retail trade. A course in retail management will discuss the basic principles of retailing, the organization of management, and the layout and organization of a store, as well as many of the problems involved in the retail industry.

Textiles. A basic course in textiles will provide information concerning different types of fabric construction, fabric weaves, the various types of dyes, and fabric finishes. With rapid technological changes occurring in the textile industry and the related needle trade industry, the buyer and his or her assistant are continuously deluged with new types of fabrics, finishes, and fibers.

Fashion Merchandising. The fashion industry is perhaps the prime force that influences the consumer in making purchases. A knowledge of the language of fashion and an in-depth study of the tools of fashion such as color, line, and design, and of the influences of the fashion designers and fashion leaders, provide the student with information that is of vital importance in selecting merchandise for the consumer.

Electronic Data Processing (EDP). The influence of the computer was discussed in Chapter 1. In a retail store, information on such business activities as sales transactions, credit and collections, charge accounts, and inventory turnover is provided by the computer. An introductory course with a managerial approach will give the student an understanding of the importance, advantages, uses of, and problems with the computer and of its future in the business environment.

Economics. A course in economics will present an overview of the American economy, a study of the determinants of level of income and employment, and an analysis of business and its various resources. The student of retailing will learn how the state of the economy can affect the spending power of the individual consumer and thus influence buying decisions.

Retail Buying. A course in retail buying will provide the student with a knowledge of the problems, policies, and techniques necessary for successful buying and selling activities in different types of retail stores. Such a course does not qualify an individual for an immediate position as a buyer; however, upon graduation many students are qualified to join junior executive trainee programs and work towards a position in upper management. Such programs will be discussed in detail later in this chapter.

Other Academic Subjects. Retailing is directly related to many other subjects that are a part of the business college curriculum, such as accounting, statistics, personnel management, business law, and report writing. Retailing draws freely from sociology; the buyer as a member of society must have an understanding of the social nature of human beings of the social world in which they live. Retailing is related to psychology, which is the study of the basic ideas and principles of human behavior. Course work in psychology will assist the buyer in attempting to determine what motivates the consumer during the selection process.

Liberal Arts Subjects. Course work in English composition that emphasizes sentence structure, the mechanics of punctuation and grammar, and paragraph development will help the student to achieve clear expression in writing. Course work in science, history, and philosophy will also broaden the student's intellectual scope, so that he or she will be a well-rounded individual on entering the realistic, complex world of business.

Attitude

Attitude is a person's mental position or feeling towards an object. Attitude or "spirit" is of vital importance to the student who is considering retailing as a profession—a strong desire for the field of retailing, with its long hours and hard work, criticism, and dejection—for the opportunity to do something for other people and to provide goods that satisfy a need—a feeling for what is new and exciting. This is the job of the retail buyer! This is the job of the assistant buyer!

Dedication to Hard Work

Dedication to hard work is dedication to standing on your feet for eight hours a day, continuously listening to people complain, confusion and turmoil, delayed deliveries, misplaced merchandise, goods marked incorrectly, and so on and so on. Hard work perhaps is in the eyes of the beholder. It is what you consider hard work that matters, but also what you consider exciting and challenging!

Dedication to Long Hours

The buyer, like most people in business, has a minimum of time that needs to be spent in accomplishing his or her work. However, when most people are relaxing, having fun and enjoying a holiday, the buyer is working. The buyer is responsible for providing all the merchandise and conveniences to encourage the shopper to return to the particular department or store. Not only is the buyer responsible for providing consumer conveniences; he or she also spends many hours doing routine paperwork, planning merchandise assortments, evaluating market conditions, and traveling to various market centers, branch stores, or store units.

Knowledge of the Trade

As a result of your experiences as a mid-management trainee or as an assistant buyer, your knowledge of the trade will develop. A knowledge of which merchandise vendors are providing the best service, the best prices, and the best merchandise lines for your particular market is essential. Trade knowledge can only come with experience, sensitivity, and confidence. As an assistant, you are exposed to the marketplace; with the guidance of knowledgeable buyers, you will soon learn your way around.

Enthusiasm

A keen interest in the field of retailing is an excellent ingredient for success. Enthusiasm for the job will bring you to work before starting time and often keep you on the job after your co-workers have gone home. It is your enthusiasm that brings you to work on Saturday morning and perhaps on the day right after a holiday. Dedication to the job and sincerity in doing a good job are all qualities basic to a good manager and, consequently, to a good retail buyer.

Managerial Ability

The scope of managerial responsibilities delegated to the new junior executive is dependent upon his or her background and experience. For a recent graduate working in the capacity of a mid-management trainee, managerial responsibilities are limited. However, handling the responsibilities delegated will provide the trainee with the necessary experience to handle more complex management decisions.

TYPES OF AVAILABLE BUYING POSITIONS

A student who states that he or she is interested in pursuing a career as a retail buyer is often unaware of the many types of merchandise within a retail store that require buyer responsibilities. Most individuals think in terms of the department-store buyer who covers the fashion market in women's apparel or in men's wear. However, buyers are also required in the area of furniture, for example, occasional and modern furniture, bedding, springs, and mattresses; in the home areas of radios and accessories, major appliances, linens and towels, china and glassware; in the budget area, for example, linens and domestics, gifts, infants' apparel and furniture, and luggage; and in the areas of pictures and picture frames, paints and artist supplies, cameras, sporting goods, and of sewing machines and piece (fabric) goods. Table 3–3 shows the merchandise categories of one type of store. The graduate should carefully investigate the merchandise breakdown of the particular store in which he or she intends to pursue a career in retailing as an assistant buyer.

OPPORTUNITIES FOR RETAIL TRAINING PROVIDED BY EDUCATIONAL INSTITUTIONS

High-school and college students often serve as an excellent source of employees for retail organizations. As a result of the availability of large sums of money from the federal government, many high schools, community colleges, and four-year colleges and universities have become more interested in vocational or career education programs. They have come to realize that many young people want and need to begin work early in life. Therefore, educational institutions throughout the United States have developed cooperative work-study programs for students interested in careers in distribution, retailing, marketing, and management.

TABLE 3–3 Merchandise categories that require buyer responsibilities.

Fashion Division

SHOES	Junior intimate	MEN'S FURNISHINGS	Active sportswear
Children's shoes	apparel	Made-to-order	Misses' sweaters
Women's shoes	Daytime lingerie	Hats and caps	Contemporary
(designer)	Sleepwear	Better-priced clothing	DESIGNER
Casual shoes	FASHION	Tailored sports clothing	CLOTHING
Men's shoes	ACCESSORIES	Shirts and ties	Tribout accessories
CHILDREN'S WEAR	Costume jewelry	Furnishings and	Couturier shop
Children's accessories	Rainwear	accessories	WOMEN'S CLOTHING
Infants' wear	Ladies' belts	Active sportswear	Better dresses
Toddler boys' wear	Sunglasses	SPORTSWEAR	Inexpensive dresses
Little girls' wear	Handkerchiefs	AND JUNIOR	Bridal salon
Boys' and girls'	Moderate-priced	SPORTSWEAR	Moderate-priced
outerwear	handbags	Better junior coats	Better knits
Boy and Girl Scouts	Small leather goods	Junior coats and suits	Casual dresses
Underwear and	Millinery	Better junior dresses	Coats and suits
sleepwear	Gloves	Junior dresses	Aprons and uniforms
INTIMATE	Hosiery	Blouses	
APPAREL	Slippers		
Foundations			
Robes and loungewear			

Home Furnishings Division

FURNITURE	Black-and-white TV	Infants' apparel and	Curtains
Bedding	Stereo-combination	furniture	Trim-a-tree
Upholstered furniture	Phonographs	Little girls' wear	Pictures, frames
Case goods	Radios and	Little boys' wear	Gift shop
Occasional furniture	accessories	Men's clothing	Candle and flower shop
Summer furniture	Records, cabinets	Luggage	Contract department
Colonial furniture	and players	Curtains, draperies	Hostess shop
Springs and	MISCELLANEOUS	Aprons, housedresses	Small electrics
mattresses	Notions, closet	Misses' dresses	Housewares, furniture
Dual sleep furniture	accessories	Women's dresses	Cookware and pantry
Modern furniture	Laces, ribbons,	Junior dresses	Bath shop
Interior design	trimmings	Gloves and umbrellas	Paints
DOMESTICS	Drugs	Hosiery	Toys
Blankets, comforters,	Fine jewelry and	Millinery	Artist supplies
spreads	clocks	HOME	Hobby
Towels	Precious jewelry	Art needlework	Cameras
Linens	Silverware	Oriental rugs	Sporting goods
China	Books	Carpets and broadlooms	Luggage
Glassware	Stationery	Domestic rugs	Sewing machines
Major appliances	Greeting cards	Lamps	Storm windows
Color TV	Candy	Custom fabric	
	Gourmet shop	Draperies	
	BUDGET		
	Linens, domestics		
	Gifts		

Cooperative work-study programs vary with the objectives of the educational institutions. Two-year colleges and senior colleges usually implement their cooperative work-experience programs in the following way: the student is employed for a specific time period (one to three semesters) during the school year with a retail organization selected by the college coordinator. The student usually receives academic credit while working. At the same time, he or she is employed by the retail organization and is receiving a planned work experience and an opportunity to apply classroom theory to on-the-job training. At the end of the training period, the student returns to college for the completion of studies. Other kinds of cooperative work-study programs permit the student to continue classroom studies while being trained in job skills on a part-time basis. The cooperative plan will vary with the educational institution and the particular retail firm. Figure 3–5 and Table 3–4 illustrate a cooperative program offered by the John Wanamaker department store in Philadelphia.

The success of these occupational programs is based on the cooperation that exists between the school and the retail firm. It is during the cooperative work-study experience that many young people have an opportunity to investigate the multitude of positions available in retailing. Here the student may begin training for the position of assistant buyer.

Figure 3–5   Cooperative work experience programs permit the student to continue classroom studies while being trained on the job. (Courtesy of John Wanamaker Department Store, Philadelphia, Pa.)

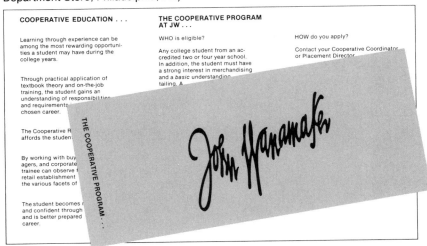

TABLE 3–4. A cooperative work experience plan used by one type of retail store.*

First week	Training	Store orientation, learn sales techniques, store procedure, cash register, training and development
Second week Third week	Sales	Apply basic selling techniques, develop good work habits, handle customer problems, develop product knowledge, learn display work, learn how to take orders, follow directions, give orders
Fourth week	Stock	Learn stock procedure, receiving, checking, marking, shipment to branch stores
Fifth week	Adjustments and complaints	Learn process involved in handling customer complaints, and returned merchandise
Sixth week	Control	Learn to handle vendor returns, defective merchandise, lost or stolen merchandise, shipments to branch stores
Seventh week	Credit	Observe techniques in credit and collections, interview new accounts, check credit references
Eighth week Ninth week Tenth week Eleventh week Twelfth week	Buyer's office	Assist in clerical work, engage in telephone contacts with vendors and branch stores, learn purchase journal procedure and inventory control, department housekeeping, scheduling of sales force, handling customer complaints, returned merchandise, and exchanges, develop good personnel relations, handle special events, learn sales promotion

*Length of time spent in each work experience is dependent upon the experience of the student as well as upon the needs of the store.

OPPORTUNITIES FOR EXECUTIVE DEVELOPMENT PROVIDED BY RETAIL INSTITUTIONS

Retail organizations provide store management training programs since most of their personnel is actively employed in the management of the store operations. However, with growth and expansion of many retail stores, man-

Figure 3–6   A Typical Pattern for Preparing New Recruits in Merchandising.

agement has found it necessary to provide training programs for individuals interested in pursuing careers in merchandising. You should review Appendix C, Selected Firms Seeking Qualified People.

Figure 3–6 is representative of a typical pattern used by a retail store for preparing new recruits for executive positions in merchandising.

Trainee

The graduate who has limited or no previous retailing experience goes through a planned training program. The length of time may vary from one to three weeks, depending on the policy of the store. The trainee is introduced to store procedure and policy, employee benefits, and cash register control, as well as other activities involved in the movement of merchandise. Trainees are usually required to work on the selling floor for a period of time to learn basic merchandise and to gain experience in meeting and working with people.

Junior Assistant Buyer

Depending on the size of the department, some buyers have more than one assistant, who in turn has helpers. The junior assistant will remain in that position long enough to prove his or her capabilities, and is then usually promoted to the next level, that of assistant buyer.

Assistant Buyer

By this time the student should have a good idea of the merchandise category that interests him or her. As stated previously, the assistant buyer is responsible for performing numerous clerical duties, managing sales personnel and stock people, keeping good telephone contacts with branch stores or other store units, following up with vendors and manufacturers, and planning neat, well-organized merchandise presentations. The assistant buyer will usually remain in this position from one to three years. However, this will vary with individual potential as well as the needs of the store. (Review Table 3–1, "A Summary of Buying Responsibilities.")

Manager

After an appreciable amount of time the assistant buyer, if working in a department store, may achieve a position in a branch store as a group manager. In a chain operation, the assistant buyer may achieve a position as a department manager. As manager of one or more departments, he or she is responsible for organizing the sales force, communicating with the buyer, analyzing consumer needs and wants, handling customer complaints, and preparing merchandise for the selling floor. In this capacity the manager learns firsthand the problems faced by retail buyers in determining consumer preferences, the problems with deliveries and lost or stolen merchandise, and the results of poor communications.

Retail Buyer

The position of retail buyer may be achieved in less than five years in most types of retail stores. The new buyer has been exposed to many of the responsibilities concerned with buying and selling, advertising, display, stock keeping, and vendor relations, as well as having experience in management. He or she is now prepared to take on the duties, responsibilities, and prestige that have been justly earned and now are deserved. (Review Table 3–1 again.)

Merchandise Manager

The merchandise manager, usually found at the head of the merchandising division, may have a number of divisional merchandise managers working under him or her, each of whom is a specialist in a particular line of merchandise. The divisional merchandise managers are responsible for the activities of the buyers of the various selling departments under the merchandise manager's jurisdiction. The buyer will consult with the divisional merchandise manager as to the seasonal merchandise plan, the amount of merchandise to purchase for a selling season, the best method of promoting sales, future market trends, and so forth. In many retail stores, the divisional merchandise manager must also sign the buyer's order form before it is sent to the vendor or manufacturer. The job of merchandise manager is considered a top executive position and one that requires a great deal of experience in the retail trade. The student should review Appendix C and D.

ADVICE TO THE NEW ASSISTANT BUYER

As stated previously, the job of assistant buyer is usually the first position in mid-management in a retail store that will provide the graduate with the experience and training necessary for an upper-management position. As a fresh recruit in the field of retailing, the new assistant buyer is immediately challenged by an entirely new set of problems and by new situations that will stimulate learning and growth. He or she is supported by the knowledge of being well enough thought of by superiors to be promoted to this new job, which is a giant step forward in a retailing career. However, this confidence should not lead the new assistant buyer to seek self-sufficiency in decision making too soon. It would be well to avoid "coming on too strong." Since inexperience is to be expected on a new job, the assistant should not be embarrassed to ask questions and should not ignore methods and procedures that have been established. The new assistant buyer will no doubt find some problems left by the previous assistant. The newcomer should accept these negative conditions without complaint and instead learn from both the errors and the achievements of those who have gone before.

The new assistant will immediately be snowed under by the attention of store employees, particularly those in the same department, of merchandise suppliers, of the customers, and of the buyer. The newcomer should listen carefully to the suggestions of peers and, most importantly, to the advice and direction of the buyer.

The buyer was chosen for both professional experience and ability as a manager. A good buyer will take the time and effort to train and instruct a new assistant properly and will provide learning experiences that will prove beneficial to buyer, assistant, and company. It is important for the assistant and the buyer to establish a good working relationship early and develop the ability to effectively communicate.[7]

THE RETAILING
SELECTION PROCESS

Too many students go looking for a job without preparing themselves. Here are a few items you should think about whether looking for a part-time or full-time position:

Preliminary Screening Interview

Usually, you are screened as soon as you walk into the personnel office. Preliminary screening is used to eliminate the obviously unqualified applicant. Poor appearance, unrelated job experience, inadequate education, poor communications skills, and poor preparation in general will lead to your elimination as a likely candidate.

Employment Application

Nearly all retailers use an application form as a tool in selecting new employees. The application collects information about your education, work experience, special skills, general background, and references. Figure 3–7 is an example of an employmnt application. Keep in mind, however, that information requested on an employment application should not lead to discrimination against applicants. Questions regarding age, sex, race, religion, national origin, or family status may violate Title VII of the Civil Rights Act of 1964.

Preparation of the Resume

Preparing a good resume is vital. You resume should be up-to-date, contain no spelling or typing errors (have a friend check it over), be concise and to the point, and above all, neat. If photocopied, copies should be of good quality and clear. Be sure to include a statement regarding your career objective, skills, experience and accomplishments, educational achievements and rewards, employment history, and references. Figure 3–8 is an example of what a resume should look like.

A Good Appearance

A good professional, business-like appearance is a definite must. Remember, the interviewer will be looking at you as a future store representative, as a candidate for management, as one who must perpetuate the image of the retailing establishment. Jeans, unkempt hair, gaudy and loud clothing and accessories, and a sloppy appearance communicate a lack of good business

Figure 3–7 Application for Employment Form.

APPLICATION FOR EMPLOYMENT						Date _____

Name _____ LAST _____ FIRST _____ MIDDLE

Social Security No. _____

Please mention any other name under which you have worked or been educated _____

Present Address _____ (No. & Street) _____ (City or Town) _____ (State) (Zip)   Tel. No. _____

What has prompted your application to our Company? _____

Positions Desired: 1. _____   Minimum Salary Required _____

2. _____   Date Available for Work _____

	NO	YES	Where		When
Have you ever been previously employed by this Company			Where		When
Have you ever previously applied for employment with this Company?			Where		When
If you are not a citizen of the United States do you have a legal right to work in this country?					
Do you have any physical defects or chronic ailments that would limit your performance in the positions stated above?			Describe		
Have you ever been convicted of shoplifting, theft or other felonies?			Describe		

EDUCATION

NAME AND ADDRESS OF SCHOOL	Dates Attended From	To	Major Study	Type of Degree	Grade Average
High School					
Address					
College of University					
Address					
Business or Technical School					
Address					
Other					
Address					

Hobbies, sports, school and other activities which may have contributed to your job skills.	Technical or business skills including special courses and training

MILITARY SERVICE

If you have served in the U. S. Armed Services, what Branch?	
Length of time spent in Military Service	Highest rank achieved
Describe duties and training _____	

sense and awareness. Refer to the Retailing Students Reference Library at the end of this chapter for references on proper attire for the job interview.

Testing

Many retailing institutions use testing as an integral component in the selection process. Tests are used to screen applicants in terms of math and verbal skills, abilities, aptitudes, interest, personality, and attitudes. Bone

PREVIOUS EMPLOYMENT

Address	To
Title or Position	Name & Title of Immediate Supervisor
Duties	
Reason for Termination	Salary

Name of Company	From
Address	To
Title or Position	Name & Title of Immediate Supervisor
Duties	
Reason for Termination	Salary

Name of Company	From
Address	To
Title or Position	Name & Title of Immediate Supervisor
Duties	
Reason for Termination	Salary

Name of Company	From
Address	To
Title or Position	Name & Title of Immediate Supervisor
Duties	
Reason for Termination	Salary

REFERENCES

NAME	POSITION	COMPANY OR INSTITUTION	ADDRESS

(SIGNATURE OF APPLICANT)

up on business math, especially, before you begin your job hunting campaign.

Interviewing

The interview is the most widely used and probably the most important method of assessing the qualifications of job applicants. Keep in mind that your interviewer will be trying to accomplish the following objectives:

Figure 3–8   What a Resumé Should Contain

Sample Resumé
GERALD A. DOUGHERTY
32 Livezey Drive
Philadelphia, PA 19107
215-972-7569

EMPLOYMENT OBJECTIVE:	Position as assistant buyer through a formal management training program in a retail department store
PERSONAL: (OPTIONAL)	Height: 6'2" Weight: 185 lbs. Health: Excellent Birth Date: May 22, 1969 Marital Status: Single
EDUCATION:	Community College of Philadelphia Associate Applied Science Degree June, 1990 Major: Fashion Buying Deans List: 1989, 1990 Philadelphia College of Textiles and Science Bachelor of Business Administration June, 1984 Major: Retail Marketing Management Class Rank: Top 10%
SCHOLARSHIPS AND AWARDS:	Community College of Philadelphia President's Award for Academic Excellence, 1989 and 1990
EXTRACURRICULAR ACTIVITIES:	President, Retail Management Club, 1989 Vice President, American Marketing Association, 1988 Member, Varsity Soccer Team, 1989, 1990
WORK EXPERIENCE: June 1989 to January 1990	Cooperative Work Period, Spring–Fall Semester, Macy's, Court, King of Prussia, PA 25 hours per week. Responsibilities included assisting department manager, department housekeeping, scheduling sales people, inventory follow-up
September 1987 to August 1988	Sales Associate, The Man's Shop, Eighth and Chestnut Streets, Philadelphia, PA Responsibilities included selling men's suits, checking and setting up merchandise, display work
REFERENCES:	Will be furnished upon request

1. Assessing your potential for advancement
2. Determining your ability to get along with others
3. Assessing your personality
4. Determining if you will fit into the organization

Figure 3–9 provides an outline of questions you should ask yourself before going on an interview.

Figure 3–9   Questions to Ask Yourself before Going on a Job Interview

1. What do I know about the company?
   Know something about the organization. Go to the business section of the library or your college placement office and locate the company's annual report. Read up on the company's financial review, accounting policies, operations reports, plans for future expansion, location of corporate headquarters. Know the type of merchandise sold, customers catered to, locations of other stores.
2. How best can I sell myself?
   Once you know something about the company, think how best you can sell yourself. Recalling the primary objectives of the interview, relate this to your own strengths and weaknesses. Be honest. Tell the interviewer about your talents and skills. If you had to drop out of school, tell the interviewer and explain why.
3. How will unrelated work experience apply?
   If your past work experience and the position you are applying for do not relate, emphasize your experience in working with people, in taking and perhaps giving orders, in showing up on time for work and perhaps staying late.
4. What salary should I ask for?
   Unless you have some idea of the salary scale (from people who work for the company or your college placement office) you may leave salary open for discussion. You may even emphasize that you are more interested in work experience than salary.
5. How does the interview begin?
   Be aware of social graces when going on an interview. For example, shake hands, remove coat and hat, smoke only if invited, do not "hog" the conversation, remove sunglasses (eye contact is very important during an interview), and do not slouch, chew gum, or wear heavy cologne or perfume.
6. What kinds of questions will be asked?
   Usually, questions will include your short- and long-range plans, reason for wanting to work at the particular company, why should you be hired, what is your definition of success, what makes you think you're a good

manager or leader, will you be furthering your education, what are your strengths and weaknesses, can you work under pressure.

7. What job am I applying for?
    Determine the kind of job you want before going to the interview. If you want sales, think in terms of the various departments in which you would like to work. If you are interviewing for an assistant buyer trainee position, think in terms of the merchandise you would like to work around.

8. What kinds of questions should I ask?
    Oftentimes, the applicant (usually because of lack of experience with interviewing) does not ask questions. Ask about salary, benefits, vacation, amount of overtime, etc. And, if the job being offered is not for you, say so.

9. Should I show that I'm a go-getter and aggressive?
    Let the interviewer know you want the job, are willing to work hard, and that you are ambitious and want to succeed. Effectively communicate that you want to grow and you want to be with a company that is interested in doing the same thing.

10. How should I follow up?
    Follow up with a short letter or a telephone call. Let the interviewer know if you have enjoyed the interview and are interested in joining the company. And thank the interviewer for taking time to see you.

Reference Checks

Once you successfully clear the interview, the retailer will usually conduct background and reference checks. The purpose of checking your background and references is to make sure the information you provided is accurate and honest. For this reason, be sure and get permission of those individuals you use as reference. Make sure you spell names correctly, and provide accurate addresses and telephone numbers. You would hate to miss out on a job because the interviewer could not get in touch with references due to incorrect addresses or phone numbers.

Job Placement

Once you have been selected for a particular position, you are now ready to receive an orientation to the job. The purpose of the orientation process is to introduce you to the company, to your job, to your co-workers. As a new recruit you must "earn your way around" in order to feel comfortable, thus, to succeed. Much of your orientation will take place on an informal basis, through conversation with other employees, or formally through training sessions.

Chapter Summary

The retail buyer is the key individual within the retail institution who is responsible for providing merchandise that will meet the needs of consumers. Buying is the purchase of consumer goods in relatively large or wholesale quantities for subsequent resale in smaller (retail) lots to the ultimate consumer.

Certain factors will affect the scope of the buyer's job, such as the organizational structure of the retail store, the types of goods offered, the store's dollar volume, and the location of store branches or units. There are three major classifications of organizational structure used by most retail stores: department and specialty stores with branches, centralized management of chain stores, and independent stores. Buying responsibilities may be categorized in the following way: management responsibilities, market forecasting, merchandise planning and selection, and working with resources and preparing merchandise for sale. (Review the list in Table 3–1.)

Successful buying depends a great deal on the ability of a buyer to work as a manager. Basic qualities a buyer must possess to be a manager are the ability to communicate, to foster team spirit, to get action, and to delegate work responsibility. Deciding who will do what job is an important phase of management. The proper delegation of work responsibility involves three steps: (1) selecting the right person for the job, (2) assigning duties and responsibilities that are exact, and (3) following up to see that the job is executed properly. The assistant buyer is an individual who has been selected for managerial potential and who is able to assume the managerial functions of the department in the absence of the buyer. This is usually the first position in mid-management in the retail store.

The merchandising function seems to be the most glamorous aspect of the retail operation and affords opportunities for advancement in many areas. For the most part, a career in retailing demands a keen interest in merchandise, an equally keen interest in people, and an understanding of the world of fashion. The student considering a job in retailing will need to have the following characteristics: a suitable educational background, a good attitude, dedication to hard work, dedication to long hours, knowledge of the trade, enthusiasm, and managerial ability. The student should be aware of the many merchandise categories in different types of retail stores that require buying responsibilities. Table 3–3 lists a number of these merchandise categories. Opportunities are provided by educational institutions for retail training through cooperative work-study plans. Retail institutions also provide executive development programs for graduates, especially in the area of merchandising. Review Figures 3–6, 3–7, and 3–8 for tips on the retailing selection process.

Trade Terminology

DIRECTIONS: Briefly explain or discuss each of the following trade terms:

1. Retail buyer
2. Buying

3. Assistant buyer

Questions for Discussion and Review

1. Define retail buyer and assistant buyer.

2. Define buying.

3. List the responsibilities of the buyer and of the assistant buyer.

4. Discuss various factors affecting the scope of the buyer's job.

5. What are the three major classifications of organizational structure used by most retail stores.

6. Discuss how the buying activity is a management function.

7. What is the cooperative work-study plan? Do you feel that such plans have any value? Explain your answer.

8. If you were asked to speak to a group of high-school students on the value of a college education in the field of retailing, what would you tell them?

9. Students often wonder why they are required to take course work in science and humanities along with their business subjects. How would you explain this requirement?

10. Refer to Table 3–3. As an assistant buyer, which merchandise category would you be interested in? Why?

11. After reading "Advice to the New Assistant Buyer," what problems would you anticipate as a fresh recruit in the field of retailing? How would you overcome these problems?

References

THE RETAIL STUDENT'S REFERENCE LIBRARY

Boosting Employee Performance Through Better Motivation. New York: NRMA, 1988.

Cash, Patrick R. and Frankel, Harold H. *Improving Apparel Shop Profits.* New York: NRMA, 1988.

Complying with the Federal Fair Employment Practice Laws & Regulations. New York: NRMA, 1988.

Complying with the Federal Wage-Hour Law and Regulations. New York: NRMA, 1988.

Effective Interviewing. New York: NRMA, 1988.

Employee Relations Bulletin. New York: NRMA, 1988.

Employer's Handbook of Federal Labor Relations Laws. New York: NRMA, 1988.

The Employment Interview. Bronx: MPC Educational Publishers, n.d.

Executive Compensation Survey of the Retailing Industry. New York: NRMA, 1987.

FUD (Fear, Uncertainty, Doubt). New York: NRMA, 1988.

Glasser, Rollin. *Retail Personnel Management.* New York: Lebhar-Friedman Inc. 1986.

Human Relations for Success in Business. Bronx: MPC Educational Publishers, n.d.

Job Orientation. Bronx: MPC Educational Publishers, n.d.

Kell, E. C. *Performance Appraisal and the Manager.* New York: Lebhar-Friedman Inc. 1986.

McLaughlin, John E. *Writing a Job Winning Resume.* Englewood Cliffs: Prentice Hall Pub. Co., 1985.

Measuring Executive and Employee Performance. New York: NRMA, 1988.

Personnel Practices of the Retail Industry. New York: NRMA, 1988.

Retail Job Analysis and Job Evaluation. New York: NRMA, 1987.

REFERENCES

1. K. Gillespie and J. C. Hecht, *Retail Business Management* (New York: Gregg/McGraw-Hill Book Company, 1970), pp. 150–152.
2. Donald L. Belden, *The Role of the Buyer in Mass Merchandising* (New York: Chain Store Publishing Corporation, 1971), pp. 1–7.
3. D. J. Duncan and C. F. Phillips, *Retailing Principles and Methods* (Homewood, Ill.: Richard D. Irwin, Inc., 1969), pp. 15–18.
4. K. Gillespie and J. E. Hecht, *Retail Business Management* (New York: Gregg/McGraw-Hill Book Company, 1970), p. 150.

5. David Blumenthal, "The Buyer as a Manager of People," in *The Buyer's Manual* (New York: National Retail Merchants Association, 1965), pp. 37–45.

6. J. W. Wingate, and J. J. Friedlander, *The Management of Retail Buying* (Englewood Cliffs, N.J.: Prentice-Hall, Inc., 1963), pp. 13–18.

7. T. W. Johnston, "You're The New Buyer—Now What," in *The Buyer's Manual,* pp. 440–448.

Buying Activity in Different Types of Stores

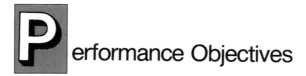

Performance Objectives

After reading this chapter, the student should be able to accomplish the following:

1. Define department store; specialty store; departmentalization.

2. Discuss methods used in departmentalization and how they are used in the department and specialty stores, chain operation, and small independent business.

3. Explain the Mazur Plan.

4. Discuss the six functional plan and how the buyer works with each division.

5. Define chain store organization and central buying.

6. Outline the various forms of central buying and its advantages and disadvantages.

7. Discuss the merchandising activity in the small independent business.

8. Relate current trends in store organization.

9. Discuss the importance of merchandising.

Buying Activity in Different Types of Stores

Figure 4–1 Departmentalization is an important aspect of the retail store organization. It is used by many types of retail firms, including chain operations and independent businesses. (Courtesy of Sergio's, Conshohocken, Pa.)

INTRODUCTION

In the previous chapter we were concerned with the scope of the buyer's job and how the degree of responsibility may be affected by the organizational structure of the retail store, types of goods offered, store's dollar volume, and location of store branches or units.

There are similarities in buying responsibilities. The buyer has a job as a manager, market forecaster, merchandise planner, and is responsible for locating the best domestic and foreign resources. The buyer is also responsible for selecting merchandise of the quality and price that best reflects the image and tastes of his or her department or store.

You also learned about the challenge of retail buying, what it takes to go into merchandising, types of available buying positions, and opportunities for retail training provided by both educational institutions and retail stores.

In this chapter we are concerned with the buying activity in different types of stores. Specifically, we will focus our attention on buying responsibilities in the large department and specialty store, the chain operation, and the independent business. Regardless of organizational structure, however, retail stores are departmentalized and divided into various functions.

There are current trends in store organization. Stores are concerned with centralizing or decentralizing and with separating the buying activity from the selling activity.

PART 1—Similarities and Differences in Buying Responsibilities

DEPARTMENT AND SPECIALTY STORES: A DEFINITION

Department stores are large retailing institutions that carry a wide variety of merchandise lines with a reasonably good selection within each line. (Examples are Strawbridge and Clothier and Stearns.) *Specialty stores are retail stores that concentrate their merchandise offerings in one broad category such as fashion apparel or home furnishings.* (Examples are Saks Fifth Avenue and Levitz.) What distinguishes the department store from the specialty store is its high degree of departmentalization.

Departmentalization is organizing different activities and functions into departments with individuals assigned to each department to see that the various activities and functions are carried out. This is a very important aspect of the retail-store organization since it enables store management to locate and eliminate weaknesses in various departments as well as to make improvements. Since organizing the business enterprise into departments is a conventional method of business organization, departmentalization is used by many types of retail firms, including chain operations and independent businesses (Figure 4–1).

METHODS USED IN DEPARTMENTALIZATION

Once the decision is made to departmentalize, however, how is this task accomplished? What methods may be used in departmentalizing? The usual ways of organizing a business into departments are by (1) functional departmentalization, (2) product-line departmentalization, (3) geographical departmentalization, and (4) a combination of these.

Functional Departmentalization

In *functional departmentalization* activities of a similar nature are grouped together in the same department.[1] Most department and specialty stores, unless they have expanded into multiunit operations, are departmentalized according to function. The theory of functional departmentalization was clearly demonstrated by Paul M. Mazur in his book *Principles of Organization Applied to Modern Retailing.*[2] Mazur set forth the four-function or four-pyramid plan, which is still widely used today. As Figure 4–2 illustrates, department and specialty store activities are classified into the following four functions: (1) merchandising, (2) publicity, (3) store management or operation, and (4) accounting and control.[3]

With growth and expansion some stores use a five-function organization whereby the store operations function is divided into two separate activities: store operations and personnel. Figure 4–3 illustrates the five-function organization. Today, however, many department and specialty stores have expanded to the suburbs, which has resulted in the addition of branch stores—the six-function organization. Figure 4–4 illustrates an organization chart of a department or specialty store with several branches.

There are other variations of functional departmentalization. For example, it is rare that a department store does not have some leased or franchised departments. A leased department may be a service department, for example, a shoe-repair service or a dry-cleaning service, or a merchandise department, for example, a leather-goods department or a wig department. In a leasing operation an outside firm will operate under the name of the department store, which takes the responsibility for providing sales personnel, advertising, and displaying the goods or services, and financial responsibility for inventory, as well as other merchandising activities. A franchised department may be run as a small store within the department store, using the store's name. However, the franchisor will assist in sales planning, manage the department, and provide trained demonstrators to stimulate sales. Many cosmetic and toiletries departments are actually franchised operations.[3]

Product-Line Departmentalization

A second method of organization, *product-line departmentalization* may be defined as organizing a business enterprise according to the various types and kinds of merchandise that it sells.

As Figure 4–5 illustrates, the merchandising division may be departmentalized into two major divisions, a fashion division and a home-furnish-

Figure 4-2 The Mazur Plan or Four-Function Plan. *Source:* Adapted from Paul M. Mazur, *Principles of Organization Applied to Modern Retailing,* New York: Harper & Row Publishers, 1927, Frontispiece.

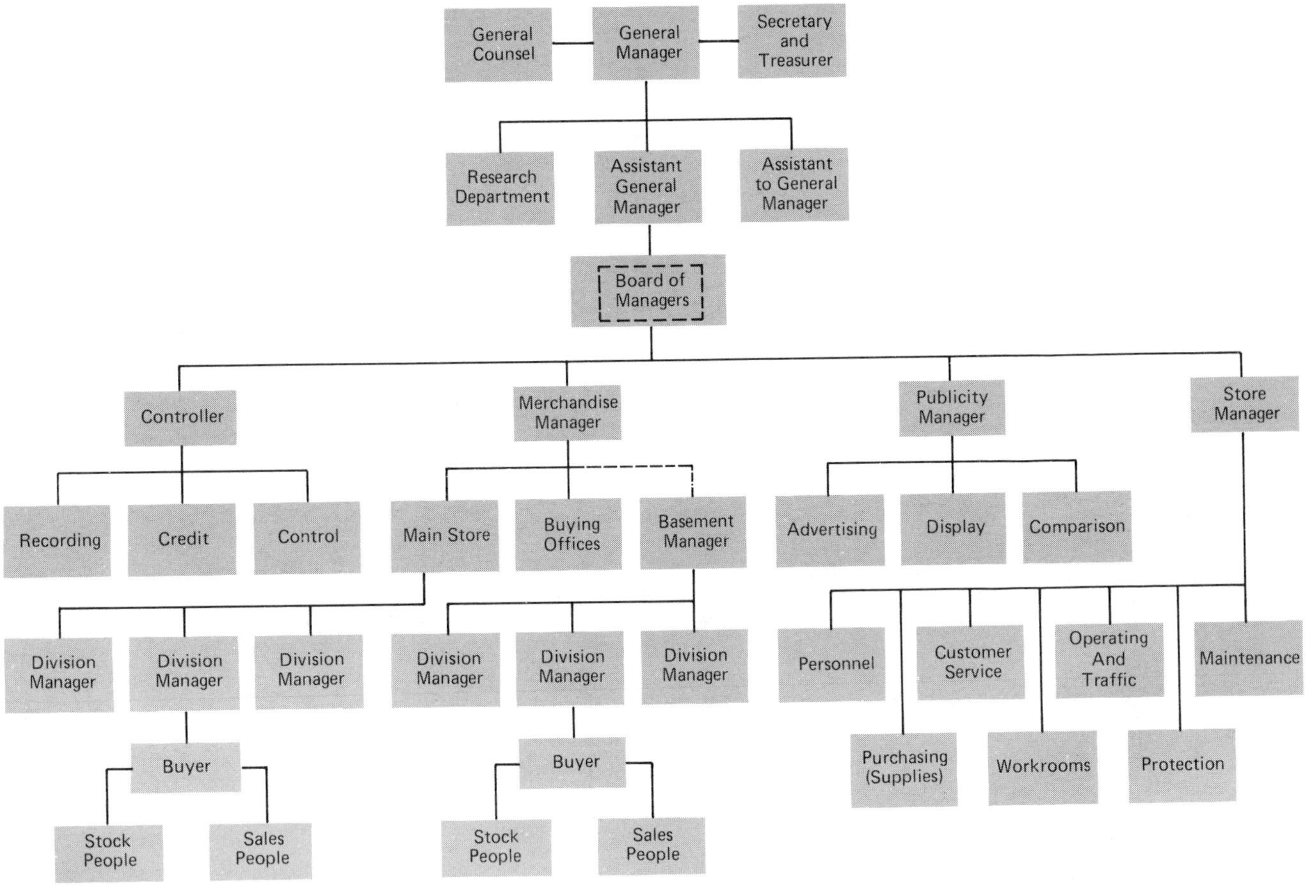

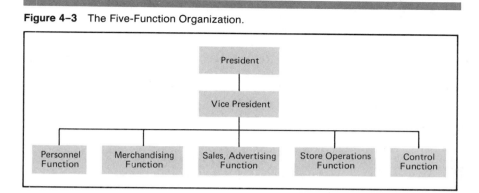

Figure 4-3   The Five-Function Organization.

ings division. The fashion division may be further subdivided into various kinds of clothes and shoes, and the shoe division, for example, is further subdivided into children's shoes, women's shoes, casual shoes, and men's shoes. This type of departmentalization is especially helpful in coordinating the many details and activities for which the buyer is responsible.

Geographical Departmentalization

A third method of organization, geographical departmentalization may be defined as departmentalizing activities on a territorial or geographical basis. This type of departmentalization is used when different markets or territories are assigned across the country. The department store or specialty store will use geographical departmentalization, particularly if it has expanded into several branches located in several cities (see Figure 4–6). Furthermore,

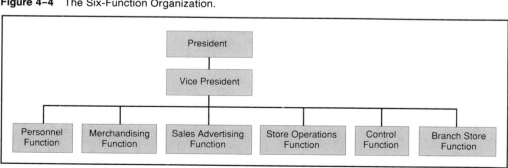

Figure 4-4   The Six-Function Organization.

Figure 4–5 The merchandising division may be departmentalized into two major divisions: a fashion division and a home-furnishings division.

Fashion Division
- Vice President General Merchandise Manager
  - Men's
  - Dresses, Coats, Suits, Furs
  - Children's Intimate Apparel
  - Sportswear Junior Apparel
  - Accessories, Intimate Apparel, Shoes, Millinery
    - DMM Shoes
  - Cosmetics

Home Furnishings Division
- Vice President General Merchandise Manager
  - Budget Store
    - Children's, Men's Wear, Home Furnishings
    - Fashion Departments
  - Smallwares, Sporting Goods
  - Home Furnishings
    - Assistant
    - Housewares Toys
    - Major Appliances, Radio, TV, Linens, Domestics, China, Glass
    - Furniture

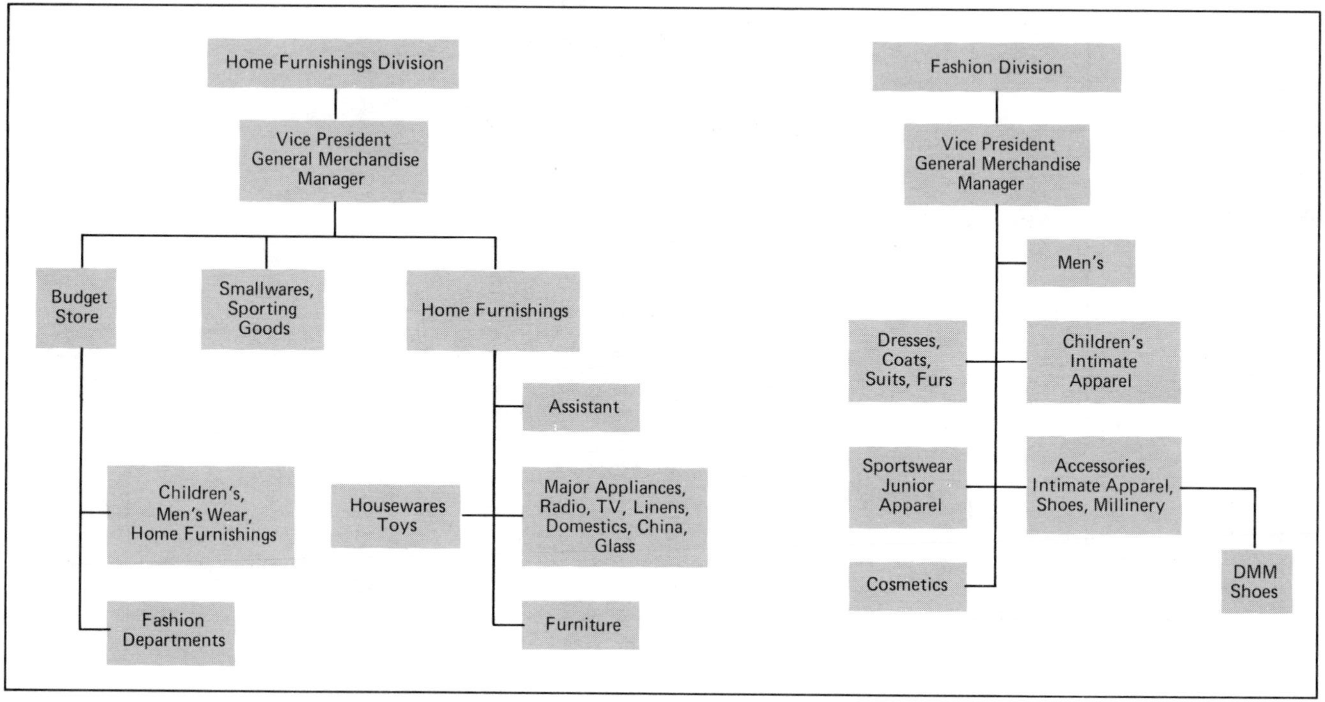

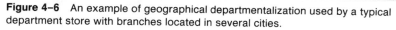

Figure 4–6 An example of geographical departmentalization used by a typical department store with branches located in several cities.

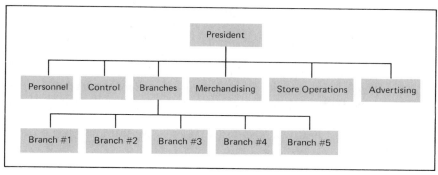

the chain-store operation will also use this method of departmentalization since it has units in various cities spread across the country. The merchandising activity is departmentalized on a geographical basis because of the importance of having the buying activity centrally controlled (central buying) to keep abreast of market changes in the immediate trade area (see Fig-

Figure 4–7 An example of geographical departmentalization used by a typical chain operation. This type of departmentalization is used when different markets or territories are assigned across the country.

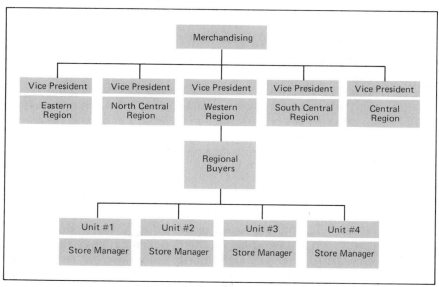

ure 4–7). The topic of central buying will be covered in detail in Part 2 of this chapter.

Departmentalization Combined

A fourth method of organization, the combined method, is self explanatory. In many large stores, combinations of the various types of organization are common. For example, a department or specialty store that is basically organized according to function (merchandising, personnel, store operations, advertising display, accounting, and control) will organize its merchandising division according to product line (fashion division and home-furnishings division) and will also organize on a geographical basis (branch store #1, branch store #2, etc.) (see Figure 4–8).

How Will a Knowledge of the Following Methods of Business Organization Help the Retail Buyer in Performing the Merchandising Activity?

1. Functional departmentalization
2. Product-line departmentalization
3. Geographical departmentalization
4. A combination of these

DEPARTMENT AND SPECIALTY STORE ORGANIZATION

As you can see from reading Figure 4.3, there are a number of functions performed by various store personnel, all of whom in one way or another have an affect on the buyer's role in the procurement process or, in this case, the merchandising function. Let us turn our attention to these other functions before discussing the merchandising function.

Personnel Function

The function of the personnel division is to provide policies and procedure on the following activities: recruitment, hiring, training, termination, and providing compensation for store personnel. Over the years the personnel function has received high priority since there has been increased wage and salary demands, more attention to unionization, and government regulations. For this reason, the placement of the personnel division within a

Figure 4–8 An example of departmentalization combined. A department store that is basically organized according to function (merchandising, personnel, store operations, advertising, accounting, and control) will organize its merchandising division according to product line (fashion division and home-furnishings division) and will also organize on a geographical basis (branch store #1, branch store #2, etc.).

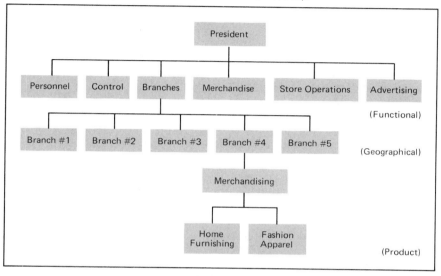

store's organization may differ from store to store. For example, in the typical department and specialty store, the personnel division is a separate entity with its own managerial support system. Other organizations may include the personnel function under the direction of the store manager (operations division) or merchandise manager (merchandising division). Regardless of the location of the personnel function in the store's organizational structure, however, store buyers must work closely with the personnel placed in his or her department. The buyer and assistants provide a leadership role in training people, providing opportunities for new learning experiences and helping the employee embark in good working relationships with all members of the department as well as the store as a whole. Therefore, it is important for the buyer to maintain a close personal relationship with the personnel working in his or her department.

Advertising/Public Relations Function

The function of the advertising/public relations division is to bring customers into the department by drawing attention to the store and its merchandise offerings. This division is concerned with all kinds of "persuasive tools" that will entice customers to buy, such as different forms of advertising (institutional and promotional), various advertising media (newspapers, radio, television, package inserts, signs, etc.), different types of display (window, point of purchase, interior), and promotional techniques (trading stamps, contests, sweepstakes). Public relations is concerned with the store's overall "image" in the community. The buyer works closely with the advertising division by providing information on "specials" that are available, popular styles that are in season, features of private and well-known brands of products, and so on.

Finance and Control Function

The function of the finance and control division is to provide a framework of "checks and balances" on the remaining divisions within the organization. Accounting, credit management, financial analysis, merchandise control systems, and budgeting are all important to the overall financial health of the store's operation.

The store's computer system is operated by the control division. As you

Figure 4–9 The retail store's computer system is operated by the control division. It is important that the buyer work closely with personnel in the control division.

will read in the chapters that follow, the buyer works closely with personnel in the control division (Figure 4–9). The following list is an example of the various reports the buyer will use to assist him or her in making merchandising decisions. A detailed discussion of this topic will be covered in Chapter 9.

Reports the Buyer Will Use in Making Fast, Accurate Decisions Regarding the Condition of the Merchandise Inventory

1. Daily Sales Reports
2. Buyer's Style Status Report
3. Vendor Summary Report
4. Suburban Store Best-Seller Report
5. Weekly Classification Sales Report
6. Unit Control-Color/Size Posting Report
7. Classification Price Line Report
8. Exception Reports

Operation Function

The function of the operation division (sometimes referred to as store-management division) is store maintenance, security, delivery, receiving, customer service, and general housekeeping chores. A number of activities performed by the operation division are vitally important to the success of the buyer's job in merchandising, such as receiving and marketing goods, delivery, and condition of stock rooms and warehouse. The buyer and assistants works closely with personnel in these areas on a daily basis in the main store and in branches.

Merchandising Function

The function of the merchandising division is to provide merchandise or service at the places, times, and prices and in the quantities that will best serve to realize the store's marketing objective. In this division are found the buying activity, selection and planning of merchandise, inventory control, sales, and stock keeping. It is within the merchandising division that we find the buyer (or department manager, as he or she may be called in some retail stores) various assistants, sales and stock people. As you recall from Chapter 3, the head of this division is called the merchandise manager.

It is here that a buyer's knowledge of the trade, managerial skills, and merchandising experience must be carried out in great depth if he or she is going to become a successful merchandiser.

Branch-Store Function

The function of the branch-store division is to give the branch manager responsibility for the operation and, in some stores, the selling functions of the store. All merchandising decisions are made by the buyer who is located in the main or parent store. The buyer makes decisions regarding merchandise selection, promotion, budget, inventory control, and so forth. Since the buyer may have little or no contact with the branch selling floor, he or she depends on various computer reports, (Daily Sales Reports, Vendor Summary Report, Suburban Store Best-Seller Report), as previously discussed in this chapter.

However, the best reporting system cannot substitute for a personal visit to a branch store. Depending on time demands, the buyer will visit each branch store routinely. The purpose of the visit is to personally talk to sales people, department managers, and the store manager regarding the status of the merchandise, and sales and stock re-orders. The branch store manager will visit the buyer in the main store to keep up to date on current fashion trends, the status of merchandise re-orders, and so forth. Figure 4–10 illustrates a partial organization chart of a department store with several branches.

Figure 4–10   A partial organization chart of a department store with branches.

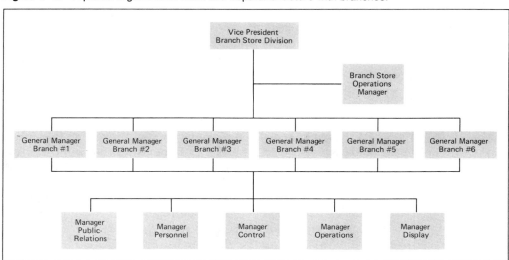

PART 2—Similarities and Differences in Buying Responsibilities: Continued

THE CHAIN-STORE ORGANIZATION: A DEFINITION

The *chain-store organization* may be defined as having two or more centrally owned and managed outlets that operate on the same plane of distribution and handle the same or similar lines of merchandise.[3] Examples of chain stores are Sears, Montgomery Ward, J. C. Penney, and Safeway.

In contrast to department or specialty stores, which emphasize local management, centralized management is emphasized in a chain-store operation. The primary reason for a centralized organization is control. Since chain stores can be very large, with hundreds and even thousands of stores under a single organization, the organizational structure must permit flexible growth as well as close control. Chain stores will vary not only in size and numbers of stores but in types of operation. Figure 4–11 illustrates the organizational structure of a typical chain operation. As you can see, there is no branch-store division; instead, you find a division called district (or unit) where central management occurs. Also, notice the merchandising division where central buying occurs and the way it is divided into product-line functions. Except for these differences, a chain operation is functionally similar to a department or specialty operation.

MERCHANDISING IN A CHAIN OPERATION

The buyers for the chain operation are located at the central headquarters, which is located in a major trading area, and are responsible for supplying merchandise to all the members of the chain. As a result of this mass purchasing power, chain-store buyers may purchase the complete output of certain manufacturers and offer the merchandise under their store's own private label. Chain stores are able to offer goods at a lower price than the department store or the independent merchant. However, since this price advantage is based upon purchasing, chain operations, such as J. C. Penney, Sears, and Montgomery Ward, usually concentrate on merchandise for which there is a steady, predictable demand. The risk factor is minimized as a result of not offering exotic or high-fashion merchandise.

VARIOUS FORMS OF CENTRAL BUYING

Let's review for a moment. *Department or specialty-store buying* has been explained as a method of buying that is accomplished by a retail specialist

Figure 4-11 The organization structure of a typical chain operation.

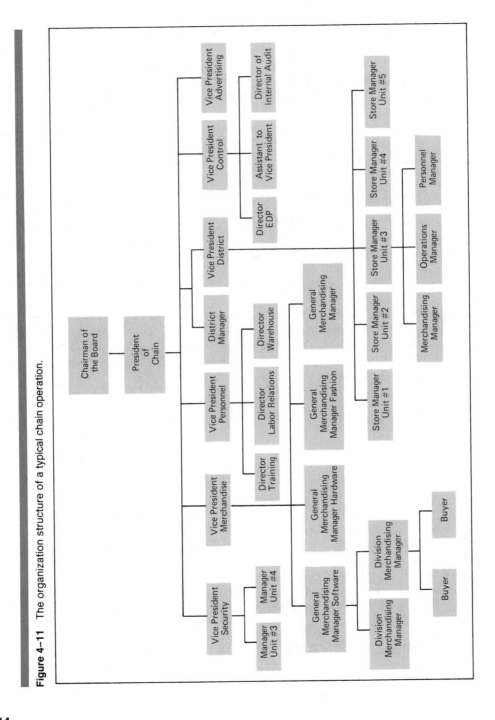

who works out of the main store and procures the necessary merchandise for the main store and its various branches. This method of buying is commonly used by small shops, boutiques, specialty shops (those that are not members of a chain operation), and various types of departmentalized stores. Recall, also, that the buying-selling activity is usually combined; thus, the responsibility for buying and selling merchandise remains with the buying specialist. However, in contrast, central buying—a method used by chain operations such as discount chains, specialty-store chains, general-merchandise chains, and variety-store chains—occurs in a main or central headquarters, with buying decisions left to central buyers who procure merchandise for all the units in the chain. The selling activity is separate, with the responsibilities for selling granted to the manager of each unit. Thus, *central buying* may be defined as the centralization of all buying activities from a central headquarters that is located in a market center, with the authority and responsibility for the selection and purchase of merchandise limited to buyers of particular merchandise categories. Remember, however, that central buying should not be confused with a chain-store operation; central buying is merely the way chain operations usually organize to procure their goods faster and more cheaply. Also, not all large chain operations use central buying; it may be adopted by small specialty stores, hardware businesses, drugstores, and food stores. Finally, a chain operation may use central buying for certain price lines, particular types of merchandise, and certain staple items. In this case you will see a combination of department-store buying and central buying.

Central buying may take one of three forms: (1) the central-merchandise plan, (2) the warehouse-and-requisition plan, and (3) the price-agreement plan.

Central Buying May Take One of Three Forms

The central-merchandise plan
The warehouse-and-requisition plan
The price-agreement plan

Central-Merchandise Plan

The *central-merchandise plan* may be defined as a form of central buying whereby the central buying authority assumes complete responsibility for buying the assortment of goods, pricing, warehousing, and distribution to the many store units. This is the most popular form of central buying for multiunit operations, especially in the area of fashion merchandise.

Since merchandise is usually purchased in manufacturers' lots, the goods may be placed in warehouses located in or near the market. Central buyers will make their purchases and have the merchandise delivered to the warehouse. Here the central buyer has an opportunity to check the goods to be sure they have been shipped as ordered according to size, color, style, and so on. Also, merchandise for several departments of one store may be consolidated and shipped at one time, minimizing freight charges. Warehousing helps ensure that goods will be available when needed by individual stores.

All multiunit operations do not have warehouses, however. If they do not, merchandise may be shipped directly to each store by the vendors or manufacturers. Problems may arise, since the goods may not be delivered on time or be the quality, size, color, or style ordered by the central buyer.

The Advantages and Disadvantages of the Central-Merchandise Plan

Advantages

1. It provides a steady flow of merchandise
2. Advanced planning by each unit is eliminated
3. It allows for more accurate forecasting
4. It provides for specialists in each merchandise category
5. Goods are inspected before delivery
6. It allows better stock control with attention on selling

Disadvantages

1. Adjustment to local conditions is difficult
2. Cooperation may be lacking
3. An enthusiastic selling force may be lacking

A variety of the central-merchandise plan is the *automatic open-to-buy plan,* which may be defined as a plan whereby a predetermined portion of funds is allotted to the central buyer after the month's purchases have been planned, with the balance allotted to the store manager. For example, if the purchases for the month of December are planned at $20,000, $8,000 may be available to the central buyer and $12,000 to the store manager. The central buyer would use his money to keep the store supplied with new and popularly priced merchandise. The store manager would use his quota for reorders of fast-selling merchandise and for ordering merchandise of special interest to his customers. The store manager will use past sales records to determine the monthly open-to-buy for the central buyer, as well as specifying quantities and price lines. The central buyer selects the styles, but the store manager usually determines the limits. With this method the store manager is given some responsibility and "say" over the selection of his inventory.

The central-merchandise plan offers many advantages as well as disadvantages.[4]

The Warehouse-and-Requisition Plan

The second form of central buying, the *warehouse-and-requisition plan,* may be defined as a form of central buying whereby the central buyer arranges for the initial stock assortment and has the merchandise shipped to the individual stores. This plan is usually used by multiunit organizations in the procurement of staple merchandise or what is often referred to as "never-out" goods. Staple goods may include office supplies, housewares, paint, wallpaper, sheets, pillowcases, and numerous other items that people will purchase continuously. Stores using this type of central buying are Sears and J. C. Penney. Drug companies and food chains also use this plan

---

The Advantages and Disadvantages of the Warehouse-and-Requisition Plan

Advantages

1. Gives the store manager some responsibility in merchandise selection
2. The store manager is usually assured of receiving the requested items
3. Reorders or fill-ins are usually filled promptly
4. There is an advantage to buying large quantities of merchandise

Does local buying offer the same advantages?

Disadvantages

1. There is little control over the composition of the merchandise selection
2. Poor warehouse control may lead to an imbalance in store inventory

Does local buying offer the same disadvantages?

in buying staple goods. This type of merchandise can be purchased in large quantities and stored in a warehouse until requisitioned by the store manager.

The plan works like this! The store manager is provided a list of the stock that is inventoried in the warehouse. He or she checks off the required merchandise in the proper quantities and sends a requisition to the warehouse, where the central buyer will see that it is promptly filled. The store manager has the responsibility for ordering enough merchandise to carry the store through the buying season. As previously mentioned, Sears is steadily turning over buying authority to its store managers (group managers) with a number of distribution centers to provide merchandise as quickly and economically as possible when requests are made.

The warehouse-and-requisition plan offers advantages as well as disadvantages.[5]

The Price-Agreement Plan

A third form of central buying is the *price-agreement plan,* whereby a central buyer working with vendors and manufacturers will agree on the retail price, color, size, style, and assortment of staple types of merchandise as well as the terms of shipping. The merchandise is then illustrated and described adequately in a catalog. Thus, the price-agreement plan is sometimes referred to as the *price-agreement* or *catalog plan.* This method of buying is used primarily by variety-store operations, for example, S. H. Green, F. W. Woolworth, and J. J. Newberry, as well as by other types of chain operations. The central buyer is responsible for prearranging the minimum amount of

---

The Advantages and Disadvantages of the Price-Agreement or Catalog Plan

Advantages

1. It develops a feeling of responsibility on the part of the store manager
2. It reduces the expense of a warehouse
3. It reduces the necessity of keeping detailed records of each unit

Disadvantages

1. Problems arise with tardy deliveries
2. Problems arise with high transportation costs

goods to be purchased by the entire chain, keeping the store catalog up to date, adding new items, seeking new merchandise resources (vendors, manufacturers), canceling old items, instructing the store manager when to take markdowns, and transferring merchandise from one store to another.

The store manager has complete authority for the composition of his or her stock. He or she places orders directly with the vendors concerned. Vendors are willing to carry reserve stocks, since the goods usually are staple goods that have a long selling life. Since arrangements have been previously negotiated by the central buyer, the store manager is assured of a supply of everything listed in the catalog.

The price-agreement or catalog plan offers advantages as well as disadvantages.[6]

THE INDEPENDENT BUSINESS: ORGANIZATION

The small independent business has been in existence since human beings first began retail transactions. It is usually owned and operated by one individual, with family members assisting the owner-manager when necessary. The corner grocery, the beauty salon, the men's wear specialty shop, the local flower shop, and children's favorite candy store are all small businesses providing goods and services for their customers. In fact, many young people first learn about retailing from working in a small business on a part-time basis while attending school. Such an experience often provides valuable training to the individual who later considers a career in merchandise management.

As the small store grows, one person can no longer handle all the necessary tasks. The owner-manager will hire employees and designate certain duties and responsibilities to them. Figure 4–12 illustrates how employees are assigned sales, stock, clerical, and maintenance duties, with the owner-manager still continuing to handle the merchandising activity as well as other management functions. As you can see, some specialization does occur. You should review Appendix D, Small Business Management Aides to Assist the New Entrepreneur.

MERCHANDISING IN A SMALL INDEPENDENT BUSINESS

In a small business, the owner-manager may be totally responsible for purchasing all the merchandise sold. As a buyer, he or she determines the needs and wants of customers and visits manufacturers or vendors in the major

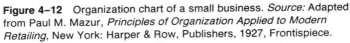

Figure 4–12 Organization chart of a small business. *Source:* Adapted from Paul M. Mazur, *Principles of Organization Applied to Modern Retailing,* New York: Harper & Row, Publishers, 1927, Frontispiece.

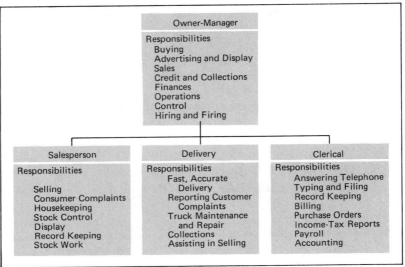

markets, or has manufacturers' representatives come to the store. Since the owner-manager is usually in the store for most of the day, he or she also supervises the activities involved with incoming merchandise. For example, the owner-manager checks the condition of the shipment, prepares records for incoming merchandise, checks contents against the vendor's invoice (bill), checks the shipment against the buyer's (purchase) order, marks the merchandise, moves it to a storage point, or places it on shelves or on racks. Once the merchandise has been moved onto the floor, the selling activity can begin. The owner-manager is literally a "one-man band" and is primarily responsible for the success of the business.

Figure 4–13 illustrates how the buying-selling activity is organized in a small furniture store. As you can see this form of organization has been adapted from the Mazur Plan (Four-Function Organization).

The store has been divided into two major functions: merchandising and store operations. In a small business the buying-selling activity will be combined, since there would be no advantage to separating it. You will note also that the furniture store has been departmentalized according to product line: Department 001, living and dining room furniture; Department 002, kitchen and patio furniture; and Department 003, bedroom furnishings.

Figure 4–13 In a small business the buying-selling activity will be combined, since there would be no advantage to separating it.

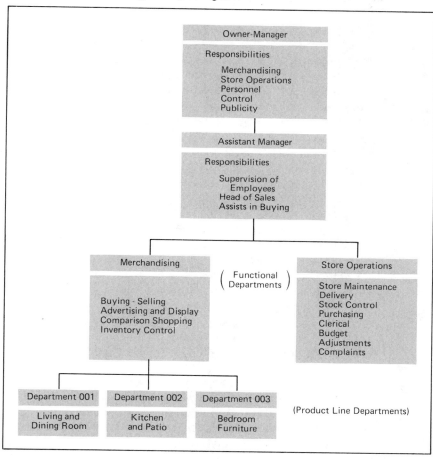

CURRENT TRENDS IN STORE ORGANIZATION

A question often asked by retailers today is "Should we centralize management activities in a central headquarters, or should we delegate it to store buyers located in the main or parent store?" This question is asked not only by the management of chain-store operations, but also by the management of department and specialty stores with branches, as well as by managers of small stores who are perhaps considering opening another store in a new shopping center. How much authority should be delegated? What kind and amount of control is required to ensure the success of the retail operation?

To Centralize or Decentralize?

Organization in the field of merchandising is continuously changing. Many chain stores appear to be moving away from centralization to decentralization, with department stores and some specialty shops moving towards a more centralized management organization. For example, Sears, a typical centralized chain operation, has determined that the best way to grow and continue to meet the competitive challenge of the marketplace is to decentralize. According to Sears, the key to decentralization is to delegate as much decision-making responsibility as possible to lower management, in this case a group manager who is responsible for twenty to thirty stores. The group manager has the responsibility of seeing that the objectives of the group's store managers are consistent with Sears' policies regarding merchandise selection, pricing policies, and advertising and promotion practices. In contrast, department stores that have merged into ownership groups, such as Federated Department Stores, Inc., Allied Stores Corporation, and Carter Hawley Hale Stores, while still retaining their original names and maintaining their own merchandising and operating procedures, seem to be moving in the direction of a more centralized management organization.

To Separate the Buying Activity from the Selling Activity?

There is really no agreement as to what is the best form of organization. The decision to centralize or decentralize must be carefully weighed by the management team. However, an important development that is closely related to the centralization program is the increasing desire to separate buying and selling activities. As we have seen, chain-store operations have long separated buying-selling activities, with the buying activity being done in a central headquarters by a central buyer and the selling activity occurring in each store unit. You have also read that the buying-selling activities of a department store are the responsibilities of the department buyer and the buyer's assistants. There are arguments for maintaining the present system of combining the buying-selling activity, and there are arguments for the separation of the buying-selling activity. The pros and cons are listed here.

Advantages of Combining the Buying-Selling Activity:

1. The individual who purchases the merchandise for resale, the buyer, should also be responsible for selling the goods.

2. The buyer is in the best position to communicate enthusiasm and interest to the selling force.

3. As the store's buying representative, the buyer can best communicate necessary produce information to the sales force and store executives.

4. The buyer must have direct consumer buying information to effectively interpret consumers' needs, wants, and desires.

5. A great deal of expense is involved in attempting to develop selling-department heads, since buyers will be required anyway.

Disadvantages of Combining the Buying-Selling Activity:

1. Since the buying activity involves a great deal of time and effort, the selling activity should be designated to a separate individual.

2. Buying and selling are different jobs, therefore, require different training, ability, talent, and personality.

3. When buying-selling activities are combined, the buying activity often takes precedence over the selling activity.

4. Effective selling can only occur when it is given the proper emphasis.

5. Separating buying from selling has been proven to be a successful method in chain stores.

THE IMPORTANCE OF THE MERCHANDISING FUNCTION

Retail institutions act as purchasing agents for consumers. Those activities associated with the planning and control of merchandise assortments are, therefore, of primary importance. You will recall that retail stores separate various business activities into major functions (store operations, control, advertising and sales, personnel, buying-selling, and so forth), and that there are similarities as well as differences in the type of organization used by stores, depending on their size, type, and the customers they are trying to please. You will see similarities and differences in organizational structure in a department store with branches (Bloomingdales); a specialty-chain store (Lane Bryant); a general-merchandise chain (Sears); or a food chain (A & P). The buying-selling activity, or merchandising function, as it is also called, may be combined, as in the small store and the department store, or may be a separate activity, as in the discount house or variety-store chain operation. However, whether a combined activity or a separate one, merchandising is responsible for the selection, arrangement, and sale of goods, and all other store functions are dependent upon the merchandising activity of the store.

Chapter Summary

There are similarities and differences in buying responsibilities depending on the size of the retail store, the types of merchandise carried, or the type of clientele the store is trying to please. The following types of stores show similarities as well as differences in organizational structure: department and specialty stores; chain operations; and small independent businesses.

Once the decision is made to departmentalize, various methods are used to organize a business into departments. They are functional departmentalization, product-line departmentalization, geographical departmentalization, and a combination of these.

The four-function or Mazur plan is still widely used by many department and specialty stores. However, the six-function plan is used by stores who have expanded into the suburbs and have opened branches. The student should review the six-function plan and how the buyer must work with personnel in each division.

The chain store may be defined as having two or more centrally owned and managed outlets that have the same plan of distribution and handle the same or similar lines of merchandise. The primary reason for a centralized organization is control. The student should review the characteristics common to many chain operations that use the central buying method. What are the current trends in store organization? To centralize or decentralize? To separate the buying activity from the selling activity?

Central buying is the centralization of all buying activities from a central headquarters that is located in a market center, with the authority and responsibility for the selection and purchase of merchandise limited to buyers.

Trade Terminology

DIRECTIONS: Briefly explain or discuss each of the following trade terms:

1. Department store
2. Specialty store
3. Departmentalizing
4. Functional departmentalization
5. Product-line departmentalization
6. Geographical departmentalization
7. Chain-store operation
8. Central buying
9. Central-merchandise plan
10. Automatic open-to-buy
11. Warehouse-and-requisition plan
12. Price-agreement or catalog plan

Questions for Discussion and Review

1. What distinguishes the department store from the specialty store?

2. What is departmentalizing? Illustrate how function, product-line, and geographical departmentalization may be used by a department store; a small business; a chain operation.

3. What is the Mazur plan? Five-function plan? Six-function plan? What types of stores would use each?

4. Discuss how the following functions or divisions may affect the buyer's role in the procurement process: personnel, advertising/public relations, finance and control, and operations.

5. What is the merchandising function?

6. Explain the branch-store function. Explain why this function is usually not used in a chain operation.

7. Explain how a merchandising division may be departmentalized in the following types of stores: discount-chain operation, boutique, and traditional department store.

8. What type of central buying would be used by a variety store? A discount chain operation? A women's specialty shop?

Case Study Number One

HANDLING SALESPEOPLE

You have been appointed assistant buyer for the small electric appliances department. After some months you discover that three full-time salespeople who have worked for the store several years are lax in regard to employee regulations. They take extended lunch hours and unscheduled coffee breaks and are late for work. You are aware that this situation has prevailed for the past year or so under your predecessor. The buyer, although aware of the problem, is unable to give it much attention, being out of the store most of the time, so has asked you to deal with it. Since you want to maintain good relations with the salespeople and also show that you can take care of the department in your buyer's absence, you have been waiting on customers in the absence of salespeople as well as doing your own work. You recognize that this situation cannot continue, since your own duties and responsibilities are beginning to suffer. As a new recruit on the job, you want to show your buyer that you can handle the situation; yet you do not want to cause friction with the salespeople. Be prepared to discuss the alternatives available in class and justify your statements.

Case Study Number Two

TOO MANY SMITHS

Bill Smith, a college student majoring in retail management, was placed in a cooperative work-study position as a mid-management trainee at Reed and Dunn's Department Store, located in a small city on the West Coast. Bill had studied retail theory and was very excited about having an opportunity to apply classroom theory to on-the-job training.

During the first two weeks, Bill attended classes on sales training, store systems procedure, customer services, and merchandise policies, adjustments, and procedures. While attending classes he was given his department assignment and was informed that he would be the junior assistant trainee to Mr. Jackson, the toy buyer. Bill and Mr. Jackson hit it off immediately. Mr. Jackson had gone through a similar type of program when he attended college and was, therefore, an excellent teacher to his new recruit.

Things were going very well for Bill Smith. He enjoyed working in the toy department, since it was the Christmas season and there was always an interesting assignment that provided a new challenge and the opportunity to learn more about the duties and responsibilities of a store buyer. He got along well with his peers, and Mr. Jackson felt he was a very capable and enthusiastic young man.

One day Mr. Jackson asked Bill to wear a pair of old trousers and an old shirt to work the next day, since he was going to be doing a great deal of heavy stock work. The following morning, according to procedure, Bill reported to the personnel office, where he punched his time card. As Bill was leaving the office to go to his department, he heard Mr. Case, the store's new personnel manager, loudly refer to his unbusinesslike attire and sloppy appearance. Mr. Case called Bill over to his desk, where he reprimanded him in front of other store employees, two of whom worked with Bill on the same floor. He said that he had been informed of Bill's sloppy appearance on numerous occasions and that he was tired of sending him notices regarding his attire on the selling floor. Mr. Case fired Bill Smith.

Bill was so surprised by the reprimand, as well as by the fact that he was fired, that he was visibly shaken. All he said to Mr. Case was that he did not understand what was going on and that he had been told to dress in jeans and an old shirt. Mr. Case, however, was shouting so loudly that he did not hear what Bill Smith was attempting to say.

Bill went to his department and informed Mr. Jackson that he had been fired because of the way he was dressed. Mr. Jackson did not understand, since he had often asked his personnel to wear casual clothing when a great deal of heavy stock work had to be done. Bill was so embarrassed and disturbed by the incident that he decided to go home.

Later that day Mr. Jackson finally caught up with Mr. Case. Mr. Case informed Mr. Jackson that he had had numerous complaints about Bill Smith's appearance on the selling floor and that several notices had been sent reminding him of the store's dress code. Now Mr. Jackson was totally confused! He was quite certain that his trainee had never received notices regarding dress code. Also, Mr. Jackson had noted that Bill had always dressed very neatly and was well groomed. Mr. Jackson insisted that some mistake had been made.

Indeed, a mistake had been made. The following day Mr. Case learned there were two Bill Smiths: one was a coop work experience trainee assigned to Mr. Jackson in the toy department; and one was a part-time salesperson. Needless to say, Mr. Case had fired the wrong Bill Smith.

Both Mr. Case and Mr. Jackson agreed that a terrible mistake had been made.

What methods would you use to solve this problem?

Case Study Number Three

MEETING THE COMPETITION

The policy of your traditional department store is that you will meet your competition's price on all types of merchandise. A customer complains that a television set your store is selling is also being sold at a nearby discount house for much less. You know the markup on the merchandise is fair, since your comparison shopping bureau has supplied you with weekly figures on market activity. You realize, however, that your competitor uses the services of a central buyer; therefore, he is in a better position to obtain merchandise at lower prices. However, the customer insists that you live up to your store's policy of "not being undersold." How would you handle the customer's complaint? How would you protect yourself from having the same situation occur in the future?

Case Study Number Four

THE TERROR OF
THE THIRD FLOOR

Mitchells' was a leading department store located in a large city in the midwest. It had expanded to eleven branch stores located in several suburban shopping centers. It had an excellent reputation for high-fashion and quality merchandise, especially in the misses' better dresses department. The buyer of this profitable and prestigious department was Mrs. Sophie Potter. She had an excellent background in women's fashions and had been the buyer of misses' better dresses for the past nine years. Since her arrival at Mitchells', she had built the department into one of the most profitable in the store. Store management was very pleased with her merchandising abilities.

However, Mrs. Potter had the reputation for being a very difficult, temperamental, and demanding person to work with. She made unreasonable demands upon her sales and stock people. She would exclude her assistant buyer from important department activities and then criticize the assistant for not doing her job. She was often heard reprimanding her assistant and salespeople in front of other employees and store customers. As a result, the misses' better dresses department had the highest employee turnover in the entire store.

The personnel department was aware of the situation. The director, Mr. Naples, had on numerous occasions spoken with Mrs. Potter about the high rate of turnover and the difficulty in finding junior assistants who were willing to work in her department. He informed her that she was getting the reputation of "the terror of the third floor" and employees were refusing work assignments to her department.

Mrs. Potter always promised that she would be more considerate and make a serious attempt to consider the feelings of her subordinates. However, her conduct continued. Finally, the fifth assistant buyer she had had in one year went to Mr. Naples and informed him that she could not tolerate the degrading and demoralizing treatment she was getting from Mrs. Potter. Mr. Naples decided the situation could not continue. He took up the matter with the merchandise manager and carefully related the numerous complaints that he had been receiving. The merchandise manager, Mr. Jackson, listened attentively. He then reminded Mr. Naples that Mrs. Potter was one of the store's best buyers and that her department was one of the most profitable. He suggested that perhaps the personnel division should do a better job in providing a high-caliber assistant capable of working with an aggressive, hardworking, and successful buyer. Mr. Jackson politely reminded Mr. Naples that "keeping employees happy" was the function of the personnel division, while merchandising was the merchandise manager's responsibility. In short, Mr. Jackson put the problem back into Mr. Naples' hands. What should Mr. Naples do?

Learning Activities

1. Interview an assistant buyer or department manager in a local department store; discount house; variety store. Make a list of the duties and responsibilities of each. How are they similar? How do they differ?

2. Make a list of the stores that you patronize on a regular basis. What kind of stores are they? Explain how the buying-selling activity is performed in each store.

3. Visit a women's specialty shop that is composed of only a few stores and a women's specialty shop that is part of a chain operation. Interview the store manager of each to determine how the buying activity is accomplished.

4. Survey your local community and determine what type of store expansion has occurred. Classify each new store according to the types of stores discussed, for example, department store, specialty store, chain, etc. What type or types of stores are widely represented? How do you account for the presence of these stores in your community?

5. Visit a traditional department store, a variety chain operation, and a boutique. Determine the buying method (department or central buying) used by each store. Is the selling activity combined with or separated from buying?

6. Interview the store manager of a branch store, a discount house, and a drugstore. Obtain an organization chart for each store. Compare each store with regard to functional organization and product-line departmentalization. How is the merchanding activity organized?

References

THE RETAIL STUDENT'S REFERENCE LIBRARY

Barry, Thomas E. *Marketing.* New York: Dryden Press, 1987.

Bennett, Peter D. *Marketing.* New York: McGraw-Hill Book Co. 1988.

Bear, R. D. *Mass Merchandising: Revolution and Evolution.* New York: Fairchild Publications, Inc. n.d.

Bluestone, Barry. *The Retail Revolution.* Boston: Auburn House Pub. Co., 1980.

Boone, Louis and Jurtz, David L. *Contemporary Marketing.* New York: Random House, 1989.

The Branch Managers Manual, New York: NRMA, 1988.

Energy Management Workbook, New York: NRMA, 1988.

Ezell, Mason Mayer. *Retailing.* Plano, Tx: Business Publications, Inc., 1988.

Gifford, John B. *Strategic Retail Management: A Lotus 1-2-3 Based Simulation.* Cincinnati: South Western Pub. Co., 1989.

Harwell, Edward. *Management Development for Discount Stores.* New York: Lebhar Friedman Inc., 1985.

Harwell, Edward and Kinslow, William E. *New Horizons in Checkout Management.* New York: Lebhar-Friedman Inc., 1988.

Leased Department Rates, Policies and Expenses in Department and Specialty Stores, New York: NRMA, n.d.

Moseley, Lloyd W. *Customer Service: The Road to Greater Profits.* New York: Lebhar-Friedman Inc., 1988.

Paperwork Systems for Centralized Merchandise Receiving, Processing and Distribution, New York: NRMA, 1988.

Productivity in General Merchandise Retailing, New York: NRMA, 1985.

Productivity: The Key to Survival in General Merchandise Retailing, New York: NRMA, 1985.

Retail Operations News Bulletin. New York: NRMA, 1988.

REFERENCES

1. Bond, Clark. "Department Store Organization," p. 16. New York: NRMA, 1987.
2. Mazur, Paul M. *Principles of Organization,* New York: McGraw Hill Book Co., 1971.
3. William J. Stanton, *Fundamentals of Marketing* (New York: McGraw-Hill Book Company, 1985), pp. 293–295.
4. Wingate J. W. and Friedlander, J. S. *The Management of Retail Buying,* Englewood Cliffs, N.J., Prentice Hall, Inc., 1983, p. 41.
5. Ibid. pp. 50–58.
6. Ibid. p. 52.
7. D. J. Duncan and C. F. Phillips, *Retailing Principles and Methods* (Homewood, Ill.: Richard D. Irwin, Inc., 1985), pp. 206–207.

SECTION

The Buyer's Role in Forecasting Consumer Needs, Wants, Desires

Understanding Consumer Behavior

Performance Objectives

After reading this chapter, the student should be able to accomplish the following:

1. Define consumer behavior.

2. Discuss various elements that compose the consumer's decision-making process.

3. Define retail consumer.

4. Outline and explain five major factors that influence consumer-buying behavior.

5. Discuss how social psychologists use social class, family interactions, and membership groups to study consumer social behavior.

6. Become familiar with the buying roles of family members.

7. Define life cycle. Discuss the nine stages of the family life cycle.

8. Compare the six social classes as classified by Warner.

9. Explain how population characteristics will assist the buyer in determining consumer behavior.

10. Analyze the five levels of needs that affect personal characteristics that influence buying motives.

11. Explain the most common patronage motives important in store selection.

12. Discuss seven techniques that may assist retail buyers to recognize their customers.

13. Become familiar with trade sources of information, government sources of information, and business sources of information.

Understanding Consumer Behavior

Figure 5–1 The consumer is an important element in retailing. Buyers must forecast as accurately as possible the needs and wants of those customers whom they expect to serve.

INTRODUCTION

As you have read in the previous chapter, buying responsibilities will differ depending on the organizational structure of the retail store, that is, department or specialty store with branches, a chain operation with many store units, or a small independent business. Regardless of organizational structure, however, retail institutions are departmentalized and may be divided into two functions, as in the small, independent business, to six functions, as in the department and specialty store, or to several more functions, as in the chain operation.

Merchandise buying in a chain operation may take on various forms, for example, the central-merchandise plan, warehouse-and-requisition plan, and price-agreement plan. There are current trends in store organization. Today, stores are concerned about centralizing or decentralizing the buying activity and separating the buying activity from the selling activity.

In this chapter, we are concerned with how the buyer is able to forecast consumer's needs and wants. In order for this to be accomplished, the retail buyer must be aware of what motivates consumers, elements that compose the decision-making process, and factors that influence buying behavior.

There are several techniques a buyer may use in recognizing potential customers. Personal contacts, basic and trade sources of information, observations and counts, competition, reporting services, and electronic systems are examples.

PART 1—Forecasting Consumer Needs and Wants

AN IMPORTANT RESPONSIBILITY

A most important responsibility of retail buyers is to forecast, as accurately as possible, the needs and wants of those customers they expect to serve. When buyers decide on merchandise selections they are going to offer to retail customers, they must be certain that the merchandise offered will appeal to that particular consumer market. A retail store, no matter how small or how large, cannot be all things to all people. A profitable store becomes reputable in the marketplace only by thoroughly understanding its customers. The retail buyer, therefore, has the responsibility to study the consumer and interpret consumer demands, as they apply both to the general objectives and policies of the retail store and to the particular department. They buyer's success in consumer forecasting will not only enhance the prestige and reputation of the retail organization but also build his or her own department through an increase in sales and profit.

Since the consumer is such an important element in retailing, the buyer must study characteristics that influence consumer buying behavior. However, at this point we should ask "What is consumer buying behavior? What elements compose the consumer's decision making process?"

CONSUMER BUYING BEHAVIOR: A DEFINITION

Consumer buying behavior may be defined as a decision-making process whereby individuals or groups of people react in a particular manner to various situations involving the planning and purchasing of goods and/or services. There are six elements that make up the decision-making process.

DECISION-MAKING PROCESS: ELEMENTS

The elements that compose the consumer's decision-making process are: (1) stimulus, (2) problem awareness, (3) information search, (4) evaluation of alternatives, (5) purchase, and (6) post-purchase behavior.[1]

Stimulus

A stimulus is a cue or drive coming from inside the consumer, such as a feeling of hunger, or an external cue coming from outside the consumer, such as seeing an advertisement for McDonald's. Cues motivate or arouse the consumer to act. In this case, the consumer felt hungry, saw the McDonald's advertisement, and acted by going into McDonald's to eat.

It is important for the retail buyer to recognize that cues direct consumers to act. A store's location, image, advertising, merchandise assortment, price, and service are examples, in this case, of external cues. If the consumer is aroused, he or she will go to the next step in the decision-making process: if not, then he or she will ignore the cues. If the cues are ignored, the decision-making process for a particular item or service is terminated.

Problem Awareness

At this stage of the decision-making process, the consumer has not only been aroused by external and/or internal stimuli but also recognizes that the product or service under consideration may solve a problem, such as an unfulfilled desire. Oftentimes it is difficult to determine why a consumer is motivated. Many consumers buy the same products for different reasons. A consumer may not know his or her particular reasons for making a purchase (subconscious). Or, the consumer may not tell the retailer the true reasons for making a particular purchase. Regardless of what motivates the consumer, however, if the consumer does not perceive the problem worthy enough to solve, then the decision-making process is terminated.

Information Search

Once the consumer determines the problem is worth solving then information is sought. The information-search process involves gathering a list of alternative products or services that will solve the problem and determining the characteristics of each alternative or, in this case, product. The list may or may not be a formal one; it may not even be in written form. A consumer with a lot of purchasing experience in a specific area (fine jewelry) will draw upon his or her personal experience to determine which product would solve the problem. On the other hand, the consumer with little background experience in making purchases of fine jewelry will be more deliberate, take more time in examining the alternatives, and probably shop around in search of information.

Evaluation of Alternatives

Once alternatives are evaluated the consumer can make a decision. This may or may not be a simple task depending on specific product characteristics. For example, if price is an important characteristic then selection may be simple. However, if characteristics such as brand name, color, image, and quality, are important along with price, then the decision may be more complex. The consumer will rank the alternatives from favorite to least favorite and wil select one product from among the list of alternatives.

Purchase

Once a product is selected from among the list of alternatives, the consumer is ready to make a purchase. To the retail buyer, this step is probably the most important element in the decision-making process. For example, the consumer must determine where to purchase the product—retail store, factory outlet, street vendor, or catalog house. Other factors such as price, method of payment, warranties, and guarantees are considered. Is the desired product readily available or on-order. Once the consumer is satisfied, the product will be purchased.

Post-Purchase Behavior

Once the product is purchased, the consumer is now concerned with post-purchase behavior, that is, will the consumer make further purchases of same or similar items or will he or she reevaluate the purchased product. This too has implications for the retail buyer who must further stimulate the consumer to return to the store or department.

When the consumer reevaluates the purchase he or she considers if the product's characteristics, such as quality, dependability, warranty, etc. perform as promised. If satisfied, the consumer may return to the original purchase place. If dissatisfied, the consumer may express unhappiness by switching stores or brands or by "spreading the word" to friends. Since many retailers recognize that consumers often express doubts regarding purchases, they offer "money back guarantees" or "liberal return" policies.

WHO IS THE RETAIL CONSUMER?

The *retail consumer* is an individual who attempts to satisfy physical and psychological needs and wants, through the purchase of goods and services. Marketing experts, manufacturers, wholesalers, and retailers attempt to analyze the current needs of consumers by forecasting their potential needs as well as determining the prices they will pay. The manufacturer, the wholesaler, and the retail buyer find that it may indeed be difficult to decide what type of merchandise assortment or services consumers will accept or reject.

FACTORS THAT INFLUENCE BUYING BEHAVIOR

Let us now turn our attention to those factors that influence the retail consumer when selecting goods or services. Consumer characteristics discussed in this chapter are (1) psychological consumer behavior, (2) sociological consumer behavior, (3) buying roles of family members, (4) population characteristics, (5) personal characteristics, and (6) patronage motives.

Major Factors That Affect Consumer Buying Motives

1. Psychological consumer behavior
2. Sociological consumer behavior
3. Buying roles of family members
4. Population characteristics
5. Personal characteristics
6. Patronage motives

Psychological Consumer Behavior

The consumer buys things for many reasons, whether in the soft-goods line, the hard-goods line, or the foods line. Today's consumer is not only concerned with basic needs, such as food, clothing, and shelter, but also strongly motivated by psychological needs to acquire a different variety of goods. Consumers not only seek to satisfy so-called basic wants, but also construct new wants or needs based on their own life-styles.

According to Melvin T. Copeland,[2] a pioneer in the psychological approach to classification of consumer motives, consumer buying motives may be divided into two categories: (1) emotional buying motives and (2) rational buying motives.[3]

Emotional Buying Motives. Emotional buying involves little logical thought (Figure 5–2). Buying decisions come from an individual's feelings rather than from thinking or rationalizing. Examples of emotional motives

Figure 5–2 Emotional buying involves little logical thought. Buying decisions come from an individual's feelings.

are many; however, some of the more common are (1) courtship and marriage, (2) care for one's offspring, (3) satisfaction of the five senses, (4) fear and anxiety, (5) rest and recreation, (6) social acceptance, (7) curiosity, (8) personal pride, and (9) distinctiveness.

Examples of Emotional Buying Motives

1. Courtship and marriage
2. Care for one's offspring
3. Satisfaction of the five senses
4. Fear and anxiety
5. Rest and recreation
6. Social acceptance
7. Curiosity
8. Personal pride
9. Distinctiveness

Courtship and marriage. The desire to appeal to the opposite sex is strong in most people. Consumer products make endless appeals to masculinity and femininity, to beauty and strength. Hair tonics, perfumes, deodorants, shampoos, fashion clothing, and automobiles—all appeal to our emotions. Newlyweds are appealed to by presentation of an array of merchandise—china, silverware, kitchen untensils, appliances, and cookbooks—that supposedly promises wedded bliss and conjugal harmony.

Care for one's offspring. Since parental love is strong in most human beings, many products make appeals to this motive. For example, the use of vitamins "will protect your child through his formative years"; or "Wise mothers never take chances, so feed your family cereal every morning." Oftentimes, we are reminded of our responsibility to care for our offspring through such advertising subtleties as "Don't let your family down, buy . . ." or "Do you know where your children are?"

Satisfaction of the five senses. Appeals to the five senses—touch, taste, sight, smell and hearing—are important influences on consumer buying habits. A TV commercial may appeal to the sense of taste through such descriptive terms as "finger-lickin' good" or "thirst-quenching." Advertisements for paper products may appeal to the sense of touch through such boastings as "squeezably soft," "tender, loving care," or "baby smooth."

Fear and anxiety. The emotions of fear and anxiety are exploited by appeals to the instincts of self-preservation and protection. We buy seat belts, burglar alarms, fire extinguishers, and vitamin pills to protect ourselves, our family, and our friends. Future uncertainties, the possibility of accident, and the occurrence of death concern us to the point where we indulge in the acquisition of insurance policies, home safety equipment, and the latest in health-care products.

Rest and recreation. Since the need for rest and recreation is basic to us as individuals, the desire to lighten the work load or perhaps to eliminate work altogether leads to a strong desire for leisure living. Today, innovations within industry have presented us with automation, power machinery, and assembly lines. As a result of these technological advances, the physical work load has been reduced; we find we are able to turn our attention to a more leisurely life-style. The three-day weekend and the four-day workweek have become popular with many businesses.

Since leisure time creates a need for activities, many appeals are designed to provide for such activities; for example, goods associated with camping and sports activities, do-it-yourself kits, indoor games and hobbies.

Social acceptance. We are strongly motivated by the desires to escape rejection and loneliness and to win approval and acceptance from our family and peers. Therefore, we, as individuals, are strongly motivated to become a part of a group. We belong to clubs, associate with a particular peer group, and live in a particular neighborhood so that we may gain confidence, security, and acceptance. We conform to particular norms to avoid being embarrassed, humiliated, or laughed at. Advertisers tell us, for example, that we should "care enough to send the very best," or "join the new Pepsi generation." Such ads appeal to our need to belong.

Curiosity. Many of us are curious individuals, and we have the desire to try things that are new, different, and exotic. That which is mysterious or enticing stimulates our sense of curiosity and tugs at our imagination. What interests other people often arouses our own curiosity. For example, a motorist "gaper-block" on the freeway often creates more problems than the accident itself. We read advertisements that suggest "romance and excitement in faraway places." Signs may read "adults only," "it's new and improved," or "more to come." We find it difficult to resist the "try it, you'll like it," appeal found in many consumer products.

Personal pride. Pride in ourselves, in the way we look, in the way we feel, have been popular retailer appeals. We have a basic desire to maintain our dignity without necessarily feeling that we must impress those around us. We have the desire to look neat and clean, to smell "fresh as an Irish spring," or to have a "kissing-sweet breath." If our home has "house-a-tosis," we have neglected our homemaking responsibilities; if the toilet bowl does not contain a blue liquid, it is unsanitary. We have been made "germ-proof," "wrinkle-resistant," "drip-dry," "longer lasting," "curl-free," "shined and waxed," and "underarm safe"!

Distinctiveness. To be distinctive or to express individuality in some socially accepted way is a desire that provides strong motivational appeal.

We may express the desire to be different through the clothes we wear, the food we eat and drink, or the automobiles we drive. During the fuel crisis of the mid-1970s, the socially acceptable "thing to do" was to drive a small, economical car or ride a bicycle to work. We became leaders in our communities and set good examples by not using Christmas-tree lights and by keeping thermostats turned down.

In the quest for distinctiveness we also seek to become specialists or to become superior in particular areas. We seek, perhaps, to become an expert or to become "number one." Perhaps the best illustration of this point is the boasting of a famous prizefighter, "I am the greatest!"

Retailers provide merchandise that appeals to the vanity of consumers. Such merchandise may "cause you to be the envy of your friends," "build a better you," or change you into the girl "girl watchers watch."

Rational Buying Motives. In contrast to emotional buying motives, *rational* or *economic motives* involve people's ability to reason or learn and to give consideration to making the most effective use of limited resources. The consumer who is rationally motivated thinks in terms of logic and gives attention to the effective use of economic resources.

Retailers who advertise merchandise that is top quality and low cost will appeal to the rational consumer. Differences in size and weight, dollar savings, and other measurable characteristics may be emphasized. Terms such as "economic," "savings," "reliable," "worthy," "practical," and "durability" are frequent appeals used by retailers to increase sales. Rational buying motives, therefore, may be classified as follows: (1) economy, (2) efficiency and durability, (3) dependability and reliability, (4) financial security, and (5) property enhancement.

Examples of Rational Buying Motives

1. Economy
2. Efficiency and durability
3. Dependability and reliability
4. Financial security
5. Property enhancement

Economy. During the past decade shoppers were faced with the problems of power shortages, fuel cutbacks, and a scarcity of food products. Since consumers had less money to spend, they would carefully shop and compare prices and would seek the best value for their money. As consumers became more budget-conscious, more retailers promoted "moneysaving coupons," "special sales days," or "super bargains." Or, as a well-known appliance ad read, "Come and get it while it lasts!"

Efficiency and durability. Since the Industrial Revolution in the nineteenth century, industry has been producing and manufacturing products in volume. Automation has provided society with the ability to mass-produce goods in highly efficient ways. As a result of this highly mechanized method of production, we have learned not only to become efficient ourselves but also to expect efficiency in the products we purchase. Warranties and guarantees provide bulwarks against dissatisfaction; labels and instruction booklets provide product information necessary to ensure the life and efficient operation of the product. We expect manufacturers to live up to their "promises," if the product does not perform satisfactorily. We look for guarantees when we purchase automobiles, appliances, home furnishings, and clothing, to name but a few products. As retailers we can appeal to the customer's desire for efficient living by emphasizing product "ease of handling" or "fast, effective performance."

Product durability is also an important motivation factor. Durability determines both how well the product will perform under certain conditions and the life expectancy of the product. Instructions for care may emphasize "hand wash in lukewarm water," "dry clean only," "do not use bleach," etc. Retailers and manufacturers are responsible for advising consumers about the care and maintenance required for merchandise. For instance, after July 1972, clothing manufacturers were required to provide information regarding the care of garments. Since that time, the consumer needs only to read the garment label, which contains specific care instructions. The consumer is now better able to extend the life of the garment. Today, if uncertain about how to care for a product, the consumer usually hesitates to purchase the item.[3]

Dependability and reliability. "You can be sure if it's Westinghouse!" Such is the promise of an appliance manufacturer. When finances become limited, the consumer may hesitate and, thus, "shop around." Wise advertisers will appeal to the consumer's cautious nature, particularly in the purchase of red-ticket or more expensive items. Not only do consumers want to purchase items which are long-lasting, but they also desire products that are of good quality. Consumers dislike surprises. They do not wish to be inconvenienced by having to return an item. The consumer becomes more expert in the purchase of retail products, and at the same time becomes more discriminating and more selective.[4] The consumer desires the "best for the money" and, in addition, desires to purchase the best in the "least amount of time." Thus, advertisements may read, "This is a top quality store." "We aim to please," or "Buy right and you'll only have to buy once."[5]

Financial security. The American culture has long fostered the concept that money in the bank will provide us with security, peace of mind, and financial independence. As consumers, therefore, we spend money with the idea that we want enough left over to guarantee us a "nest egg" for a happier tomorrow. Banks tell us that pennies saved today will increase our financial security for the future. We join Christmas Clubs to ensure the availability of cash during the holiday season. We join vacation clubs to have "a little something extra" for next year's family excursion. We give our children piggy banks and encourage the teenager to open a savings account when the first paycheck is received. As one TV commercial says, "My kid is smarter than I was at his age; he's opened a savings account at Federal Savings . . . !" Service institutions encourage us to save at their banks, purchase their insurance, buy through their real-estate offices, or buy stocks from their brokerage houses. Why? Because each one knows the "best way of increasing your money!"

Property enhancement. Improvement or upkeep of personal property has a rational appeal to the consumer. Our neighbors "paint up, fix up, and clean up" during the spring of the year and, usually, so do we. We know that property value is best insured by yearly maintenance and repairs. However, as stated earlier, since we desire freedom from work, we turn our attention to economical worksaving devices. During the spring, retailers provide window displays and newspaper advertisements that demonstrate "no-peel paint," "longer-lasting window screens," "maintenance-free aluminum siding," "quick-drying cement," or "easy-to-install screen doors."

An understanding of psychological motives, both emotional and rational, may assist the retail buyer to interpret and explain why consumers buy certain kinds of products or various product lines. However, we know less about why people buy *specific* merchandise and *specific* brands. Consumers in different trading areas may purchase goods for a variety of different reasons, depending on their needs and the influence of others. Since each consumer is influenced by a wide range of different buying motives, emotional motives may be strongest in one consumer, while rational or economic motives predominate in another. For example, one consumer may elect to "put himself into debt," ignoring the desire "to save" and, instead, fulfilling a stronger emotional motive.

By understanding consumer buying motives, the retail buyer can enhance the abilities to better serve the retail consumer and to provide a successful merchandise assortment. A buyer's own initiative and insights about how particular consumers behave in determining their wants, coupled with retailing experience, can foster development of a distinctive marketing strategy that will be far superior to the average plan utilized by competitors.

Up to this point we have been discussing approaches to the understanding of consumer buying behavior that can be developed from psychology. However, consumer buying attitudes may be determined not only by psychological drives but also by relationships with others. Therefore, we will turn our attention to sociological factors that motivate consumer buying.

Sociological Consumer Behavior

Sociological factors are a second major influence that affects consumer selections of goods or services. As previously stated, the consumer is a most important element in retailing, although perhaps the least understood, both individually and collectively. Retail buyers are most anxious to understand their customers better, but they have difficulty in gathering, sorting, and utilizing available data. Knowledge of human behavior that has been gathered by social psychologists and sociologists will certainly prove helpful in studying consumer behavior in terms of social interactions arising from (1) social class, (2) family interactions, and (3) membership or reference groups.

Social Class. A first help in studying consumer social behavior is a study of social class. Social class has long been identified as part of American society. Much consumer behavior may be explained in terms of social class. This is not to say that an individual is superior or inferior because he or she is in a particular social class. But social standing and social aspirations do motivate buying behavior. Some people aspire to enter a higher class, since they find its values more to their liking; others prefer the standards of their own group and are happy to remain there.

One of the goals of retailers should be to learn the characteristics and typical behavior patterns of each social class. Such knowledge will help retailers to better serve their customers and thus enable development of unique marketing strategies oriented toward particular markets.

W. Lloyd Warner, a social psychologist, developed a class system for cities in the 10,000 to 25,000 population range.[6] *Social class* refers to groups of people who share the same goals and attitudes toward life. Members of the same social class are more or less equal to one another in income, prestige, and community standing, and interact formally or informally, readily, and regularly.

Warner's classification is based on source of income, type of occupation, house type, and residential area.

The six social classes are, starting from the highest, (1) upper-upper class, (2) lower-upper class, (3) upper-middle class, (4) lower-middle class, (5) upper-lower class, and (6) lower-lower class (see Table 5–1).

Upper-upper class. Often referred to as "the elite," individuals from this group are very wealthy, come from prominent families, live in the finest homes, and buy the most expensive clothing. This is the smallest of the six classes and represents approximately 1.4 percent of the total population.

Lower-upper class. This class consists of individuals who have achieved first-generation wealth or who are "nouveau riche." Families are composed of professional people, such as doctors and lawyers, who desire a leisurely lifestyle and work successfully to achieve it. This class represents approximately 1.6 percent of the total population.

TABLE 5–1   The Warner Social Class System—an overview.

Social Class	Characteristics	Percent of Population
Upper-Upper Class	Very wealthy; old wealth; prominent families; expensive clothing and home	Approximately 1.4% of the total population
Lower-Upper Class	Nouveau riche; first generation wealth; professional, educated	Approximately 1.6% of the total population
Upper-Middle Class	Reflect value of leisure living, fairly successful in top management	Approximately 10% of the total population
Lower-Middle Class	White-collar workers; highly paid blue-collar workers; strive for right neighborhood; save money; practical	Approximately 28% of the total population
Upper-Lower Class	Semiskilled; labor unions; enjoy life day to day; uninterested in future savings	Approximately 33% of the total population. Represents the largest class.
Lower-Lower Class	Unskilled workers; unemployed ethnic groups; fatalistic, apathetic attitudes; little concern for self-improvement	Approximately 25% of the total population

Upper-middle class. This social class is composed of fairly successful individuals who have achieved top-management positions in business. This group reflects the value of leisure living as reflected in the first two classes. This social class represents approximately 10 percent of the total population.

Lower-middle class. Individuals within this group are white-collar workers—teachers, office workers, entrepreneurs, and most salesmen—and some highly paid blue-collar workers. Members of this class are essentially practical people. Respectability, living in the "right neighborhood," saving for a college education, and saving money are important. This group represents approximately 28 percent of the total population.

Upper-lower class. These are assembly line workers, members of labor unions, the semiskilled, and those employed by small service establishments. Members of this group are interested in enjoying life on a day-to-day basis rather than in saving for the future. This group represents the largest class, accounting for approximately 33 percent of the total population.

Lower-lower class. This class consists of many unskilled, unemployed ethnic groups. Its members are frequently fatalistic, apathetic, and show little concern for self-improvement or planning for the future. This group represents approximately 10 to 25 percent of the total population.[7]

SIGNIFICANCE
OF SOCIAL CLASS

What does social class mean to the retail buyer? Since social class is based on source of income, type of occupation, house type, and residential area, it is often quite significant in attempts to analyze consumer buying habits, store preferences, and communications media and product likes and dislikes. The various classes patronize different stores, buy different merchandise lines, and have different cash or credit attitudes. Various classes may read quite different meanings into a single retail advertisement. One advertisement for plastic automobile seat covers showed the plastic covers on the seats of a new Cadillac. Unhappily for the advertiser, the lower class associated plastic seat covers with less-expensive and used cars. The "prestige image" of the Cadillac did not spur the consumer to buy plastic seat covers; and the owners of Cadillacs felt that if they could afford the car, they could afford to keep it clean![8]

Class differences may also affect the type of merchandise carried by the retailer. For example, members of the more affluent classes, such as the upper and upper-middle classes, may prefer period or traditional furniture, handcrafted and expensive, whereas members of less-affluent classes may prefer mass-produced, lower-priced furniture, selected strictly for function rather than style. Lower-class buyers may be confused by the variety of furniture styles available and look to the retailer for advice in furniture selection. On the other hand, upper-class buyers are usually more knowledgeable and, even if they are not, have often had the advice of an interior decorator; they are likely to be more confident when making a selection.

It is important for the retail buyer to carefully analyze his or her particular consumer market before planning marketing strategies. Consideration should be given to the type of occupation, source of income, educational achievement, and family goals and aspirations. All may affect the social-class standing of various members. Therefore, the retailer may have problems distinguishing among individual consumer needs within each social class.

Family interactions. Understanding family interactions is a second aid to the retailer in efforts to understand consumer social behavior. Since many buying decisions are made within the structure of the family, individual family members are often influenced by the rest of the family in their selections of products and services. Often, the family is consulted before a buying decision is made. The family, therefore, provides a frame of reference that guides its members in the purchase of goods that will benefit most of the family members. A significant fact is that one person in the family usually makes most of the purchases. The retail buyer needs to learn the identity of the decision maker who is the most influential in selection of goods and services.

Traditionally, the housewife was considered the chief decision maker of the family. Today, however, due to increased emphasis on leisure living and to growth of shopping centers in or near outlying residential areas, more and more men make purchases. Such shopping centers enable whole families to participate in buying decisions. The head of a family, however, is usually consulted when expensive, or "red ticket," items are considered. Perhaps both husband and wife may share in the decision-making process.

The buyer must be aware of the different roles of each family member in regard to various buying responsibilities (not to mention the great variation in reaction among separate families when faced with choices among merchandise).

Membership or reference groups. A third help in studying consumer social behavior is knowledge of a consumer's *membership* or *reference group, the group of people that the individual looks to when formulating concepts, beliefs, opinions, and attitudes.* Reference groups may be organized according to age, sex, religion, ethnic background, occupation, income, life-style, or likes and dislikes.[9] An individual may be a member of many reference groups, depending on what he or she finds appealing and comfortable. Retailers need to be aware of the kinds of reference groups within their particular consumer markets since buying decisions may be based upon "what the rest of the crowd is wearing (eating, or driving)." Different ethnic groups may be reached by promoting Indian cottons, African caftans, natural hairstyles, or Peruvian embroidery. Convenience foods appeal to the large group of working wives and mothers, who hear radio commercials describing food products that may be prepared by just "adding water at breakfast time," "'adding to' at lunchtime" or "'mixing into' at dinnertime." She can cook food in a microwave oven, pop it into a toaster, or serve it precooked from the can!

In summary, human beings' interactions with those around them, with their families, and with particular groups of individuals have far-reaching effects upon their buying decisions and thus upon retailers. Information about people, their ability to purchase, and what influences their motivation to buy is necessary if retailers are to identify their consumer markets.

The Consumer May Be Studied in Terms of Social Interactions

1. A knowledge of social class
2. Family interactions
3. Membership groups

How will information about these help the retail buyer?

Buying Roles of Family Members

The buying roles of individual family members is a third major factor that influences consumer's buying motives. Family buying assumes five specific roles: (1) initiator, the family member who first recognizes the problem; (2) user, the family member who will actually use or consume the product or service; (3) decision maker, the member who decides what will be bought and at what time, place, and source; (4) decision influencer, the family member who has input or affects the choice of the decision maker; and (5) purchasing agent, the family member who actually visits the store and makes the purchase.[8]

The Family Life Cycle: Definition and Stages

It is also valuable for the retail buyer to know the stage in the family life cycle of consumers who patronize the department or store. *Life cycle may be defined as a series of stages of marital status and child raising through which most people move in the course of their lives.* The nine stages of the family life cycle are as follows:[10]

1. Bachelor Stage. Young, single people who live alone. Usually have few financial burdens and spend sparingly on basic household goods. However, they spend more on clothing, automobiles, and recreation.

2. Young Married Couples with No Children. These couples are better off financially since both partners work and they have no children. They have a high purchase rate of consumer durable goods such as appliances, furniture, and automobiles.

3. Full Nest I: Youngest Child Under Six. Both partners are less likely to be working. Expenditures are highest for housing and household operations. Expenses are also high for toys, medical care, baby products, and perhaps child care. The family has little to spend on luxuries.

4. Full Nest II: Youngest Child Over Six. Usually the family's financial situation is improved since the wife has returned to work, and the husband's salary has increased. The family will spend more money on recreation and clothing while it spends less on housing and household furnishings.

5. Full Nest III: Older Married Couples with Dependent Children. In this stage, the family is in better financial condition than the previous stage since even more women are working. Expenditures for housing usually declines, however, expenditures for home furnishings increase as the family upgrades its living standards.

6. *Empty Nest I: Older Married Couples with No Dependent Children.* The head of the household is working. Since there are no dependent children the couple is comfortable financially. They are interested in travel, education, recreation, and luxury items.

7. *Empty Nest II: Older Married Couples with No Dependent Children.* In this stage the head of the household is retired. Family income declines while expenditures for health care and personal comfort become important.

8. *Solitary Survivor I: Survivor Is Working.* The survivor who is in the labor force is financially comfortable. However, the one survivor usually sells the home and begins to rent. Expenditures for recreation and travel usually increase.

9. *Solitary Survivor II: Survivor Is Retired.* Since survivor is retired, there is a decline in income. However, most expenditures also decline, except for medical and personal care.

Population Characteristics and Income Data

A fourth major factor that affects consumer buying motives is the population with which the retailer must work—and average income of that population. The retailer must be constantly aware of changes in population, such as shifts in population from the urban to the suburban market of changes in age distribution within a population. A sudden growth in one area may create a demand for new shopping centers, while existing facilities may be more than adequate in other areas. A change in age distribution of a population may alert the retailer to the necessity to increase stocks of merchandise that will appeal to the dominant age groups.

Populations are composed of people, and people are consumers. Retailers must know where people are today and where they will be tomorrow. Population figures for only a single year fail to reveal the full potential of consumer markets. For example, the U.S. population has been growing continuously since the founding of the country, and it more than doubled from 1910 to 1970. However, the population did not increase equally over the entire nation. Some states have grown rapidly; others have grown at a slower rate. Since it is certain that the U.S. population will continue to grow, retailers must ask themselves "how much, how fast, and where?" As a result of present-day attitudes toward marriage, women working, educational opportunities, family planning, and family size, population trends should be watched carefully.

If the members of the population are going to purchase products, they must have money to spend. Income data should be studied by retailers, since the amount of money available will affect the type of goods consumers are likely to purchase. Also, unless a person has money or the assurance of acquiring it, he cannot be regarded as a potential customer. Income is an important ingredient in purchasing power.

Income, which is measured in money, is derived from producing and selling goods or services in the marketplace.

Four standards that may be used to measure the output and the growth of the economy are:

1. *Gross national product (GNP),* which represents the total output of goods and services produced in a year;
2. *National income (NI),* the sum of employees' earnings, proprietors' income, corporate profits, rental income, and net interest for a given year;
3. *Personal income (PI),* calculated by first subtracting undistributed corporate profits, taxes on profits, and social security taxes from national income and then adding to it all transfer payments (payments unrelated to current production, such as social security benefits and pensions);
4. *Disposable personal income (DPI),* the income that persons have available for saving or spending; the most useful measure of income for retailers. Disposable personal income may be determined by subtracting personal taxes from personal income.

Disposable income refers to that part of income that may be spent by the consumer. However, since most families do not have to spend their entire disposable income, a distinction needs to be made between disposable income and actual expenditures. Many households allocate a portion of their income to necessities, such as food, rent, and household furnishings. A family's purchase of luxury items comes from what remains, called the discretionary income. Discretionary income is important because its availability increases purchasing power for luxury items. If the consumer lacks discretionary income, sales of luxury items suffer.

An important point to remember is that individuals' needs for necessities may continue to grow, perhaps to a point where needs exceed purchasing power. Once a retail buyer has determined total expenditures in his or her particular trading area on goods that he or she stocks, then that buyers' particular share of the business must be estimated. The buyer must consider the possibility of attracting both new customers and customers presently shopping the competition.

Consumer expenditure patterns are closely related to population characteristics. Population and income data are pertinent because such information assists retailers to identify particular consumer markets. When such data are evaluated, a clearer picture of consumer life-styles and spending habits will provide better insight into present as well as future buying activities. This provides the retailer with information on how different kinds of consumers live and spend their money, thereby guiding the retail buyer in the decision-making process.[11]

How Will Information About the Following Help the Buyer in Determining Consumer Spending Power?

1. Gross national product (GNP)
2. National income (NI)
3. Personal income (PI)
4. Disposable personal income (DPI)

Personal Characteristics

A study of personal characteristics, the fifth major factor that affects spending, will provide information on that part of the consumer personality concerned with preservation of "the self." Each of us has a mental image of "ourself," and these ego-related images are of great importance in attempts to understand consumer buying behavior. A majority of consumer purchasing decisions are related in some way or another to the questions, "What will this do for me?" or "How will this impress those about me?" Many of us need the approval of those around us to give us self-confidence and, thus, reinforce our self-concept.

We all have certain needs and wants. Some needs may be physiological, concerned with an individual's physical body, while others are psychological or sociological. The presence of unsatisfied needs or wants leads to efforts to obtain satisfaction. Psychologist A. S. Maslow proposed five levels of needs, in ascending order of importance to the individual. They are:

1. Physiological needs: hunger, sex, thirst, etc.
2. Safety needs: the need for security, protection, order or routine.
3. Love needs: the need for affection and belonging.
4. Esteem needs: the need for self-respect, prestige, success.
5. Self-actualization needs: the need for self-fulfillment.[12]

Individual consumers attempt to satisfy, first, the needs they regard as most important to them. However, the *total* needs of each consumer are both partially satisfied and partially unsatisfied. That is, certain needs are given high priority, but not to the complete exclusion of other needs. For example, the need for food may be given high priority, but not all of the consumer's income will be spent on food. Once an adequate food supply has been purchased, the consumer will allocate money to satisfy another high priority need, such as housing, clothing, entertainment, or whatever else is important at that time. An important point to remember is that one product may satisfy several needs at the same time.

Consumers are pictured as wanting to improve their self-images. Some social psychologists view individuals as having several "selves": (1) the way an individual really is, (2) the way the individual sees himself, (3) the way the individual would like to be, and (4) the way the individual thinks others perceive him. Each consumer, therefore, is trying to develop a better "self." It goes without saying that products and services that offer means of self-image improvement will be very successful in the marketplace.

Retail buyers will find that there are problems when trying to study consumer personality.

1. Not all psychologists agree on the same set of theories, nor are the theories developed necessarily compatible.

2. One psychological theory might not be helpful in explaining the behavior of a particular type of consumer.

3. Consumers may not be willing to discuss or perhaps may not even be aware of the motivations that drive them to strive to meet particular needs, wants, and desires.

Figure 5-3   Why do consumers favor one store over another? Patronage motives explain why a customer purchases products or services from one retail store rather than another. (Courtesy of O'Shea's, Laconia Mall, Laconia, N.H.)

4. Consumers may act at three levels of awareness: conscious, preconscious, and unconscious. At the conscious level consumers are aware of their motivations and are willing to talk to their neighbors about them. At the preconscious level consumers may be aware of motives but would rather not discuss them. At the unconscious level consumers are not even aware of what forces are driving them. Keep in mind that several motives may be affecting consumer buying simultaneously, perhaps at different levels of awareness.

Patronage Motives

Why do consumers favor one store over another (Figure 5–3)? What influences where they will buy? Up to this point we have been discussing buying behavior in terms of why individuals buy *what* they do. Let us now turn our attention to why they buy *where* they do.

The sixth major factor in consumer buying behavior is *"patronage motives,"* which may be emotional or rational. Patronage motives explain why a consumer purchases products or services from one retail store rather than from another. This, needless to say, is a matter of great concern to the retail buyer, since he must first get the customer into his store before he can sell merchandise.

Retailers must ask themselves, "What can we do to get customers into our stores?" "How can we make our stores more attractive than the competition?" The motives listed below are the most common.[13]

Price. The value received for merchandise sold may be the single most important factor in store patronage, particularly during poor economic periods. The discount revolution has emphasized "low prices" and has influenced pricing policies of all types of stores, from department stores to specialty shops. Where have you not seen such signs: "discount bakery," "discount furs," "discount gasoline," or even "last sale day before Christmas." Since there is no simple formula for determining the most attractive price, retailers must keep abreast of economic forecasts, rates of unemployment in their particular trading areas, consumer spending, and income levels of their consumers.

Convenience. The location of your store may be a decisive factor in influencing the consumer to shop at your store instead of at your competition. Large shopping centers contain branch stores, chain operations, supermarkets, discount operations, specialty stores, and many small businesses. A shopping center emphasizes the one-stop concept by providing a variety of merchandise under one roof. The consumer may drive to the shopping center, find plenty of parking space, and leisurely select merchandise from a number of stores that provide various assortments of merchandise in varying price lines. A good location is essential to the retailer, particularly one mer-chandising food, gasoline, or other basic consumer goods.

Integrity. The store's reputation for fair dealing may influence the con-sumer, particularly when the product is an intangible or service, such as banking, shoe repair, dry cleaning, or food. To build repeat business and develop store loyalty, retailers must establish a record of honest dealings with consumers.

Quality and Assortment of Goods. Quality of the merchandise line is often the basis for many appeals made by retail buyers. Such appeals as "We sell only name brand lines," "Quality is the only consideration!" "Shop here for the best!" will attract consumers, since quality is equated with depend-ability. As consumers become more experienced shoppers, they tend to become more selective shoppers. Quality becomes an important factor in store patronage.

The *assortment of goods offered by a particular store* is often a reason why consumers patronize a store. However, with new products, new styles, and new adaptations saturating the market, consumers often become con-fused and hesitate to spend. Retailers must be careful to supply a merchan-dise assortment that will appeal to but not confuse the customer. Such appeals as "See our special line from Paris!" or "Your choice of three colors," or "We have the best selection in town!" may be used in advertisements. A merchandise assortment provides more convenience for the consumer because fewer stops need to be made while shopping for particular items.

Services Offered. A service is *an intangible offered by the retailer to encour-age patronage.* Services may include credit, delivery, gift wrapping, a baby-sitting service, tailoring and alterations, or a return policy. Service is a tech-nique used by retailers to distinguish their stores from competitive stores. In good economic conditions, when consumers have more money to spend, they will often patronize stores with liberal service policies. Service often increases the price of the merchandise sold; however, some consumers want a great deal of service and are, therefore, willing to pay.

Courteous Personnel. Consumers will shop in retail establishments where personnel are likable, friendly, and courteous. Particular products may require advice and explanation from sales help; if such advice is not avail-able, the retail buyer has found that consumers will not purchase. Courteous personnel are a part of the store's reputation for integrity and of its overall image. Therefore, the more courteous and helpful the store's personnel, the more likely it is that customer spending will increase.

Retailers may use such advertising appeals as "Fast, friendly, courte-ous service awaits you!" or "You're number one!" or "You're the only one who counts."

How Will a Knowledge of Patronage Motives Help Explain Why Consumers Shop at One Store Rather than at Another?

1. Price
2. Convenience
3. Integrity
4. Quality and assortment of goods
5. Courtesy of personnel

PART 2—Recognizing the Customer

Up to this point, we have discussed factors that influence consumer buying behavior and how an understanding of those factors will greatly assist buyers in selecting merchandise assortments. Let us now discuss techniques a retail buyer may utilize in recognizing a particular customer that will patronize a particular store.

CUSTOMER-RECOGNITION TECHNIQUES

How can the buyer learn about the customer? How does a buyer determine the sex, age, income level, habits, occupations, and aspirations of each man, woman, or child entering his or her retail establishment? The following seven techniques may help retail buyers to recognize customers.

Techniques the Buyer May Use in Recognizing Customers

1. Personal contacts
2. Basic sources of information
3. Trade sources of information
4. Observations and counts
5. Competition
6. Reporting services
7. Electronic systems

Personal Contacts

Whenever possible, the buyer should attempt to be on the selling floor to personally evaluate buying-selling activity. As a result of talking to sales personnel and consumers, a buyer may gain insight into why merchandise offered for sale is or is not selling. For instance, customer complaints that a particular brand of swimsuit is vulnerable to fading and will not hold up for one season's wear may be overheard. This may indicate that such merchandise is low quality and will be difficult to sell. A customer may return a pair of men's slacks because the seams fell apart after one washing; later, other customers may come into the store with the same complaint. The buyer may then suspect that that particular shipment of men's slacks was defective and that the goods will have to be returned to the manufacturer. Since consumers are usually free with their opinions about merchandise offered for sale, the buyer may hear clues about the kinds of styles, colors, and fabrics that are popular with his or her particular market. It is an advantage to have personal knowledge of what customers like and dislike.

The buyer is responsible for personal contacts with salespeople, not only in the main store but also in the branch stores. A major problem with personal-contact activity, however, is that the buyer is so completely absorbed with merchandising activity that it is difficult to get out onto the selling floor. In these circumstances the assistant buyer may prove invalu-

TABLE 5–2   Federal government sources.

Federal Government Sources

Alphabetical Index of Occupations and Industries	Census of Business
	County Business Patterns
	Retail Trade Area Statistics
	Small Business Administration Pamphlets

Business Sources

Barrons National Business & Financial Weekly	Newsweek
Business Horizons	New York Times
Business Week	Occupational Index
Dun's	Sales Management: The Marketing Magazine
Fortune	Time
Franchise Journal	U.S. News & World Report
Journal of Marketing	The Wall Street Journal

able in assisting the buyer by gathering valuable market information. As you recall, however, in some department and specialty stores (and in chain operations) the buyer must depend on the department or store manager for this information.

Basic Sources of Information

Basic consumer information is readily available to the retail buyer from a variety of federal government and business publications. Table 5–2 represents a partial listing of sources. These basic sources of business information provide consumer data by states, cities, counties, and specific trading areas. By reading such material, retail buyers may gather data about population growth and projections, population age groupings, population shifts, employment, family income and expenditures, and family life-styles. For example, a daily newspaper, such as *The Wall Street Journal,* relates current economic trends, consumer spending patterns, and environmental conditions that affect business in general. The buyer may apply basic business information to his or her particular retail market.

Trade Sources of Information

This information serves the common interests of firms in the same business on a local or national basis. Sources of trade information are (1) resident buying offices, (2) noncompeting stores, (3) vendors and manufacturers, and (4) trade papers and trade associations.

Trade Sources of Information

1. Resident buying offices
2. Noncompeting stores
3. Vendors and manufacturers
4. Trade papers

Resident Buying Offices. Resident buying offices, described in Chapter 4, are responsible for providing buyers with information about market trends, styles, sizes, and assortments available; conducting consumer surveys; and forecasting seasonal trends. Resident buying offices not only inform buyers of demands in their particular trading areas but also of demands in different parts of the country. Resident buying offices offer a variety of services that may prove effective in assisting buyers to identify their customers.

Noncompeting Stores. Noncompeting stores are frequently organized into groups for purposes of quantity buying. Since buyers from such stores are not in direct competition with one another, they are often willing to exchange information about the types of merchandise that sold successfully or unsuccessfully in their particular stores. Information from noncompeting stores provides a buyer with knowledge of what is selling in other areas and what may soon be in demand locally.

Vendors and Manufacturers. Vendors and manufacturers are in close contact with designers of new merchandise lines and usually possess knowledge of sales results in stores to which they sell. Sales figures from vendors are likely to be accurate, because vendors' success is based upon their ability to obtain orders, and such orders require accurate record keeping. Buyers may

TABLE 5-3   Various trade papers and publications.

Fashion and Fashion Accessories

Boot and Shoe Recorder	Daily News Record	Leather and Shoes
Boutique Fashions	Fabric and Fashion Maker	Men's Wear
California Apparel News	Footwear Forecast	New England Apparel
California Men's Stylist	Fur Age Weekly	Retailer
Clothes	Jewelers' Circular	Women's Wear Daily

Home Furnishings

Bedding Magazine	Hardware Merchandising	New England Furniture News
Casual Living Magazine	Home Furnishings Daily	Pacific Marketeer
Contract Magazine	Home Goods Retailing	Professional Furniture
Decorating Retailer	Interior Design	Merchant
Furniture Field	Interiors	Small World
Furniture and Furnishings	Juvenile Merchandising	Southwest Furniture
Furniture Methods and	Market Place	Western Furniture
Materials	National Hardwood	Western Merchandiser Inc.
Furniture World	Magazine	

General Trade Sources

American Druggist	Discount Merchandiser	Merchandising Week
American Vocational Journal	Drug Topics	Modern Retailer
Chain Store Age	Journal of Retailing	Progressive Grocer
Department Store	Journal of Marketing	Stores
Management		Supermarket News

obtain information from vendors' and manufacturers' salespersons, catalogs, fashion bulletins, and fabric swatch cards; or information may be issued directly from vendors' and manufacturers' showings. Vendors may inform buyers about which styles other retail stores have ordered, and they are particularly anxious to pass on information about "best sellers." Reorders are usually an indication of customer acceptance; therefore, reorder information is important to the buyer.

Trade Papers and Trade Association. There are different types of buyers for various merchandise lines. Since nearly every line of merchandise has its particular trade paper or magazine, each buyer will subscribe to those trade journals that provide the most interesting and accurate information in his or her particular field of interest. Trade papers provide information regarding the newest styles or trends and what is selling in particular markets in different parts of the country, as well as vendor advertisements, notices of market showings, and arrivals of buyers in the marketplace, to name but a few types of information. Examples of various trade papers and trade publications are listed in Table 5–3. Trade associations also provide useful information to retail buyers, for example, Fashion Group, Inc. (Table 5–4 and Figure 5–4).

Observations and Counts

A fourth technique used by buyers to aid recognition of customers is observing individuals and groups in the immediate trading area. For instance, if a men's shirt buyer is interested in learning about styles, colors, and patterns popular in the immediate trade area, the cut and style of shirts worn by men at business meetings, social gatherings, and sporting events may be observed, and also the age, social class, and life-style of the men wearing particular colors, patterns, and price lines. In addition, trade papers may print detailed reports of costumes worn by men considered to be leaders of fashion, which may give some indication of future popular demand.

A buyer of lamps and accessory items may notice that a particular kind of lamp or style of lampshade is in demand. Observations of shoppers, in both main and branch stores, may indicate shopper merchandise preferences, as well as regional differences in preferred merchandise items. For example, some items that are not selling well in urban stores may be showing good sales results in branch stores. This difference may arise from differences in shopper types: the shopper typically found in the suburban shopping center is a more affluent, leisurely shopper than the urban customer, who may feel pressed for time, more hurried and concerned with meeting specific needs.

TABLE 5-4   Trade associations also provide useful information to retail buyers.

American Advertising Federation
American Hardware Manufacturing Association
American Millinery Manufacturers Association
American Printed Fabrics Council
Association of Buying Offices
Chamber of Commerce of the Apparel Industry
Clothing Manufacturers Association of the U.S.A.
Cosmetic, Toiletry, Fragrance Association
Costume Designers Guild
Cotton Council
Council of Fashion Designers of America
Custom Tailors and Designers
Daytime Apparel Institute
Fashion Group, Inc.
Fur Brokers Association of America
Fur Information and Fashion Council
Greater Blouse, Skirt and Undergarment Association
Handkerchief Industry Association
Industrial Association of Juvenile Apparel Manufacturers
Infants' and Children's Wear Salesmen's Guild

International Association of Clothing Designers
Intimate Apparel Associates
Knitted Outerwear Foundation
Lingerie Manufacturers Association
Master Furriers Guild of America
Men's Fashion Association of America
Men's Tie Foundation
Menswear Retailers of America
Merchandise Mart Apparel Association
Millinery Displayer's Association
Millinery Institute of America
National Association of Blouse Manufacturers
National Association of Daytime Dress Manufacturers
National Association of Hosiery Manufacturers
National Association of Men's and Boys' Apparel
National Association of Men's Sportswear Buyers
National Association of Textile and Apparel Wholesalers
National Association of Women's and Children's Apparel Salesmen
National Costumers Association
National Dress Manufacturers Association
National Fashion Accessories Salesmen's Guild

National Glove Manufacturers Association
National Handbag Association
National Hand Embroidery and Novelty Manufacturers Association
National Knitwear Manufacturers Institute
National Neckwear Association
National Outerwear and Sportswear Association
National Retail Hardware Association
National Retail Merchants Association
National Skirt and Sportswear Association
National Women's Neckwear and Scarf Association
Silk and Rayon Manufacturers Association
Sportswear Salesman's Association
Textile Association of Los Angeles
Undergarment Accessories Association
Underwear-Negligee Associates
United Better Dress Manufacturers Association
United Infants' and Children's Wear Association
United Fur Manufacturers Association
Upholstery and Decorative Fabrics Association of America

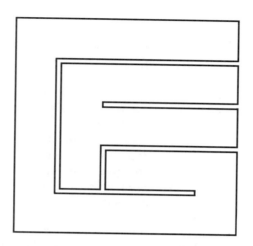

Figure 5–4 The Fashion Group is an international organization of over 6,000 women executives who represent all aspects of the fashion industry: retailing, manufacturing, advertising, accessories, cosmetics, media, design, home furnishing, textiles/fibers, education, and public relations. Headquartered in New York, with 39 Regional Groups in major fashion centers throughout the United States, France, Canada, Australia, Mexico, Japan, England, Korea, and South Africa, The Fashion Group services and inspires those who conceive, design, manufacture, promote, and distribute fashion and beauty. (Courtesy of Fashion Group, Inc.)

Competition

Study of merchandising techniques used by competing stores is a fifth technique in customer recognition. Buyers may study competition advertisements, which will give a base for price and quality comparisons and represent the competitor's judgment about what people will buy. Buyers may observe competitors' window displays, since they indicate what the competition thinks may be best sellers, as well as showing how the merchandise relates to other style trends. Buyers may also "shop" competition by actually going into a particular store and looking over the merchandise assortment, talking to salespeople, observing the number of items sold or not sold, and perhaps even buying merchandise to compare price and quality. Buyers or their representatives may shop many competing stores during "rush hours" to observe which counters or departments are doing the most business. Such observations may indicate items that customers are *not* interested in purchasing as well as items for which there is great popular demand. Buyers may find that stocked merchandise would move faster if it were displayed differently or perhaps marked down or, unhappily, that merchandise they do not even carry is in demand. Buyers who are responsible for much of the activity in their own stores often do not have time to visit competitors. Therefore, assistant buyers, department managers, salespeople, comparison shopping bureaus, and resident buying offices may provide the needed information.

Along with observations of competitors' merchandise, buyers must compare the merchandising *policies* of their own stores with those of the competition. Often a store emphasizes quality and service along with price. A buyer may recognize that the competition is only interested in selling cheaply, forsaking customer service. The buyer who emphasizes quality merchandise with top-quality service may still "beat out" the competition despite the price difference.

Reporting Services

Buyers may receive assistance from reporting services responsible for predicting styles and trends in the consumer market. A number of trade papers, fashion magazines, resident buying offices, consumer magazines, and special reporting bureaus undertake market research valuable to retail buyers. Such information may be analyzed and published weekly or monthly in specific trade papers or sent directly to buyers. Contents of these trade papers include announcements of the arrival of the lastest fashions from Europe, reports on conditions of manufacturing facilities in Hong Kong and economic conditions in South American markets, announcements of the newest fabrics and textures or of new colors and coordinates. Perhaps the most useful trade service is the type that reports specific items that are selling well in leading stores throughout the country. The following list is representative of retail reporting services:

Retail News Bureau. Provides reports on current promotions of New York City retailers. This reporting agency also provides advanced market reports from Seventh Avenue. Figure 5–5 is an example of the kind of information available to retail buyers who use this service.

Retail Memo. The American Newspaper Publishers Association offers news of particular interest to retailers on a weekly basis.

Tobe Service. An independent fashion consulting service, Tobe Service issues bulletins reporting fashion trends and market activities that are of interest to the fashion trade.

Beryl Tucker Young Trends. An independent consulting service that provides current information to those who specialize in children's fashions.

Ram Services, Inc. A reporting agency that provides data on how particular styles of misses' dresses are selling in department stores representative of a particular region.

The Use of Electronic Systems

As stated previously electronic systems cannot be overlooked as an excellent source of information to assist retail buyers in fast, accurate decision making (Figure 5–6). When the electronic cash register (ECR) is combined with a computer, an electronic point-of-sales (POS) system is developed. This system automatically reads or scans special labels on merchandise, verifies prices, and registers sales. This and similar systems will help the buyer, who can more readily obtain information about peak sales periods, take accurate customer counts, and determine amounts and types of merchandise that are "best sellers."

Figure 5–5   A retail news report. (Courtesy of Retail News Bureau.)

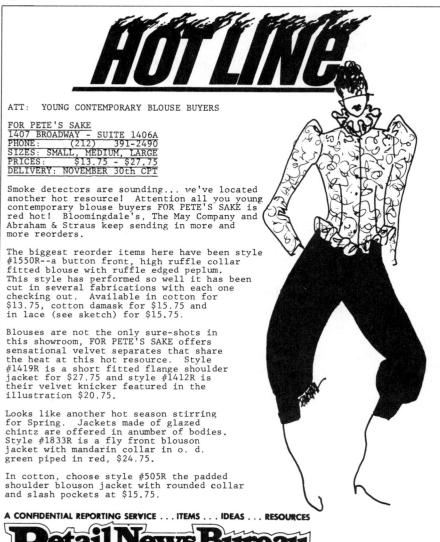

ATT: YOUNG CONTEMPORARY BLOUSE BUYERS

FOR PETE'S SAKE
1407 BROADWAY - SUITE 1406A
PHONE: (212)   391-2490
SIZES: SMALL, MEDIUM, LARGE
PRICES: $13.75 - $27.75
DELIVERY: NOVEMBER 30th CPT

Smoke detectors are sounding... we've located
another hot resource! Attention all you young
contemporary blouse buyers FOR PETE'S SAKE is
red hot! Bloomingdale's, The May Company and
Abraham & Straus keep sending in more and
more reorders.

The biggest reorder items here have been style
#1550R--a button front, high ruffle collar
fitted blouse with ruffle edged peplum.
This style has performed so well it has been
cut in several fabrications with each one
checking out. Available in cotton for
$13.75, cotton damask for $15.75 and
in lace (see sketch) for $15.75.

Blouses are not the only sure-shots in
this showroom, FOR PETE'S SAKE offers
sensational velvet separates that share
the heat at this hot resource. Style
#1419R is a short fitted flange shoulder
jacket for $27.75 and style #1412R is
their velvet knicker featured in the
illustration $20.75.

Looks like another hot season stirring
for Spring. Jackets made of glazed
chintz are offered in anumber of bodies.
Style #1833R is a fly front blouson
jacket with mandarin collar in o. d.
green piped in red, $24.75.

In cotton, choose style #505R the padded
shoulder blouson jacket with rounded collar
and slash pockets at $15.75.

A CONFIDENTIAL REPORTING SERVICE . . . ITEMS . . . IDEAS . . . RESOURCES

RetailNewsBureau

232 MADISON AVENUE • NEW YORK, N.Y. 10016

NEW YORK REPORTS   •   CALIFORNIA REPORTS   •   DALLAS REPORTS •

Errors subject to corrections. Reproduction in whole or in part in any form whatsoever forbidden.

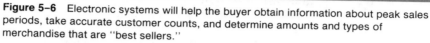

Figure 5-6 Electronic systems will help the buyer obtain information about peak sales periods, take accurate customer counts, and determine amounts and types of merchandise that are "best sellers."

Chapter Summary

A most important responsibility of the retail buyer is to forecast as accurately as possible the needs, wants, and desires of customers he or she expects to serve. The buyer needs to understand consumer buying behavior and the elements that comprise the decision-making process.

Retail consumers are individuals who attempt to satisfy physical and psychological needs, wants, and desires through the purchase of goods and services. Students should review psychological consumer behavior, sociological consumer behavior, population characteristics, personal characteristics, and patronage motives; and also the lists provided in Part 1 of this chapter.

What factors influence retail consumers when selecting goods or services? There are emotional buying motives and rational buying motives. Examples of emotional motives are courtship and marriage, care for one's offspring, and satisfaction of the five senses. Examples of rational buying motives are economy, efficiency and durability, and dependability and reliability. Buying motives may also be studied in terms of social interactions by social class, family interactions, and membership groups.

The buyer must be aware of buying roles of family members. It would also be valuable for the retail buyer to know the stage in the family life-cycle of consumers who patronize the department or store.

Population characteristics affect consumer buying motives. Retailers must continuously ask themselves "how much, how fast, and where is the population growing?" A study of income data goes hand in hand with the study of population characteristics. Four standards may be used to measure the output and growth of the economy: gross national product (GNP), national income (NI), personal income (PI), and disposable personal income (DPI). Important in consumer motivation is that part of the consumer personality concerned with preservation of "the self." In relation to this, psychologist A. S. Maslow proposed five levels of needs: physiological, safety, love, esteem, and self-actualization needs. Patronage motives, which may be emotional or rational, explain why a consumer purchases products or services from one retail store rather than another. Examples of patronage motives are price, convenience, integrity, quality and assortment of goods, and courtesy of personnel.

There are a number of sources of information that retail buyers may use to assist in recognizing customers: personal contacts, federal government and business publications, trade sources of information, observations and counts, competition, and reporting services. A representative list of federal and business publications is included in this chapter. There are a number of trade sources of information that will assist buyers in recognizing customers, such as resident buying offices, noncompeting stores, vendors and manufacturers, and trade papers. A list of general trade sources of information is provided, as well as a list of trade associations that may provide useful information. Reporting services also provide market information, and students should review the examples of reporting services in this chapter.

Trade Terminology

DIRECTIONS: Briefly explain or discuss each of the following trade terms.

1. Consumer buying behavior
2. Life-cycle
3. Retail consumer
4. Emotional buying
5. Rational or economic motives
6. Social class

7. Membership or reference groups
8. Income
9. Gross national product
10. National income
11. Personal income
12. Disposable personal income
13. Patronage motives

Questions for Discussion and Review

1. Why is it important for buyers to know what motivates consumers to purchase particular items?

2. Develop a list of characteristics that may be referred to when determining consumer buying motives. Explain.

3. What is the difference between a rational motive and an emotional motive?

4. What is the Warner Social Class System? Describe the characteristics of each class in Warner's system. Do you feel this system is applicable today?

5. What is a reference group? Name five reference groups that buyers may find in an urban consumer market.

6. How can the four standards used to measure economic output and growth help buyers to determine consumer purchasing power?

7. How can retail buyers apply Maslow's five levels of needs when selecting merchandise assortments?

8. Develop a list of ten patronage motives that may influence consumers to shop at one store instead of another. Why have you selected these particular patronage motives?

9. How do personal contacts help buyers to a better understanding of their customers?

10. To what business sources would you refer to predict consumer income level? economic trends? an area buying trend?

11. What trade sources of information are popular in the fashion apparel trade? home furnishings trade? menswear industry? footwear trade?

References

THE RETAIL STUDENT'S REFERENCE LIBRARY

Bedient, John. *Marketing Decision-Making Using Lotus 1-2-3*. Cincinnati: South Western Pub. Co., 1990.

Brightman, Richard W. and Dimsdale, Jeffrey M. *Using Computers in an Information Age*. Cincinnati: South Western Pub. Co., 1986.

The Conference Board Inc. A Guide to Consumer Markets. New York: Yearly Edition).

Dubrin, Andrew J. *Essentials of Management*. Cincinnati: South Western Pub. Co., 1986.

Hetzel, William and Adams, David R. *Computer Information Systems Development: Principles and Case Study*. Cincinnati: South Western Pub. Co., 1985.

Keyes, Ruth. *Essentials of Retailing*. New York: NRMA, 1986.

Milton, Shirley. *Advertising for Modern Retailers*. New York: NRMA, 1986.

Paganetti, J. and Seklemian, M. *The Best in Retail Ads*. New York: NRMA, 1986.

Pitts, Gerald N. *Victory at "C"*. Cincinnati: South Western Pub. Co., 1989.

Pochtrager, Frances P. *The Best of New York Shoe Windows*. New York: NRMA, 1986.

Reiss, Levi. *Using Computers: Managing Change*. Cincinnati: South Western Pub. Co., 1989.

Schelf, Eileen. *Changes in Boston's Retail Landscape*. New York: NRMA, n.d.

Sheth, Jagdish and Garrett, Dennis E. *Marketing Management: A Comprehensive Reader*. Cincinnati: South Western Pub. Co., 1986.

Smith, Allen N. and Medley, Donald B. *Information Resource Management*. Cincinnati: South Western Pub. Co., 1987.

Walters, C. Glenn and Bergeil, Blaise J. *Consumer Behavior: A Decision-Making Approach*. Cincinnati: South Western Pub. Co., 1989.

References

1. Barry Berman and Joel R. Evans, *Retail Management* (New York: Macmillan, 1983), pp. 121–28.

2. Melvin T. Copeland, *Principles of Merchandising* (New York: A. W. Shaw Co., 1924), pp. 155–67.

3. Ibid., p. 162.

4. John G. Udell, "A New Approach to Consumer Motivation," *Journal of Retailing,* 40, no. 4 (Winter 1964–1965), pp. 6–10.

5. Ibid., pp. 8–9.

6. W. Lloyd Warner, "Classes Are Real," *Issues in Social Inequality,* ed. Gerald W. Thielbar and Saul D. Feldman (Boston: Little, Brown and Company, 1972), pp. 8–9.

7. W. Lloyd Warner, Marchia Mecker, and Kenneth Eels, *Social Class in America* (Chicago: Science Research Associates Inc., 1949).

8. Dale M. Lewison and Wayne M. DeLozier, *Retailing.* (Columbus, Ohio: Merrill Pub. Co., 1986), p. 123.

9. Calvin Hall and Gardner Lindzey, *Theories of Personality* (New York: John Wiley & Sons, Inc., 1957).

10. William D. Wells and George Gubar, "Life Cycle Concept in Marketing Research," *Journal of Market Research,* 3 (November 1966), p. 362.

11. Pierre Martineau, "The Personality of the Retail Store," *Harvard Business Review,* 36, no. 1 (January–February 1958), pp. 47–55.

12. A. H. Maslow, "A Theory of Human Motivation," *Psychological Review,* 50 (1943), pp. 370–96.

13. Pierre Martineau, "The Personality of the Retail Store," pp. 47–48.

The Importance of Fashion

6

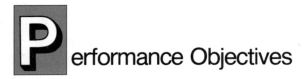

Performance Objectives

After reading this chapter the student should be able to accomplish the following:

1. Define fashion, style, fad, silhouette, detail, good taste, classic, and haute couture.

2. Explain how fashions differ according to age groups, geographic location, ethnic groups, and vocational or occupational groups.

3. Discuss human tendencies that condition fashion.

4. Explain the reasons for changes in fashion.

5. Illustrate the six stages every fashion passes through as it rises in response to consumer demand and then eventually declines.

6. Outline the merchandising responsibilities of the fashion coordinator in the department store, the chain store, the boutique, the specialty store, and the resident buying office.

7. Define fashion department and fashion trend.

8. Discuss the role of the buyer in fashion coordination.

The Importance of Fashion

Figure 6–1 A scene from the finale of the SFA/USA gala. Left to right (with models): Mary McFadden, Adolfo, and Geoffrey Beene. (Courtesy of Saks Fifth Avenue, New York, N.Y.)

INTRODUCTION

As you have read in the previous chapter, a most important responsibility of retail buyers is to forecast, as accurately as possible, the needs and wants of those customers they expect to serve. The buyer's success in consumer forecasting will not only enhance the prestige and reputation of the retail organization but also build his or her own department through an increase in sales and profit.

Since the consumer is such an important element in retailing, the buyer must study characteristics that influence consumer buying behavior such as psychological and sociological factors, population characteristics, personal characteristics, and patronage motives. The buyer should also be aware of customer-recognition techniques such as personal contacts, basic and trade sources of information, observations and counts, competition, reporting services and electronic systems.

In this chapter we are concerned with the importance and application of fashion information. Buyers, whether of hard goods or clothing apparel, must be aware of fashion terminology, the way fashions differ according to age groups, geographic location, and ethnic and vocational groups, since this too will affect consumers' buying behavior.

There are human tendencies that condition fashion and may account for fashion changes. However, fashion trends and the fashion cycle may also be affected by such things as consumer boredom, outstanding and dominating events, ideals, and social groups.

Fashion coordination—the job of the fashion coordinator—is a major activity in merchandising. Various approaches used in fashion coordination in different types of stores will also be discussed.

PART 1—The Language of Fashion

ALL DEPARTMENTS

The fashion director for a leading department store was asked, "What departments within a retail store are influenced by fashion?" Reply: "All departments."

A knowledge of fashion is of vital importance to the retail buyer (Figure 6–1) since all merchandise lines are affected in one way or another by the fashion influences of the time. Fashion is everywhere. It is found in the clothing apparel industry (the most obvious representative of fashion influences), in home furnishings, in appliances, in automobiles, in education, and in recreation, to name but a few.

Fashion has existed since the beginning of time. When a human being first added colored beads and fancy ornaments to his or her wardrobe of hides and skins, he or she was, perhaps, feeling a desire for change, wanted to try something new, or was giving way to the fundamental human desire for originality. If this early human was a leader among the tribespeople, he or she was emulated and copied by the members of the village. Thus he or she became a "fashion leader."[1]

Fashion is a powerful force that affects us not only as individuals but also as members of society. It satisfies our desire for conformity, for status and prestige, for security, and for distinctiveness. Since fashion influences what we wear, what we eat and drink, the way we decorate our homes, and the environment in which we live, it is important to understand the workings of fashion.

BASIC
FASHION TERMINOLOGY

In studying such a complex and exciting topic, the student needs to be aware of the various terms that are used over and over within the retail trade. Such terms may seem simple, yet their use by different people at different times may affect their meanings. If the student is to acquire an understanding of fashion, he must learn the following basic terminology. Basic fashion terminology includes: (1) fashion, (2) style, (3) fad, (4) silhouette, (5) detail, (6) good taste, (7) classic, and (8) haute couture.[2]

Fashion

Fashion may be defined as a distinctive method of expression that has been accepted and adopted by a number of people as the result of common thought. It is what the majority of people have accepted at a given time in a particular consumer market.

Fashion is not a universal phenomenon. What is accepted as a fashion in one geographic area is not necessarily a fashion in another geographic area and perhaps is not even acceptable. For example, the short skirt of the 1960s was popular with women in most metropolitan cities; however, in more conservative areas of the country women wanted longer skirt lengths.

Different fashions exist for different age groups. For example, during the 1970s some prevailing styles in the youth market were the ankle-length skirt, argyle knee socks, raglan-sleeved sweaters, and high platform shoes.

Fashion Is Not Universal.
Fashions Differ According To:

1. Geographic location
2. Age groups
3. Ethnic groups
4. Occupational or vocational groups

Mature women, on the other hand, found conformity and self-assurance in pantsuits, the double-breasted blazer, body shirts, and medium-heeled shoes. The coordinated look of the pantsuit, worn with a variety of accessories and accented with interesting color combinations, was so popular that it has since found a place in the wardrobes of the career woman, the housewife, and the mother.

The menswear industry has also experienced the influence of fashion in different consumer markets. The young men of the early 1980s were find-ing strong fashion influences in sports clothing.

Not only do fashions differ according to geographic location and age groups but also according to ethnic groups. Members of different ethnic groups often wear clothes that are representative of their native countries. For example, the natural hair style of black people during the 1970s, the corn-row hair style of the early 1980s, and the caftan dress decorated with African prints had tremendous impact on this particular ethnic consumer market. Other ethnic fashions, such as the sari from India, the kimono from the Orient, the fringed suede vest from the American Indian, have found their way into the apparel trade; and their design motifs and fabrics have influenced other trades as well. Madras fabric, batik prints, and Oriental and African designs have been used in automobile interiors, wallpaper design, art objects, and kitchen appliances.

Different vocational or occupational groups, such as students, teachers, hairdressers, doctors, and lawyers, have been influenced by fashion. Cotton denim jeans have dominated the college campuses since the 1970s. Jeans or denims have been tie-dyed and bleached, patched and embroidered, and studded with rhinestones.

Since different groups have different fashion tastes, fashions may be divided according to the group to which they appeal. Therefore, *high fashion* may be defined as high-priced fashion, usually created by a famous designer, in limited editions and accepted by an elite group of consumers who are the first to accept the new style. In contrast, a *mass fashion* is a style or design that is mass-produced at a moderate price and is widely accepted by the majority of consumers.

Being "in fashion" indicates conformity, social adaptation, and a cer-tain feeling of superiority or self-assurance. Fashion helps the individual to fulfill many emotional and practical needs. Fashion is influenced by such aspects of human behavior as the desire to be alike and the tendencies to act in common, to have the same or similar tastes, to have similar instincts or desires, and to respond in similar ways to the same impulses.

Fashion, therefore, has the power to satisfy many of the buying motives that you have studied in Chapter 5, "Understanding the Retail Consumer."

Human Characteristics That Influence Fashion:

1. The desire to be alike
2. The tendency to act in common
3. The tendency to have the same or similar tastes
4. The tendency to have similar instincts or desires
5. The tendency to respond in similar ways to the same impulses

Style

Since fashion is an art form, *style* may be defined as the characteristic of one fashion that makes it different from another. Style is the distinctive quality of an art form that makes it different from other art forms in the same category. There are styles in architecture, styles in home furnishings, styles in writing, and styles in speech. A fashion style is distinctive enough to express the tastes and feelings of the majority of people and to become associated with a particular fashion period. For example, dresses worn by women during the early 1980s were worn in various lengths, ranging from floor length to six inches above the knee. Skirt styles included the wraparound skirt, the accordion-pleated skirt, the bias-cut skirt. Each was a different fashion style that appealed to a variety of consumer markets.

Since styles are often associated with a particular fashion period, their return as a fashion influence is often recognized. For example, the flapper style of the 1920s with the skirt worn above the knee influenced fashion again during the mid-1960s and again in the late 1980s. And styles worn during the 1950s were reflected in fashions of the early 80s. However, *it is important to remember that when a style returns to a new fashion period, some details of the style are changed to meet the needs and tastes of the new period in which it appears.* Also, unless the style is accepted and adopted by a number of people, it is not a fashion. For instance, a style adopted by you or me alone has no influence on fashion.[3]

Fad

Fad may be defined as a minor fashion that has been adopted by a group of people for a short period of time. A fad is usually taken up with exaggerated zeal and quickly abandoned. Fads, like fashion, have also invaded every field. There are fads in children's toys (skate boards), in furniture (the water bed), and in works of art (pop art). For brief periods of time we are interested in pet rocks and mood rings, such hobbies as macramé and decoupage, and natural foods. Then we lose interest and go on to cross-country skiing, karate, jogging, racquet ball or bicycling.

The youth market is especially vulnerable to fads, since fads originate as novelty fashions that stimulate and excite the young consumer. In recent years, we've had fads of rhinestone-studded T-shirts, disco jewelry, signature jeans, and star rocks.

Many fashions that begin as fads continue for many seasons. The length of time the fad is popular is dependent upon (1) the type of fad, (2) the market to which it appeals, (3) the amount of market saturation that has occurred, and (4) the strength of other fads prevalent at the time. *What is important to remember, however, is that a fashion is far-reaching and includes many consumer markets, whereas that which is insignificant and includes few consumer markets is a fad.*

> ### How Long Is A Fad Popular?
>
> It depends on:
>
> 1. Type of fad
> 2. The market
> 3. Amount of market saturation
> 4. Strengths of other popular fads

Silhouette

The overall shape or contour of a costume is called the *silhouette*. It is the basic ingredient that changes slightly with each new season (Figure 6–2). The silhouette or general outline of both men's and women's garments is one of the dictates of fashion that progresses from one standard of beauty to another over a period of from five to ten years. Silhouette is also revealed in home furnishings, in which it seems to last for several years, and in architecture, where the popularity of particular shapes or silhouettes may last for decades.

It is oftentimes difficult to determine the start of a particular fashion silhouette, since its beginnings are almost always overlapped by preceding fashions and its endings are lost in the oncoming new fashion wave. For example, the fashion tendency to shorter skirts was apparent during the 1920s. However, the movement was influenced twenty-five years previously with the growing popularity of the bicycle in about 1895. Bicycling costumes for women had skirts shortened to provide utility and comfort. Such costumes soon led to the development of "short," confortable walking skirts. The mod period of the mid-1960s also gave us the short-skirt silhouette, with skirts ranging in length from the micro-mini to the midi-length of the 1970s and knee length during the mid-1980s. In recent years, because of technological innovations and numerous external environmental influences, the time-period of a silhouette has become shortened, in the apparel industry and in other industries as well.

Detail

The design lines that are held within the silhouette are the *details* of the silhouette (Figure 6–3). The features or cut of the design may include waist, neckline, or bodice treatment and trimmings and decoration. These individual segments that make up the silhouette may gradually lead to changes in silhouette. For example, skirt lengths in the mid-1960s were extreme in brev-

Figure 6–2 The overall shape or countour of a costume is called the *silhouette*. It is the basic element that changes slightly with each new season. (Courtesy of Saks Fifth Avenue, New York, N.Y.)

ity, to the point where the silhouette reversed itself and lengths dropped to the ankle during the early 1970s. Such changes are predictable; however, the time period involved and the particular markets that will be affected are oftentimes unpredictable. For example, women wore ankle-length skirts and skirts three to six inches above the knee during the day. During the 1970s short skirts were predicted for evening wear. As a result, long skirts were worn to the office, while short dresses were worn to the theater. The silhouette was beginning to reverse, as it did during the 1980s.

Variations in design line offer variety and change to both the consumer

Figure 6–3   The design lines that are held within the silhouette are the details of the silhouette. (Courtesy of Saks Fifth Avenue, New York, N.Y.)

and the retail merchant. Unlimited opportunities for individuality may be offered to the customer, while the retailer is able to meet competition by offering many variations of an accepted fashion silhouette.

Good Taste

Good taste is essential to an understanding of fashion. *Good taste* implies a knowledge of the proper use of materials, design, and color. For some people good taste comes naturally, while other people may have to learn or struggle to attain it.

Good taste may be influenced by common sense. Good taste is understanding of when and where it is appropriate to wear a fashion, as well as of the correct way to accessorize the garment. Good taste is a concept that changes from year to year; consequently, it is necessary to recognize such changes within the retail environment as well as changes within ourselves. What is considered in good taste one year may be considered the wrong thing or in poor taste another year. For example, a new style is considered daring when first introduced; therefore, it may be in doubt in considerations of good taste. The more people who accept the style and the more "fashionable" it becomes, the more it will be considered in good taste.

An exposure to fashion over a period of time will develop good taste and thus provide the knowledge and understanding necessary to become an authority.

Classic

Those styles which remain in good taste over a long period of time may be referred to as *classic*. Minor changes may occur, such as skirt length, the width of the cuff, the shape of the collar, and variations in the neckline. Most of us have some classics in our wardrobe, while others of us have an entire wardrobe of basic, traditional clothing. Classics are usually not derived from fad influences, since they appeal to a great number of people for a long period of time. The shirtwaist dress, the V-neck sweater, and the button-down shirt are but a few examples of classics. The crewneck sweater, which originated during the 1920s, has long been a classic of the wardrobe. The crewneck returned to the fashion picture during the 1980s, called the "preppy" look with minor neckline variations influenced by the period.

Haute Couture

Haute couture refers to an expensive original style created by a French fashion designer or manufacturer in limited editions for a group of people considered leaders of fashion. Such designs are usually in advance of mass-market fashions and, therefore, appeal to a limited number or elite group of fashion-conscious people. The retail buyer is usually interested in viewing the couture openings in Paris and other European cities, since high fashion is representative of something new and different. However, many high-fashion designs usually never become accepted as mass-merchandise items, since they are usually far in advance of the needs, wants, and desires of the majority of fashion consumers. For example, the French designer Courrèges influenced the look of the 1960s with the short white boots that he designed. Madame Chanel gave us her famous "Chanel suit"; Yves Saint-Laurent gave us the "Crusader Cross." Bill Blass, Bonnie Cashin, Betsy Johnson, and many other American designers have a tremendous influence on the American mass market, perhaps more so than the European designers.

How Will a Knowledge of the Following Fashion Terminology Help You as a Retail Buyer?

Fashion	Detail
High fashion	Good taste
Mass fashion	Classic
Style	Haute couture
Fad	Silhouette

WHY FASHIONS CHANGE

Fashion, as stated previously, is conditioned by the human tendencies to be alike, to act in common, to have the same or similar tastes, to have similar instincts or desires, and to respond in similar ways to the same impulses. A question that should be considered at this point is, "What causes changes in fashions?" Why are short white boots fashionable during one period and out of fashion the next? Social historians relate that fashion in clothing and accessories, home furnishings, food and drink, and other merchandise classifications reflect the economic, political, and social feelings of the time. That we as consumers create a fashion by accepting it; and we end or cause a fashion to change by rejecting what we actively dislike. For example, most women refused to accept the mid-length style created by designers during the early 1970s. As a result, manufacturers were forced to abandon the style and continue to produce shorter lengths. Reasons for changes in fashion, therefore, may be classified as follows: (1) boredom, (2) outstanding and dominating events, (3) dominating ideals, and (4) dominating social groups.[4]

Reasons for Fashion Change:

1. Boredom
2. Outstanding and dominating events
3. Dominating ideals
4. Dominating social groups

Boredom

The most simple explanation for desiring something new in fashion is boredom. We become tired of looking at the same old thing hanging in the closet or on the wall or furnishing the dining room. In other words, we find those sensations tiring that are constantly experienced. Clothing that has been worn throughout a season has tired the senses of sight and touch and has aesthetically fatigued the wearer. Fashion designers continue to create styles or variations of styles that cause already existing fashions to become obsolete and tiresome. Naturally, a demand for something new develops. Expensive items (and the definition of expensive depends on our own value concepts) will remain fashionable longer than inexpensive items. Accessory items are usually worn more often and, therefore, we grow tired of them sooner. Shoes, jewelry, ties, shirts, hats, scarves, sweaters—the list is unending—are worn frequently and soon become monotonous and uninteresting.

Another consideration that affects the development of boredom is that apparel and accessories of bright colors, busy or outstanding designs, and popular or "in" fabrics will bore or fatigue the wearer sooner than muted or soft colors, fabrics, and textures will.

Outstanding and Dominating Events

Examples of outstanding and dominating events that may influence the character and direction of fashion movements may be events such as wars, world's fairs, art exhibits, technological innovations, and scientific explorations, to name but a few.

The Vietnam conflict influenced the fashion industry with jump suits, battle jackets, and bullet belts. The space explorations of the 1960s and early 1970s gave us shiny metallic fabrics, brightly colored geometric-shaped jewelry, and bubble silhouetted hats and helmets. The moon walk influenced furniture departments to display transparent tables and chairs in a variety of colors and patterns. Art exhibitions influence fabric designs, the use of texture, and new color combinations.

All phases of retailing are affected by such occurrences. The fuel shortage of the 1980s encouraged the manufacture of small economy cars by the automobile industry. Thus, the fashionable autos of the time became Ford's Escort, Chevrolet's Chevette, Chrysler's K car and Toyota's Corolla. And, high fuel costs fostered an interest in wood burning stoves and kerosene heaters.

Dominating Ideals

Ideals or philosophies that tend to blend the thoughts and actions of a large number of people also affect fashion movements. Many examples of people's ideals during the 1960s may be cited. President John Kennedy emphasized youth, physical fitness, and freedom. Such ideals were reflected in youthful looking styles in men's and women's apparel, in homes with brightly colored appliances and gayly printed wallpaper. The Vietnam conflict generated ideals of love and peace. Lovebeads, smocked dresses, sandals, and long hair—all portrayed the feeling of freedom and the urge to "do your own thing."

Women's greater activity outside the home affected the textile industry's successful development of carefree, drip-dry, wrinkle-resistant fabrics. The food industry capitalized on this movement with advertisements of timesaving convenience foods. Not only were the textile industry and the food industry influenced by the new role of women but the garment, automobile, appliance, and home furnishings industries also geared themselves to producing an easy, free environment for the working mother and wife.

The environmental crisis of the 1970s and the problems with air pollution, noise pollution, water pollution, and the 1980's energy shortage had an effect on fashion. Among other things, the use of recycled paper in magazines and books, increased interest in electric-battery-powered automobiles, and a return to use of natural fibers were brought about by the rising respect for the natural environment. And our changing relationship with China has brought about a renewed interest in Oriental influences and the use of silk fabric.

Dominating Social Groups

Society is dominated by particular groups of people or fashion leaders who influence the rest of society. Such groups may include a particular economic group, such as the very wealthy. Normally, new styles first appear among the wealthy, then filter down to the lower income levels. Because of complex, advanced marketing systems and well-developed techniques in mass-production, fashions of quality are made available to all consumer markets in a wide range of prices.

Other groups who influence fashion may be of a religious, ethnic, or political nature. Today, many fashions start among young people, who influence their elders. For instance, the youth market influenced the automobile industry in its choice of such names as "Pinto," "Charger," and "Maverick." The buyer, manufacturer, and designer need to be constanty alert to those fashion leaders who inspire fashion trends.

FASHION TRENDS

What happens to a fashion after one season? two seasons? a year? Does it return to fashion? Do we ever see it again? Such questions are often asked,

Figure 6–4 The life cycle of a fashion. *Source:* Wingate, J. W. and Weiner, J. D., *Retail Merchandising,* Cincinnati: South Western Publishing Company, 1963, p. 177.

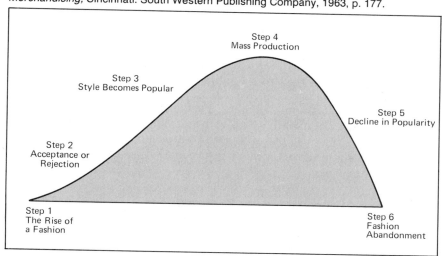

and the best way to answer them is to study the trends in fashion. A *fashion trend* is the direction in which a style or fashion is moving. Fashions move continuously through their life cycles at varying, individual speeds. The art of predicting what the current fashions are, estimating how popular they are, and estimating future demands requires careful recognition of fashion trends.

Every fashion passes through definite stages as it rises in response to consumer demand and then eventually declines. Fashion goes through a series of six stages to complete a "life cycle." The stages are: (1) the rise of a fashion, (2) acceptance or rejection, (3) style becomes popular, (4) mass production, (5) decline in popularity, and (6) fashion abandonment. This life cycle may be called the *fashion cycle*[5] (see Figure 6–4).

Feminine apparel and accessories have a high fashion turnover. Consumer appeal, price, and aesthetic qualities all affect how fast a style will pass through each stage. For example, some fashions are abandoned shortly after they are introduced and never reach the mass consumer market. Fashions in accessory items, such as jewelry, scarves, and handbags, have short life cycles. Styles of suits, coats, and jackets may appeal to consumers for longer periods of time. Home furnishings, appliances, and linens, as well as other products, follow the same cycle; however, the length of the fashion cycle may be a year or longer because of the nature of the goods. The life cycles of fashions in carpeting, china, glassware, utensils, and upholstered goods may take several years to complete.

STEPS IN
THE FASHION CYCLE

Step 1—The Rise of a Fashion

Where do fashions originate? Fashions begin with designers or manufacturers, who are usually the first to introduce the new fashion influence. New designs may be presented at the European couture openings; however, since the fashion life expectancy in the market is still untried, these fashions are very expensive.

Step 2—Acceptance or Rejection

Once the styles are introduced to manufacturers, decisions are made concerning the style, color, or texture that will appeal to a majority of people. Acceptance of the design by an increasing number of people will lead to steadily increasing sales. Rejection of the design is evidenced by a lack of sales.

Step 3—Style Becomes Popular

After the style has been accepted in the marketplace, its popularization with consumers follows rapidly. The fashion is in demand. Buyers will place their orders with those manufacturers who are able to supply the merchandise quickly.

Step 4—Mass Production

As a result of consumer demand, certain styles are mass-produced by the manufacturers. Once the fashion is mass-produced, it is mass-distributed and sold at prices within reach of a majority of the people in particular consumer markets.

Step 5—Decline in Popularity

In time, consumer boredom, outstanding and dominating events, changes in ideals, and the influence of the "Beautiful People" or fashion leaders will bring about a decline in demand for the fashion. Consumers start experimenting with new styles that have been introduced.

Step 6—Fashion Abandonment

A style is totally abandoned when it is no longer manufactured and cannot be sold at any price. The item has saturated the market to the degree that it is of no interest to the consumer. As buyers would say, "You can't give it away!"

A CONTINUOUS PROCESS

One can conclude that fashion is a never-ending, continuous process (Figure 6–5).[6] It influences the clothes we wear, when we wear them, and how we accessorize them. There are fashions in home furnishings, fashions in food, and fashions in recreational activity.

Fashion influences the designer, the manufacturer, the retail buyer, and the consumer. We all interact with one another in creating a fashion. As consumers we reveal our feelings about a particular style by buying or not buying. We learn to discriminate and compare. As retail buyers we determine whether or not particular goods will sell, depending upon consumer reactions. The retail buyer passes the information on to the manufacturer, who, in turn, communicates with the designer. The designer then creates a style that will have a psychological, aesthetic appeal to the consumer. Thus, the process begins again.

Figure 6–5 Fashion—a Continuous Process

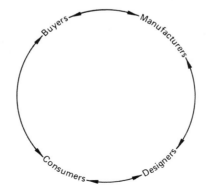

PART 2—Fashion Coordination in Retail Stores

A *fashion department* may be defined as a department that sells masculine or feminine outer apparel and accessories. The merchandise offerings of a fashion department must be timed to coincide with peak fashion demands if the merchandise is to sell. Not only must fashion departments be coordinated with each other but also with departments not usually considered fashion departments; for example, children's clothing and intimate apparel must offer merchandise of the "right type." This takes a great deal of teamwork and coordination. If the store's customers are to be able to find fashionable merchandise, a store must provide a suitable merchandise assortment, adequately train salespeople to sell fashion goods, effectively display and advertise the merchandise, and offer promotional events that will develop a favorable store image. The individual usually responsible for such activities is called a fashion coordinator. Therefore, a *fashion coordinator* may be defined as an individual who is responsible for promoting the sale of fashion merchandise throughout the entire store.[7]

Regardless of the size or type of retail store, the objective of the fashion coordinator is the same, that of coordinating and promoting the sale of fashion merchandise throughout the entire store. However, the manner in which this objective is achieved and the methods used will vary with the store type and size. For example, the approach used in a chain operation will differ from that used in a department store, which, in turn, will differ from the approach of the boutique. Since the retail buyer is directly affected by the efforts of the fashion coordinator, the approach used in the following types of retail firms will be discussed: (1) the chain-store approach, (2) the department-store approach, (3) the boutique approach, (4) the specialty-store approach, and (5) the resident-buying-office approach.[8]

VARIOUS FASHION APPROACHES USED

The Chain-Store Approach

Since the chain operation is usually national in scope, the fashion coordinator will restrict the fashion assortment to proved and accepted styles; that is, each style will be considered from the viewpoint of fashion popularity, quality, price, and whether or not it will meet the fashion image projected by the store. The fashion coordinator of large chain operations has recognized the power of fashion and its ability to move huge volumes of apparel and accessories and home furnishings. Evidence of this is revealed in the catalogs of large chain operations, such as J. C. Penney Company and Sears,

Roebuck and Company, who have made tremendous efforts toward upgrading both the breadth and quality of their fashion assortments and, thus, their images as fashion stores. The chain-store fashion coordinator has the responsibility:

1. To work closely with the firm's merchandise executives, central and regional buyers, marketing experts, and trade specialists.
2. To be responsible for market trips to both domestic and European markets to view major collections and shows.
3. To make arrangements to purchase original designs that the coordinator feels could be incorporated into the fashion assortments to be featured by the firm.
4. To arrange to have famous fashion designers create exclusive models, which would eventually be manufactured by the firm under its own label.
5. To be responsible for providing current information to chain-store personnel on current trends, style changes, and future market potentials in both the apparel and home furnishings trades.
6. To attempt to pinpoint customer preferences as well as determine the best methods for coordinating fashion presentations in each store throughout the chain.
7. To insure that fashion merchandise will be distributed en masse on the basis of consumer interest, good taste, moderate price, and fashion appeal.

The Department-Store Approach

The fashion coordinator in a department store also has an awesome job, which, however, does not require as much experience or training as the job of fashion coordinator in a large chain operation. The fashion coordinator of a department store may have been a former buyer or a former assistant to a large store's fashion coordinator. The department-store fashion coordinator has the responsibility:

1. To provide fashion information for the main store as well as its various branches. The fashion assortment presented in the branches must represent the fashion image of the store as a whole, as well as meet the diverse needs of consumers in the different local trade areas. To accomplish this task, the fashion coordinator will attend all market openings, both at home and abroad, maintain close contact with market specialists, and attend social gatherings usually frequented by fashion leaders to determine what is "in" for the upcoming season.
2. To carefully observe fashion trends, since any decision on trend

directions will affect the development of the store's seasonal fashion themes.

3. To be responsible for (1) communicating fashion trends to store executives and buyers, (2) conducting fashion shows and merchandise seminars, (3) assisting buyers in all departments in merchandise planning, (4) working with advertising and display departments to develop storewide fashion themes, and (5) training salespeople and new store personnel by providing pertinent fashion information about the various kinds of merchandise they have been hired to sell.

Depending on the size of the department store, the job of the fashion coordinator may be divided among several assistants, with a fashion coordinator for each major fashion division within the store. For example, a large department store may have one fashion coordinator for women's, children's, and accessories departments; another for home furnishings departments; and yet another for men's and boy's fashions. In this type of organization the store's top fashion executive is called a "fashion director" (see Figure 6–6).

The Boutique Approach

Boutique is a French word that means "shop." The boutique has come to be associated with unique and distinctive types of fashion goods usually presented in dramatic displays. Oftentimes, once a fashion offered by a boutique becomes popular, the boutique will abandon it and go on to newer fashions. The fashion coordinator in a boutique, whether it is a small independent store or a special department within a large store, has the opportunity to present distinctive, well-coordinated, and expensive merchandise that consumers can purchase in a single visit. The fashion coordinator will seek apparel and accessories that are representative of the more "avant-garde" or "way-out" tastes of well-to-do women, as well as goods that represent newness, exclusiveness, and one-of-a-kind designs. The boutique located in a department store is strikingly different from other sales departments of the store. The department-store boutique is decorated and merchandised to meet the special interests of particular customers, in the same way as the small independent business is. The boutique fashion coordinator must be constantly aware of the higher fashion that appeals to these consumers and continuously seek unique and distinctive kinds of goods.

The Specialty-Store Approach

The fashion coordinator of a specialty store may also be the merchandise manager of the women's apparel and accessories department who has worked up from a buyer's position and who enjoys working closely with fash-

Figure 6–6 A large department store may have one fashion coordinator for fashion apparel and one for home furnishings.

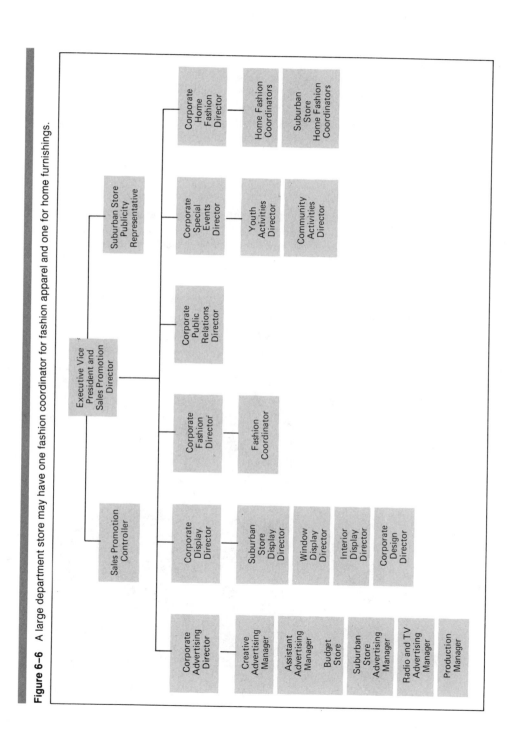

ion specialists. Like the fashion coordinator of larger stores, the specialty-store coordinator will visit the market centers, view manufacturer and designer collections, plan the store's fashion seasons, consult with executives and fashion buyers from other stores, and continuously analyze current fashion trends in terms of the store's merchandising policies, fashion image, and customer demand. Since the merchandise offerings of the specialty store are not as vast as those of the chain operation or the large department store, the merchandise-manager-fashion coordinator is able to offer well-stocked, well-balanced, and distinctive fashion assortments. See Figure 6–7.

Figure 6–7   The fashion coordinator of a specialty store will visit the market centers, view manufacturer and designer collections, plan the store's fashion seasons, and consult with executives and fashion buyers from other stores. (Courtesy of Saks Fifth Avenue, New York, N.Y.)

The Small-Shop Approach

The small independent shop differs from the boutique in not being dedicated primarily to new and exclusive styles but rather to the current fashion demands of the store's clientele. The fashion coordinator of the small shop is usually the owner-manager, who is responsible for the management of the entire store as well as for the buying function. As in the boutique, the fashion coordinator of the small shop will attempt to present coordinated apparel and accessories to meet the needs of special groups of customers. For example, a small shop may devote its apparel line to maternity clothes; career fashion, country, and leisure-living clothing; or clothing for young people with high fashion tastes but ready-to-wear budgets. In this case, the owner-manager-fashion coordinator must visit local markets, attend fashion shows, consult with trade specialists, train salespeople, and be continuously aware of the fashion interests of the store's clientele. The store owner is not only responsible for the entire operation of the business but also has the responsibility for projecting the shop's fashion image to its clientele as well as throughout the community.

The Resident-Buying-Office Approach

As you will read in Chapter 10, the resident buying office has the same or similar personnel that a retail store has. There is a buyer working with each department in the retail store; there is a merchandise manager who directs the activities of the buyers; and there is a fashion coordinator who pulls together all fashion activities of the resident buying office and its member stores. The fashion coordinator is sometimes called the fashion director in a resident buying office, and is solely responsible for covering the ready-to-wear, the sportswear, the casual, and the accessories markets. Therefore, the coordinator may have a number of assistants to help cover the numerous and varied markets. It is the fashion director's duty:

1. To bring together the entire fashion operation through careful planning, organizing, researching, and follow-through.
2. To coordinate the buyer's efforts for both the resident buying office and its member stores.
3. To act as a clearinghouse for fashion information regarding current fashion trends, colors, popular fabrics and textures (see Figure 5–10).
4. To be responsible for arranging fashion shows for the major seasons: a January fashion show to present spring merchandise, and a June fashion show to present fall fashions.
5. To discuss with individual buyers the fashion trends and promotions for the coming season.

6. To visit textile mills, fabric houses, and manufacturers to determine the most popular fashion trends.
7. To send fashion bulletins to member stores containing information on selling techniques, fashion forecasts, the best fashion sellers, new display techniques, fashion show themes, important fashion accessories, and new trends in interior designs.

The fashion coordinator of a resident buying office is usually a seasoned buyer or merchandiser and has had a wealth of experience in the retailing business.

In Each of the Following Stores the Fashion Coordination Approach Differs. In What Respects Do They Differ? What Are Their Similarities?

The department store	The small store
The boutique	The resident buying office
The specialty store	The chain store

THE ROLE OF THE BUYER IN FASHION COORDINATION

Unlike buyers in large, departmentalized stores, fashion buyers in small stores are responsible for merchandising several related classifications of merchandise. A single buyer may have to purchase goods for several accessory departments, for example, jewelry and belts; wigs, scarves, and hats; ties and socks. In a large chain operation several buyers may be responsible for buying fashion accessories. For example, there may be separate buyers for jewelry, for scarves and neckwear, for rainwear, for wigs and hairpieces, and so on. The fashion buyer must plan purchases, promotions, displays, and special sales events.

Special problems arise in buying fashion merchandise. How long customers will continue to purchase certain fashions or fads is oftentimes a guess. As a result of the unpredictable tastes of the retail consumer, the individual fashion buyer must work with market specialists, especially those in the buyer's particular area of expertise; must analyze fashion trends in terms of the store's merchandising policies, customer reactions, and fashion image. If several buyers are working as a team, it is a relatively simple matter to get them together to work out a coordinated fashion picture for the store. In coordinating the small-store operation, the owner-buyer-coordinator will display entire outfits that are easily viewed and compared by the shop's customers. In addition, it is easier for salespeople in a small store to keep one another informed about the likes and dislikes of their customers and to communicate such information to the owner-buyer.

PLANNING THE FASHION SEASON

The fashion coordinator, whether a buyer, merchandise manager, or owner-manager, must plan the fashion season for the store or department. To accomplish this task, the fashion coordinator must plan a consumer or retail calendar as well as be aware of the trade calendar of events that will affect the planning of the store's seasonal fashion theme. A basic consumer calendar is important to a retail operation because it provides information regarding the time period when fashion merchandise must be in the store; a trade calendar is important because it informs the buyer of trade activities that occur throughout the fashion season. The student may wish to refer to Chapter 11 for a detailed discussion of trade activities.

When fashion coordinators are aware of what is happening at both the retail and the trade levels, they can plan their work accordingly. Fashion coordinators must work with top store executives, as well as with buyers of various departments, and continuously supply up-to-date fashion information that will assist fashion buyers when selecting merchandise for resale. It is the fashion coordinator's job to provide interesting and exciting fashion themes that will promote a store's fashion image, stimulate sales, and provide customers with quality fashion assortments.

Chapter Summary

A knowledge of fashion is of vital importance to the retail buyer, since all merchandise lines are affected in one way or another by the fashion influences of the time. In studying such a complex and exciting topic as fashion the student needs to be aware of the various terms that are used over and over within the retail trade. The student should review the following basic fashion terminology: fashion, high fashion, style, fad, mass fashion, silhouette, detail, good taste, classic, and haute couture.

Fashion is not a universal phenomenon. It will differ according to age groups, geographic location, ethnic groups, and occupational or vocational groups. Being "in fashion" indicates conformity, social adaptation, and a certain feeling of superiority or self-assurance. The student should review the human tendencies that condition fashion. Fashions reflect the economic, political, and social feelings of the times. Reasons for changes in fashion, therefore, may be boredom, outstanding and dominating events, dominating ideals, and dominating social groups.

The direction in which a style is moving is called a fashion trend. Fashions move continuously, but at varying and individual speeds, through life cycles. The student should review the six stages through which every fashion must pass as it rises in response to consumer demand and then eventually declines. Fashion is a never-ending and continuous process. The student should review how fashion influences the designer, the manufacturer, the retail buyer, and the consumer.

A fashion department is one that sells feminine or masculine outer apparel and accessories. The fashion coordinator is the individual responsible for promoting the sale of fashion merchandise throughout the entire store. The student should review the numerous merchandising responsibilities of a fashion coordinator as they are listed in Part 2 of this chapter. The job of the fashion coordinator will vary with the type and size of the retail firm. The student should review the approach used by the following types of stores: the chain store, the department store, the boutique, the specialty store, and the resident buying office. The buyer of fashion merchandise must work closely with the fashion coordinator to determine the unpredictable tastes of the retail consumer. The fashion coordinator, whether a buyer, merchandise manager, or owner-manager, must plan the fashion season for the store or department.

Trade Terminology

DIRECTIONS: Briefly explain or discuss each of the following trade terms:

1. Fashion	9. Classic
2. High fashion	10. Haute Couture
3. Mass fashion	11. Fashion trend
4. Style	12. Fashion cycle
5. Fad	13. Fashion department
6. Silhouette	14. Fashion coordinator
7. Detail	15. Boutique
8. Good taste	

Questions for Discussion and Review

1. Do you agree with the statement that "fashion is everywhere"? Explain your answer by citing examples.

2. Select a popular fashion and trace it through the six stages in the fashion cycle. In what stage is the fashion currently? How long do you predict it will remain in stage five? stage six?

3. Who are the fashion leaders in your particular age group? ethnic group?

4. What fashions are popular in your particular occupational group? geographic area?

5. What is the difference between a fashion and a fad? Cite an example of each.

6. How does the fashion coordination approach differ for each of the following stores: the chain operation, the boutique, the specialty store?

7. What is the difference between a fashion department and a nonfashion department?

8. What is the role of the fashion buyer in fashion coordination?

Case Study Number Five

THE WOMEN'S BOUTIQUE

The women's boutique at Hoffman's Department Store is one of the store's most profitable departments. One reason is the great ability of the boutique buyer; another is that the store is located in an area occupied by many firms that employ large numbers of female employees. During the past several months, however, while the rest of the store continues to meet its past year's sales figures, the women's boutique has been plagued with slow sales, high inventory, and numerous markdowns. The boutique buyer, realizing she was overconfident in her sales projections, is uncertain of how to correct the situation. She realizes, however, that she must keep the boutique customer in mind while attempting to solve her problem.

Be prepared in class to discuss the methods you would use in this buyer's place to secure information about your customers. What additional information would you require to help you solve the problems of slow sales, high inventory, and numerous markdowns?

Case Study Number Six

SHOULD UPTOWN
SHOPPERS GO DOWNTOWN?

Kittering & Blake operated a high-quality, profitable women's specialty shop in Society Hill, a fashionable shopping and cultural section of Philadelphia. Since K & B was located in this high-rent area, it concentrated on offering well-known national brands of merchandise, with price emphasis upon the moderate to upper income groups. The store offered a well-rounded assortment of both classic types of merchandise, and currently popular fashions. Its philosophy of business was to provide personalized selling in attractive and pleasant surroundings.

Mr. Kittering, one of the store's owners, learned that the city was planning to provide a special "cultural loop" bus, which would carry business people, shoppers, and out-of-town visitors for a minimum fee to visit various historical and cultural centers throughout the city. The route, of course, included Society Hill. Upon examining the store's charge account records, he discovered that many of K & B's customers came from the immediate residential area, composed of townhouses, condominiums, and high-rise apartments. He discussed his findings with Mr. Blake; together they decided that a new advertising campaign should be developed to encourage shoppers from uptown to come to Society Hill and shop at K & B, especially since transportation was readily available.

However, there were some factors to consider.

First, Kittering & Blake's advertising efforts had been limited to local newspapers and magazines with an occasional ad appearing in one of the city's larger newspapers. A major problem was that K & B was operating on a limited advertising budget; therefore, it advertised only in smaller, less-expensive newspapers and magazines.

Second, since K & B was a small specialty shop, it had limited purchasing power in the marketplace; it often had difficulty in obtaining exclusives and other specials when dealing with merchandise sources. As a result, Kittering & Blake might not be able to provide a merchandise assortment that could meet demands of customers from such a variety of socioeconomic backgrounds.

Finally, K & B would have to offer merchandise in heretofore unrepresented price ranges. This would require locating new merchandise sources. Since the business was small, locating new sources was likely to prove difficult.

Considering the above factors, do you think K & B should develop a new advertising campaign to attract more customers?

Case Study Number Seven

TOO MUCH CONSERVATISM?

The women's specialty shop in which you are employed has maintained a policy of taking as few risks as possible in purchasing fashion merchandise. The store does not purchase the more popular lines of merchandise until other stores have tested them and found them to be acceptable by customers. As a result, your store's fashion image has become less appealing and your more fashion-conscious clientele are going elsewhere. You have been promoted to the position of fashion coordinator for the entire store. Your store manager has informed you that you may have a free hand in the development of the store's fashion image. However, you must be careful not to offend the existing clientele. The manager has also emphasized the fact that the store must upgrade its fashion image so that it will attract the more fashion-conscious customer. Be prepared in class to outline the merchandising responsibilities of a new fashion coordinator in a specialty shop.

Case Study Number Eight

THE NEW LOOK

Henson's is a twelve-store large volume discount chain that specializes in women's fashion apparel and accessories. It is an aggressive company that caters to the middle- to low-income groups in a large metropolitan area. During the past year, however, it was decided that Henson's was going to "trade-up"; that is, offer fashion apparel and accessories that would attract the upper-middle class and wealthy class type of clientele.

Mr. Blackmore, Henson's divisional merchandise manager, met with Ms. Skinner, the merchandise manager of the store's resident buying office, to discuss the change in Henson's merchandise policy. Mr. Blackmore felt that it was necessary to improve the store's fashion image to attract the higher-income clientele. He felt that Henson's would have to initiate an ambitious merchandising program to achieve its goal. Ms. Skinner suggested that Mr. Blackmore seek the advice of Mrs. Alexander, the fashion coordinator of the resident buying office. Mr. Blackmore agreed.

Mrs. Alexander was informed of Henson's intent to offer higher-priced fashion merchandise and of the store's intent to upgrade its fashion image. Mrs. Alexander immediately went to work. She consulted with various fashion buyers and developed a list of manufacturers and vendors who supplied high-fashion merchandise. She developed promotional themes that would tie in store advertising and display, sales events, fashion shows, and special public relations events. She developed a seasonal fashion calendar and made suggestions for special in-house fashion shows. This she felt was necessary to provide sales personnel with up-to-date information.

A meeting was called for the following week. Mr. Blackmore, Ms. Skinner, several store buyers, several resident buyers, and Mrs. Alexander met to discuss the development of Henson's new look. All agreed that improvement of store image was a number-one priority. They also agreed that store advertising and promotion campaigns should be coordinated to give the store a total fashion picture.

However, when Ms. Skinner asked Mr. Blackmore when he was going to hire additional buyers for the new high-price fashion departments, trouble started. Mr. Blackmore stated that the store's regular buyers would also buy for the new fashion departments. The entire room was silent. Ms. Skinner and Mrs. Alexander insisted that such a task was impossible because the regular store buyers were totally unfamiliar with the new resources. Mr. Blackmore insisted that the resident buying office had the responsibility for providing assistance in seeking new resources. Ms. Skinner agreed, but only to the extent that store buyers were able to come into the market and view the lines. This, she said, was extremely important due to the nature and price of the goods. Ms. Skinner further suggested that the regular store buyer would be too busy with existing buying responsibilities and would not have the time or the energy to view the additional vendors and manufacturers who offered high-fashion goods. In fact, she further stated that the fashion accessories markets alone would require the work of two or three store buyers. Mr. Blackmore disagreed. He stated that the store did not have the money to go out and hire additional buyers and that a good fashion coordinator would be able to provide the necessary fashion information. Mrs. Alexander agreed, but only to the degree that adequate market coverage on the part of store buyers was available. The meeting ended.

Considering the facts just stated, do you think that Henson's will accomplish its new merchandising objectives?

Learning Activities

1. Select a store advertisement from local newspapers for each of the following types of stores: a men's and boys' specialty shop; a discount house; a department store; a variety store; a chain-store operation. Evaluate each advertisement to determine the consumer appeal of each ad. Do you feel that each store's advertising reflects the social-class values of its potential customers?

2. Refer to the list of trade publications in this section. What trade publications would you subscribe to if you were a buyer of furs and fur accessories? of curtains and draperies? of hardgoods, such as kitchen utensils, pots and pans, and small electrical appliances? of children's furniture and accessories? of expensive furniture and furnishings?

3. Refer to the list of trade organizations in this section. What trade organizations would you join if you were a buyer of fabrics (piece goods) and sewing notions? of cosmetics, toiletries, and perfumes? of millinery, scarves, and neckwear? of lingerie and intimate apparel? of men's sportswear?

4. Interview the fashion coordinator of a department store; a boutique; a chain store operation. Prepare a list of questions on the topic, "How do you predict fashion trends for the coming season?" Are there similarities in the methods used by each? How do they differ?

5. Interview a buyer of fashion merchandise; a buyer of nonfashion goods. Determine the techniques used by each in determining the life-cycles of the merchandise they handle.

6. Develop a list of the fads that are currently popular on your college campus. Are these fads popular as a result of ethnic influence? geographic location? age group? occupational or vocational group?

References

THE RETAIL STUDENT'S REFERENCE LIBRARY

Bertrand, Frank. *Progressive Apparel Production.* New York: Fairchild Pub., Inc. n.d.

Cumming, James C. *Making Fashion and Textile Publicity Work.* New York: Fairchild Pub., Inc. 1985.

Diehl, Mary Ellen. *How to Produce a Fashion Show.* New York: Fairchild Pub., Inc. 1985.

Dolber, Roslyn. *Opportunities in Fashion.* New York: Fairchild Pub., Inc. 1985.

Gioello, Debbie Ann. *Fairchild's Designer's/Stylist's Handbook.* New York: Fairchild Pub., Inc. 1985.

Gold, Annalee. *How to Sell Fashion.* New York: Fairchild Pub., Inc. 1985.

The History of Menswear Industry: 1899–1950. New York: Fairchild Pub., Inc. n.d.

Jaffe, Hilde. *Children's Wear Design.* New York: Fairchild Pub., Inc. n.d.

Kawashima, Masaaki. *Men's Outerwear Design.* New York: Fairchild Pub., Inc. n.d.

Oerke, Bess V. *Dress—The Clothing Textbook.* Peoria, Ill: Chas. A. Bennett Co., Inc., n.d.

Packard, Sidney. *Strategies and Tactics in Fashion Marketing.* New York: Fairchild Pub., Inc. n.d.

Roberts, Edmund. *Fundamentals of Men's Fashion Design: A Guide to Casual Clothes.* New York: Fairchild Pub., Inc. 1985.

Rosen, Selma. *Children's Clothing: Designing, Selecting Fabrics, Patternmaking, Sewing.* New York: Fairchild Pub., Inc. 1985.

Salomon, Rosalie Kolodny. *Fashion Design for Moderns.* New York: Fairchild Pub., Inc. 1985.

Sixty Years of Fashion. New York: Fairchild Pub., Inc. n.d.

REFERENCES

1. George Simmel, "Fashion," *The American Journal of Sociology,* 57, no. 6 (May 1957), pp. 541–43.
2. Paul Nystrom, *Economics of Fashion* (New York: The Ronald Press Company, 1928), pp. 3–7.
3. Bernice G. Chambers, *Color and Design* (Englewood Cliffs, N.J.: Prentice-Hall, Inc., 1951) pp. 160–61.
4. M. D. Troxell and B. Judelle, *Fashion Merchandising* (New York: McGraw-Hill Book Company, 1971), pp. 20–28.
5. John W. Wingate and J. Dana Weiner, *Retail Merchandising* (Cincinnati: South-Western Publishing Company, 1963), pp. 176–78.
6. Troxell and Judelle, *Fashion Merchandising,* pp. 71–74.
7. *Fashion Coordination* (New York: ITT Educational Services, Inc., 1969), pp. 5–7.
8. Troxell and Judelle, *Fashion Merchandising,* pp. 323–30.

SECTION 3

The Buyer's Role in Merchandise Management: Planning and Controlling

The Merchandise Planning Process: Dollar Planning

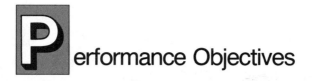

Performance Objectives

After reading this chapter, the student should be able to accomplish the following:

1. Discuss three components that make up the planning process. Describe types of records used in planning.

2. Define merchandise budget. List the elements that are essential to a good merchandise budget.

3. Outline the factors considered important when planning the merchandising budget.

4. Discuss the top-down plan; the bottom-up plan.

5. Calculate the following equations: BOM stock method; the percentage-variation (or deviation) method; the weeks' supply method; the stock-sales ratio method.

6. Write three formulas that may be used to compute stock turnover.

7. Define merchandise shortage; merchandise overage; and employee discount.

8. Calculate the markdown and the markdown percent. Explain why markdowns are necessary.

9. Calculate the initial markup, the markup percent, and the maintained markup.

10. Write the formula for computing gross margin and for net profit.

11. Write the formula used when planning purchases.

The Merchandise Planning Process: Dollar Planning

Figure 7-1 Retailers must plan ahead if they are to maintain their position in a complex, highly competitive, and aggressive business environment.

INTRODUCTION

As you have read in the previous chapter, fashion is everywhere. It is found in clothing apparel (the most obvious representative of fashion influences), in home furnishings, in appliances, in automobiles, in education, and in recreation, to name a few. You became aware of the various trade terms that are used in the retail business and the importance of understanding why fashions change, as well as what influences trends in fashion. Furthermore, fashion is a never-ending process. It influences the designer, the manufacturer, the retail buyer, and the consumer.

The retail buyer and the fashion coordinator must work closely together to insure that a unified fashion image is communicated throughout various departments within the store. However, the manner in which this objective is achieved and the methods used will vary with the store type and size. For example, the approach used in a chain operation will differ from that used in a department store which in turn will differ from the approach of the boutique.

In this chapter we are concerned with how the retail buyer plans merchandise whether for a fashion department, for departments carrying hard goods (appliances, furniture, small electrical appliances) or departments carrying soft goods (linens, curtains, draperies).

Merchandise planning is a process. The merchandise planning process first begins with the formulation of objectives, establishment of policies, and the implementation of procedures necessary to carry out department or store objectives. The planning process includes both dollar planning in terms of merchandise budgets and unit planning in terms of merchandise lists. Unit planning will be discussed in detail in Chapter 8.

Effective planning requires accurate record keeping. Top management in conjunction with store buyers must plan and thereby set specific policies for the following types of records used in most retail establishments: cash receipts and disbursements, expenses, sales, purchases, stocks and inventories, and profit-and-loss statements.

A successful retail operation requires a merchandise assortment of the right type, in the right place, and at the right price. To accomplish this task, activities such as profit and loss, sales, inventory, purchases, markups, markdowns, and expenses must be planned at least six months in advance by buyers and managers. This plan, called the merchandise budget, forecasts specific merchandising activities in terms of dollars for a department or store for a specified period of time. The merchandise budget is also referred to as the six-month merchandise plan.

Part 1—Merchandise Planning Process: Importance and Application

WHY PLAN?

Until recently, retailing has been primarily a day-to-day business. Plans have been based on short-range seasonal activities and monthly sales promotions. Buyers were concerned with beating last year's sales figures *today.* However, population shifts, urban redevelopment, the shortage of natural resources, and other environmental factors have forced retailers to take a second look at their merchandising policies and philosophies. Retailers must plan ahead if they are to maintain their position in a complex, highly competitive, and aggressive business environment (Figure 7–1).

THE PLANNING PROCESS

When planning the business enterprise, the manager should give consideration to the three components that make up the planning process: (1) objectives, (2) policies, and (3) procedures.[1]

Objectives

Objectives provide the framework for business planning; therefore, the formulation of business objectives during the early stages of planning is a must. A *business objective* may be defined as the goal toward which the management activities of the business establishment are directed. Business objectives may be stated in broad terms, that is, they may present a general picture of what the company hopes to achieve; or they may be stated in very specific terms. It is important to remember that all of those involved in retailing, whether a chief executive, a mid-management trainee, or a first-line supervisor, must give attention to company objectives and the methods used to achieve them.

Examples of business objectives may be illustrated as follows: a retail store may wish to offer exclusive or unique products, such as handcrafted items or imports not usually carried by other retailers; it may provide store customers with the newest, high-fashion styles and, therefore, will step up its foreign buying program; or it may wish to have the "dependable-store" image. Another specific store objective may be to appeal primarily to upper-middle and upper price bracket customers. This could be accomplished through store advertising and promotion appeals. Or, the store may have a policy of only selling merchandise that will be consistent with its objectives regarding quality and dependable merchandise offerings.

Policies

Business policies provide management with a frame of reference for decision making that is consistent with planned objectives. If policy statements are written clearly and concisely, they will provide the necessary guidelines for dealing consistently with problems and issues. Policies may be broadly stated to provide latitude to upper management, or they may be stated in specific terms. Usually more authority will be granted in policy interpretation to those in upper management, for example, members of the corporate board, store managers, and merchandise managers, while less latitude in

Figure 7–2   Breadth of policy interpretation.

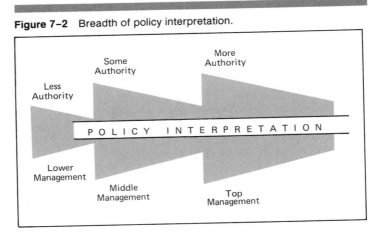

Figure 7–3   An example of one store's merchandising philosophy and policies.

We in Merchandising have the fundamental objective of developing "Maximum Sales Volume at a Maximum Rate of Profitability."

We, therefore, in Merchandising, perform the functions of planning our stocks and assortments aimed to satisfy our customer's demands—to then buy this merchandise—to promote it through advertising and display— and to have it sold at a price that will give us a sufficient gross margin which, after expenses, will return a net profit.

How we are to arrive at that goal and how our Company should accomplish the profitable volume and growth result we wish to obtain is set forth in the "Merchandising Philosophy and Policies" manual which was distributed to all executives as well as all of our associates. I am sure that you have all received a copy and I trust you have read it carefully. Our Merchandising Philosophy and Policies as to the kind and type of store that we wish to be are clearly set forth. It is the responsibility of all of us in merchandising to implement these objectives and policy statements.

policy interpretation is granted to those holding lower management positions (Figure 7–2). Figure 7–3 is an example of one store's merchandising philosophy and policies as presented to an executive training group by the vice-president of merchandising. As you will note, the store's broad objective is developing "maximum sales volume at a maximum rate of profitability."

Procedures

Procedures are necessary steps that must be followed to implement a given policy. When management sets up procedures for implementing store policies, it should emphasize whether or not the particular procedure is a *rule,* that is, a statement that must be obeyed, or a *guide,* which is a statement

---

What Type of Stores Will Plan the Following Objectives, Policies, and Procedures?

Objectives	*Policies*	*Procedures*
Provide mass-produced goods at discount prices	No cash refund; credit only	All employee packages must be checked before leaving the store
Provide one-stop shopping for food items, hard goods, soft goods	Cash and carry; no charges accepted	Smile and be courteous when on the selling floor
Offer exclusives and imported merchandise assortments	"The customer is always right"	Use authorized employee exits
Provide special services not found in competing stores	Personal and friendly service	Never ring anyone else's time card

---

that recommends an action be taken and is not necessarily mandatory. For example, Figure 7–4 illustrates the importance of store regulations that *must be observed* by employees since a violation of these rules can result in immediate dismissal. Figure 7–5 illustrates how one store provides information to employees to *guide* them in the performance of their duties. The store suggests that employees "smile," "be telephone-conscious," "be host to the public," "give courteous service," and "talk up the store."

Figure 7–4 An illustration of the importance of store regulations that must be observed by employees, since a violation of these rules can result in immediate dismissal.

Important Store Regulations!

You can understand and recognize the importance of a retail store as large as ours providing rules of conduct both for your protection and for the protection of our customers. We ask your full cooperation and understanding in observing all store regulations for a violation can result in immediate dismissal.

1. Use of intoxicating liquor or illegal drugs during store working hours or reporting to work under their influence.
2. Excessive tardiness or absences, or failure to report absences promptly.
3. Unauthorized presence in freight elevators, stock rooms and other areas unless authorized.
4. Unauthorized personnel are prohibited from entering the receiving and marking areas unless specifically authorized.
5. Handling merchandise in departments other than that to which they are assigned is prohibited.
6. Registering time for anyone other than yourself or permitting anyone else to register time for you is a violation of store rules which is cause for dismissal.
7. Improper procedures in handling cash or cash registers. You are responsible, particularly at the end of the day, to prevent not only the theft of cash but leaving the day's receipts and bank funds in a department overnight.
8. Gambling.
9. Violation of other Company rules and policies.

Thank You

PLANNING PROCESS AND EFFECTIVE RECORD KEEPING

A primary objective of any business is to make a profit. However, to determine whether or not the business is profitable, top management in conjunction with store buyers must plan thereby setting specific policies for effective record keeping. Specific policies will be set for the following types of records used in most retail establishments: (1) cash receipts and disbursements, (2)

Figure 7–5 An illustration of how a store guides its employees in the performance of their duties. (Courtesy of John Wanamaker Department Store, Philadelphia, Pa.)

IT'S A WANAMAKER CUSTOM

TO SMILE Everyone agrees that we're all more attractive when we smile. A gracious smile is the easiest way to make friends for Wanamaker's. This applies to all personnel, for no matter what your line of duty, you are a public relations representative for Wanamaker's. Of course the public can see your smile on the selling floor. But the public can feel your smile in a letter or from behind the telephone. So let's smile more and more: when we talk, when we write, and when we phone.

TO BE TELEPHONE CONSCIOUS Telephone business is big business. You'll be making good impressions if you answer promptly, in a clear, interested voice, give correct and complete information, eliminate side tone noises, and hang up carefully . . . without that bang in the ear. And remember, seconds seem like minutes when someone is left holding the line.

Automatic phones are used for intra-store communication in order to keep Bell phones free for customer service.

TO BE HOST TO THE PUBLIC "Make every visitor feel like a welcomed guest in your home," John Wanamaker said that. Just remember your manners, for they are always showing. When you use the passenger elevator stand aside to permit customers to enter first. You are permitted to use the passenger elevators for all purposes, except to carry freight and while in an elevator it's wise to refrain from shop talk, eating, or loud talking. Escalators should be used wherever possible so that the public can be served more efficiently.

TO GIVE SERVICE Of course selling merchandise is Wanamaker's principal service. But there are additional services that create good will. To give direction and information accurately and graciously also pays off. When you don't know the right answers, just ask. There are information centers in all stores. Our public is important. Without it, we wouldn't be here. The impressions we make keep the doors open for all of us. So let's always remember to treat each day as though it were our first . . . in this way we are bound to make it our best.

TO TALK UP THE STORE Make Wanamaker history. Rouse your customers, your relatives, your friends. Spread the news about the store. Talk current and coming store events. Let the people know . . . *THE EAGLE SPEAKS*, your publication, tells you regularly about the store family and its activities.

8

credit, (3) expenses, (4) sales, (5) purchases, (6) stocks and inventories, and (7) profit-and-loss statements.

Cash Disbursements and Receipts

Cash disbursements refers to the amount of cash paid out by a business. A buyer will keep a record of all cash paid out for expenses such as inventory, sales help, clerical items, advertising, display, and so forth. *Cash receipts* refers to the amount of money taken into the business throughout the day. Usually, cash receipts come from sales and from payment on account by customers. The store will set policies regarding the amount of money a buyer or department has to spend, as well as the amount of money or profit the department is responsible for earning. Management will provide a *cash budget,* which is an estimate of the department or store's cash receipts and cash disbursements over a specified period of time. The cash budget, as well as other types of budgets, will be discussed later in this chapter.

Credit

The decision as to the amount and kind of credit that will be extended to store customers will depend on the overall merchandising policies of the business. Management may decide that sales will be made on a cash-only basis and thus eliminate the problem of credit and collections. This may be the credit policy of a small businessperson who must have adequate amounts of working capital to buy stock and inventory. A specialty shop may adopt a conservative credit policy to provide a service to its clientele as well as to keep up with competition. A discount house may offer a liberal credit policy to encourage shopping as well as to keep up with the merchandise techniques used by similar stores.

A large department or specialty store or chain operation may maintain its own credit records and set up its own type of in-house credit system, or it may offer credit but use the resources of an outside agency such as a bank to operate and manage the credit system. Typically, the retailer realizes most of the benefits associated with the in-house credit system while eliminating many of the problems associated with credit management.

Credit plans may take on three forms: (1) open account, (2) installment credit, and (3) revolving credit.

Open credit, often referred to as the regular charge, allows customers to buy merchandise and to pay for it within a specific time period, usually 30 days, without an interest charge. Some stores, however, will extend the due date to either 60 or 90 days to promote a special occasion, for example, Christmas season.

Installment credit allows the customer to pay the total purchase price, less down payment, in equal installment payments over a specified time period, which may be weekly, quarterly, or monthly. This method of payment is used when purchasing expensive or high ticket items, such as automobiles, appliances, furniture, fur coats, and so forth.

Revolving credit combines the convenience of the open credit and installment credit. The customer can make multiple purchases, as in open credit, up to a limit, for example $500, and pay the amount within 30 days at no charge, or the customer can pay in installments at an interest rate specified in advance.

In addition to offering in-store credit services, many retailers accept one or more of the credit cards issued by outside institutions. Referred to as third-party cards, the most common types of credit cards are those issued by banks (Master Card and Visa) and entertainment card companies (American Express, Diner's Club, and Carte Blanche). Stores usually advertise the acceptance of various credit cards by displaying a symbol of the credit card company near the cash register. Many customers prefer this method of charging merchandise, since it eliminates carrying a credit card for each individual store.

Expenses

Records are kept of the expenses incurred by the store or department. The merchant will keep records of those expenses that involve direct cash outlays; however, those records do not provide information about all expenses. One way to classify retail expenses for monthly, semiannual, or annual analysis is to set up expense categories. The chart that follows is an illustration of "natural" expense classification as recommended by the National Retail Merchants Association.[2]

Retailers may classify expenses according to a "natural" expense category

Payroll—salaries, wages
Property Rentals—all property used in the business
Advertising—all payments for various media used
Interest—on borrowed funds, and assets
Taxes—all local, state, federal taxes
Supplies—wrapping, delivery, office, repairs
Services Purchased—purchase of cleaning, repair, delivery, light, heat, power
Travel—transportation and hotel accommodations
Unclassified—cash shortages, supper money, etc.
Communications—postage, telephone, telegrams
Pensions—retirement allowances
Insurance—fire, public liability, etc.
Depreciation—building, equipment, fixtures
Professional Services—legal, accounting, resident buying office
Donations—charitable, welfare, educational
Losses from Bad Debts—bad checks, etc.
Equipment Rentals—cash registers, computer, delivery trucks

Expenses may also be classified as direct and indirect expenses.

Direct expenses are paid out directly for the benefit of the department; the department manager or buyer is responsible for keeping control of these expenses. Examples are the payroll of full-time and part-time salespeople;

the department manager's and assistant's salary; advertising, promotions, and special events expenses; selling materials and supplies; travel expenses and hotel accommodations; and miscellaneous expenses.

Indirect expenses are those that serve the whole store. Examples are utilities (heat, light), rent, taxes, insurance, and the payroll of sales-supporting departments. Thus, if a department's sales are $20,000, the cost of goods sold is $14,000, and direct expenses are $4,000, the department will be responsible for contributing $2,000 to the store as a whole to help cover the store's indirect expenses as well as contributing to the store's profit. The following example illustrates how a department will contribute to the store's overall expenses:

Department Sales	$ 2 0,000
Cost of Goods Sold	− 14,000
Total	$ 6,000
Direct Expenses	− 4,000
(salaries, promotions, advertising, etc.)	
Total	$ 2,000

Sales

Sales records will tell the merchant how much is sold each day, according to classification, style, prize, size, color, and so forth; how much is sold each week and during a particular season; and how much is sold in branches or other store units. Some buyers, especially during storewide sales, will take hourly sales readings to determine whether or not their predetermined sales goals will be reached.

As you recall from our previous discussion of sales reports, sales analysis may be accomplished manually or electronically. A small business will usually use a manual type of control system. For example, at the end of the day, the owner-manager or assistant will count the day's receipts (cash and charge) and total the sales. Thus a sales total is derived for the entire store, with little consideration given to merchandise classification, style, price, color, size, etc. As the store expands, however, the owner-manager may determine sales by classification, style (remember the discussion of style cards), and so forth.

Most chain operations, department stores, variety stores, and other types of retail stores with more than one unit will use electronic controls to obtain sales information. Every sale is automatically recorded by price, department number, salesperson, date sold, and other information deemed necessary by the store. The information is printed out in a sales report and made available to store managers, buyers, assistants, or to whomever has a need for the reports.

Purchases

The department-store buyer or central buyer will keep a record of merchandise purchased from vendors, suppliers, and manufacturers for the department for which he is responsible. This record is called the *purchase journal.* Each department keeps a separate record *(billing record)* of all invoices (bills) received from various merchandise resources. The purchase journal and billing record contain invoices that provide information on department transfers, vendor returns, short shipments, damages, lost merchandise, and other claims.

As Figure 7-6 illustrates, the purchase journal will contain the following information: vendor's name, invoice date, style number, quantity, cost per unit, unit retail cost, the receiving apron number, total cost, total retail discounts, and balance paid or owed. The purchase journal is a most important record, since it is used to compare dollar amounts of merchandise receipts against planned purchase figures. This information will tell the buyer what has been received and what is on order, so that he or she can

Figure 7–6   A Purchase Journal

| Department Name Girls' wear Department Number 476 | Month Oct. 1 | Year 19 | Page Number 2 |

VENDOR	Ven-dor No.	In-voice Date	Style No.	Quant.	Cost per Unit	Cost at Retail	Apron No.	Total Cost	Total Retail	Disc.	Bal. Pd.	Bal. Due
Sweet and Sour, Inc.	17	10/3	75	432	8.95	17.95	1103	3,866.40	7,754.40	80.17	3,517.28	
Lemon Twist	12	10/5	12	108	7.85	15.00	1301	847.80	1,620.00	90.03	572.31	
Big Girl, Inc.	6	10/9	80	95	11.94	22.50	1400	1,134.30	2,137.50	50.41	1,410.10	
Four Foot Two	10	10/12	14	230	12.50	25.00	1403	575.00	5,750.00	82.71	2,826.32	

decide whether to increase or slow down the inventory turnover to conform to the merchandise budget.

Stocks and Inventories

The retailer may take a physical inventory, that is, actually count the goods on hand (merchandise on the shelves, on racks, and in bins, both on the selling floor and in the stockroom). This may be done semiannually or annually. In this way old, lost, or damaged merchandise may be found and thus eliminated from the inventory through preinventory clearance sales.

Figure 7-7 An EDP report will provide information on inventory turnover. Figures are recorded not only for department totals, but also for totals according to merchandise class and subclass. The buyer can use stock records to determine those merchandise classifications that are above or below the merchandise plan. (Courtesy of John Wanamaker Department Store, Philadelphia, Pa.)

```
                    WEEKLY CLASS SUMMARY REPORT
          DIV 29 DEPT 517 WEEK 4 ENDING 11/03 PERIOD 09    PG.    1

                 SALES              STOCK     SALES  LY
                 UNITS               UNITS      UNITS
          C   THIS  PER TO    $    THIS WEEK  THIS  NXT  FOLL
          L   WEEK  DATE    TOTAL  OH   OO    PER   PER  PER
                            PER

          090 P                                            1
              W                                            1
          TOTAL                                            1

          100 P                                            1
              A
              N     1       22
              EH                              2            3
          TOTAL     1       22                2            4

          110 P   8    25    538             23    20     49
              A   1    2     30                          9
              J        2     24              13    42     80
              W   1    6     111             14    31     96
              C        1     22              32    53    202
              SP  5    17    256             16    31     70
              PL  1    5     584             22    89    101
              N   4    7     115              7    23    107
              EH  3    8     117              7    56     88
              EX  2    5     72
          TOTAL  25   78    1869            134   345    802

          117 P                              2
              C                              1     3      1
          TOTAL                              3     3      1

          120 P   11   51   1014            110   173    306
              A    4   20    405             13    35    153
              J    4   28    566            103    72    319
              W    6   20    405             43    73    220
              C    3   48    940             72    93    471
              SP   7   48    963             83   152    473
              PL   7   33    655             78   116    429
              N    8   43    843             79   201    340
              EH   5   48    941             33   128    331
              EX   7   33    656
          TOTAL  62  372   7388            614  1043   3042
```

(We shall discuss opening and closing inventories in the section "Profit-and-Loss Statements.")

As Figure 7–7 illustrates, stock and inventory records show the amount of inventory on hand, or order, actual sales results, planned sales and stocks, and the sales and stocks for the same period of the previous year. If EDP is used, figures are recorded not only for department totals but also for totals according to merchandise class and subclass. A buyer, therefore, can use stock records to determine those merchandise classifications that are above or below the merchandise plan. Also, stock records will show the individual needs of branch stores or store units; thus, the buyer can either replenish the merchandise assortment or transfer goods to another store.

Profit-and-Loss Statements

The department *profit-and-loss statement,* also called the *income statement* and the *operating statement,* may be defined as a summary of the transactions conducted by a business during a specific period of time such as one month, six months, or a year. It shows the relationship that has prevailed for the period among sales, cost of goods sold, and expenses. The buyer will receive reports on the financial standing of each department, which includes information on actual and planned dollar sales figures for all phases of merchandising operation. As Figure 7–8 illustrates, the buyer will obtain information on gross sales, customer returns and adjustments, markdowns, purchases, gross margin of profit, operating expenses, cash discounts, and so on.

You will notice that the profit-and-loss statement starts with net sales and deducts cost of goods sold. The result is called *gross margin.* From gross margin the operating expenses are deducted, and the result is *net profit.* Each term will be discussed individually as follows:

Net Sales. Net sales is the difference between gross sales (all the sales that were made) and customer adjustments or returns. For example, the profit-and-loss statement for the women's blouse department shows net sales of $10,890. The following example illustrates how net sales were calculated.

Gross Sales	$11,259.00
Returns and Adjustments	− 369.00
Net Sales	$10,890.00

Cost of Goods Sold. The *cost of goods sold* is the amount of money paid for merchandise sold during a particular period covered by the profit-and-loss statement. The $25,290 figure was calculated as follows: at the beginning of June all the blouses in stock were counted and the cost value of the stock was figured. This cost value of stock is called the *opening inventory.* Thus, the opening inventory at cost is $18,990. However, purchases were made during the month that were added to the inventory value. For example, 500 blouses were purchased at $12 each. Thus the purchase cost is $6,000. Also, there was a shipping cost on the blouses. This amounted to $300. The total cost of purchases may be calculated as follows:

Cost of Goods Sold:		
Opening Inventory		$18,990.00
(cost value)		
Purchase Costs	$6,000	
Cost of Shipping	+ 300.00	
	$6,300.00	+$ 6,300.00
Total Cost of Purchases		$25,290.00

Once a determination is made of what was in stock at the beginning of the month (opening inventory $18,990) and what was added during the month (purchase costs plus shipping $6,300), it is important to determine what is left at the end of the month (closing inventory). A closing inventory figure of $17,400 is assumed. Thus, if we take the total cost of purchases ($25,290) and deduct the closing inventory, $17,400, the result is the *gross cost of goods sold,* which includes what was sold during the month as well as merchandise lost, damaged, stolen, or worn. This may be calculated as follows:

Opening Inventory		
(cost value)		$18,990.00
Purchase Costs	$ 6,000.00	
Shipping Costs	+ 300.00	
	$ 6,300.00	+6,300.00
Total Cost of Purchases		$25,290.00
Closing Inventory		
(cost value)		−17,400.00
Gross Cost of Goods Sold		$ 7,890.00

However, the buyer is allowed cash discounts for paying his bills within a certain period of time. Therefore, if the buyer was granted a 1 percent discount for paying the invoice (bill) within 20 days after receipt, he may deduct the following amount:

Cash Discount = Cash Discount % of Purchase Costs
$60   = 1% of $6,000

Since the entire purchase cost of $6,000 is figured in total goods handled, it is now necessary to deduct the cash discount to determine the net cost of goods sold. Net cost of goods sold may be calculated as follows:

Figure 7–8 Profit-and-loss statement, women's blouse department, month ending October 31.

INCOME			
Gross sales		$11,259.00	
Customer returns and adjustments		− 369.00	
Net sales		$10,890.00	$10,890.00
COST OF GOODS SOLD			
Open inventory (cost value)		$18,990.00	
Purchase costs	$6,000.00		
	+		
Shipping costs	300.00		
Total purchase costs	$6,300.00	+ $ 6,300.00	
Total purchases		$25,290.00	
Closing inventory (cost value)		− 17,400.00	
Gross cost of goods sold		$ 7,890.00	
Cash discount		− 60.00	
Net cost of goods		$ 7,830.00	−$ 7,830.00
Gross margin			$ 3,060.00
OPERATING EXPENSES			
Buyer's salary		$ 600.00	
Sales help salaries		1,200.00	
Advertising and promotions		240.00	
Rent		450.00	
Utilities		+ 150.00	
Total operating expenses		$ 2,640.00	−$ 2,640.00
NET PROFIT			$ 420.00

Opening Inventory (cost value)		$18,990.00
Purchase Costs	$6,000.00	
Shipping Costs	+ 300.00	
	$6,300.00	+ 6,300.00
Total Cost of Purchases		$25,290.00
Closing Inventory (cost value)		− 17,400.00
Gross Cost of Goods Sold		$7,890.00
Cash Discount		− 60.00
Net Cost of Goods Sold		$ 7,830.00

Gross Margin. *Gross margin* is the amount of profit before operating costs are deducted. It is determined by subtracting the net costs of goods sold ($7,830) from the net sales ($10,890). Thus:

Income			
Gross Sales		$11,259.00	
Returns and Adjustments		369.00	
		$10,890.00	
Net Sales			$ 10,890.00
Cost of Goods Sold			
Opening Inventory (cost value)		$18,900.00	
Purchase Costs	$ 6000.00		
Shipping Costs	+ 300.00		
	$ 6,300.00	+ 6,300.00	
Total Cost of Purchases		$25,290.00	
Closing Inventory		−17,400.00	
Gross Cost of Goods Sold		$ 7,890.00	
Cash Discount		60.00	
Net Cost of Goods Sold			−7,830.00
Gross Margin			$ 3,060.00

Operating Expenses. As previously stated, expenses may be classified as *direct* and *indirect.* The two together make up *operating expenses,* which may appear in the profit-and-loss statements as follows:

Operating Expenses	
Buyer's Salary	$ 600.00
Sales Help Salaries	1,200.00
Advertising and Promotion	240.00
Rent	450.00
Utilities	+ 150.00
Total Operating Expenses	$ 2,640.00

Net Profit. *Net profit* is determined by deducting operating expenses from gross margin.

Now, let's review for a moment. There are five key factors important in the formulation of the profit-and-loss statement: net sales, cost of goods sold, gross margin, operating expenses, and net profit. The student should determine how a profit-and-loss statement is developed by reviewing each step in the procedure. Refer to Figure 7–8 again for a complete picture of what the profit-and-loss statement looks like.

Key Factors Important in the Formulation of the Profit-and-Loss Statement Are:

1. *Net Sales*
   Net sales = Gross sales (−) Customer adjustments or returns
2. *Cost of Goods Sold*
   Opening inventory + purchase costs and shipping costs = total purchases (−) closing inventory = gross cost of goods sold (−) cash discount
3. *Gross Margin*
   Gross margin = net sales (−) net cost of goods sold
4. *Operating Expenses*
   Total operating expenses = direct expenses + indirect expenses
5. *Net Profit*
   Net profit = net sales (−) net cost of goods (−) total operating expenses

Planning Requires Accurate Record Keeping.

How Will the Following Types of Records Assist You in Merchandise Planning?

Records of cash receipts and disbursements
Credit records
Expense records
Sales reports
Purchase journal
Stocks and inventory records
Department profit-and-loss statement

PLANNING PROCESS
AND EFFECTIVE BUDGETING

The budget is an important tool used by management in planning and controlling business systems. It is a document that outlines in quantitative terms the planned operations of the retail business for a specified period of time. However, the size and type of retail establishment will determine the number and the extent of budgetary controls used. The procedure involved in setting up the budget will occur during the planning stages. The retailer, therefore, will plan different types of budgets even before the merchandising activity begins. The important types of budgets used by most retail establishments, regardless of size or type, are: (1) operations budget, (2) cash budget, (3) capital budget, and (4) merchandise budget.

Operations Budget

The *operations budget* may be defined as a forecast of expected sales along with expected costs for a specified time period. The operations budget is sometimes referred to as the revenue-and-expense budget. This type of budget is usually made up a year in advance, though estimates may be made for as long as three to five years. The revenues portion of the budget is based on estimated sales for the coming year, especially in a retail operation where the sale of goods and services constitutes the chief source of operating income.

The buyer, as well as other store executives, will hold several meetings throughout the year to determine if present sales figures are keeping pace with sales projections. For example, the buyer and merchandise manager of a department store will refer to daily sales and stock reports to guide them in determining whether they will be able to meet planned sales objectives in the parent store and in branches during a particular selling season, such as the Easter season. In a chain operation the central buyer and corporate executives will also utilize daily sales and stock reports to tell them how much merchandise is selling in each unit throughout the chain.

Merchants must pay close attention to daily flash reports, sales analysis, inventory turnover, exception reports, and so forth when determining if sales figures are meeting projected goals. However, they must also consider internal as well as external business factors that may affect the accomplishments of sales goals. For example, the small business owner may fall ill, which may require that the business be closed for a few days, so that customers go elsewhere to purchase goods. This is an internal business factor. Other factors include labor strikes, poor morale, inefficient management, poor control systems, and so forth. External business factors are always present in the retailer's environment. As you recall from chapter 1, the merchant must be aware of economic conditions, changes in consumer spending patterns, changes in federal legislation, income and age levels of the population in the immediate trading area, and so forth.

Estimated costs or expenses, as you recall, may be classified as direct or indirect expenses. Usually, expenses are controlled and fixed throughout the budgetary period. Controllable expenses are those expenses directly

Figure 7-9 An example of an operations budget for the Santiago's Appliance Store.

		Actual 19		Budget 19
Sales		$35,000		$42,000
Cost of goods sold		−21,000		−25,000
Gross profit		$14,000		$17,000
Operating expenses				
Salaries of sales help	$5,100		$5,200	
Advertising & promotion	1,200		1,800	
Miscellaneous	200		250	
Total selling expenses	$6,500		$7,250	
Rent	$1,200		$1,200	
Utilities	450		500	
Taxes	350		450	
Insurance	150		150	
Miscellaneous	600		800	
Total general expenses	$2,750		$3,100	
Total operating expenses		$ 9,250		$10,350
Operating profit		$ 4,750		$ 6,650
Income taxes		$ 600		$ 1,050
Net profit		$ 4,150		$ 5,600

attributed to a specific department. If a department is discontinued, these expenses end. Fixed expenses are continuing storewide expenses, which will remain even if one or two departments within the store close down.

Figure 7-9 is an example of an operations budget for Santiago's Appliance Store.

Cash Budget

The *cash budget* is an estimate of the retail business's cash receipts and cash disbursements for a specified period of time. The cash budget will tell management how much cash is required during future periods. In a small business, this is a useful tool in determining the need for a short-term loan for a forthcoming selling season. Depending on the size of the business, the cash budget may extend over a year, with cash receipts and disbursements estimated on a monthly basis. If cash balances are very large, as in chain operations, discount houses, and department stores, closer and more sophisticated controls are used, for example, EDP. Figure 7-10 is an example of the cash budget for Santiago's Applicance Store for one month.

Figure 7–10   An example of a cash budget for one month for Santiago's Appliance Store.

	Jan.	Feb.	March	April	May	June	July	August	Sep.
Cash receipts									
Cash sales	$1,500	$1,000	$2,000	$3,000	$1,500	$1,000	$1,000	$1,500	$2,500
Credit & collections	3,000	2,000	1,000	2,000	3,000	1,500	1,000	1,000	2,000
Total receipts	$4,500	$3,000	$3,000	$5,000	$4,500	$2,500	$2,000	$2,500	$4,500
Disbursements									
Purchases	$3,500	$5,500	$1,000	$1,000	$3,500	$2,000	$1,250	$3,500	$2,000
Wages	400	400	500	500	400	400	400	400	500
Rent	100	100	100	100	100	100	100	100	100
Utilities	75	75	75	50	50	50	75	75	75
Taxes			600			600			600
Total disbursements	$4,075	$6,075	$2,275	$1,650	$4,050	$3,150	$1,825	$4,075	$3,275
Monthly cash flow Cash in; cash out	+$ 250	−$3,175	+$ 675	+$3,150	+$ 300	−$ 750	+$ 100	−$1,695	+$1,325
Beginning cash	$ 750								
Cash minimum	$ 750								
Cash overage; cash shortage	−$ 500	+$2,925	−$2,250	+$ 900	+$1,200	−$ 450	+$ 550	−$1,125	+$ 400
Anticipated monthly loans	$2,925		$2,250				$1,125		

Capital Budget

The *capital budget* will plan for the investment of assets that will last longer than a year. It contains a list of future investment projects, with a justification for each proposal listed next to each item. For example, a department store may propose to open two new branch stores during the year 1990, one in 1992, and one in 1994. The plan would include a careful analysis of the geographical region, income level, competition, and the number of support businesses (banks, food markets, shoe repair stores, drug stores, etc.) also estimated for the area. Capital budgets are usually planned by the store's research division. However, the buyer has additional responsibilities for merchandising each time a new branch is added, and therefore must be included in a store's future plans.

Merchandise Budget

The *merchandise budget* is planned by the buyer together with other store executives. Since the maintenance of an inventory that meets the needs and wants of customers and is within the financial plan set by management is a primary responsibility of store buyers, this topic will be covered in detail in the second part of this chapter.

Why Are the Following Types of Budgets Used by Most Retail Establishments?

What kind of information is contained in each?

Operations budget
Cash budget
Capital budget
Merchandise budget

PART 2—Merchandise Planning Process: The Merchandise Budget

THE MERCHANDISE BUDGET

A successful retail operation requires a merchandise assortment of the right type, in the right place, and at the right price. To accomplish this, factors such as profit and loss, sales, inventory, purchases, markups, markdowns, and expenses must be planned at least six months in advance by buyers and managers. This plan is called the *merchandise budget* and may be defined as a plan that forecasts specific merchandising activities for a department or store for a specified period of time.

The buyer will work with numerous store executives in developing a plan to guide him or her in the various phases of the merchandising activity. For example, the control manager will provide detailed information on previous years' sales activities for the parent store and branches in a department store or for each store unit in a chain operation. The financial manager will provide information regarding the availability of funds, future cash needs, and figures on cash receipts and disbursements. The merchandise manager will provide valuable guidance based on company objectives and procedures, and will maintain a proper balance among the departments under his or her jurisdiction with regard to departmental opportunities and needs. A buyer who is also the owner-manager, as in the small independent business, will rely on past experience and on his or her ability as a manager and merchandising objectives when planning a workable merchandise budget.

WHAT THE
MERCHANDISE BUDGET INCLUDES

Once all available information regarding business conditions, consumer trends, market and supply conditions, competition, business philosophies, and future forecasts are gathered, actual planning for the period ahead may begin.

The small store will usually adopt a six-month plan that is very simple. For example, the desired results of the various merchandising activities for a specific period are put down on paper in the form of dollar figures, and comparisons and adjustments are made at frequent intervals in relation to the actual performance. The budget items may consist solely of sales, purchases, expenses, and stocks. However, in the department store or chain operation, a separate merchandise budget is made for each department and will contain, in addition to those items mentioned, markdowns, employee discounts, stock shortages, stock turnover, customer returns, gross margin, net profit, and average sales. Thus the buyer and the store executives will develop a merchandise budget based on planned: (1) sales, (2) stocks, (3) reductions, (4) markups, (5) gross margin and operating profit, (6) expenses, and (7) purchases.

It is important to note that management plans the budget in terms of dollar figures, since dollar figures formulate the store's overall profit objective. Also, buyers will plan in units, that is, they will estimate what they expect to sell during a season or period according to merchandise classification, sub-class, size, color, price, or whatever, and determine inventory needs based on this plan. Once unit needs are determined, dollar figures are arrived at by multiplying the number of units times prices. This topic will be covered in detail in Chapter 8.

Figure 7–11 is an example of a six-month merchandise budget or plan. You should refer to the illustration to understand the relationship among the factors discussed on the following pages.

Planned Sales

Sales planning is the first step in the merchandise budget and is the *key element in planning.* Most plans span the time from February 1 to July 31, and from August 1 to January 31. Sales are planned first because it is easier to adjust stocks, markups, and expenses to sales potentials than to attempt to plan these factors and to reach a sales goal consistent with them.

Figure 7–11 An example of a six-month merchandise budget, a plan that forecasts specific merchandising activities for a department or store for a specified period of time.

Department Number: 714							
Department Name: Budget Housewares					The Six-Month Merchandise Plan		
Profit Goal $12,000				Actual Profit Goal			
Operating Expenses $10,000				Actual Operating Expenses			

Fall 1990	Aug.	Sept.	Oct.	Nov.	Dec.	Jan.	Season
Last Year's Sales	$13,400	$20,200	$23,400	$19,000	$17,400	$13,000	$106,800
Planned Sales	15,400	20,200	26,000	21,000	19,000	13,400	115,000
Actual Sales							
Stock Last Year	$24,000	$34,000	$40,000	$32,000	$22,000	$18,000	$ 25,000
Planned Stocks	13,000	33,000	36,000	31,000	24,000	20,000	28,300
Actual Stock							
Reductions	$ 220	$ 320	$ 440	$ 300	$ 420	$ 400	$ 2,100
Planned Reductions	220	320	300	400	400	400	2,040
Actual Reductions							
Markup Last Year	45%	33%	50%	53%	40%	50%	
Planned Markups	45%	33%	45%	50%	45%	50%	
Actual Markups							
Profit Last Year	$ 2,500	$ 1,500	$ 2,000	$ 2,000	$ 1,500	$ 3,500	$ 12,000
Planned Profit	2,000	1,500	2,500	2,500	1,500	2,000	12,000
Actual Profit							
Expenses Last Year	$ 420	$ 480	$ 600	$ 480	$ 340	$ 280	$ 2,600
Planned Expenses	500	540	660	540	420	340	3,000
Actual Expenses							
Purchases Last Year	$23,400	$26,200	$15,400	$13,000	$13,800	$ 9,000	$100,800
Planned Purchases	22,400	23,700	21,000	18,000	15,000	9,400	109,000
Actual Purchases							
Comments	Rainy Month	Turned Cool	News-paper Strike	Sales Pro-motion	Fair Weather	Snow Storm	

Merchandise Manager	Buyer	Store Controller
L. L. Allen	M. S. Smith	H. I.

Important Factors to Consider When Planning the Merchandise Budget. They Are Planned:

1. Sales
2. Stocks
3. Reductions
4. Markups
5. Gross margin and operating profit
6. Expenses
7. Purchases

The first step in planning sales is to refer to department sales records and consider the overall past sales performance of the store or chain operation as a whole, as well as sales trends for each department in individual branches or units. Consideration should be given to factors within the store that may aid or hinder sales activity. For example, a store may decide to upgrade its fashion image, add a new branch, close two store units, develop a discount merchandising philosophy, or change to a self-service operation. Next, the buyer must consider outside factors that may affect sales, such as economic trends, the rate of employment and unemployment, the growth of shopping centers, competitive conditions, etc. For example, management may determine that a 7 percent gain in sales storewide is necessary to meet rising costs due to increased fuel expenses, scarcity of building supplies, demands of labor unions, and changes in overhead and operations, to name but a few. Management may determine that the unpainted furniture department could increase its sales activity by 6 percent, whereas the kitchen appliances department offers little opportunity for increased sales activity. Therefore, only a 2 percent sales increase would be planned for the kitchen appliances department.

After considering the store's sales opportunities as a whole, the buyer must next consider how the department or departments will achieve the sales goals based on the store's overall projections. The buyer must consider sales planning according to each classification, price line, size, color, or other subdivision that is felt to be important.

The Monthly Sales Plan. To plan the six-month budget realistically, buyers and management must first plan for each of the six months on a monthly basis. Sales goals will be set for each month, since all months will not contribute equally to the six-month plan. For example, the months of November and December will have a higher sales goal than the months of July and August, due to changes in seasonal demand patterns. Easter and the back-to-school period are peak periods for most fashion departments; therefore, the sales goals for the corresponding months (March and April; September) will be higher. Or a store may plan a preinventory clearance sale during the month of January, which would account for a higher sales goal then as opposed to goals for a month where no significant sales promotion was planned. Finally, a department that sells seasonal goods, for example, patio and outdoor furniture, will plan for higher sales activity during the months of June and July due to weather patterns.

As stated previously, management will plan in terms of dollar figures, and in addition the buyer will plan in terms of units of merchandise according to classification, price line, size, color, or other breakdowns that are applicable. For example, if you are a buyer of men's sweaters, you may find that the classic crewneck sweater is featured as an important fashion look for the fall season. You will plan your stock in units with the crew neck classification given priority, while less popular styles are offered in a limited selection.

Methods Used in Planning Departmental Sales. Buyers and managers will not only consider the points just discussed but also will plan in general terms, that is, in terms of store needs and individual departmental needs. Two methods used in planning departmental sales are (1) the top-down plan and (2) the bottom-up plan.

Top-down planning may be defined as the planning of overall sales management based on economic trends, external conditions, and changes in store policies. Such goals are further broken down into plans for each department in the store, and if the store is a branch or chain system, into plans for each department or each store. If there is a central buying system, the departmental sales plans will include the sales in all the selling units within each store. In this case, buyers have their sales goals planned for them by top management and can only make suggestions for adjustments in the sales figures presented to them.

Bottom-up planning may be defined as the planning for a specific department, whether it is located in one store or in many units. In this method, the initial planning is accomplished by those directly responsible for implementing the sales plan, and storewide plans are primarily built up from the plans formulated from within each department and selling unit. This is the most favored plan used by retail stores; however, flexibility and realistic thinking are prime requisites for its success. For example, after the buyer has formulated the sales plan for the coming season, he must confer with the merchandise manager, who is aware of the goals and objectives set by top management. If the buyer's plan falls short of the overall objectives of the store, research is required to establish how a particular department may increase sales.

> ### How Will the Following Techniques Help the Buyer When Planning Department Sales?
>
> Department sales records
> Store policies and procedures
> The monthly sales plan
> Top-down planning
> Bottom-up planning

Planned Stocks

The second step in the merchandise plan is to maintain a balanced stock in relation to anticipated sales. It is interesting to note, however, that inventory costs are closely linked to economic booms and recessions. Buyers tend to overstock when prospects of increased sales are good and to understock when prospects are bad. Often, a relatively small increase in sales leads to excessive buying and excessive production.

    The buyer will plan the stock in terms of the specific items of merchandise he believes will serve his customer's needs and wants. However, stock planning also includes: (1) an understanding of the various methods used to plan needed stocks, (2) the computation of stock turn, (3) computation of the average inventory, (4) an understanding of methods of increasing stock turn, (5) an understanding of the different rates of stock turn, and (6) stock planning for branches and store units.

Various Methods Used to Plan Needed Stocks. A most important responsibility of all types of buyers is to plan stock accurately and efficiently, whether for the forthcoming season or for merchandise replenishment at any time. Four methods may be used when planning stock: (1) the basic stock method, (2) the percentage-variation (or deviation) method, (3) the weeks' supply method, and (4) the stock-sales ratio method.

    The basic stock method shows the necessity of having a *basic stock* (which in this case refers to the difference between the average stock and the average amount sold monthly) on hand at all times. Beginning-of-the-month (BOM) stock is determined by the following equation:

BOM = Planned Sales for the Month + (Average Stock at Retail − Average Monthly Sales)

    For example, during the six-month period, season sales may be planned at $57,000; planned turnover, 3; June sales may be estimated at $15,000 and July sales at $17,000.

Stock, June 1 $15,000
  Average Stock at Retail
  = $57,000 ÷ 3
  = $19,000
  Average Monthly Sales
  = $57,000 ÷ 6
  = $ 9,500
  Stock, June 1 = $15,000 +
  ($19,000 − $9,500)
  = $15,000 + $9,500
  = $24,500

Stock, July 1 $17,000
  Average Stock at Retail
  = $57,000 ÷ 3
  = $19,000
  Average Monthly Sales
  = $57,000 ÷ 6
  = $9,500
  Stock, July 1 = $17,000 +
  ($19,000 − $9,500)
  = $17,000 + $9,500
  = $26,500

The student will note that this plan increases and decreases stock at the first of each month in approximately the same amount of dollars as sales increase or decrease. In the example, July sales are approximately $2,000 higher than June sales, and stocks are also $2,000 higher. Since the basic stock is constant throughout the season, stocks for the first of the month may be found by adding the sales for the month to the basic stock.

A second method of stock planning, *the percentage-variation (or deviation) method,* is based on the premise that BOM stock is increased or decreased from the planned average stock by approximately 50 percent of the sales variations from the average monthly sales. The formula may be expressed as follows:

$$\text{BOM Stock} = \text{Average} \frac{\text{Yearly Sales}}{\text{Turnover}} \times \left[\frac{1}{2} \left(1 + \frac{\text{Sales for the Month}}{\text{Average Monthly Sale}} \right) \right]$$

For example, the planned yearly sales may be $48,000; the planned sales for the month of September, $2,500; and the planned yearly turnover, 6.

Then:
Retail Stock September 1
  (BOM Stock)

$$= \frac{\$48,000}{6} \times \frac{1}{2} \left(1 + \frac{\$2,500}{\$48,000} \div 12 \right)$$

$$= \$8,000 \times \frac{1}{2} \left(1 + \frac{\$2,500}{\$4,000} \right)$$

$$= \$8,000 \times \frac{1.625}{2}$$

$$= \$8,000 \times .8125$$

$$\text{BOM Stock} = \$6,500$$

A third method of stock planning, known as *the week's supply method,* is to plan stock on a weekly basis and to set stocks equal to a predetermined number of weeks' supply, depending upon the stock turn desired. For example, if approximately eight turns a year are desired, the stock should equal approximately six weeks' supply. The calculations are as follows:

$$\text{Weeks' Supply} = 52 \text{ Weeks} \div \text{Desired Stock Turn}$$
$$= 52 \div 8$$
$$= 6.1$$

Estimates are made, therefore, to cover sales about six weeks ahead.

A fourth method of stock planning, known as the *stock-sales ratio method,* uses the monthly stock-sales ratio as the basis for stock planning. With this method, the planned sales volume for the month is multiplied by the planned BOM stock-sales ratio to determine the planned BOM stock. The formula may be written as follows:

BOM Stock = Planned Monthly Sales Volume × Planned BOM Stock-Sales Ratio

The stock-sales ratio is the BOM stock expressed as a ratio of sales. It shows the number of months that would be necessary to dispose of BOM stock at the rate of the sales for that month. The formula may be written as follows:

$$\text{Stock-Sales Ratio} = \frac{\text{Beginning Stock}}{\text{Sales}}$$

For example, it may be found that the January stock-sales ratio for a shoe department is 5. This means that the stocks on the first of January are usually 5 times the January sales. Thus, if the department sales forecast is $15,000 for January, this figure is multiplied by the stock-sales ratio of 5 to determine planned stocks of $75,000 for January 1.

$$\text{Stock-Sales Ratio} = \frac{\text{BOM Stock}}{\text{Month's Sales}}$$

$$\text{Stock-Sales Ratio} = \frac{\$75,000}{\$15,000}$$

$$\text{Stock-Sales Ratio} = 5$$

BOM Stock = Planned Monthly Sales Volume $\times$ Planned BOM Stock-Sales Ratio

BOM Stock = $15,000 $\times$ 5

BOM Stock = $75,000

The Computation of Stock Turnover. Stock turn or stock turnover is the rate at which stock is disposed of or depleted and replaced in a given period of time. Every buyer should understand stock turnover to make more profitable use of his capital investment, control inventories, and maximize profits. Stock turn may be computed by one of the following formulas:

1. $\dfrac{\text{Stock Turn}}{\text{Retail Basis}} = \dfrac{\text{Net Sales}}{\text{Average Stock at Retail Price}}$

2. $\dfrac{\text{Stock Turn}}{\text{Cost Basis}} = \dfrac{\text{Cost of Goods Sold}}{\text{Average Cost of Stock}}$

3. $\dfrac{\text{Stock Turn}}{\text{Unit Basis}} = \dfrac{\text{Number of Units Sold}}{\text{Average Number of Units in Stock}}$

For example, if the retail store keeps records of the retail value of the stock, then the retail basis for computing stock turnover is used. When information regarding stock is available only in terms of cost, the cost basis of computing stock turnover is preferred. The unit basis is useful in studying the number of items or units carried in relation to the number sold.

Stock turn may be computed for any period, such as a year, a month, or a week. However, when the term *rate of stock turn* is used, a period of one year is understood.

Average inventory. To find the average inventory, you would find the sum of all the inventories in a period and divide by the number of inventories. Many buyers use the average of the actual stocks as determined by a physical inventory at the beginning and at the end of the year. For example:

Inventory on Hand at Retail

January 1		$ 30,000
February 1		17,000
March 1		22,000
April 1		25,000
May 1		+ 23,000
Total Inventory	=	$117,000

$$\text{Average Inventory} = \frac{\text{Total Inventory}}{\text{Number of Inventories}}$$

$$\text{Average Inventory} = \frac{\$117,000}{5}$$

$$\text{Average Inventory} = \$ 23,400$$

It must be remembered, however, that the stock remaining at the end of a selling period is not an accurate reflection of the average stock carried throughout the year. For example, stock at the end of the year (December 31) is usually below the true yearly average because more goods have been disposed of, primarily through store inventory clearance sales. A more accurate method of determining the average inventory is by dividing the sum of the stocks on the first of every month, plus the ending stock, by 13. The number 13 is used because the retailer is starting with the beginning-of-the-month inventory and there will be an additional 12 times (each month throughout the year) when inventory is counted. A physical inventory is not necessary because a monthly book inventory may be utilized. An example follows:

Inventory on Hand at Retail

January 1	$ 30,000
February 1	$ 27,000
March 1	$ 26,500
April 1	$ 22,000
May 1	$ 25,500
June 1	$ 19,500
July 1	$ 24,000
August 1	$ 21,400
September 1	$ 27,000

October 1	$ 22,600
November 1	$ 25,000
December 1	$ 23,000
December 31	+$ 20,000
Total Inventory	= $313,500

$$\text{Average Inventory} = \frac{\text{Total Inventory}}{\text{Number of Inventories}}$$

$$\text{Average Inventory} = \frac{\$313,500}{13}$$

$$\text{Average Inventory} = \$24,115$$

Increasing stock turn. The buyer who maintains a small, clean inventory will find this the fastest method of increasing stock turn. Since profit is not realized until the inventory is turned back into money, the higher the stock turnover, the greater the profit returned on the dollars invested. The following is a list of methods the buyer may use to keep inventory to a minimum without jeopardizing sales.

Stocks may be kept to a minimum by:

1. Reducing the number of price lines carried
2. Limiting the number of brands carried
3. Reducing duplicate styles
4. Carrying smaller reserve stocks
5. Avoiding the accumulation of unsalable goods
6. Eliminating unsalable goods
7. Closely following the buying plan

Different Rates of Stock Turn. Another major consideration in the planning of stock is the different rate of stock turn. The rate of stock turnover will depend on certain factors, which are listed here.

1. Different lines of merchandise have different rates of stock turn. The rate of stock turn for a gourmet food department is faster than the rate for a small-appliance department due to the nature of the goods.

2. Types of goods also influences stock turn. Convenience goods will have a faster rate than shopping goods. Convenience items are articles for which there is an immediate need or which are bought on impulse. Shopping goods, because they cost more and are less frequently needed, require more careful consideration and selection.

3. Type of retail institution influences stock turn. Discount stores will have faster rates than traditional department stores. Discounters concen-

The Merchandise Assortment

A primary responsibility of the buyer is to provide a merchandise assortment that reflects the needs and wants of the store's clientele. How will the following factors assist the buyer in accomplishing this task?

Various Methods Used to Plan Needed Stocks

The basic stock method, the percentage-variation (or deviation method), the week's supply method, and the stock-sales ratio method

The Computation of Stock Turnover

Retail basis, cost basis, unit basis

Average Inventory

$$\text{Average inventory} = \frac{\text{Total inventory}}{\text{Number of inventories}}$$

Increasing Stock Turn

Advantages and disadvantages

Different Rates of Stock Turn

Rates according to different merchandise, the types of goods carried by the department and the type of retail institution

Planning Stock for Branches and Store Units

Plan stock separately, seek advice, recognize that each branch or unit has its own set of unique characteristics

---

trate on the fastest-moving merchandise, even though stock assortment may be thrown out of balance. Department stores, on the other hand, will provide a full line of merchandise to offer the customer a variety of choices in each category.

Planning Stock for Branches and Store Units. A final major consideration in planning stock is the number of branches or units for which you are responsible. For example, if you are a local buyer for a department store, you may have to purchase goods for your department in the parent store and for the same department in a number of branches, depending on the size of the operation. If you are a central buyer for a chain-store operation, you may have to purchase large quantities of merchandise for your particular department in many store units, perhaps 30 to 40 or 300 to 400. Or you may be a resident buyer offering assistance and advice to a number of client stores that require goods for the particular department or departments you represent.

Planned Reductions

The third step is to plan retail reductions. *Retail reduction* may be defined as the allowance for the difference between the original retail value of merchandise and the actual final sales value of the merchandise. It consists of three major factors: (1) merchandise shortages and overages, (2) employee discounts and discounts for other special groups, and (3) markdowns.

Merchandise Shortages and Overages. As previously explained, a *merchandise shortage* is the difference between the book inventory and the physical inventory when the book inventory is larger. In most stores today, merchandise shortages exceed 1 percent of the store's sales; and since the buyer is the person responsible for the inventory, his competence as a merchandiser is in question when inventory shortages are high. Also the gross margin of the department will suffer because shortages will cut into the buyer's profit, and gross margin is one of the important factors by which management judges the buyer's performance.[3]

The buyer and his manager require sound facts to determine the extent of merchandise shortages as well as their causes. A most important step toward improving the shortage problem is to make sure that all records are kept as accurate as possible. For example, if a handbag department receives 10 units of handbags and the report lists 12 units, 2 units may be presumed to be lost. It is important that all personnel within the department, from the stockboy upward, be trained to count and recount actual merchandise units against the figures recorded. For instance, if a buyer decides to transfer 20 dresses at $35.95 each to a branch store or another unit, the assistant buyer or department manager should check the count, price tickets, style number and whatever else is necessary to ensure that the right merchandise in the right amount is going to the right place. And, in turn, someone at the branch or store unit should check and count the incoming merchandise to make sure that the right goods in the right amount have been received.

If accuracy in record keeping is maintained, methods may be developed that will assist the buyer in pinpointing the source of the shortage problem and thus serve to discourage carelessness, dishonesty, and waste.[4] (The subject of shoplifting will be covered in detail in Chapter 15.)

The formula used to determine inventory shortage is illustrated as follows:

Merchandise Shortage = Book Inventory − Physical Inventory
For example:

Net Sales	$150,000
Purchases	70,000
Opening Inventory	160,000
Physical Inventory	70,000

Then:

Opening Inventory	$160,000
+Purchases at Retail	70,000
Total Handled	$230,000
—Net Sales	150,000
Book Inventory	$ 80,000

When comparing the physical inventory with the book inventory, we find:

Book Inventory	$80,000
Physical Inventory	70,000

Apply the formula:

Merchandise Shortage = Book Inventory − Physical Inventory = $80,000 − $70,000
Merchandise Shortage = $10,000

A *merchandise overage* is the difference between the book inventory and the physical inventory when the physical inventory is larger. In this case there may be an error in the physical count. The formula is as follows:

Merchandise Overage = Physical Inventory − Book Inventory

For example:

Net Sales	$150,000
Opening Inventory	160,000
Purchases at Retail	70,000
Physical Inventory	70,000

Then:

Opening Inventory	$120,000
+Purchases at Retail	70,000
Total Handled	$190,000
—Net Sales	150,000
Book Inventory	$ 40,000

When comparing the physical inventory with the book inventory, we find:

Book Inventory	$40,000
Physical Inventory	70,000

Apply the formula:

$$\text{Merchandise Overage} = \text{Physical Inventory} - \text{Book Inventory}$$
$$= \$70,000 - \$40,000$$
$$\text{Merchandise Overage} = \$30,000$$

Employee and Other Discounts. The *employee discount* is a price reduction granted to store employees. Such discounts are also granted to other groups, such as charitable organizations and various religious orders. The dollar amount of discounts for the period may be illustrated as follows:

Net Sales for May $200,000
Employee Discounts for the Month   2,000

Employee Discount %

$$= \frac{\text{Employee Discounts for the Month}}{\text{Net Sales}} = \frac{\$2,000}{200,000}$$

Employee Discount % = 1%

Markdowns. The retail buyer will mark down his merchandise in an effort to keep his prices at a level that will reflect consumer demand. A reduction in price from the original retail price is called a *markdown.* The markdown equation may be written as follows:

Original Retail Price	$5.00
− Markdown Price	4.00
Dollar Markdown	$1.00

The *markdown percent* is the difference between the net dollar markdown and the original retail price divided by the net sales. The markdown equation may also be expressed in terms of a percent (%). The formula is as follows:

$$\text{Markdown \%} = \frac{\text{Net Dollar Markdown}}{\text{Net Sales}}$$
$$\text{Markdown \%} = \frac{\$1.00}{\$5.00}$$
$$\text{Markdown \%} = 20\%$$

Figure 7–12 A retail buyer will plan markdowns because it is frequently necessary to reduce merchandise to sell it. Clearance sales will induce customers to come to the store seeking bargains.

Why Markdowns Are Necessary. The buyer will plan markdowns because it is frequently necessary to reduce the price of items to sell them (see Figure 7–12). This is particularly true of fashion goods that have become slow sellers. There are two major reasons for markdowns: (1) to sell merchandise to which customers have not satisfactorily responded, and (2) to induce customers to come to the department or store seeking bargains and thus stimulate sales for regularly priced goods.

Why Markdowns Are Necessary

1. To sell merchandise to which customers have not responded
2. To induce customers to seek bargains, thus stimulating sales

There are many reasons why goods must be sold at a price lower than the retail price. For example, buying errors may occur, such as purchasing too many goods in one size, price, fabric, or color; careless selling may result in return of merchandise; pricing errors may occur, as when goods are priced too high.

How Are the Following Formulas Used When Planning Reductions?

Merchandise shortage formula
Merchandise overage formula
Employee discount percent
Markdown equation
Markdown percent

Planned Markups

The fourth step in the merchandise plan is to plan markups. A retail buyer must sell merchandise at a price that will cover the cost of the goods and the expenses incurred as a result of acquiring the goods and that will yield a profit. The term *markup* may be defined as the difference between the cost price and the retail price of an item. The formula may be written as follows:

Dollar Markup = Retail Price − Cost Price
Dollar Markup = $20.00 − $10.00
Dollar Markup = $10.00

Most retail buyers think of markup in terms of percent. The markup equation as expressed in percent *(markup percent)* may be written as follows:

$$\text{Markup \% at Retail} = \frac{\text{Markup}}{\text{Retail Price}}$$

$$\text{Markup \% at Retail} = \frac{\$10.00}{\$20.00}$$

$$\text{Markup \% at Retail} = 50\%$$

The markup percent is usually calculated as a percent of retail price because all operating costs and profit or loss are determined as a percentage of net sales.

The buyer should seek the following information to plan a satisfactory markup:

1. Total amount of sales for the planned selling season
2. Planned expenses for the season
3. Planned reductions such as markdowns, shortages, and employee discounts
4. Profit goal planned for the season

Markup may apply to individual pieces of merchandise, to a group of items, or to the entire stock.

In addition, the buyer should give consideration to the initial and maintained markup. *Initial markup* (also known as mark-on or original markup) is the difference between the cost price and the retail price of goods. *Maintained markup* is the difference between the cost price and the final retail price. For example, if a pair of shoes costs $10 and is retailed for $20, the difference between the retail and the cost is $10; this is the initial markup. However, if the shoes do not sell at $20 but instead sell at $15, the difference between the cost price and the final selling price is $5; this is the maintained markup. The $20 price may be called the original retail selling price and the $15 price the sale price.

When planning the initial markup, the buyer must consider the following:

Considerations When Planning the Initial Markup

1. To cover costs and expenses and to make a profit (the initial markup formula)
2. Consumer demand: how high or how low to attract customers?
3. Types of store clientele: low-income group? average-income? well-to-do?
4. Kind of merchandise carried by the store: top quality? discount? prestige item?
5. Type of retail store: discount house? traditional department store? boutique?
6. Competition: what kind of a markup does my competition take?

How Are the Following Formulas Used When Planning Markup?

Markup equation
Markup percent
Initial markup
Maintained markup

Planned Gross Margin and Operating Profit

The fifth step in the merchandise plan is to plan gross margin and operating profit. Gross margin, as previously explained, is the difference between net sales and the cost of goods sold. Gross margin represents what is available for operating expenses and profit. It is what is left after costs have been deducted but before operating expenses have been considered. The formula is as follows: Net Sales − Cost of Goods Sold = Gross Margin. For example:

Net Sales	$5,549.00
− Cost of Goods Sold	1,320.00
Gross Margin	$4,229.00

Operating profit may be defined as that part of the gross margin which remains AFTER operating expenses have been deducted. As you recall, operating expenses are the expenses incurred during the operation of the department or store. For example:

Operating Expenses:

Buyer's Salary	$ 400
Sales Help Salaries	350
Asst. Buyer's Salary	200
Sales Promotions	100
Rent	200
Utilities	+ 100
Total Operating Expenses	$1,350

Once operating expenses have been planned for the month, the *net profit* may be computed by deducting the total operating expenses from the gross margin. For example:

Gross Margin	$4,320
− Total Operating Expenses	1,350
Net Profit	$2,970

The retail buyer is always faced with the task of determining how best to forecast a realistic gross margin figure that will yield, after expenses have been deducted, a satisfactory and reasonable net profit. Planning techniques should include not only the buyer's previous experience, but also all pertinent information that is available.

Planned Expenses

The sixth step in planning the merchandise budget is to plan expenses for the store as a whole and for each department. Expense planning is a most important activity for all buyers in all types of stores, since it provides a control system that assists in analyzing and forecasting the costs involved in merchandising and thus safeguards the store's profit objective. Expense planning consists of a series of dollar estimates of the various expenses a retail business will incur in a specified (budgeted) period. The primary objective of expense planning is to make careful and accurate forecasts of expenses so that proper controls can be established to meet them. Top store management and buying specialists have the responsibility for estimating future expenses and thus preparing the expense plan or budget. However, management will plan for all store units and branches, while buying specialists (local or central) will plan for departmental needs.

A major advantage of expense planning is that remedial action may be taken where and when required. For example, the department executive may need additional sales help as a result of increased sales activity due to an upswing in the economy. He will submit a sales help request to his merchandise manager, who will approve or disapprove the request, depending on the status of the expense budget and the relationship to anticipated sales.

Review the Methods Used to Plan Expenses

1. Plan figures for the store's overall expenses
2. Plan expenses for individual units or branches
3. Estimate expenses for each department

Planned Purchases

The last step in planning the merchandise budget is to plan the dollar amount of goods that can be brought into the department or store during a specified period or season. The buyer can determine planned purchases by adding together planned sales, planned reductions, and planned stock (stock planned for the end of the month or for the beginning of the next month) and subtracting from the total needs for this month the planned stock at the beginning of the month. The formula is as follows:

> Planned Sales
> + Planned Reductions
> + Planned End-of-Month Stock
> = Total Needs for the Month
> − Beginning-of-the Month Stock
> = Planned Purchases

The Merchandise Budget

A well-planned merchandise budget will assist store managers and buying specialists in meeting the profit objectives of the business. How will the following information be useful in meeting this objective?

I Planned sales

Departmental sales records
The buyer's diary
Store policies and procedures

The monthly sales plan
Top-down planning
Bottom-up planning

II Planned stocks

Various methods used to plan needed stocks
Computation of stock turnover
Average inventory

Increasing stock turn
Different rates of stock turn
Planning for branches and store units

III Planned reductions

Merchandise shortages and overages
Employee discounts and special groups
Markdowns

IV Planned markups

Markup equations
Markup percent

Initial markup
Maintained markup

V Planned gross margin and operating profit

Gross margin
Net profit

Total operating expenses

VI Planned expenses

Figures for the store's overall expense plan
Expenses for individual units or branches
Estimated expenses for each department

VII Planned purchases

Equation for determining purchases

For example:

Planned Stock, October 1	$100,000
Planned Sales, October 1–31	140,000
Planned Markdowns, October 1–31	70,000
Planned Stock, October 31	120,000

What are the planned purchases?

Then:

Planned Sales	$140,000
+ Planned Reductions	70,000
+ Planned End-of-Month Stock	120,000
= Total Needs for the Month	$330,000
− Beginning-of-the-Month Stock	100,000
= Planned Purchases	$230,000

Purchases are planned at retail prices and then converted to cost value by applying the planned markup percent.

For the buyer to plan and control purchases effectively, a measure called the open-to-buy is used. The open-to-buy is the amount of retail dollars that a buyer is permitted to spend for merchandise inventory within a certain time period based on formulated plans. The buyer's objective in using open-to-buy planning is to avoid having too much money tied up in inventory, which may require a large amount of capital and add to the rise of markdowns. Nor does the buyer wish to have too little merchandise available, which will lead to out-of-stock conditions and lost sales. The open-to-buy is based on a broad dollar scale, rather than on individual units or even small groups of units, which may help in preventing such problems. This topic will be discussed in detail in Chapter 9.

Chapter Summary

Planning is a very important function of the buying activity. However, the means used to achieve the planning objectives are based upon the business's objectives, policies, and procedures. Planning requires accurate record keeping. Specific policies will be set for the following types of records used in most retail establishments: (1) cash disbursements and receipts, (2) credit, (3) expenses, (4) sales, (5) purchases, (6) stocks and inventories, and (7) profit-and-loss statements. The student should review the discussion of each in Part 1 of this chapter.

There are several types of budgets used in a business; however, the plan used by the buyer to guide him in the merchandising activity is called the merchandise budget or six-month merchandise plan. This is a control measure that enables the buyer to follow a definite course of action as well as to evaluate current activities. Certain elements should be present for the merchandise plan to accomplish its objectives. The student should review the list under "The Merchandise Budget" in Part 2. A merchandise budget may be planned for a week, a month, or six months. Referring to the six-month merchandise plan illustrated, we see that seven important factors should be considered when planning: (1) sales, (2) stocks, (3) reductions, (4) markups, (5) gross margins and operating profits, (6) expenses, and (7) purchases.

Sales planning is the first step in the merchandise plan and is the key element in planning. Sales are planned first because it is easier to adjust stocks, markups, and expenses to sales potentials, rather than attempt to plan these factors and then to reach a sales goal consistent with them. The buying specialist should review several kinds of records used when planning sales. Two methods may be used in planning department or store sales: (1) the top-down plan, and (2) the bottom-up plan.

The second step in the merchandise plan is to maintain a balanced stock in relation to anticipated sales. Stock planning includes an understanding of the various methods used to plan needed stocks, the stock turn, the average inventory, increasing stock turn, and the different rates of stock turn. Four methods are used when planning needed stocks: (1) the basic stock method, (2) the percentage-variation (or deviation) method, (3) the week's supply method, and (4) the stock-sales ratio method.

Planned reductions is the third step in the merchandise plan. Retail reductions consist of three major factors: (1) merchandise shortages and overages, (2) employee and other types of discounts, and (3) markdowns. A reduction in price from the original retail price is called a markdown. The markdown percent is the difference between the original retail price and the markdown price. The buyer will plan markdowns because it is frequently necessary to reduce merchandise for various reasons.

Planned markups is the fourth step in the merchandise plan. Most retail buyers think of markup in terms of percent. The markup percent is usually calculated as a percent of the retail price because all operating costs and profits or loss are determined as a percentage of net sales. The buyer should review several kinds of records when planning the markup. Initial markup, also known as mark-on or original markup, is the difference between the cost price and the retail price of the goods. The maintained markup is the difference between the cost price and the final selling price. Consumer demand, initial markup formula, store clientele, etc., should also be considered when planning the initial markup.

The fifth step in the merchandise plan is to plan gross margin and operating profit. Gross margin is the difference between net sales and the cost of goods sold. Profit is that part of the gross margin that remains after operating expenses have been deducted. Once operating expenses have been planned for the month, net profit may be computed by deducting the total operating expenses from the gross margin.

The sixth step in the merchandise plan is to plan expenses. There are two types of operating expenses: (1) direct expenses, and (2) indirect expenses. Expense planning is a method of control that will help safeguard the store's profit objective. A major advantage of expense planning is that remedial action may be taken where and when needed.

The last step in planning the merchandise budget is to plan the dollar amount of goods that can be brought into the department or store during a specific period or season (planned purchase). The buyer can determine planned purchases by adding together planned sales, planned reductions, and planned stock and subtracting from the total needs for the month the planned stock at the beginning of the month. To control purchases effectively, a device called the open-to-buy (OTB) is used. The OTB is the amount of merchandise, either at cost price or at retail price, that the buyer is open to receive into inventory during a certain time period, based on the plans formulated. For the OTB to be effective, careful checks are made of all orders placed with vendors.

Trade Terminology

DIRECTIONS: Briefly explain or discuss each of the following trade terms:

1. Business objectives
2. Business policies
3. Procedures
4. Cash disbursements
5. Cash receipts
6. Direct expenses
7. Indirect expenses
8. Purchase journal or billing record
9. Profit-and-loss statement
10. Net sales
11. Cost of goods sold
12. Gross margin
13. Operating expenses
14. Net profit
15. Operations budget
16. Cash budget
17. Capital budget
18. Merchandise budget
19. Top-down planning
20. Bottom-up planning
21. Retail reduction
22. Merchandise shortage
23. Merchandise overage
24. Employee discount
25. Markdown
26. Markdown percent
27. Markup
28. Markup percent
29. Initial markup or mark-on
30. Maintained markup
31. Operating profit

Questions for Discussion and Review

1. It has been stated that the tempo of retailing has accelerated. Do you agree with this statement? Cite specific examples of forces that have affected the planning activity of merchandisers.

2. Explain the differences among objectives, policies, and procedures. How would each be applied to: a small independent pet-supply store; a women's specialty chain operation; a general store?

3. What are the functions of the following types of records used by most retail stores: cash disbursements and receipts, credit, expenses, profit-and-loss statement?

4. Summarize the seven steps you would follow when preparing the merchandise budget. Explain why "sales planning" is considered the first step in budget planning.

5. As the new buyer for an electrical-appliance department, how would you proceed to estimate your stock needs for the next six months?

6. Assume that you have recommended the use of the merchandise budget to a buyer in a small retail store who has not used this method previously. What words of caution would you give this buyer? What results might he or she expect from using the merchandise budget?

7. What is the difference between initial and maintained markup?

8. Write the formula for each of the following: finding the retail price; finding the stock turn at cost price; finding the average inventory.

9. Would it be wise for the buyer to adopt a policy of taking approximately the same markup percent on all kinds of merchandise? What would be the pros and cons of such a practice?

10. How does the open-to-buy operate as a control feature of the merchandise budget?

11. Why is it common to recalculate the planned purchases and the open-to-buy every week to ten days?

References

THE RETAIL STUDENT'S REFERENCE LIBRARY

Anderson, Rolph E., Hair, Joseph F., and Bush, Alan J. *Professional Sales Management.* New York: McGraw-Hill Book Co., 1988.

Annual Survey of Operating Expenses for Men's Wear Stores. Washington, D.C.: The National Association of Retail Clothiers and Furnishers, n.d.

Basic Stock Lists, Infants and Children's Wear. New York: NRMA, n.d.

Bedient, John. *Marketing Decision-Making Using Lotus 1-2-3.* Cincinnati: South Western Pub. Co., 1990.

Brightman, Richard W. and Dimsdale, Jeffrey M. *Using Computers in an Information Age.* Cincinnati: South Western Pub. Co., 1986.

DuBrin, Andrew J. *Essentials of Management.* Cincinnati: South Western Pub. Co., 1986.

Established Cash Discounts to Retailers. New York: NRMA, n.d.

Expenses in Retail Businesses. Dayton: National Cash Register Company, n.d.

Hetzel, William. *Computer Information Systems Development: Principles and Case Study.* Cincinnati: South Western Pub. Co., 1985.

Internal Control and Documentation of EDP. New York: NRMA, n.d.

Let the Expert Tell You About Electronic Data Processing. New York: NRMA, n.d.

198 Ways to Control Markdowns. New York: NRMA, n.d.

Operating Results of Furniture Stores. Chicago: National Retail Furniture Association, n.d.

Retail Control. New York: NRMA, n.d.

The Retail Inventory Method in Practical Operation. New York: NRMA, n.d.

REFERENCES

1. Jerry B. Poe, *An Introduction to the American Business Enterprise* (Homewood, Ill.: Richard D. Irwin, Inc., 1972), pp. 128–132.
2. I. Wingate and J. D. Weiner, *Retail Merchandising* (Cincinnati: South Western Publishing Co., 1963), pp. 448–449.
3. *The Buyers Manual* (New York: National Retail Merchants Association, 1965), p. 248.
4. Beatrice Judelle, *The Fashion Buyer's Job* (New York: National Retail Merchants Association, 1971), p. 74.

The Merchandise Planning Process: Unit (Assortment) Planning

8

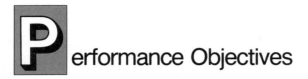

Performance Objectives

After reading this chapter, the student should be able to accomplish the following:

1. Relate eight factors a buyer should consider in assembling stock.

2. Become aware of five factors affecting unit (assortment) planning decisions.

3. Cite information necessary to plan staple stocks.

4. Plan a model stock that includes a staple assortment, a fashion assortment, and a seasonal assortment.

5. Calculate the formulas used in determining periodic fill-ins for staple goods; for fashion stocks; for home furnishings.

6. Plan a seasonal assortment for soft goods based on fashion apparel seasons.

7. Discuss four important factors to consider when determining the quantity of merchandise to purchase.

The Merchandise Planning Process: Unit (Assortment) Planning

Figure 8–1 Unit (assortment) planning can easily be seen in a retail store where many kinds and types of merchandise are found. (Courtesy of L. S. Ayre, Indianapolis, Ind.)

INTRODUCTION

As you read in the previous chapter, we are concerned with a most important managerial function—the planning function. We are concerned with how the retail buyer plans merchandise, whether for a fashion department, for departments carrying hard goods, or for departments carrying soft goods.

Merchandise planning is a process. The merchandise planning process begins with the formulation of objectives, the establishment of policies, and the implementation of procedures necessary to carry out department or store objectives. The planning process includes both dollar planning in terms of merchandise budgets and unit planning in terms of merchandise lists.

Since effective planning requires accurate record keeping, top management, in conjunction with store buyers, must plan and thereby set specific policies for various types of records used in most retail establishments.

A successful retail operation requires a merchandise assortment of the right type, in the right place, and at the right price. To accomplish this objective, activities such as profit and loss, sales, inventory, purchases, markups, markdowns, and expenses must be planned at least six months in advance by buyers and managers. This plan is called the merchandise budget. It is also referred to as the six-month merchandise plan.

In this chapter we are concerned with the amount of inventory the retail buyer should carry—how many separate items (assortment) and how many units of each item.

At this point we should ask the question, "What should a well planned assortment contain?" Factors such as quality, price range, brands, good taste, timing, product life cycle, and product mix affect assortment planning.

Since no one retail store can carry all products available in the marketplace, decisions about which merchandise assortment to carry are not left to chance but are based on a number of important factors such as the type of retail institution, past sales records, determination of consumer wants, internal and external sources of information, the type of goods offered, and elimination of merchandise items.

Unit (assortment) plans may be developed in two ways. The first method is through the use of a basic stock list; the second method is through the use of a model stock plan. All merchandise assortments can be planned by using either of these methods; however, the method used depends on the kind of merchandise under consideration. When determining unit (assortment) plans, consideration must also be given to the quantity of units to purchase.

PART 1—Factors Affecting Unit (Assortment) Planning

WHAT SHOULD A WELL-PLANNED ASSORTMENT CONTAIN?

No aspect of retailing is more subject to close and constant scrutiny than is the selection of merchandise assortments (Figure 8–1). The buyer must not only determine the selection of a particular merchandise classification or category, but also must decide whether or not to offer the classification at all. The buyer must determine the quality of the merchandise, the price range, and the number of brands as well as the number of lines within each classification. Other important factors are: (1) the quality of the merchandise offered for sale; (2) price range; (3) choice of national brands or private store brands; (4) good taste; (5) proper timing; (6) life cycle of the product; (7) variety of product lines; and (8) depth vs. breadth vs. common assortment.[1]

Factors the Buyer Should Consider in Assembling Stock.

1. The quality of the merchandise offered for sale
2. Price range that will meet consumer demand
3. National brands or private (store) brands
4. The essence of good taste
5. Proper timing
6. The life cycle of the product
7. Variety of product lines
8. Depth vs. breadth vs. balanced assortment

Quality of the Merchandise Offered for Sale

Merchandise quality may be defined as the best or finest material available, or superior to that of lesser quality or standards. Usually a high-quality merchandise line will boast a higher price range, while merchandise of low or inferior quality may be found in the lower price ranges. However, with the merchandising evolution brought about by discounters, hypermarkets, and catalog houses, good-quality merchandise may be offered at lower prices.

Merchandise quality will reflect the image of the store. Those stores that cater to clientele in the upper income bracket will offer merchandise representative of high standards and excellent quality. Such merchandise will "wear well," "last longer," or "never wear out," as we say. On the other hand, you may have walked through a store and felt its merchandise presentation to be "junky," "low-quality," or "not worth the money." Perhaps you felt this retail store was offering merchandise that was not consistent with your standards of quality.

Price Range

Price range and quality usually interact with each other during the selection process. There is no specific correlation between price and quality; however, a general correlation does exist. Better-quality merchandise is usually offered at a higher price, whereas lower-quality or inferior merchandise is usually found in lower price ranges. Since a store normally cannot offer merchandise of all price ranges, management must determine particular price lines and suitable quality. The buyer must follow the pricing policies of the store when selecting the merchandise assortment. A detailed discussion of the formulation of pricing policies will appear in Chapter 14.

National Brands or Private (Store) Brands

The established store policy may call for offerings of national brands as well as store or private brands. Private brands give the buyer an opportunity to be exclusive, to offer a variety of different goods, and to avoid direct competition. National or standard brands, however, are usually easily recognized by the store's customers and, therefore, readily accepted. Today most stores have adopted the policy of offering a selection of popular-brand items along with private-brand items that are consistent with store standards of quality and price.

Good Taste

As you read in Chapter 6, good taste is not easily defined. What is in good taste for one individual may be in poor taste for another. The buyer must determine what will be esthetically pleasing to all customers. Buyers are responsible for providing a selection of goods that will be appropriate in design, express the moods and feelings of the season, and appeal to the majority of people. Trade papers and journals in both the hard-goods line and the fashion apparel markets are usually able to predict trends in consumer preferences. However, many buyers will tell you of costly mistakes resulting from inaccurate prediction of consumer likes and dislikes.

Proper Timing

Timing is of vital importance, especially when introducing a new item. Some new items become staples, others convenience goods, while still others may become important fashions. The buyer, therefore, not only has the problem of deciding what to offer; the best time to introduce new items must also be decided. Does the store want to become a leader in the market or wait until the new item has been accepted. Each department must develop policy guides as to how often new items will be experimented with and at what risk, and how soon previously existing merchandise lines should be dropped from the stock.

Product Life Cycle

Maintaining a regular stock assortment is important to most types of goods. For example, staple convenience goods, shopping goods, and specialty items must be available for ample replenishment. Even fashion lines must be available to ensure continuity of individual colors, styles, sizes, and prices.

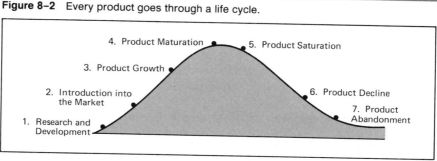

Figure 8–2 Every product goes through a life cycle.

However, factors such as changing consumer wants and needs, a higher standard of living, the growing youth market, and the mass media have all contributed to a constantly changing retail environment. These factors, as well as others, have affected the life cycle of individual products.

A product's life cycle may be divided into seven stages. They are: (1) product research and development; (2) introduction into the market; (3) product growth; (4) product maturation; (5) product saturation; (6) product decline; and (7) product abandonment[2] (see Figure 8–2).

The length of the life cycle will depend upon the product. As you recall from Chapter 6, "Importance and Application of Fashion Information," a fad may last only a few weeks, while a fashion may last two to three seasons or even several years. Staple goods may last for several decades. A product will usually yield the greatest amount of profit for the department or store late in the growth stage and will decline in profit yield late in the maturation stage of its life cycle.

Variety of Product Lines (Product Mix)

A *product line* may be defined as a broad category of products having reasonably similar characteristics and similar end uses. The variety of product lines or product mix offered may be limited, as in the specialty store, which offers only a few lines of merchandise, or may be numerous, as in the department store. The buyer must be informed whether the "sky is the limit" or if buying must be done within the confines of only a few related lines of merchandise. Such information will help determine where to place greatest emphasis as to type, variation, sizes, colors, and styles. Also, decisions about lines to be de-emphasized must be made.

Over the past several years there has been a rapid expansion of product lines, which has made the buyer's selection process more complex. Consumers are always willing to purchase products that are more innovative, more attractively designed, and offer more advantages. With the increased interest of consumers in fashion apparel and home furnishings and the desire to try something new each season, manufacturers and retailers have increased their sales. In the area of housewares, consumers have become more interested in kitchen appliances that are fashionably decorated and in electrical appliances that are not only useful but also tie in to the color and decorating theme, such as early American, Spanish, or contemporary, of the kitchen or dining area.

Depth vs. Breadth vs. Balanced Assortments

The last factor the buyer should consider is the breadth and depth of the assortment. Working with the money available in the inventory budget, the buyer must make a decision about the breadth of the assortment with respect to its depth, and vice versa. The balanced assortment must also be considered.

Assortment depth may be defined as a characteristic of an inventory assortment offering limited versions of proved popular styles. This kind of assortment is spoken of as a "narrow and deep assortment." Mass merchandisers usually use this method of stock inventory, since it has been proved the most efficient from a cost point of view. Its advantages are: (1) it has a faster turnover; (2) it is easier to stock; (3) it uses less room and display area; (4) it is easier to reorder, check and receive; (5) counting is simplified; and (6) markdowns are easier to avoid. A major disadvantage, however, is that consumers are not offered a wide selection of products and may have to shop in competing stores to find what they want.

Assortment breadth may be defined as a characteristic of an inventory assortment offering a large number of different categories or classifications, but not a large stock of any one style. This is a "broad and shallow assortment." Stores and departments catering to middle- and upper-income consumers usually use this kind of inventory assortment. The advantages of this type of assortment are: (1) presentation of a wide variety of goods; (2) a high degree of stopping and pulling power; and (3) slant to those customers of discriminating taste. The major disadvantage is that, due to shallowness of the assortment, alert and frequent reordering is needed to keep everything in stock. Consequently, this is a costly method of inventory.

The *balanced assortment* may be defined as an inventory assortment using both assortment breadth and depth to develop an assortment that is balanced. For example, broad assortments are used early in the season, when new styles are still being tested for consumer acceptance; however, narrow and deep assortments are used later in the season, when demand is clearly defined. The balanced type of assortment may be used by mass merchandisers as well as by stores boasting a high-fashion image. In fact, this may be considered a normal compromise. Breadth and depth comprise a retailer's *product mix,* which may be defined as all the products and services offered for sale.

FACTORS AFFECTING UNIT (ASSORTMENT) PLANNING DECISIONS

As previously discussed, in unit (assortment) planning, the merchandise manager and the buyer together must determine where to place the greatest emphasis. Just as no one retail store can carry all products available in the market, so no one store can offer all available merchandise categories. Therefore, decisions about which merchandise assortments to carry are not left to chance but are based on a number of important factors: (1) the type of retail institution, (2) past sales records, (3) a determination of consumer wants, (4) the types of goods offered for sale and (5) the elimination of merchandise lines.[3]

The Type of Retail Institution

Needless to say, a discount house usually will not offer high-priced, one-of-a-kind types of merchandise, a variety chain will not stock Oriental rugs, and a department store usually will not carry landscaping and gardening supplies. Customers usually expect to find merchandise consistent with a store's image, merchandise that meets their individual needs and interests and reflects the store's reputation in the business community. Since no single store can be all things to all people, the buyer must work within certain limitations set up by top store management. Such limitations as (1) the availability of capital resources, (2) the particular trading area served by the store, (3) the nature of the goods carried, and (4) the amount and kind of competition represented in the trading area may affect the buyer in attempting to plan the merchandise assortment.

Capital Resources Available. A retail store must have sound financing, since it often takes time to gain consumer acceptance for new lines of merchandise. Ample capital resources permit the heavy promotion campaigns necessary to hasten product recognition and, eventually, acceptance. Sound financing will absorb the costs of increased inventories and markdowns that may occur during the introduction period. Retailers with limited capital may adopt a merchandise plan that leads to fast turnover of stocks, offers limited service, and offers a narrow merchandise assortment, such as the kind usually found in a discount house.

Particular Trading Area. No store can cater to all people in all areas; differences in consumer tastes, occupations, incomes, and life-styles make this impossible. Wise management will realize that the general character of a particular trading area may be self-limiting. For example, the trading area may be either very rich or very poor; consequently, the merchandise assortment offered may be either lower-priced staple goods or high-priced fashion goods. Most stores, however, attempt to cater to that considerable portion of middle-class consumers who are price-conscious yet who are willing to make discretionary expenditures. Many stores located in urban environments cater not only to middle-class consumers but also to those of lesser economic means, perhaps even to those who are dependent upon public assistance. Urban stores often expand into suburban shopping centers in attempts to draw more affluent, fashion-conscious shoppers.

Nature of the Goods Carried. A merchandise plan that calls for a fashion assortment is certainly more important to a women's specialty store than it is to a variety store. A wide selection of staple merchandise is more important to a department store than it is to a discount house. The nature of the merchandise assortment offered, whether it be fashion goods or staple goods, will clearly depend upon the character of the retail institution and the type of consumer it caters to.

Competition Represented in Trading Area. Every type of retail store has some kind of competition. Not only is there competition among similar stores, but also among different types of stores. For example, department stores soon realized that they had to offer special promotion sales to offset the sales of discount houses. As mentioned in Chapter 1, a great deal of merchandise scrambling has occurred among department stores, discount houses, variety stores, and specialty shops. If a store is going to continue to attract customers and build its trade, its merchandise plan must include the successful offerings provided by its competition.

Explain How the Following Limitations Will Affect the Buyer's Merchandise Plan.

1. Capital resources available
2. Particular trading area
3. Nature of the goods carried
4. Competition represented in the trading area

Past Sales Records

The second factor the buyer must consider when planning the merchandise assortment are records of past sales. As you have already learned sales records provide valuable information about sales made and lost, about returned goods, and about customer complaints. There are numerous records available that can supply the sales information, such as unit control records, special promotion records, charge accounts, and files from the adjustment office. Personal observations on the selling floor, as well as conversations with salespeople, will also prove helpful.

Because sales of different product lines fluctuate from year to year and from season to season, the wise buyer will examine records of the previous year or, perhaps, of the past two or three years and use the information as a basis for planning sales in any given season. The buyer's sales records should contain notes that refer to weather conditions, economic trends, labor strikes, supply conditions, market opportunities, and whatever else affected sales activity in a particular period.

Determination of Consumer Wants

A third factor a buyer must consider when planning the merchandise assortment is the consumer. With the growth of the middle-income group, we have developed into a more affluent society. Thus, there has been a demand for a greater assortment of goods, which has led to quicker product replacement and an increase in impulse buying. Today, the consumer can afford new and attractive variations of a particular item or product. The modern shopper does not wait until a set of dinnerware is cracked and chipped before purchasing a new set, but will purchase a new set of dinnerware to improve the appearance of the dinner table as well as taking advantage of new designs and patterns. As a result of having more money to spend and an increase in consumer education, the modern shopper is more critical in merchandise selection. Shoppers read labels carefully, check the warrranty or guarantee, and compare before buying.

The buyer is the purchasing agent for store customers. The goods purchased for resale will reflect the buyer's judgment and ability to forecast what customers will like. The student may wish to review "Customer-Recognition Techniques" as discussed in Chapter 6, "Importance and Application of Fashion Information."

The Type of Goods Offered

A fourth factor the buyer must consider when planning the merchandise assortment is the type of goods offered for sale to the retail consumer. As stated previously, the type of goods offered will depend upon the merchandise policies of the store.

Merchandise can be categorized as fashion goods or seasonal goods. Merchandise can also be classified according to the amount of consumer shopping effort, such as convenience goods, shopping goods, and specialty goods. The way merchandise is classified will be introduced in Part 1 of this chapter; however, the way each classification is used in unit (assortment) planning will be discussed in Part 2.

How Merchandise May Be Classified.

1. Fashion goods
2. Seasonal goods
3. Convenience goods

4. Shopping goods
5. Specialty goods

Figure 8–4 Seasonal goods are in demand only at certain times of the year, for example, Christmas decorations. (Courtesy of The Gift Gallery, Havertown, Pa.)

Fashion Goods. Fashion goods may be defined as new merchandise that appeals to consumers for a short period of time and has a relatively short life cycle (Figure 8–3).

We said earlier that "fashion is everywhere," and this is undoubtedly true. However, the degree of fashion influence will depend upon the merchandise and the target market to be served. Fashion may be seen in kitchen appliances, furniture, stereo equipment, and food items; however, buyers who purchase these lines of goods will not be influenced by seasonal changes as much as the buyer of soft goods. As you will read later in this chapter, fashion apparel and accessories will change with each new season, that is, every three to four months, while the buyer of hard goods will have two market seasons, that is, one every six months.

Seasonal Goods. Seasonal goods may be defined as merchandise that is in demand only at certain times of the year or for particular seasons of the year (Figure 8–4). Nearly all departments in all types of retail stores are affected by the Christmas season, so buyers of soft goods, hard goods, and food items must be aware of merchandise that will appeal to Christmas shoppers. Buy-

Figure 8-5 Goods that are always in stock, or *never-out* goods, are demanded by consumers year in and year out. (Courtesy of Duckwall Stores, Inc., Abilene, Kan.)

ers will plan assortments for seasons such as fall, back to school, spring, summer, transitional, and resort. Assortments may be planned for special promotional events such as Mother's Day, Father's Day, Columbus Day, Washington's Birthday, Valentine's Day, and so forth.

A firm's seasons will depend upon the merchandise policies of the store. For example, most department stores will have some type of "founder's day sale" or "anniversary sale." A discount operation may have a "special bargain days sale" or "big values sale." The small shop owner may have a "Mother's Day specials sale" or a "back-to-school event," and a variety store may feature "Halloween specials." Regardless of the season, however, the buyer must plan the assortment carefully to include special events and seasonal merchandise lines that will enable him or her to have a full share of the market.

Convenience Goods. Convenience goods can be defined as those goods consumers expect to have readily available at a convenient location. These goods are usually inexpensive and may include such products as candy, notions, small housewares, drug items, hardware items, and beauty and medical aids. Convenience goods can be further classified into staple, impulse, and emergency goods.

Staple goods may be defined as goods that should always be in stock since they are demanded year in and year out (Figure 8–5). Never-out goods is a term used synonymously by the buyer. You will find staple goods in many types of retail stores. Have you ever noticed the kind of merchandise found alongside the checkout counter of a food market or a variety store? There you will find chewing gum, assorted types of candy, razor blades, film, deodorant, and magazines (Figure 8–6).

Impulse goods may be defined as goods purchased by consumers on impulse, that is, with little logical thought. Impulse goods may include snack foods, costume jewelry, cigarettes, and whatever else appeals to the impulsive mood of the consumer.

Emergency goods may be defined as goods purchased by consumers when a severe need arises. For example, a sudden downpour may cause you to purchase an umbrella from a street vendor, or a home accident may cause you to purchase gauze or adhesive tape from the local pharmacy.

Shopping Goods. Shopping goods may be defined as those products for which a consumer will accept no substitute and about which the consumer

Figure 8–6   Have you ever noticed the kind of merchandise found alongside the checkout counter of a self-service store? (Courtesy of Duckwall Stores, Inc., Abilene, Kan.)

does not have a thorough knowledge. This includes merchandise for which there is no replacement or no alternative in the mind of the customer. Since consumers usually do not have a thorough knowledge of the item, they will go from store to store and compare the different prices, colors, product features, styles, guarantees, and warranties, as well as other characteristics. Usually, the consumer will decide on a brand of merchandise to purchase; thus, the retail buyer will make an effort to provide the customer with specific information and advice on the product sought, as well as offering deals, customer service, prompt delivery, and credit terms. Examples of shopping goods are television sets, stereo equipment, radios, cameras, automobiles, small appliances, gift items, and furs (Figure 8–7).

Figure 8–7　When shopping for gift items, the customer will usually go from store to store to compare prices, colors, product features, and the selection offered for sale.

Figure 8-8 A buyer of specialty goods will plan to have as wide an assortment as possible, realizing that customers will be satisfied once they locate the specific item.

Specialty Goods. Specialty goods may be defined as those products of which the consumer will usually accept only a well-known brand and of which the consumer has full knowledge. For example, a buyer of fine china is providing specialty merchandise. The consumer may wish to increase a set of china-ware and will return to the store for the particular pattern or design. Buyers of specialty goods will plan to have as wide an assortment as possible, since consumers will surely be satisfied once they locate the specific item (Figure 8-8). Examples of specialty goods are brand-name items, silverware, furniture, pianos, watches, kitchen appliances, household appliances, and cosmetics.

Eliminating Merchandise Items

The final factor the buyer must consider when planning the assortment is the elimination or dropping of certain items from the merchandise plan. As more items are added to the assortment, a limit to what can be carried by the store or department, considering the financial investment involved and the amount of space required to store the goods, becomes evident. Therefore, the buying specialist must include in the assortment plan the elimination of certain items. The buyer must also consider whether or not the items to be dropped are fashion goods, since, due to their short selling life, such goods must be eliminated before they become out of style. If the goods to be dropped are staple types of merchandise, they must be eliminated before they become obsolete or outdated.

Mistakes in assortment planning are made by many retailers, but are more common in the small business, since the entrepreneur does not have the facilities (electronic data processing), the team of management experts or the market specialists (for example, the resident buying office) to assist in assortment planning. However, retailers large and small have a tendency to stock too many similar brands or types of merchandise. Often one item is simply a substitute for another; therefore, it is not necessary to stock both. How, then, does the buying specialist or manager determine which items should be eliminated from stock?

1. The buyer will give close attention to stock turnover and the rate of sales for each item found in the assortment. Large retailers are provided with sales and exception reports on a daily basis, for branch stores as well as for each store in the unit. Sales reports will inform the buying specialist what items, price lines, styles, colors, or sizes are selling in a particular merchandise classification as well as subclass.

2. The buyer may discover that a substitute has been developed that offers better merchandising opportunities. This often occurs in the area of hard goods or staple goods, where innovations or improvements have taken place in the design, material, construction, or usefulness of the products. Many consumers have the financial ability to throw away the old and try the new. Recognizing this fact, the buying specialist must be aware of new products, changes in consumer demand, and the availability of substitutes.

3. Items may be eliminated from the line if changes in merchandising efforts have failed to improve the sale of goods. For example, a buyer may learn from daily sales reports that a style of cashmere sweaters is not selling. She will visit branch stores, talk to department managers, and perhaps decide that the merchandise should be displayed differently and moved to better selling locations. However, the buyer may be informed that the sweaters are too expensive for the clientele patronizing the department. As a result, several markdowns may have to be taken to sell the merchandise before the season ends.

4. The buyer will eliminate items from the assortment that contribute little or nothing to the sales of other products. This is, the items do not "tie in" or relate to those items already available. A certain style of costume jewelry may be obsolete in design, of inferior quality, out of place, or too expensive for the rest of the line. Thus, it will be eliminated from the assortment plan.

Explain Why the Buying Specialist Should Consider the Following Factors When Planning the Merchandise Assortment.

1. Type of retail store
2. Past sales records
3. Determination of consumer wants
4. Study of internal and external sources
5. Types of goods offered for sale
6. Elimination of merchandise items

PART 2—How Unit (Assortment) Plans are Developed

Unit (assortment) plans are developed in one of two ways. The first method is through the use of a basic stock list; the second method is through the use of a model stock plan. All merchandise assortments can be planned by using either of these methods; however, the method used depends on the kind of merchandise under consideration.

Assortment Plans May Be Developed by Two Methods.

Method 1. Through the use of a basic stock list
Method 2. Through the use of a model stock plan

PLANNING A BASIC STOCK LIST

In a retail store, basic stock lists are composed of staple types of merchandise. For example, in a variety store, staple goods may include toothpaste, deodorants, socks, underwear, detergents, light bulbs, and sewing thread.

Figure 8-9 An example of a basic stock list used by a buyer in a notions department. *Source:* Adapted from "Basic Stock List for the Notions Department." Copyright, National Retail Merchants Association.

Item No.	Item	Brand	Manufacturer	Description Type	Color	Size	Retail Price	Min. Stock	Quarters 1st	2nd	3rd	4th
1	Cotton thread	Cordo	Cordo	Mercer	All	Fine	59	100	25	50	20	5
2	Silk thread	Cordo	Cordo	Fine	All	Fine	69	100	25	25	25	25
3	Nylon thread	Cordo	Cordo	Fine	All	Fine	49	100	25	25	25	25
4	Linen thread	Cordo	Cordo	Medium	Red, Wh	Med.	59	200	50	50	50	50
5	Elastic thread	Cordo	Cordo	Medium	White	Med.	59	200	75	25	50	50
6	Darning thread	Elso	Elso	Fine	All	Fine	29	300	100	100	50	50
7	Carpet thread	Gruner	Gruner	Thick	Black	Thick	89	100	25	50	20	5
8	Buttonhole thread	Finely	Finely	Thick	All	Thick	49	200	50	50	50	50
9												
10												

MC 7 Sheet No.: STAPLE LIST Date April 1

Class: Sewing Notions-Sewing Thread   Dept. 428-Notions

The list will specify in detail the items to be carried in stock. Figure 8–9 illustrates a basic stock list.

When planning staple merchandise assortments, buying specialists should consider (1) homogeneous and heterogeneous staples and (2) seasonal and nonseasonal staples.

When Planning Staple Merchandise Assortment, the Buyer Should Consider:

1. Homogeneous and heterogeneous staples
2. Seasonal and nonseasonal staples

Homogeneous and Heterogeneous Staples

Homogeneous staples may be defined as staple goods that are all of the same size, color, fabric, and style ("homogeneous" means "the same or similar"). For example, light bulbs are manufactured by Westinghouse and General Electric. The 100-watt bulbs produced by each company are alike in that they are the same size, provide the same amount of light, and fit into standard lightbulb sockets. Another example is the glass used in picture frames. The glass looks the same and performs the same function, yet it is produced by different manufacturers, for example, Pittsburgh Plate Glass and Corning Glass.

Heterogeneous staples may be defined as staple goods that are alike but not identical ("heterogeneous" means "containing dissimilar elements"). For example, shoelaces of the same length and width will come in assorted colors, patterns, and texture, though they all perform the same function. Hairpins or bobby pins of the same size come in different colors, to be worn by blondes, brunettes, or redheads. The buyer must plan the staple stock according to the similarities that exist among the staple goods available, as well as the differences.

Seasonal and Nonseasonal Staples

A second factor the buyer should consider is seasonal and nonseasonal staples. Items offered in the staple category should be available at all times of the year or at least during recurring seasons of demand. For example, some staples may be in demand regularly for years and not be affected by seasonal variations. This is true for hardware, foodstuffs, and toiletries. On the other hand, many staples tend to be seasonal, since sales will vary throughout the year or during specific times of the year in a manner that is predictable. For example, Easter egg decorations may be staples only during the Easter season, Christmas tree trimmings during the Christmas season, Halloween costumes during the fall season, and ski poles during the winter season.

PERIODIC FILL-INS OF STAPLE STOCKS

To ensure a well-balanced assortment of merchandise, it is essential that staples be reordered periodically. However, the buyer must have certain information available before reorder formulas can be applied. The necessary information is summarized below. This topic will be discussed in detail in Chapter 9.

1. The normal sales rate expected during the delivery and reorder periods
2. The delivery period
3. The reorder period
4. The reserve
5. Stock on hand
6. Merchandise on order

When stock is checked between the normal reorder dates, the length of the review inventory period should also be known. The unit of measurement used in calculating stocks, orders, and sales is usually expressed as the number of pieces. Or it may be expressed in terms of cases or dozens where the stock value is large.

The following formulas best illustrate how this information is used when determining the periodic fill-in of staple stocks.

The first formula may be used to determine the maximum or total amount of staple goods to be on order and on hand:

Maximum = (Reorder Period + Delivery Period) Rate of Sales + Reserves

$$M = (RP + DP) \times S + R$$

or: Maximum = (Lead Time) Rate of Sales + Reserve, where Lead Time = RP + DP.

$$M = (RP + DP) S + R, \text{ or } M = (LT) S + R$$

For example, you want to determine the total number of goods on order and on hand, or the *maximum*. You know that the item is selling at 100 items per week (S), with 58 units left in reserve (R). To ensure that you will have an ample supply of stock to cover the reorder period of four weeks and the delivery period of two weeks, you must have enough goods to carry you through the six-week (RP + DP) period; also, you must continue to carry an additional 58 units in reserve (R) for unexpected sales fluctuations. Thus:

$$
\begin{aligned}
M &= (RP + DP) S + R \\
&= (4 + 2)100 + 58 \\
&= 6 \times 100 + 58 \\
&= 600 + 58 \\
&= 658
\end{aligned}
$$

The total number of staple goods on order and on hand, or the maximum amount, is 658 items.

The second formula is used to determine the unit open-to-buy (OTB), or the quantity of stock that needs to be reordered when minimum stock is opened:

Unit open-to-buy = Maximum − On-hand orders − Outstanding orders

$$OTB = M - OH - O$$

Inserting the parenthesis, the equation becomes:

Unit open-to-buy = Maximum − (On-hand + Outstanding orders)

$$OTB = M - (OH + O)$$

Let us say you know that you have 200 units on hand (OH) and 58 units still on order (O) from your supplier. Your total number of goods on hand, or the maximum (M), is 658 units.

Thus:

$$OTB = M - (OH + O)$$
$$= 658 - (200 + 58)$$
$$= 400$$

The quantity of stock that needs to be reordered, or the unit open-to-buy, is 400 units.

Another formula may be used when you wish to determine the reserve period or safety time period required to maintain a maximum reserve level. Management considers this method a 99 to 100 percent protection against reserve depletion:

$$\text{Reserve} = 2.3 \times \sqrt{(\text{Lead Time}) \text{ Sales}}$$

Recalling that Lead Time = Reorder Period + Delivery Period, the equation may be stated:

$$R = 2.3 \times \sqrt{(RP + DP)S}$$

For example, you want to determine the number of items you must have in reserve to cover unexpected sales. The Poisson distribution table of probability reserves,[5] which is based on estimates of 99 percent, states that reserves should be 2.3 times the square root of the reorder period (RP), which in your case, we will say, is four weeks, added to the delivery period (DP), which is two weeks, multiplied by the rate of sales (S), which you know to be 100 units per week.

Thus, 99 to 100 percent protection:

$$R = 2.3 \times \sqrt{(LT) S}$$
$$= 2.3 \times \sqrt{(6) 100}$$
$$= 2.3 \times \sqrt{600}$$
$$= 2.3 \times 25$$
$$= 57.5 \text{ (rounded to 58)}$$

The number of items you must have in reserve, based on the 99 to 100 percent protection to cover unexpected sales, is 58 units.

A fourth formula may be used when management feels that 95 percent protection is adequate to maintain a maximum reserve level:

$$\text{Reserve} = 1.6 \times \sqrt{\text{(Lead Time) Sales}}$$

$$\text{or: } R = 1.6 \times \sqrt{\text{(RP + DP)S}}$$

Ninety-five precent protection means that one lost sale in 20 reorder periods will occur.

Thus, 95 percent protection:

$$
\begin{aligned}
R &= 1.6 \times \sqrt{\text{(LT) S}} \\
&= 1.6 \times \sqrt{(6)\ 100} \\
&= 1.6 \times \sqrt{600} \\
&= 1.6 \times 25 \\
&= 40
\end{aligned}
$$

The number of items you must have in reserve, based on the 95 percent protection to cover unexpected sales, is 40 units.

How Do the Following Formulas Assist the Buying Specialist When Determining the Periodic Fill-In of Staple Stocks?

$$M = \text{(RP + DP) S} + R$$
$$OTB = M - \text{(OH + O)}$$
$$R = 2.3 \times \sqrt{\text{(LT) S}}$$
$$R = 1.6 \times \sqrt{\text{(LT) S}}$$

PLANNING
THE MODEL STOCK

The model stock plan is the second method a buyer may use to develop the assortment plan. A *model stock* may be defined as the desired assortment of stock broken down according to predictable factors, such as classification, price, material, color, and size, based on consumer demand. The model stock plan is used by buyers of fashion goods to plan fashion assortments since, unlike staple goods, fashion items are identified by general characteristics rather than by specific details. In planning a model stock, accurate sales and stock information is necessary to achieve maximum sales from the merchandise assortment. The buyer of fashion apparel and of home furnishings must be guided by current trends as well as by previous sales patterns. As you will learn in the next chapter, the buying specialist will develop a specific buying plan that gives consideration of what to buy, when to purchase, and when to have merchandise delivered for the model stock plan to be fulfilled.

What the Model Stock Includes

An assortment of staple goods
  Goods always in stock
  Goods in demand year in and year out

An assortment of fashion goods
  Goods that appeal for a short period of time
  Goods that have a short life cycle

An assortment of seasonal goods
  Goods in demand only at certain times of the year
  Goods that have a life cycle as long as the season

The model stock plan is used to plan the ideal assortment; thus, it will include an assortment of staple goods, fashion goods, and seasonal goods.

An Assortment of Staple Goods

The amount and kinds of staple items found in the model stock plan will differ. For example, the buyer of boutique fashions may develop a different basic stock list from that developed by the buyer of mass fashions. The bou-

Figure 8–10 Model stock plan, women's blouse department.

Department Stock in Dollars		
Total, April 1		$30,000
Major Breakdown		
Special promotional stock		3,500
Stock left over		1,500
Model stock		25,000
Total		$30,000
Distribution of Model Stock Based on Classification		
Short-sleeved	35%	$10,000
Printed silks	25%	6,250
Evening prints	20%	3,750
Suit blouses	15%	1,250
Sporty knits	5%	1,250
Total	100%	$22,500

tique buyer may consider tie-dyed scarves, jeweled sweaters, and plastic jewelry to be part of the basic stock assortment, whereas the buyer of mass fashions may consider such items too innovative, fad-oriented, or expensive; the basic mass-fashion assortment may include plain silk scarves, basic sweaters, and proved styles of costume jewelry. The staple fashion assortment is used for the normal stocking of fashion items that the customer expects to find available (convenience items). (See Figure 8–10.)

An Assortment of Fashion Goods

The model stock plan will include a fashion assortment. Fashion stock in both apparel and home furnishings is the most difficult of all classes of merchandise to plan for because of the many choices of styles, colors, materials, vendors, and manufacturers, and the many new items available. Since fashion goods have a short life cycle, the risks in fashion buying are high. Five characteristics of fashion merchandise will assist the buyer in determining the fashion assortment. They are (1) classification, (2) price, (3) size, (4) material, and (5) color.

Planning the Fashion Assortment

Characteristics of the Fashion Assortment That Are Predictable:

1. Classification
2. Price
3. Size
4. Material
5. Color

Classification. In planning by classification, the buyer will break each general line of merchandise down into subdivisions. For example, furs can be broken down into fun furs, expensive furs, and fur accessories.

The consumer demand for merchandise in each classification is usually predictable by the buyer, who therefore can determine fairly accurately the quantity of merchandise to buy. Often further subdivisions may be used if the subdivision becomes too cumbersome (for example, fur stoles may be further subdivided into expensive, medium-priced, and low-priced within the fur classification).

Price. Since most retail stores attempt to cater to consumers representing many income levels, a variety of price lines is found within each classification of fashion goods. The buyer will plan the fashion assortment to include at least three price lines tailored to the income brackets of the customers who patronize the store. Such planning will enable the customer to have a choice in the price of the item bought. Once the price norm in each classification is determined, the buyer can predict with considerable accuracy future demands in lower and higher price ranges as well as a specific price range.

Size. Size is an important factor with most fashion merchandise. This is true not only of fashion apparel but also of many home furnishings. The buyer must determine the customer demand for each size and buy accordingly. The size distribution of the items sold during the past season is usually an indication of future demands.

Material. A knowledge of textiles and the kinds of materials available will help the buyer determine customer wants. For example, wide customer acceptance of cotton denim during the past decade caused retail store buyers to stock fashion apparel, such as jeans, hats, swimsuits, and handbags, made of denim. The automobile industry followed the trend by using the "denim look" in automobile seat covers; the furniture industry was influenced by the popularity of the fabric and used denim as an upholstery fabric. Knowledge of customer acceptance of materials will assist the buyer in stocking a well-balanced fashion assortment with proper emphasis given to particular materials in demand.

Color. Color plays an important role in the selection of fashion goods. Since each new season popularizes specific color combinations, the buyer can predict the color or color combinations most consumers will seek. Basic colors usually account for the majority of sales; however, fashion colors or seasonal colors have promotional value and are used to attract fashion-conscious customers into the department. The buyer must be careful not to overstock that which is new and popular while neglecting the standard and more conventional colors.

An Assortment of Seasonal Goods

Finally, the model stock plan will contain an assortment of seasonal goods. Many staple stocks and fashion stocks will also reveal a pattern of seasonal variations, whereby goods are in demand only at certain times of the year and their life cycle is only as long as the season. Good planning will provide for seasonal coverage, whether on a six-month basis or broken down into monthly or weekly subdivisions.

Major seasons usually include showings by the majority of manufacturers in the fashion apparel and accessory trades. Manufacturers who spe-

TABLE 8–1. Fashion apparel seasons.

Season	Type	Length of Time	Merchandise Line Affected
Fall season	Major	Late August to December	Sportswear, coats, dresses, suits, accessories
Holiday season	Minor	November to December	Eveningwear, dresses, special Christmas merchandise
Cruise and resort	Minor	January to March	Sportswear, swimwear, casual clothing
Spring season	Major	March to April, depending on occurrence of Easter Sunday	Coats, dresses, suits
Summer	Major	May to June	Sportswear, coats, suits, dresses, accessories
Transitional	Minor	July to August	Casual wear in lightweight fabric in dark colors
Back to school	Minor	Late August to October	Children's wear, casual clothing, and accessories

cialize in certain types or lines of products participate in minor season showings.

Staple products and home furnishings also have seasons. They are the fall season, from August until March, and the spring season, from April until July. Manufacturers' openings are generally held in January and July (refer to Table 8–1).

PLANNING FILL-INS FOR THE MODEL STOCK PLAN

Both staple and fashion stocks require accurate assortment planning and careful controls. However, the control measures used differ in two respects: first, fashion assortments must be reviewed more frequently, usually on a weekly basis, whereas most staple or basic stocks require review only every three to four weeks. Second, fashion reorders are generally based on the heterogeneous assortment such as a style, price line, or size within a classification, whereas in the staple stock assortment each different item may require a separate control measure.

Formulas may be used to determine periodic fill-ins of fashion stocks. The following formula may be used when a particular style becomes popular and needs to be reordered several times during the selling season. (As you recall, this formula was also used for reordering staple goods.) This topic will be discussed in detail in Chapter 9.

Maximum = (Reorder Period + Delivery Period) Rate of Sales + Reserve or:

$$M \quad = \quad (RP \quad + \quad DP) \quad \times \quad S \quad + \quad R$$

where (RP + DP) = Lead Time, the equation is either:

$$M = (RP + DP)S + R \text{ or: } M = (LT)S + R$$

Suppose that you want to determine the total number of women's blouses on order and on hand, or the maximum. You know that the blouses are selling at 100 pieces per week (S), with 58 units left in reserve (R). To ensure that you will have an ample supply of blouses to cover the reorder period of four weeks and the delivery period of two weeks, you must have enough goods to carry you through the six-week selling season (RP + DP); also, you must continue to carry an additional 58 pieces in reserve (R) for unexpected sales fluctuations.

Thus:

$$
\begin{aligned}
M &= (RP + DP)\,S + R \\
&= (2 + 4)\,100 + 58 \\
&= 6 \times 100 + 58 \\
&= 600 + 58 \\
&= 658
\end{aligned}
$$

The total number of women's blouses on order and on hand, or the maximum amount, is 658.

Along with various kinds of reports, a popular technique used by buyers to determine periodic fill-ins of fashion goods is the style-out. The *style-out technique* may be defined as a method used to detect trends in customer preferences. The technique works like this: the buyer of, for example, handbags and leather goods will select from stock some of the best-selling items—

for example, three popular styles of handbags in each classification, such as shoulder bags, clutch bags, and pouch bags. He or she will carefully examine each to determine a feature that is characteristic of all. For example, the common denominator may be the color, fabric, type of closing, shape, or whatever. Once the feature is noted, for example, the type of closing, the buyer will confer with the buyer of better handbags and the budget-store buyer to seek their opinion. As a result, each buyer may reorder handbags with this particular feature for the store's forthcoming pre-Christmas sales promotion.

PERIODIC FILL-INS AND HOME FURNISHINGS

In the home furnishings field there are many types of merchandise, for example, bedroom furniture, dinette sets, living-room furniture, bedding, and major appliances, to name a few, that are sold largely from samples. Since many of these products must often meet specific consumer requirements, such as fabric covering or addition of extra parts, they need not be reordered periodically. Instead, the finished product is shipped to the customer directly from the manufacturer's warehouse. However, if the merchandise is stocked in the store's warehouse, then a periodic control system must be maintained among the store, the particular selling department involved, the vendor, and the customer. Samples on the selling floor will usually carry tickets that report the current stock availability, particular fabrics and colors available, or whatever. The ticket will also note the length of time required to prepare the merchandise to meet customer specifications, as well as the delivery date.

How Will the Following Information Assist the Buyer When Planning Period Fill-Ins for Fashion Goods and Home Furnishings?

$M = (RP + DP) S + R$
Vendor selling reports
Buyer's style status report
Daily sales report
The unit open-to-buy
The style-out technique
The periodic fill-in of home furnishings

THE QUANTITY TO PURCHASE

The buyer who has decided *what* merchandise to purchase for resale then faces the question of *how much* merchandise should be purchased for particular time periods. The buyer may utilize the judgment of a *buying committee,* which acts in behalf of a single buyer and assists in decision-making policies regarding the procurement of specific merchandise categories. However, if the buyer has complete responsibility for the buying-selling activity, as do the department-store buyer or the small business owner-manager, decisions may rest on four important factors: (1) the period for which purchasing is done; (2) estimated sales for the period; (3) merchandise on hand and on order; and (4) the desired merchandise at the end of a particular period.

When Determining the Quantity of Goods to Purchase, the Buyer Should Consider These Important Factors:

1. Period for which purchasing is done
2. Estimated sales for the period
3. Merchandise on hand and on order
4. Desired merchandise at the end of a particular period

Period for Which Purchasing Is Done

The time period for which purchasing is done may differ with the type of goods sold, the type of store in which the goods are sold, and the nature of the period itself. For example, a fashion goods buyer may purchase winter coats for the winter season, which is approximately three months long; a buyer of contemporary furniture may make purchases based on a six-month selling plan; while a buyer in a gourmet food department may work on a buying period of one to seven days. There are six factors that may influence the period for which purchasing is done: (1) the open-to-buy; (2) hand-to-mouth buying; (3) speculative buying; (4) quantity discounts; (5) supply conditions; and (6) storage facilities.

The Open-to-Buy. The *open-to-buy* (OTB), as stated previously, is the amount of retail dollars that a buyer is permitted to spend for merchandise inventory within a certain time period based on formulated plans, for example, the six-month merchandise budget. The buyer's objective in using open-to-buy planning is to avoid having too much money tied up in inventory, which may require a large amount of capital and add to the rise of markdowns. Nor does the buyer wish to have too little merchandise available, which will lead to out-of-stock conditions and lost sales.

Hand-to-Mouth Buying. Hand-to-mouth buying may be defined as the practice of limiting orders to immediate needs and ordering goods for immediate delivery rather than well in advance. The practice of limiting orders to current needs rather than placing them on a basis of future sales usually occurs during periods of price fluctuations in the marketplace. For example, a buyer of men's expensive suits will delay buying as long as possible if there is evidence that the longer buying is delayed, the lower the wholesale price will be. Also, the practice of letting orders go until the last minute will increase the vendor's risk, because a vendor must carry a reserve that is subject to price fluctuations and may require warehouse expenses.

Hand-to-mouth buying also suggests the trend toward carrying minimal stocks, which may lead to a loss in sales. The buyer must be constantly alert to market conditions when using this buying method. There must always be an up-to-date inventory count to ensure an ample reserve, which will take care of possible sales variations as well as problems resulting from faulty deliveries. Needless to say, this buying practice would be curtailed during periods of rising prices, since the buyer who purchased early would get the best prices.

Speculative Buying. Speculative buying may be defined as the decision to purchase goods based on an expected rise or fall in the price level. The buyer who expects rising prices will place large orders in anticipation of reselling at the higher prices. The buyer who expects falling prices will adopt the policy of hand-to-mouth buying. Speculative buying may help the buyer obtain a larger gross margin; however, a buyer is not in business to speculate, but rather to purchase goods for the purpose of making a merchandising profit and not a speculative profit.

Quantity Discount. Quantity discount is a reduction in wholesale price based upon a specific quantity of merchandise purchased from the vendor or wholesaler. For example, the buyer may be informed that purchases in lots of 100 or more will get a 2 percent discount off the regular wholesale price. Quantity discounts are often used by vendors and manufacturers to encourage advance ordering. Usually, the buyer of staple merchandise is able to take advantage of quantity discounts, since such a buyer is able to stock the merchandise for longer periods of time with a minimum of concern for risk due to obsolescence. The fashion buyer will also take advantage of quantity discounts, especially if the department is included in a special store promotion. A fashion buyer will order promotional goods before they are needed, store them in a warehouse, and thus take advantage of a quantity discount offering. This topic will be covered in detail in Chapter 14.

Supply Conditions. If delivery periods are uncertain, the buyer will place orders early to ensure receiving merchandise on time. Vendors, trade journals, resident buyers, and newspapers serve as excellent sources of information on the conditions of supply in the marketplace. The time required to have merchandise delivered will, therefore, affect the period for which purchasing is done.

Storage Facilities. The retailing specialist must consider whether or not there are adequate storage facilities when considering the length of the purchasing period. If a warehouse is available or if there is adequate storage space within the store itself, the buyer may place the order in advance and have the merchandise delivered before the actual selling period. However, if warehousing is costly and in-store storage space is limited, the buyer may have to plan carefully the delivery period to avoid storage problems. Thus, lack of storage facilities may restrict the length of the period for which the retail buyer can purchase.

Explain How the Following Factors May Affect the Period for Which Purchasing Is Done:

1. The open-to-buy
2. Hand-to-mouth buying
3. Speculative buying
4. Quantity discounts
5. Supply conditions
6. Storage facilities

Estimated Sales for the Period

A second important factor the buyer should consider when determining the quantity of goods to purchase is the estimated sales for the particular selling period.

The estimate of sales for the forthcoming buying period is usually based on past sales with allowances for changes in business conditions as well as actions taken by competition. The impact of economic conditions, unemployment, and fashion trends may modify planned sales figures as well.

The buyer must remember that a careful estimate of sales may vary with the type of stock as well as from one seasonal period to another. For example, a buyer of fashion goods or perishable goods may require careful estimates, since excessive purchases will result in large markdowns or in spoilage. On the other hand, staple goods purchased in excess may result in larger than necessary inventories, with inventory capital tied up for a longer period of time. However, in periods of price fluctuations, particularly in periods of falling prices, overestimates of sales for staple goods may lead to significant losses in inventory.

When considering the estimated sales from one seasonal selling period to another, the buyer must consider the nature of the selling season. For example, Christmas has traditionally been the retailer's largest and most profitable selling season. Therefore, sales estimates are usually higher for that period than for the spring season, Mother's Day, or Independence Day.

Merchandise On Hand and On Order

A third important factor the buyer should consider when determining the quantity of goods to order is the amount of merchandise on hand and on order.

Information as to the merchandise on hand may be obtained in the following ways: (1) observations and counts and (2) up-to-date inventory records. Observations and counts are self-explanatory. A perpetual inventory system may be used in large retail stores whereby, through the use of a computerized system, the buyer is kept constantly informed as to the color, size, style, and price of each unit of merchandise remaining in stock, not only in the main store, but in each branch or in each store unit. As a result of the perpetual inventory system, the buyer is provided with an up-to-the-minute picture of stock conditions. This topic will be discussed in detail in Chapter 9.

Information regarding merchandise on order may be obtained from the buyer's own records. It is relatively simple to determine the unfilled orders, since the buyer's records generally include duplicate copies of every unfilled order placed with vendors or manufacturers. As you recall, this file will be found in the buyer's purchase journal.

Desired Merchandise at the End of a Particular Period

A final important factor the buyer should consider when determining the quantity to buy is the planned or desired stock at the end of the particular selling period. The following conditions may determine whether or not the buyer decides to build up a large end-of-period stock or reduces the end-of-period inventory:

1. Sales trend—have marketing surveys indicated an increase or decrease in demand for the product?
2. Popularity of the fashion—has the item become an accepted fashion that will remain in style several seasons, or has it become a fad, which will only remain one or two seasons?
3. Stage in the product life cycle—is the product in the growth stage? The maturation stage? The obsolescence stage?
4. Price fluctuations in the marketplace—has the wholesale price fluctuated? Has there been an increase in price? A decrease in price?
5. Availability of supplies and materials—are manufacturers able to procure materials and supplies to meet production schedules? Have there been shortages in materials? In supplies?
6. What types of goods remain in stock? If staple goods, can they be stored for several seasons? If fashion goods, will they go out of style or become obsolete if stored over a period of time? If seasonal goods, will they be popular next season?
7. Type of retail institution—if a discount house, can the buyer afford to have leftovers and costly markdowns? If a department store, can the merchandise be sent to branch stores? If a small retailer, can he afford to tie up his capital?
8. Supply conditions—can the vendor deliver the merchandise as scheduled?
9. Availability of discounts—will quantity discounts be available? If so, are they worth the risk?
10. A new item? If the merchandise that remains is new on the market, is this the result of consumer resistance? Poor store promotion? A poor product?

All of these factors must be taken into consideration when the buyer determines the desired or planned stock at the end of the particular period. Not only does the buyer need to plan merchandise for the beginning of a new selling period, but merchandise must be on hand at the end of a period so that it will be available for use at the beginning of the next period, and so on. For example, merchandise that remains at the end of the Christmas season will continue to be sold at the beginning of the winter season; however, it may be sold as "an inventory clearance" or "special after-Christmas sale" or "a January white sale."

Chapter Summary

The buying specialist must exercise careful planning techniques when selecting the merchandise assortment. The following should be considered when planning the assortment: quality, price range, brand (store or private), good taste, proper timing, product life cycle, product mix, and depth vs. breadth vs. balanced assortment. Decisions as to which merchandise assortments to carry are not left to chance, but are based on a number of important factors. The student should review each of the following: (1) the type of retail institution, (2) past sales records, (3) determination of consumer wants, (4) the types of goods offered for sale, and (5) the elimination of merchandise lines.

The buyer will work within limitations set forth by store management. The limitations to consider are: (1) the availability of capital resources, (2) the particular trading area served by the store, (3) the nature of the goods carried, and (4) the amount and kind of competition represented in the trading area.

Sales records may be used as a basis for planning sales in any given season. However, to be effective, they must contain a breakdown of specific information.

The type of goods offered in the merchandise assortment will depend upon the type of retail store. Merchandise can be categorized as fashion goods or seasonal goods. Merchandise can also be classified according to the amount of shopping effort such as convenience goods, shopping goods, and specialty goods. The student should review the definition of each.

The plan for the merchandise assortment may be developed in one of two ways. The first method is through the use of a basic stock list; the second method is through the use of a model stock plan.

Basic stock lists are composed of staple types of merchandise. When planning the staple merchandise assortment, the buyer should consider (1) homogeneous and heterogeneous staples, (2) season and nonseasonal staples, and (3) periodic fill-ins of staple stocks. When determining the periodic fill-in, certain information is necessary to calculate the formulas. The student should study carefully the formulas listed in the same section.

The model stock plan is the second method a buyer may use to develop the assortment plan. It is used to plan fashion assortments, since, unlike staple goods, fashion items are identified by general characteristics rather than by specific detail. The model stock will include an assortment of staple goods, an assortment of fashion goods, and an assortment of seasonal goods. The student should review the sections on fill-ins for fashion goods and home furnishings to determine how the buyer will plan.

To buy the proper quantity of merchandise, a good retail buyer must give close attention to details and must plan. The buyer must consider the period for which purchasing is done, estimate sales for the period, merchandise on hand and on order, and the desired merchandise at the end of a particular period.

Trade Terminology

DIRECTIONS: Briefly explain or discuss each of the following trade terms:

1. Merchandise quality
2. Product line
3. Assortment depth
4. Assortment breadth
5. Balanced assortment
6. Fashion goods
7. Staple goods
8. Seasonal goods
9. Convenience goods
10. Impulse goods
11. Emergency goods
12. Shopping goods
13. Specialty goods
14. Homogeneous staples
15. Heterogeneous staples
16. Model stock
17. Classification
18. Style-out technique
19. Buying committee
20. Hand-to-mouth buying
21. Speculative buying

Questions for Discussion and Review

1. What is the importance of good planning? What should a well-planned assortment contain?

2. Define the following: assortment depth, assortment breadth, balanced assortment. What points should the buyer consider when determining the breadth and depth of the assortment?

3. The merchandise plan a buyer adopts for a particular store or department may depend on five factors. What are they?

4. Why must a buyer consider eliminating goods when planning the assortment?

5. Define fashion goods, staple goods, seasonal goods, convenience goods, shopping goods, and specialty goods.

6. What is the difference, if any, between a basic stock list and a model stock plan?

7. Describe a homogeneous and a heterogeneous staple stock. Cite examples of each.

8. Why is fashion planning more difficult than staple planning? What are the predictable characteristics of a fashion assortment?

9. What are the fashion apparel seasons? Why are there more seasons in fashion apparel than in home furnishings? In staple goods? Explain.

10. How does the time period for which purchasing is done differ? Cite examples. What factors may influence the length of the selling period? Explain.

11. You are a buyer of women's fashion apparel. You have not decided whether you want to build a large end-of-period stock or slowly reduce your end-of-period inventory. What conditions should you consider when determining the amount of merchandise remaining at the end of the selling season?

References

THE RETAIL
STUDENT'S REFERENCE LIBRARY

Drew-Bear, R. *Mass Merchandising: Revolution and Evolution.* New York: Fairchild Pub., Inc., n.d.

Ferguson, Frank. *Efficient Drug Store Management.* New York: Fairchild Pub., Inc., n.d.

Frank, Bertrand. *Progressive Apparel Production.* New York: Fairchild Pub., Inc., n.d.

The Independent Store Policy Manual. New York: NRMA, n.d.

Keyes, Ruth and Cushman, Ronald A. *Essentials of Retailing.* New York: NRMA, 1985.

Kreiger, Murray. *Creative Markdown Practices for Profit.* New York: NRMA, 1985.

Leather Sales Tactics. New York: Leather Industries of America, n.d.

Lewis, R. Duffy. *Lewis Merchandise Control Kit.* New York: NRMA, 1985.

Marketing, Sales Promotion, Advertising Planbook. New York: NRMA, n.d.

Minsky, Betty Jane. *Gimmicks Make Money in Retailing.* New York: NRMA, 1985.

Paganetti, J. *The Best in Sales Ads.* New York: NRMA, n.d.

Profitable Merchandising of Men's Clothing. New York, NRMA, n.d.
A Retailer Visits the Market. New York: Fairchild Pub., Inc., n.d.
Swimwear Merchandising. Washington, D.C.: National Education Association, n.d.
Taylor, C. G. *Merchandise Assortment Planning.* New York: NRMA, n.d.
Techniques of Fashion Merchandising. Indianapolis: ITT Pub. Co., n.d.
Tepper, Bette K. and Godnick, Newton E. *Mathematics for Retail Buying.* New York: NRMA, 1985.

REFERENCES

1. E. Jerome McCarthy, *Basic Marketing: A Managerial Approach* (Homewood, Ill.: Richard D. Irwin, Inc., 1985), pp. 335–36.
2. Ibid.
3. *The Buyer's Manual* (New York: NRMA, 1970), pp. 240–41.
4. *The Buyer's Manual,* pp. 276–77.
5. Beatrice Judelle, *The Fashion Buyer's Job* (New York: NRMA, 1971), p. 80.

The Merchandise Control Process: Systems and Applications

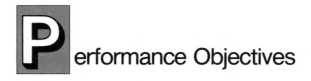

Performance Objectives

After reading this chapter the student should be able to accomplish the following:

1. Evaluate the elements contained in a control system; discuss the requirements of a good control system.

2. Explain two methods of merchandise control.

3. Illustrate the formula used to determine the periodic inventory system.

4. Demonstrate how the retail value of stock on hand may be reduced to a cost basis.

5. Define merchandise inventory, perpetual inventory system, and periodic inventory system.

6. Determine the figure for net sales under the physical inventory system.

7. Explain inventory systems for use in unit control other than the periodic system and the perpetual system.

8. Identify characteristics that differentiate retail inventories from inventories carried by most other types of businesses.

9. Explain the reasons for taking a physical inventory; outline the procedure used.

10. Write the formulas for the following: the cost method of inventory, the book method of inventory value, and the retail method of investment value.

11. Define open-to-buy; illustrate the formula used to calculate the open-to-buy.

12. List the advantages and limitations of merchandise control.

The Merchandise Control Process: Systems and Applications

Figure 9–1 Retail buyers must be aware of certain control measures that will assist in merchandise planning and ensure prompt reordering.

INTRODUCTION

In the previous chapter you learned that unit (assortment) planning is concerned with the amount of inventory the buyer should carry in a department—by the number of separate items and by the number of units of each item. Since no one retail store can carry all products available in the market place, decisions about which merchandise assortment to carry are not left to chance but are based on a number of important factors.

Unit (assortment) plans may be developed in two ways: The first method is through the use of a basic stock list. The second method is through the use of a model stock plan. All merchandise assortments can be planned by using either of these methods; however, the method used depends on the kind of merchandise under consideration.

In this chapter we are concerned with the control function of management and its application to merchandising. Control is often thought of as the fifth stage in the management process of planning, organizing, staffing, directing, and controlling. However, as previously noted, a good control system will be built into management's business objectives during the initial planning stage. Control provides a way to inform top management if established standards are or are not functioning according to plan. Control also provides a basis for making changes to correct problems that are already present.

There are two major forms of merchandise control (dollar control and unit control) that are regulated by two types of inventory systems (the perpetual inventory system and the periodic inventory system).

Another approach to the periodic system of unit control is the physical inventory system. A major concern of store buyers is to determine the actual worth of the inventory on hand. Three methods may be used to determine inventory value: (1) the cost method, (2) the book method, and (3) the retail method. Other types of systems used in unit control are visual, tickler, warehouse, want slip, and the physical inventory.

In most retail stores, the largest monetary investment is usually in the merchandise inventory. Unlike inventories of merchandise carried by most other types of businesses, inventories carried by retail stores have certain differentiating characteristics. Because the merchandise inventory is so varied, the problems of inventory planning and control become major ones. A physical inventory, therefore, becomes a necessity.

The open-to-buy is a major tool used by retail buyers to control future inventories. Other control methods include the use of various inventory reports, and electronic controls (the computer), which may be used in a variety of retailing applications. However, retailers have found that control measures also offer limitations along with their many advantages. Therefore, close attention must be given to both when determining which control system is best for the individual store or department.

PART 1—Control Systems: Merchandise Applications

ELEMENTS OF A CONTROL SYSTEM

No matter what activity is being controlled in the retail establishment, whether it is personnel, operations, finance, or merchandise, there are certain elements that should be present in every control system (Figure 9–1). Three elements important to a good control system are (1) establishment of control standards, (2) measurement of performance, and (3) analysis and correction of deviations from planned standards.[1]

Establishment of Control Standards

Every type and size of retail establishment has certain goals and objectives it is striving to attain. *Control standards* represent a business firm's objectives and goals. A retail store will establish certain *monetary standards* or goals for each department, for example, the quota that the average sales department must attain during certain selling periods, such as special sales promotions, Mother's Day, and the Easter season. Another example of a monetary control standard is the number of sales required of each salesperson; a monetary standard may include cost of store overhead, such as labor, utilities, and rent, in ratio to the amount of profit earned by each department.

A retail store will also have certain *physical standards.* For example, if a chain store opens a new unit, there will be certain physical characteristics—the design of the store exterior and interior, window displays, store signage—that will readily identify the store as a member of a particular chain operation. A franchise operation emphasizes certain physical standards (for example, McDonald's golden arch) throughout all its franchises.

Finally, a retail store will establish certain *intangible standards,* such as "quality" service, "good performance," or store "loyalty." Intangible standards, however, are often difficult to measure because they cannot be precisely stated in either monetary or physical terms. We cannot necessarily see, touch, or feel such factors as "loyalty," "good performance," or "quality."

Measurement of Performance

If control standards have been properly established and communicated to store personnel, then the measurement of performance resulting from application of these standards should be a relatively simple task. A department manager may measure the performance of a management trainee by using a rating form based on ratings of good, average, or poor (see Figure 9–2). The performance of a store executive may be rated according to such descriptions as needs improvement, average expected for position, or above average (see Figure 9–3). Performance measurement, however, is not as simple as it appears. For example, definitions of terms such as "good," "average," and "poor" may differ. One evaluator may have a very strict standard regarding what constitutes a good performance, whereas another evaluator may be much more lenient.

Figure 9–2   A department manager may measure the performance of a management trainee by using a rating form based on such factors as good, average, or poor.

Date Sent to Department _____ Date to be Returned to Personnel _____

EXECUTIVE DEVELOPMENT TRAINEE

Progress Review

(six and twelve months)

Date _____

Name _____ No. _____ Department _____

Starting Date: _____ Age _____ Education _____

Department Manager _____

Department Manager: Please evaluate the above trainee by answering the following questions. After you have completed this review of your trainee's progress, discuss your evaluations with him and then *forward the review to the Divisional Merchandise Manager for his comments.*

1. Please evaluate your trainee on the following factors:

	Good	Average	Poor			Good	Average	Poor
Dependability					Maturity			
Initiative					Aggressiveness			
Appearance					Cooperation			
Tact					Loyalty			

2. What responsibilities has your trainee been given? Please describe briefly below.

Supervising Salespeople: _____

_____

Handling Classifications: _____

_____

Meeting resources: _____

_____

Advertising and/or Display: _____

_____

Responsibility for department while you are away: _____

_____

Figure 9–3 An example of a form used to rate a store executive. (Courtesy of John Wanamaker Department Store, Philadelphia, Pa.)

EXECUTIVE PERFORMANCE REVIEW

Date of Review

NAME	DEPT.	EMP. NO.	SALARY	LAST INCREASE	AMOUNT	TENURE DATE	POSITION	STORE

ANNUAL FOLLOW-UP	RATED BY	DATE	INTERVIEWED BY	DATE

INCREASE	NEW SALARY	EFFECTIVE DATE	APPROVED BY	DATE	PERSONNEL DEPT. APPROVAL	DATE

1. JOB FACTOR CHECKLIST: For each statement use 1, 2, or 3 to indicate how the employee is performing relative to standard.

(1.) Needs improvement
(2.) Average expected for position
(3.) Above average

_____ Is a self starter
_____ Accepts responsibility for his actions
_____ Makes effective use of interstore reports, e.g. productivity, best seller, etc.
_____ Demonstrates cost awareness and constructive control
_____ Has creative, yet practical ideas and foresight
_____ Solves problems and makes decisions carefully, yet rapidly
_____ Communicates effectively to supervisors
_____ Trains subordinates to prepare them for promotion
_____ Understands all merchandising facets of his job
_____ Understands all operational aspects of his job
_____ Understands and follows store policies and procedures
_____ Sells himself and his ideas
_____ Follows through
_____ Communicates to subordinates
_____ Demonstrates sense of timeliness

If past records are available and information regarding department sales, inventory turnover, purchases, and expenses are provided, then fulfillment of monetary standards may be measured more accurately. The store buyer can plan department sales, purchases, and expenses based on past performance and use this information as a guide through selling seasons. In some departments, such as notions, greeting cards, gift wrapping, and stationery, monetary standards have been established for certain selling seasons, and sales projections for staple types of merchandise become fairly routine.

Analysis and Correction of Deviations from Planned Standards

What happens when the owner-manager of a small variety store does not make the sales quota for the Christmas season and has to take several markdowns? What does a buyer who has not requested enough sales help for the week-long "Founder's Day Sale" do when the store is swamped by customers? Obviously, the owner-manager overestimated sales potential, and the department manager underestimated the need for sales personnel. Why? How will each correct the situation?

A good control process will include as part of its system the ability to analyze and correct any deviations from established standards. For example, the owner-manager will have to refer to projected sales goals and determine corrective action to prevent the same mistake from recurring. The buyer may have to take another look at the budget and determine how to correct the understaffing situation in light of past information.

There are certain elements that should be present in every control system.

Review each of the following.
Why are they necessary?

1. Establishment of control standards
   a. Monetary standards
   b. Physical standards
   c. Intangible standards
2. Measurement of performance
3. Analysis and correction

REQUIREMENTS OF A GOOD CONTROL SYSTEM

The kind of control system required by a retail business will depend upon its merchandising policy, the size of the store, and the clientele it serves.

However, there are certain requirements that should be a part of any control system. A good control system should (1) call attention to deviations, (2) suggest a means of solving the problem, (3) be accurate and timely, (4) be understood by the members of the organization, and (5) be economical.[2]

A good control system should:

1. Call attention to deviations
2. Suggest a means of solving the problem
3. Be accurate and timely
4. Be understood by the members of the organization
5. Be economical

Call Attention to Deviations

Well-planned control systems will be applied to those store activities with which management is most concerned. For example, inventory control is watched carefully by large and small retailers alike. In the large departmentalized store, merchandise inventory is usually controlled by the use of electronic data processing (EDP), since EDP has proved to be an excellent method of fast, accurate, efficient information retrieval. In contrast, the owner of a small hardware store may use "eyeball" checks to determine the amount of merchandise sold, the amount of goods left in the stockroom, and the amount and type of inventory that must be reordered.

A good control system should be able to determine errors, mistakes, and any other problems that require the immediate attention of the buyer; and should be able to locate problem areas before a complete breakdown occurs in some part of the system. Suppose that a salesperson working in a greeting-card shop sees a reorder card appear in the bin or on the rack. When this occurs, the reorder card should be turned over to the department manager or store buyer so that merchandise can be reordered promptly; or the department manager or buyer should alert the manufacturer's representative to the necessity of reorders when the agent visits the store.

Suggest a Means of Solving the Problem

Once attention is called to a problem, a good control system should provide a means of solving it. The store's EDP system may have corrective measures built in for some types of variations from standards. The manager of a variety store that is a member of a large chain operation may receive a computer-prepared stock list indicating that a particular stock item has been discontinued; however, the stock list also suggests a reasonable substitute. As a result the buyer will be able to maintain both a continuous flow of stock and a balanced stock assortment. Even less automated systems should alert management to areas that require improvement.

Be Accurate and Timely

A good control system should provide accurate corrective information in time to allow effective decision making. Often, however, it is difficult to achieve a balance between accuracy and time. For instance, the manager of a cosmetic and perfume department may wish to offer a new line of fragrance. However, uncertainty about the success and, therefore, the profitability of the fragrance causes the manager to hestitate. Trade journals are read, manufacturing representatives consulted, and buyers in noncompeting stores are sought out for advice. While all this information accumulates, the competition may enter the market with the new line. Needless to say, if the new line proves successful, and if the merchandising philosophy of the manager's store is based upon being a leader in offering new lines of merchandise, this manager has "missed the boat." When accuracy and time come into conflict, store management must ask which is more important. The answer will depend on the merchandising philosophy of the store and the time pressure under which retailers are working. One store may offer only items that are well established and proved to be profitable, while another store may wish to be a leader when it comes to offering new lines of merchandise.

Be Understood by the Members of the Organization

Even the most sophisticated control system is worthless if it is not understood by those who must use the information it provides (Figure 9–4). Management must carefully explain both the purposes and objectives of the control system and how to use it. If a new credit procedure is introduced, the data-processing division must inform store managers or merchandise managers and buyers about the new procedure, and they, in turn, will pass the information on to members of their staff. Perhaps the store's personnel division will offer special training sessions, to sales personnel especially, to instruct them about the procedures involved in implementing the new credit procedure. When the control system is understood by the members of the organization who must use it, it is likely to increase managerial effectiveness and improve profitability.

Be Economical

A good control system will remain consistent with the overall profit objectives of the retail firm. The amount of money spent on a control system will

Figure 9–4 Even the most sophisticated control system is worthless if it is not understood by those who must use the information it provides.

depend on both the relative importance of the division or system to be controlled and the size of the operation. Sophisticated computer systems used by many retail organizations require not only elaborate installation, maintenance, and repair but also intensified training sessions for those who will operate them. All of this is expensive; the necessity for such complex systems should be thoroughly considered before implementation. Management should not spend more money collecting and analyzing data than they will save by improvements that result from the addition of the control system.

CONTROL SYSTEMS USED IN MERCHANDISING

Up to this point, we have discussed general characteristics of control systems. Let us now turn our attention to the specific application of control systems to merchandising divisions of retail stores. An important control measure used by store managers, buyers, and small business managers alike to assist them in data collection is called merchandise control. *Merchandise control* may be defined as the maintenance of a stock of merchandise that is adjusted to the needs of consumers and prospective consumers.[3]

The type of merchandise control system that a retail store uses will depend upon the type and size of the business, the kind and amount of data required, the methods employed by the store's competition, and the store's business objectives. The owner-manager of a small retail store may determine the amount of stock on hand by simply inspecting or counting items on the shelves and in the stockroom. Because the business is small, this visual count of merchandise will help to determine which items are selling and which are not, as well as which items should be reordered. In a large department store, the buyer may seek the assistance of salespeople and stock personnel, who are assigned to specific areas or departments. The buyer will use more formal means of stock control because of the amount and value of the stock and the need for more detailed information concerning particular stock units. In a chain operation, the central buyer will refer to both reorder requests from store managers and supply information from warehouse managers to determine the amount and kind of merchandise on hand as well as items of merchandise that need to be replenished.

There are two major forms of merchandise control: (1) dollar control and (2) unit control.

Dollar Control

Dollar control may be defined as the amount of dollars at retail prices invested in the merchandise inventory. Dollar control usually involves maintaining records designed to provide accurate information in terms of retail prices by answering the question, "How much?" This information can be used as a guide to buying and reordering. The small store buyer will usually use this method of control throughout the entire store. If the small store grows and expands, however, the dollar control method becomes more specific; that is, the dollar control method may be applied (1) to departments, (2) to classifications, or (3) to specific price lines.[4]

Departmental Control. *Departmental control* refers to the use of dollar control on a departmental basis. Through the use of sales records, customer returns, returns to vendors, markups and markdowns, physical inventory counts, and rate of stockturn, the buyer or department manager can determine his or her department's profit picture in comparison with other store departments and with the profit objectives of the company. Departmental dollar control will assist store management to determine weaknesses and strengths in each department and thus lead to the development of measures that will improve individual department operations.

However, depending on the size of the store, many retailers have found that dollar information compiled at the department level is inadequate.

"Over" and "under" conditions of sales, purchases, markdowns, stock, and open-to-buy are grouped together, thus concealing information that may be vital for effective management decision making. These retailers, therefore, use a more detailed analysis called classification control or classification merchandising.[5]

Classification Control. Classification control or *classification merchandising* refers to the use of dollar control based upon classifications of related types of merchandise within individual departments. For instance, in a ladies sportswear department information regarding dollar investment may be recorded separately for each classification of merchandise, such as active sportswear, casual sportswear, and spectator sportswear. Because this type of control is so popular today, many retailers have shown a tendency to subdivide broad classifications of merchandise into even smaller groups based on "consumer end-use"! Activity sportswear, for example, may be further subdivided into tennis wear, boating attire, or golf clothing.

Price-Line Control. Price-line control refers to the use of dollar control based upon a single retail price. A department or a classification of merchandise may be broken down by particular price lines, such as $5.99 for a certain classification of men's shirts or $19.95 for all men's shirts sold in the men's furnishings department. In some cases, a buyer or department manager may use price-line control in place of merchandise control; furthermore, price lines may also be broken down according to size, style, fabric, or some other desired category.

Unit Control

Unit control, a second major form of merchandise control, may be defined as an organized method of recording the individual units or pieces of mer-

---

Explain the major forms of merchandise control:

1. Dollar control
   Answers the question "how much?" May be applied to:
   a. Department—departmental control
   b. Classifications—classification control
   c. Price—price-line control
2. Unit control
   Answers the question "what?"
   Considered a supplement to dollar control

chandise found in the inventory. This type of control is usually concerned with purchase orders, inventories, and sales. It involves the maintenance of records designed to provide accurate information in terms of physical units rather than in terms of dollars. Unit control attempts to answer the question "What?" This type of control is usually considered a supplement to dollar control; therefore, both types of formal control are essential in stock maintenance and in regulating stocks to consumer demand.

TYPES OF INVENTORY SYSTEMS THAT REGULATE DOLLAR CONTROL AND UNIT CONTROL

Dollar control and unit control may be achieved either through a perpetual inventory system or a periodic inventory system. A *perpetual inventory system* may be defined as a system where sales figures are derived from sales and purchase records of merchandise on hand—reported at regular intervals, such as every day, week, or month—in terms of goods that have been received and goods that have been sold. Tally records kept by salespeople on control cards or computer tape that is punched when the cash register is operated are two examples of sales records that yield information that will provide a basis for a perpetual, or ongoing, inventory system. This system is suitable for high-priced and fashion merchandise, since such merchandise is subject to high risk because of the short selling season. Inexpensive staple merchandise generally does not require sales information on a daily basis, since this type of merchandise has a longer selling period.

The basic procedures for calculating a perpetual inventory in dollars may be illustrated as follows:

      Opening inventory
  + Purchases
  ———————————
  = Total inventory on hand
  − Sales
  − Markdowns
  ———————————
  = Ending inventory on hand

The *periodic inventory system* may be defined as an inventory method that derives sales figures from inventory and purchase data by periodically adding opening inventory and purchases and subtracting the sum of the closing inventory and markdowns. This is the commonly used method for staple goods and may be illustrated as follows:

      Opening inventory
  + Purchases
  ———————————
  = Total inventory on hand

> — Ending inventory on hand
> = Sales and markdowns
> — Markdowns
> = Sales

Dollar Control and the Perpetual Inventory System

When using the perpetual inventory system in dollar control, it is necessary (1) to use the retail inventory method of accounting (discussed in detail in Part 2 of this chapter) for the store as a whole and for each department, classification, and price line, or (2) to analyze sales data and inventories without attempting to determine initial markup or gross margin. A major problem under the perpetual inventory method is to obtain complete and accurate information. To solve this problem, many retailers have installed information systems capable of reporting all relevant transactions. However, some retail stores, particularly smaller stores, still use clerical help to obtain necessary information. Whether done with clerical assistance or with information systems, the perpetual inventory method provides a cumulative record of stocks on hand, sales for a particular period, and reorder periods.

Dollar Control and the Periodic Inventory System

When using the periodic inventory system in dollar control, three important records must be kept, whether the system affects the store as a whole, individual departments, classifications, or price lines. Records that must be kept, all at retail prices, are (1) records of inventory, (2) records of purchases, and, (3) records of markdowns. These records will provide valuable information either on a semiannual basis or at other designated intervals. An illustration follows:

Sales from retail inventories, retail purchases, and markdowns may be analyzed on a semiannual basis as follows:

Retail Stock on hand—May 1	$25,000
(whole store, department, classification, or price line)	
Retail Purchases—May 1–October 31	+ 50,000
Total Retail Stock on Hand—October 1	$75,000
Retail Stock on Hand—October 31	− 30,000
Sales and Markdowns—May 1–October 31	$45,000
Markdowns—May 1–October 31	− 5,000
Derived Sales (including stock shortages)	$40,000

When an average rate of stock shortages for the store, department, classification, or price line is known, actual sales may be determined. For example, the derived sales may be divided by 100% plus the shortage percentage to determine the estimated net sales. If the shortage percentage is 2% of net sales, $40,000 may be divided by 102% to give estimated sales of $39,215.

Actual or net sales = Derived sales − (100% + shortage percentage)
$39,215 = $40,000 ÷ 1.02 (100% + 2%)

The periodic inventory method may also be used to determine the maintained markup, the difference between cost price and final selling price. A markup percentage may be obtained by recording opening inventory and retail purchases at both cost price and retail price. By calculating the cost percent, which is 100 percent − markup percent, the retail value of the stock on hand may be reduced to a cost basis. The gross cost of merchandise sold and the gross margin figures may be obtained by this procedure; however, stock shortages must be closely estimated. An example follows:

	At Cost	At Retail	Markup %
Retail Stock on Hand—May 1	$15,000	$25,000	
Retail Purchases—May 1–October 31	+ 30,000	+ 50,000	
Total Retail Stock on Hand	$45,000	$75,000	40.0%
Retail Stock on Hand—October 31		− $30,000	
Cost Stock on Hand—October 31	$18,000		
Sales and Markdowns—May 1–October 31		$45,000	
Markdowns—May 1–October 31		− 5,000	
Sales and Shortages		$40,000	102.0%
Estimated Sales ($40,000 ÷ 1.02)		$39,215	100.0%
Gross Cost of Goods Sold	− $27,000		
Maintained Markup	$12,215		31.1%

A major advantage of the periodic inventory method of dollar control is that it is simple to use. Unfortunately, its usefulness is limited, since information is provided only at designated intervals.

Unit Control and the Perpetual Inventory System

As a result of using the perpetual inventory system in unit control, a continuous feedback of information on merchandise moved into and out of a department is readily available. To obtain this information, however, the buyer must establish a method of recording sales, receipts of merchandise, and merchandise returns based on a unit control system. Because the buyer receives this information on a weekly or even daily basis, inventory levels can be adjusted accordingly. This method of control also helps the buyer to determine stock shortages at the time inventories are taken.

The perpetual inventory system in unit control is commonly used for merchandise of high unit value that has a short selling season, such as women's apparel, fashion accessories, and men's clothing. This type of merchandise must be watched carefully to avoid taking high markdowns because of obsolescence. The method is practical because sales are easily recorded by units and reorders are common. The system enables the buyer and other store officials to keep a close watch on the progress of a specific line of merchandise or a specific merchandise classification.

In most department stores and chain operations the perpetual system of unit control is electronically operated. The computer issues daily, weekly, or monthly sales reports on styles, colors, sizes, price lines, vendors, and merchandise classes. However, for smaller stores other methods may be more practical. For example, the owner-manager of a small women's boutique keeps track of merchandise by using style cards. A separate style card is used for each style represented in the assortment. Each style card contains information on all transactions involved—orders, returns, markdowns, damages, price changes, colors, and sizes. The style card is kept either in a file box or on a rack. With ths system the store owner can see at a glance what styles are selling fast; what styles need to be reordered; what styles are slow sellers; and what colors, fabrics, and sizes are popular.

Unit Control and the Periodic Inventory System

The periodic inventory system in unit control is based upon periodic inventory counts, which may be taken as frequently as desired (for example, weekly, monthly, or semiannually). This is the basic system used for the control of staple, low-value merchandise and of items with a long selling life that are replaced as they sell out, such as men's underwear, classic sweaters, men's socks, and women's hosiery. When using the periodic system, buyers or store managers should make frequent counts of fast-moving items, especially at the beginning of a season when they are watching for trends. Classic and basic merchandise items are counted less frequently but at regular intervals. Special attention should be given to merchandise that often sells out between counts. This system can be a basis for decisions about dropping merchandise lines that show little or no sales activity between counts. The buyer should continually check past sales figures, because even basic merchandise categories can show upward or downward trends.[6] Staple merchandise is usually in continuous demand; consequently, markdowns are less likely.

Unit Control and Other Types of Inventory Systems

Other types of inventory systems, in addition to perpetual or periodic systems, have been developed for use in unit control: (1) visual control, (2) tickler control, (3) warehouse control, (4) want-slip control, and (5) the physical inventory.[7] These systems are used when visual inspection indicates that stock will soon be in short supply. They are designed to minimize lost sales caused by merchandise being out of stock and to maintain adequate assortments of stocks based on consumer demand. Selection of one or all of these inventory systems depends upon the special needs of the individual business.

Visual Control. Visual control is used when there is a reserve quantity of stock that has been separated from the rest of the stock by a divider or a banding device. When it becomes necessary to break into the reserve, a control ticket attached to the reserve stock is forwarded to the buyer for his evaluation on whether or not to reorder. In visual control, stock people or salespeople simply make a notation of the need to reorder whenever they observe that stock is low or depleted. This system is usually used for staple merchandise with a steady turnover, for example, greeting cards.

Tickler Control. Under this type of control, lists of items to be counted (usually staples, such as drugs and cosmetics) are kept in a tickler file. A *tickler file* may be defined as a system that serves as a reminder and is arranged to bring matters to timely attention. For example, lists of cosmetic items to be counted each day are kept in a tickler file. They are so arranged that the list for any given day appears at the front of the file on that day and, thus, automatically comes to the attention of the buyer. The advisability of reorder is determined at this point. This system is most useful for goods having a steady turnover.

Warehouse Control. Merchandise commonly displayed in the store only in the form of floor samples, such as furniture, refrigerators, and washing machines, with delivery to the customer made from warehouse stock, may be controlled from the retail store, from the warehouse, or from both places. When the sale is made, a copy of the sales check is sent to unit control, where the transaction is entered into the control book. Control information is readily available to buyers, salespeople, and warehouse personnel alike to help eliminate overselling with consequent inability to deliver merchandise.

Want-Slip Control. A want slip is a simple form filled out by salespeople regarding either out-of-stock items or items not sold by the store but requested by customers. It is a method of unit control that tells the buyer or store manager of sales that might have been made. A want-slip system may indicate to a buyer that a new trend is starting, a particular fad is developing, or a particular color or fabric is becoming popular.

Types of inventory systems that regulate merchandise controls

Dollar control
Perpetual inventory system
Periodic inventory system
Unit control
Perpetual inventory system
Periodic inventory system

Visual control
Tickler control
Warehouse control
Want-slip control
Physical inventory system

How will each of the above assist the buyer in making effective merchandising decisions?

INVENTORY VALUATION

Another approach to the periodic system of unit control is the physical inventory system. Under this system a figure for net sales is obtained by adding the former physical inventory to the purchases received from vendors minus the ending physical inventory. Steps in taking a physical inventory will be discussed in Part 2 of this chapter.

Former Physical Inventory	$15,000	
+ Purchases Received from Vendors	+ 30,000	
Total	$45,000	
− Ending Physical Inventory	− $ 5,000	($15,000 − $10,000)
Net Sales	$40,000	(Physical inventory minus merchandise sold)

A major concern of store buyers is to determine the actual worth of the inventory on hand. Calculating the value of the inventory is essential if sound financial planning and control is to be accomplished.

Three methods may be used to determine inventory value: (1) the cost method, (2) the book method, and (3) the retail method.

> **Methods used to determine the value of closing inventory**
>
> 1. The cost method—goods are recorded at cost price
> 2. The book method—a record of inventory
>   book inventory = stock on hand + purchases − goods sold
> 3. The retail method—a combination of the cost method and book method at retail prices

The Cost Method

In the *cost method of inventory,* goods are recorded at cost price and the ending inventory values are determined by actually counting the merchandise in stock and recording values at cost prices. The cost price of each item is usually recorded in code on the price ticket. Most codes are expressed in such a way that the value is not apparent to customers or even to those employees who do not need to possess such information.

This valuation of inventory is based on the assumption that present in-stock goods have the same worth as they had when they were bought. However, this may not always be true, since some inventories can depreciate in value. For example, factors that may contribute to merchandise depreciation are (1) obsolescence, (2) damaged merchandise, (3) a drop in wholesale price, (4) change in consumer demand, and (5) the type of goods (that is, staple or fashion). The inventory, therefore, should be evaluated at less than cost or at the current market value. For example, if a toy buyer bought bicycles at $50 and priced them at $150, they may have to be sold for $105 if they are still on the selling floor when new models appear. The inventory value of the bicycles can be determined as follows:

Original Cost Price	$ 50.00	
+ Markup Price	+100.00	(200% Markup)
Original Retail Price	$150.00	
New Cost Price (at Cost or Market, whichever is lower)	$ 35.00	(devalued due to obsolescence)
+ New Markup Price	+70.00	(200% Markup)
New Price (Markdown)	$105.00	

The inventory value or new cost price is $35.00. Note that the same markup of 200% is maintained.

If prices remained constant, there would be little, if any, problem concerning valuation of inventory. However, when changes occur with no relationship to cost of initial purchases, buyers and store managers have a difficult task when they attempt to place values on inventory at cost or market price, whichever is lower. There are two methods that may be used to calculate inventory value: (1) the First-in First-out Method (FIFO) and (2) the Last-in First-out Method (LIFO).

Under the FIFO method of inventory evaluation, larger profits result during periods of rising prices because higher values are placed on ending inventories than on the merchandise on hand at the beginning of the year. The difference is added to profits. For example, a buyer of children's toys will usually attempt to sell items that were bought earliest because they have been in stock for the longest period of time and they initially cost less than merchandise purchased later. Thus, goods included in the beginning-of-the-year inventory would be the first units sold. The FIFO method is one way of keeping stocks fresh and up to date. It is also used to keep profits high due to price increases of end-of-year inventories.

A second method of inventory valuation, the LIFO method, assumes that those goods purchased recently are sold first. Once a retail organization decides to use this method of inventory valuation, it must do so continuously. This method also requires that total markdowns must be deducted from the retail sales figure in calculating the net markup figure. This method of inventory is gradually being accepted by most retail organizations, primarily because of the continued upward trend of retail prices.

The following illustration compares the FIFO method and the LIFO method in a period when costs are increasing.

A buyer purchased 100 items at $5 each and 100 additional items at $7 each, a total of 200 items at $1,200. During the season, 100 items were sold, leaving 100 items remaining in stock. The 100 items that were sold brought a retail price of $10 each.

	FIFO		LIFO	
Retail Sales				
100 items @ $10	$1,000		$1,000	
Cost of Goods Sold				
100 items @ $5	− 500;	100 items @ $7	− 700	(increased
Profits Before Taxes	$ 500		$ 300	costs)
Ending Inventory Value				
100 items @ $7	$ 700;	100 items @ $5	$ 500	

The student should note that under the FIFO method, profits are $200 higher and ending inventory values are $200 higher. Under the LIFO method, profits before taxes are $200 lower, which leads to lower taxes, and ending inventory values are $200 lower.

When costs are decreasing, the above illustration is reversed. The LIFO method shows inflated profits, taxes, and ending inventory, and the FIFO method results in lower profits before taxes and lower ending inventory. Needless to say, during a period of steady costs, the buyer will not gain from either the FIFO method or the LIFO method.

The Book Method

Many stores, such as discount houses, specialty chain operations, variety stores, and drugstores, require continuous information about the value of the merchandise inventory, even though it is impractical to take a physical inventory more than twice a year. The *book method of inventory* is the record of stock that should be on hand in terms of what has been purchased and what has been sold. What should be on hand is called the closing book inventory. No actual counting of the merchandise is required for the book inventory; however, what is counted twice a year is called the physical inventory. The book inventory method, if calculated every day, week, or month, is called a perpetual inventory. It may be kept either in terms of dollar value or in terms of units of merchandise. The excess of book inventory at the end of every six months over physical inventory is the merchandise shortage. In recording information for a book inventory, values may be recorded at either cost or retail prices. Most retail stores employ the book method of inventory at retail prices. An example follows:

At Retail

Physical Inventory, August 1	$10,000
Purchases, August–January	+ 15,500
Total Merchandise Handled	$25,500
Goods Sold, August–January	− 15,000
Book Inventory, January 31	$10,500
Physical Inventory, January 31	− 10,000
Merchandise Shortage	$ 500

The retail buyer will subtract from the book inventory those markdowns he may have taken before he compares it with the physical inventory.

The Retail Method

The *retail method of inventory* is a combination of the cost method of inventory with the book method of inventory at retail prices. When inventory is calculated at retail prices rather than at cost prices, it is necessary to subtract the cost or market price from the total retail value to figure profit or loss. Every six months all purchases are recorded at both cost and retail prices. The markup on all purchases, including the opening inventory, is determined. This markup is applied to the closing inventory at retail to arrive at the cost or market value. An example of this procedure follows.

	At Cost	At Retail	Markup %
Beginning Inventory	$3,050	$ 5,000	40%
Purchases	+5,950	+10,000	
Total Merchandise Handled	$9,000	$15,000	
Closing Physical Inventory at Retail		$ 2,500	
Closing Physical Inventory at Cost or Market Value ($2,500 × 60%)	$1,500		

Eventually, the merchandise in the entire store must be physically counted. It is highly unlikely that a physical count will show agreement of the book inventory and the physical inventory. When the physical inventory is greater than the book inventory, there is a *merchandise overage;* when the physical inventory is less than the book inventory, there is a *merchandise shortage.*

A merchandise shortage usually indicates an actual loss of inventory in the department, whereas a merchandise overage probably indicates an error in the physical count.

PART 2—Control Systems: Merchandise Applications: Continued

CHARACTERISTICS OF THE MERCHANDISE INVENTORY

In most retail stores, the largest monetary investment is usually in the *merchandise inventory,* merchandise that is available for sale to the ultimate customer. Unlike inventories of merchandise carried by most other types of businesses, inventories carried by retail stores have certain differentiating characteristics.

Merchandise Inventories:

1. Constitute an exceptionally large part of the assets, usually more than 50%.
2. Fluctuate daily, monthly, or seasonally.
3. Are constantly changing as new items are added and old items deleted.
4. Contain only the most appealing and up-to-date lines of merchandise.

5. Contain large numbers of many different types of items.
6. Are perishable; that is, they will deteriorate as soon as new items enter the market.
7. Are subject to stock deterioration; therefore, markdowns become a major consideration.
8. Are vulnerable to shoplifting and pilferage.
9. Are difficult to safeguard, since they are displayed and stored in many locations.
10. Must be readily available to meet consumer demands.

WHY TAKE A PHYSICAL INVENTORY?

Because the merchandise inventory is so varied, the problems of inventory planning and control become major ones for store managers and buyers. A physical inventory, therefore, becomes a necessity. A *physical inventory* may be defined as the actual counting and recording of the merchandise or stock on hand at a specified time, together with the cost or the retail price of each item.[8] There are several reasons for taking a physical inventory.

First: Preparation of Financial Statements

A retailer must take a physical count of merchandise on hand to determine the total value of his stock. This information is necessary for the preparation of financial statements, such as the profit-and-loss statement. Business statements provide management with a detailed analysis of the financial condition of an individual department or of the store as a whole. We discuss financial statements and other important business records in greater detail in Chapter 10.

Second: To Familiarize Personnel with the Stock Assortment

By taking a physical count of stock on hand, all personnel—merchandise managers, central and local buyers, assistants, salespeople, and stock people—will have an opportunity to know what merchandise is in stock. Since the merchandise inventory contains thousands of many different types of items, merchandise may often remain unnoticed or "lost." Think, for example, of the number of items you can find in a variety store, a hardware store, or a discount house! By taking a physical count, items are brought to the attention of salespeople, who, in turn, will adapt selling techniques to selling that merchandise.

Third: Inventory Analysis

At a specific time, the physical inventory relates the quantities, kinds, and values of the items found in stock in the entire store and in individual departments. If there are branch operations, an inventory analysis is also taken of the stock in each branch store. In a chain operation, a count is taken of all merchandise in each individual unit. In a storewide inventory, stock is analyzed according to merchandise classification, price line, and physical units by season or age group. With this information, buyers or store managers can adjust stock on hand according to consumer demand by marking down old stock that has accumulated or by shipping that merchandise to a branch store or unit where the merchandise as proved more appealing.

Fourth: Determine Stock Shortages and Overages

By taking a physical count of merchandise in stock, buyers may compare actual counts with stock records to determine the amount of stock shortage or overage. This information will help buyers to take corrective measures. It provides a basis for checking and correcting unit control and other stock records.

Fifth: Sales Determination

Sales records are usually kept for the entire store, for individual departments, and for each merchandise classification for each store and its branches (if a branch operation) or for each unit in the chain (if a chain-store operation). The physical count may be taken for subgroups, for price lines, or for special stock items. If a count is taken by these breakdowns at specified periods and if purchase records are maintained for each, valuable sales data may be obtained that will assist buyers or managers to determine slow sellers, best sellers, markdowns, and so forth.

STEPS IN TAKING THE PHYSICAL INVENTORY

If you ever worked in a retail store, large or small, you were probably involved either directly or indirectly in taking a physical inventory. However, methods used by different stores and the time periods involved vary with the type and size of the retail establishment. Some types of retail operations require little advance preparation (for example, the grocery store where stock personnel simply count merchandise on the shelves and in the stockroom and record the counts on special forms). However, in a department store and chain operation the procedure of taking a physical inventory is far more complex. The procedure discussed in the following pages is the one used primarily by these stores. The inventory procedure may be broken down into three steps.[9] (1) The times of the inventory—annually or semiannually; (2) The planning stage—careful advance planning is a *must;* (3) Counting, recording, checking—must be thorough to insure accuracy.

The Times of the Inventory

In most retail stores, it is the practice to take two inventories a year. In fashion apparel stores and in general merchandise chain operations these inventories are usually taken during the months that are considered to be the end of selling seasons, for example, January and July. In stores where inventory is taken only once a year (an annual inventory) the complete inventory is usually taken at the end of January. Management must consider when counting times will occur during the specified inventory period and determine whether to close down the store during the period in which inventory is taken, to take the inventory after business hours or on weekends, or to conduct the inventory during store hours and close the store early. Most retail store managements decide to conduct inventory counts during business hours and, in some cases, close the store early to complete the physical inventory procedure. Many times a store notifies customers of a store inventory through such advertisements as "We will close today at 3:00 P.M. to take our annual inventory" or "Early closing due to storewide inventory."

Planning Stage

Careful advance preparation is a must if accuracy in recording and thoroughness in counting are to result. Advance preparation includes six types of activities: (1) classifying and grouping merchandise by type, price, and style; (2) placing all merchandise information on the price ticket; (3) planning sales to reduce stock; (4) preparing a layout chart; (5) obtaining the necessary forms; and (6) issuing inventory instructions to sales and stock personnel.

Classifying and Grouping Merchandise by Type, Price, and Style. By this means, the speed of the count will be increased and the buyer will be sure that all merchandise is included. For example, the buyer or department manager of the handbag department will direct assistants and sales and stock personnel to group the merchandise according to shoulder bags, clutch bags, evening bags, etc. Once merchandise is classified, the counting procedure may proceed with counts recorded according to the specified merchandise classification. This also assists the buyer by increasing his or her own information regarding what is in stock.

Figure 9–5 Price ticket information should include price, department, classification, style, season, size (where applicable) and vendor.

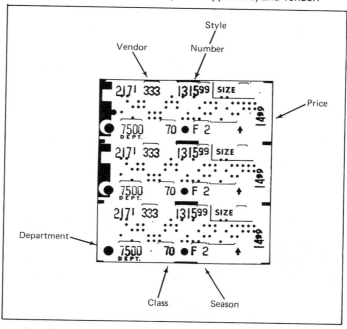

Placing All Merchandise Information on the Price Ticket. If an accurate count is to occur, the buyer must be certain that all merchandise information is on the price ticket. Ticket information should include price, department, classification, style, season and size (where applicable), and vendor number. Figure 9–5 illustrates the kind of information found on most price tickets.

Planning Sales to Reduce Stock. As a result of classifying and grouping merchandise by type, price, or style, the buyer may discover that certain stock items may be included in special sales-promotion activities, for example, an "Inventory Clearance Sale." In this way, the buyer may clear out unwanted, slow-moving merchandise before the actual inventory count begins.

Preparing a Layout Chart. The buyer or department manager should prepare a layout chart of the entire department that indicates the position of each fixture that contains stock items. This information is sent to the controller who, in turn, issues inventory sheets that mark specific sections in each department. This is one way to ensure that all merchandise is included when the count is taken.

Obtaining the Necessary Forms. Three types of forms may be used by a store for recording and listing stock: (1) the inventory sheet, (2) the inventory tag or ticket, and (3) the punch card.

The *inventory sheet* allows recording a large number of items on one sheet and includes such information as description, quantity, price, style or lot number, season letter, classification, vendor, and other desired information. If selling continues while the count is being taken, a special deduction sheet is made out. (The deduction sheet is the same as the regular inventory sheet but is clearly marked to differentiate it.) Salespeople must carefully fill out the deduction sheet as sales are made; otherwise inventory figures will not agree with information obtained from previous inventory records.

The *inventory tag* or ticket is not as popular as the inventory sheet. The information required is similar, but a separate tag is required for every different style or lot number and for the same article in different locations. Since these tags are filled out in advance of the inventory period, deductions are made between the time the tag is filled out and the time the inventory is completed. Figure 9–6 illustrates an inventory tag that can be attached to merchandise in the furniture department.

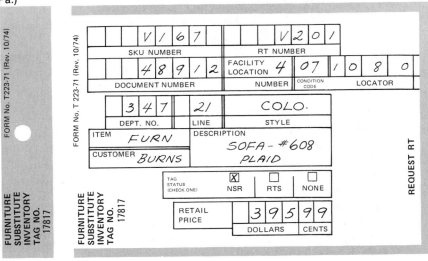

Figure 9–6   An illustration of an inventory tag that can be attached to merchandise in the furniture department. (Courtesy of John Wanamaker Department Store, Phladelphia, Pa.)

Figure 9–7 An example of a punch card. The punch card is punched by the computer with an identifying mark before it is attached to the merchandise or its ticket. (Courtesy of John Wanamaker Department Store, Philadelphia, Pa.)

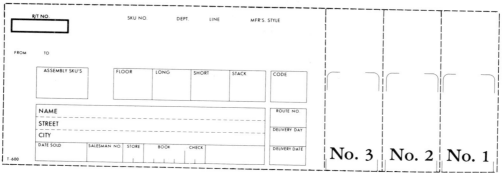

Since electronic data processing has become so popular, some retail stores have adopted *punch cards* or tape to facilitate inventory computations. A punching machine may be used, and while one person calls out the description and quantity of each stock item, another person operates the machine, which punches a card for every item (see Figure 9–7).

Issuing Inventory Instructions to Sales and Stock Personnel. It is important for sales personnel to understand completely the technique of inventory taking. Usually the merchandise manager or store manager issues instructions to department assistants, salespeople, and stock personnel before the

---

Why are each of the following planning activities important when taking a physical inventory?

1. Classifying and grouping merchandise by type, price, and style
2. Placing all merchandise information on the price ticket—style, vendor, price, class, season, size, department
3. Planning sales to reduce stock—"Inventory Clearance Sale"
4. Preparing a layout chart—the position of each fixture that contains stock
5. Obtaining the necessary forms—the inventory sheet, the inventory tag or ticket, the punch card
6. Issuing inventory instructions to sales and stock personnel—explain the entire procedure to merchandise personnel

Figure 9–8   Issuing inventory instructions to sales people.

TO: Furniture Divisional Merchandise Manager
           All Furniture Buyers, Assistant Buyers
           Branch Store Furniture Divisional Merchandise
              Managers
           Branch Store Furniture Group Managers
           All Branch Store Operations Managers

FROM: Arthur Kimmel   AK

**Furniture Inventory Instructions
For Taking Inventory on the
Selling Floor—All Locations**

Inventory will be taken on January 31, 1983, in all selling locations for the following furniture departments:

51-21   51-23   51-26   51-28   51-24   51-22   51-25

A.   *Preparation for Inventory*

 1.   Prepare a floor plan of the area to be inventoried.
 2.   Divide the floor into area of responsibility and assign
       same to individuals.
 3.   Beginning immediately, individuals assigned to an area
       must inspect each piece of furniture in his assigned
       area to be sure that the appropriate tag with at least
       one stub is affixed to each piece of furniture.
 4.   For pieces of furniture without the appropriate tag with
       at least one stub, a request must be made. This re-
       quest is to be made by contacting the terminal control
       area.
 5.   The following information must be available:

       a. Department Number
       b. Line
       c. Manufacturer's Style
       d. Article
       e. Description

 6.   Issuing inventory instructions to sales and stock per-
       sonnel: explaining the entire procedure to merchandise
       personnel.

inventory period begins and carefully explains the importance of accuracy and thoroughness when counting and recording stock items. Figure 9–8 illustrates the first page of instructions issued to merchandise personnel that explain the entire procedure involved in taking a physical inventory of, in this case, a furniture department.

Counting, Recording, Checking

The third step in taking a physical inventory involves counting the merchandise (both on the floor and in the stockroom), recording the counts on the inventory sheets, and checking for accuracy (Figure 9–9). Before counting begins, it is important to ensure that no merchandise will be moved onto the selling floor from the stockroom. Movement of merchandise during the inventory count increases the possibility of double counting; that is, counting the same item, both in the stockroom and on the selling floor.

Some stores count their complete forward stock (that is, stock on the selling floor) in advance to avoid difficulties in handling sales during inven-

Figure 9–9 The actual counting of merchandise, both on the floor and in the stockroom, is an important step in taking a physical inventory.

tory. Warehouse and reserve-stock inventories may also be taken in advance, and careful records must be kept of all goods sent to the selling floor or received in the stockroom or warehouse. Addition and deduction sheets are used, along with the regular counting forms, such as inventory sheets, inventory tags or tickets, or punch cards. Employees usually work in pairs with one person calling and one recording. To ensure accuracy, the person recording the count may change places with the person counting and do a recount. However, because this method slows down inventory taking, spot checks or partial recounts are frequently taken. Unless spot checks indicate the existence of many errors, the inventory count is assumed to be correct.

METHODS USED TO CONTROL FUTURE MERCHANDISE INVENTORIES

Open-to-Buy: A Major Tool

A major tool used by retail buyers to control future inventories is a device called the open-to-buy (OTB) and may be defined as the amount of merchandise, either at cost price or at retail, that the buyer is open to receive into inventory during a certain time period based on the plans formulated. It contains figures agreed upon by store executives in consultation with finance and control personnel and is based on the expectations of the merchandising division. It may be prepared weekly or monthly, and provides a method of allocating purchases so that planned stock levels may be maintained. It may be broken down according to separate merchandise categories within a department or into specific quantities of individual items of merchandise. The breakdown depends on the amount and extent of control that management feels is necessary. For example, a large discount chain operation would use EDP replenishment controls to keep stock replenished and balanced according to sales, classification, style, size, color, or whatever.

The OTB may be calculated either in dollars or in units. For example, let us say that a woman buyer has planned purchases for the month of August at $2,000. By August 20, she has spent $1,500 for merchandise that has been received or that will be received into the department before the end of the month. This leaves $500 for her to spend during the remaining time; therefore, she is open to buy $500 worth of merchandise on August 20. The dollar open-to-buy formula may be calculated as follows:

Planned Purchases	$ 2,000
− Merchandise on Order	1,500
= Open-to-buy	$ 500

In practice, however, the open-to-buy formula is far more complicated than this illustration shows. Adjustments are often necessary due to fluctuations in reductions, sales, and availability of goods. Also, merchandise ordered but not yet received may further complicate the open-to-buy figure. For example:

Planned Sales	$ 50,000
+ Planned Reductions	10,000
+ Planned End-of-month Stock	40,000
= Total Needs for the Month	$ 100,000
− Beginning-of-month Stock	25,000
= Planned Purchases	$ 75,000
− Merchandise on Order	30,000
= Open-to-buy	$ 45,000

The OTB figure shows how much merchandise may be received into a particular department or merchandise classification during the course of a month without exceeding the planned inventory at the end of the month.[4]

For the OTB to be an effective control measure, however, careful checks must be made concerning all orders placed with vendors; therefore, merchandise must be ordered on the appropriate form or purchase order.

Other Control Methods: Inventory Reports/Electronic Controls

Inventory Reports. Another method used to control future merchandise inventories is the use of inventory reports. Once a physical inventory is taken, all information derived from the various inventory forms (inventory sheets, tags, punch cards) are analyzed by inventory price, classification, season, and by department in relation to sales.

If the punch-card method is used to take inventory, sorting by department, classification, season, and price line is accomplished automatically. If inventory sheets or tags are used, the information is sent to the computer center, where a card is punched for each item appearing on the inventory sheet or on each inventory tag. These cards are then fed into the computer, which issues a typed, classified report. When department totals are added, the result gives the dollar value of merchandise in the entire store. The buyer can then determine whether he should reduce his present inventory.

If a number of slow sellers are discovered, an effort is made to clear out old stock by listing these items on special slow-selling sheets. An inventory is taken of slow-selling merchandise, either daily, weekly, or monthly. Additional markdowns may be necessary to move the stock.

Sales and stock reports assist buyers or store managers in making decisions regarding inventory conditions. The following list is representative of the kinds of reports buyers and managers receive on a daily, weekly, or monthly basis.

Reports used by buyers and store managers to assist in decision making regarding inventory conditions

1. Daily sales reports
2. Sales by style, vendor, best seller, classification, color and size, price line
3. Exception reports

Daily sales reports. The daily sales report shows how rapidly or how slowly inventory is being converted to sales. It is a day-to-day indication of progress toward the department's or store's sales goals and serves as a reminder to adjust inventory. It informs the buyer of possible changes in consumer demand, either throughout the entire store or in particular departments. If daily sales figures are high or low for several days running and there is no obvious explanation, such as unusual weather conditions, special sales promotions, or changes in economic conditions, then the buyer should carefully search for possible reasons.

Sales by style, vendor, best sellers, classification, color and size, price line. A type of reporting system used by some department stores is a computerized system called the SABRE System. It provides sales activity reports to buyers or group managers on a weekly basis, both in the parent store and in the branches. Figure 9–10 is an example of a Weekly Buyers Style Status Report that shows unit sales for the entire week, one week ago, month to date, and season to date. Sales totals in units are given by style, class, subclass, and department. Within each classification, the percentage of each store's weekly unit sales is compared to the total corporate unit sales.

The buyer may also receive a Vendor Summary Report (Figure 9–11), which provides unit sales information for all styles of each vendor within a department by location. The frequency of the report is predetermined by the buyer, and the report may be received once a week, twice a week, quarterly, or upon request of the merchandise manager. Unit sales by vendor are provided for the week to date (WTD), one week ago (1WA), month to date (MTD), and season to date (STD). The Vendor Summary Report contains information by classification, selling price, vendor, style, and branch store.

In many cases the selling activity of the parent store tends to outweigh each branch store's selling activity; therefore, the buyer will request a Suburban Store Best Seller Report (Figure 9–12). This report isolates the ten best selling styles by dollar volume by department for each separate branch or suburban store. Sales in units are provided for this week (T.W.), last week (L.W.), and two weeks ago (2 wks. ago). The report may be distributed once

Figure 9-10 Weekly Buyers Style Status Report shows unit sales for the entire week, one week ago, month to date, and season to date. Sales totals in units are given by style, class, subclass, and department. (Courtesy of John Wanamaker Department Store, Philadelphia, Pa.)

CLASS	Selling Price	Vndr.	Style	STORE	Week To Date	One Week Ago	Month To Date	Season To Date
21	356000	01	1021	02		1		5
				07		2		3
			TOTAL			3		28
21	360000	02	2115	04	1		1	1
			TOTAL		1		1	2
21	380000	02	2116	02		1		2
				06	1		1	1
			TOTAL		1	1	1	5
21	400000	01	1095	05	2		2	2
				10		1		1
			TOTAL		2	1	2	5
21	400000	01	5017	02		1		1
			TOTAL			1		1
21	400000	02	4331	01		1		1
			TOTAL			1		1
21	410000	03	3629	07		1		1
			TOTAL			1		1
21	412500	01	1022	05		1		1
				11		1		1
			TOTAL			2		2
21	416905	48	0244	01	1	2	1	7
				03	1		1	1
				10		1		2
				11				3
			TOTAL		3	3	3	14
21	420000	02	3362	05	1		1	1
			TOTAL		1		1	2
21	425000	61	0116	07		2		2
			TOTAL			2		2
21	425000	67	7777	07		1		1
			TOTAL			1		1
21	425001	51	2200	01	1		1	1
				04	1		1	1
			TOTAL		2		2	2
21	440000	33	6290	03		1		1
			TOTAL			1		2
21	450000	33	6300	02		1		1
				08		1		1
			TOTAL			2		3
21	468500	11	0240	04		1		6
			TOTAL			1		46
21	475000	11	0000	02		2		3
				05		1		1
				07		1		1
			TOTAL			4		5
21	475000	11	0210	01	1		1	1
				06	1		1	1
				11	1		1	1
			TOTAL		3		3	4

Figure 9-11 Vendor Summary Report provides unit sales information for all styles of each vendor within a department by location. (Courtesy of John Wanamaker Department Store, Philadelphia, Pa.)

CLASS	Selling Price	Vndr.	Style	STORE	Week To Date	One Week Ago	Month To Date	Season To Date
22	325000	12	0050	08	1		1	6
			TOTL		1		1	1
			TOTL		1		1	1
22	350000	13	0111	11	1		1	1
			TOTL		1		1	4
22	400000	13	0222	01		1	1	1
			TOTL			1	1	5
22	400000	13	0850	01		1	1	3
			TOTL			1	1	4
22	450000	13	0290	06		1	1	2
			TOTL			1	1	23
22	475000	13	0240	05		1	1	1
			TOTL			1	1	2
22	525000	13	0261	11	1		1	1
			TOTL		1		1	5
22	600000	13	0290	05		1	1	5
			TOTL		1	1	2	8
31	400000	11	0500	02	1		1	2
				04		1	1	1
				05	1		1	1
			TOTL		2	1	3	6
31	400000	11	0850	01		2	2	2
				02				
				03				
				04				
				05		1	1	2
				06				
				07		1	1	2
				08		1	1	2
				09	1		1	1
				10				
				11				
			TOTL		1	5	6	8
31	400000	13	0950	01		1	1	1
			TOTL			1	1	3
31	550000	11	0222	04	2		2	2
			TOTL		2		2	4
31	750000	11	2250	02	1		1	1
			TOTL		1		1	5
31	800000	01	0000	04	1		1	1
			TOTL		1		1	1
31	800000	11	3250	05		1	1	1
			TOTL			1	1	3
32	400000	13	0222	09	1		1	1
			TOTL		1		1	2
32	525000	13	0260	09	1		1	1
			TOTL		1		1	1
40	275000	12	0030	02	1		1	1

a week, usually on Monday morning, to the divisional merchandise manager, the buyer, and the general manager for all departments for each branch store. The report contains information according to classification number and name, vendor number and name, style number, single unit price, and total store dollars.

Figure 9–12 Suburban Best Seller Report. This report identifies a suburban store's ten best selling styles by dollar volume by department for each separate branch or suburban store. (Courtesy of John Wanamaker Department Store, Philadelphia, Pa.)

```
REED - LEISURE RECR                      BEST SELLERS REPORT                                    FMSPR068

DPT NO    DESCRIPTION      VENDOR NAME       VEN  STYLE  UNIT     TOTAL        U N I T S
CLASS                                       NO.  NO.    PRICE    DOLLARS    T.W.  L.W.    2 WKS AGO

075-00    LUGGAGE          WYNNEWOOD                       BEST SELLERS REPORT        WEEK ENDING  03/15/75

60  CANVAS LUGGAGE        YORK LUGGAGE CORP   015  0526   55.00    110        2
21  WOMENS LUGGAGE        ATLANTIC PRODUCTS   054  8824   43.99     88        2
21  WOMENS LUGGAGE        AMERICAN TOURISTER  001  1027   72.50     73        1
22  WOMENS LUGGAGE        LARK LUGGAGE        020  0021   54.00     54        1
21  WOMENS LUGGAGE        SAMSONITE           002  5629   45.00     45        1
21  WOMENS LUGGAGE        YORK LUGGAGE CORP   015  1220   42.50     43        1
40  BRIEF CASE ATTACHE    SAMSONITE           002  0443   42.00     42        1
31  MENS LUGGAGE          SAMSONITE           002  2133   42.00     42        1
31  MENS LUGGAGE          SAMSONITE           002  3352   40.00     40        1
21  WOMENS LUGGAGE        YORK LUGGAGE CORP   015  1214   40.00     40        1
                                        TOTALS                    577       12
```

In addition to the Suburban Store Best Seller Report, buyers and merchandise managers receive a Weekly Classification Sales Report (Figure 9–13), which summarizes unit and dollar sales by class on a weekly basis and is used as an input into the classification "open-to-buy." It is usually distributed once a week. The report contains regular unit and dollar sales and percent to classification and markdown unit and dollar sales and percent to classification, as well as total department regular and markdown dollar sales. The percentages are comparisons of each store's *class* units and dollars with each store's *department* total units and dollars.

For departments (usually fashion) where unit control is based on color and size, the Unit Control-Color/Size Posting Report (U/LC) shows unit sales at these levels by store. This report may be distributed twice a week, with one copy sent to the unit control office. The form contains information on vendor, style, color, size, class, and price. Unit control keeps a daily record of basic merchandise, of deductions, and of what has been received into inventory.

Besides the Unit Control-Color/Size Posting Report, the buyer and merchandise manager receive a monthly Classification Price Line Report, which provides information in units for each department by location for each price line within each classification. The report contains information on class number, price, store, unit sales for each month of a season, and total dollar sales for price line by classification for each store.

Exception reports. It is important that the buyer locate problems as well as opportunities in stock-sales relationships to ensure effective merchandise replenishments. Most stores use a computerized system that simplifies the problem of locating exceptions; hence, the use of exception reports. Once certain sales and inventory standards have been planned for a specific period in a department, the information is sent to the computer center. The computer periodically prints out information on stock items that do not meet predetermined standards and are, therefore, exceptions. When an exception report is received, the buyer carefully reviews why sales are low or why sales are high on certain items. Immediate action should be taken to rid the department of merchandise items that are slow sellers by using new display techniques, markdowns, store transfers, special sales promotions, and so forth. The exception report that shows best sellers is important to the buyer because it enables prompt identification of fast-selling sections of the

Figure 9–13 Weekly Classification Sales Report. This report summarizes unit and dollar sales by class on a weekly basis for regular and markdown dollar sales. (Courtesy of John Wanamaker Department Store, Philadelphia, Pa.)

LEISURE RECR — DEPARTMENT 075-00 — WEEKLY CLASSIFICATION SALES REPORT — FMSPR12

		REGULAR				/	MARKDOWN				/	TOTAL SUBCLASS			
		UNITS	%	DOLLARS	%	/ UNITS	%	DOLLARS	%	/	UNITS	%	DOLLARS	%
S-CLASS 000	04	1	100	36	100	/				/	1	100	36	100
SUBCLASS TOTAL		1	100	36	100	/				/	1	100	36	100
S-CLASS 010	02	2	100	65	100	/				/	2	100	65	100
SUBCLASS TOTAL		2	100	65	100	/				/	2	100	65	100
S-CLASS 020 WOMENS LUGG	01	1	4	48	6	/				/	1	4	48	5
	03	1	11	30	8	/				/	1	11	30	8
	11	1	20	50	26	/				/	1	20	50	26
SUBCLASS TOTAL		3	4	128	4	/				/	3	4	128	4
S-CLASS 021	01	12	57	462	59	/ 1	100	30	100	/	13	59	492	61
	03	8	88	337	91	/				/	8	88	337	91
	04	5	83	251	83	/				/	5	83	251	83
	05	7	70	290	67	/				/	7	70	290	67
	06	3	75	109	70	/				/	3	75	109	70
	07	4	100	284	100	/				/	4	100	284	100
	08	1	33	25	34	/				/	1	33	25	34
	11	3	60	114	61	/				/	3	60	114	61
SUBCLASS TOTAL		43	68	1,872	72	/ 1	100	30	100	/	44	68	1,902	72
S-CLASS 022	01	8	38	263	34	/				/	8	36	263	32
	02	1	100	25	100	/				/	1	100	25	100
	04	1	16	50	16	/				/	1	16	50	16
	05	3	30	138	32	/				/	3	30	138	32
	06	1	25	45	29	/				/	1	25	45	29
	08	2	66	47	65	/				/	2	66	47	65
	11	1	20	22	11	/				/	1	20	22	11
SUBCLASS TOTAL		17	26	590	22	/				/	17	26	590	22
CLASS 020 WOMENS LUGG	01	21	40	773	41	/ 1	100	30	100	/	22	41	803	42
	02	1	12	25	9	/				/	1	12	25	9
	03	9	60	367	67	/				/	9	60	367	67
	04	6	40	301	52	/				/	6	40	301	52
	05	10	43	428	46	/				/	10	43	428	46
	06	4	80	154	95	/				/	4	80	154	95
	07	4	44	284	62	/				/	4	44	284	62
	08	3	42	72	38	/				/	3	42	72	38
	11	5	71	186	72	/				/	5	71	186	72
CLASS TOTAL		63	43	2,590	48	/ 1	100	30	100	/	64	43	2,620	68

assortment for the purpose of determining specific areas in which consumer demand is strong (color, size, style, etc.) and can possibly be made stronger.

How will the following information assist the buyer or store manager in making fast, accurate decisions regarding the condition of the merchandise inventory?

1. Daily sales reports
2. Buyer's style status report
3. Vendor summary report
4. Suburban store best seller report
5. Weekly classification sales report
6. Unit control-color/size posting report
7. Classification price line report
8. Exception reports

Electronic Controls. Many small businesses, general merchandise operations, department stores, variety stores, specialty shops, and food stores have turned to electronic controls to facilitate counting procedures and forecast future merchandising activities. The computer is used by retail executives in many aspects of retailing; however, it is especially suited to the control of merchandise inventories. For example, most large department stores and specialty shops are using sales registers which record on tape the department number, classification, style number, amount of sale, and number of the salesperson for each sales transaction. At the end of the day, register tapes are taken to the computer center, where they are processed. The following day, the store buyer is furnished with a detailed report of the previous day's sales. Daily information concerning net sales, customer returns, fast-selling items, slow sellers, and merchandise on hand will assist buying specialists to make decisions affecting markdowns, reorders, vendor returns, and consumer demand. The computer also issues a list of all stock items to be counted on any given day, and by means of an optical scanner, it will provide a complete list of merchandise in stock. Provision of fast, accurate data retrieval to ensure correct merchandising decisions has been achieved by the use of EDP equipment.

The National Retail Merchants Association (NRMA) has developed a group EDP service, whereby small businesses may make arrangements to send register tapes of sales and inventory data to the NRMA computer service bureau. The NRMA computer sorts the transactions into merchandise classifications and sends back printed sales and inventory reports for classifications and departments as well as for the entire store.[7]

In the multiunit chain operation, EDP is a more elaborate, sophisticated procedure. A variety store chain may use an automatic replenishment system that keeps track, by means of a special tape, of each order placed by each store in the chain. The computer keeps a record of each item shipped and from the monthly on-hand reports it knows how many items are sold. By correlating each store's merchandise history with its monthly on-hand reports, the data-processing center can forecast and order shipment of the quantities of each item (usually staple goods) that will be required by each store over a certain period of time. It is important for each store to accurately record merchandise on hand, so that the store will not overstock or run out of an item. An inventory should be taken at least every two weeks; more often, if needed. At inventory time, the store manager or the staff will check to see how many units of merchandise are on hand, both on the selling floor and in the stockroom. A report is then sent to the data-processing center, where items will be either reordered or canceled.

In between the monthly on-hand reports, the store buyer may notice that the store is out of an item, very low on an item, or, upon receipt of a shipment, has more of an item than it needs. If this is the case, another report will be prepared to tell the EDP center that figures for store totals of that item need adjustment. Once this report is sent to the EDP center, immediate action is taken to adjust the store's stock by changing the amount of merchandise that will be shipped in the future.

As you recall, a good control system must be accurate, timely, and understood by the members of the organization if it is to be an effective tool in managerial decision making. Thus, an EDP center should issue guidelines that store personnel may use for reference and as reminders when filling out various EDP forms. Guidelines may include instructions to write numbers legibly; refrain from stapling, folding, or tearing reports; and record numbers accurately.

ADVANTAGES AND LIMITATIONS OF MERCHANDISE CONTROLS

The purpose of a good control system has already been stated: (1) to assist store managers, department store buyers, and small-store owners to make effective purchases, (2) to ensure prompt reordering, and (3) to prevent purchase of merchandise that is unacceptable to the consumer. However, retail stores have found that control measures also offer limitations along with their many advantages, and close attention must be given to both when determining which control system is best for the individual store or department. The following list of advantages and limitations should be consulted by all retailers when considering the adoption of merchandise controls.

Advantages of Merchandise Controls

Ensure Meeting Consumer Needs and Wants. An important responsibility of retailers is to provide merchandise that consumers need and want, at a price they are willing to pay, in a convenient location. Since consumer demand may change from day to day, season to season, and year to year, a merchant often has difficulty in determining such demands. Merchandise controls that are effectively implemented will assist the buyer by indicating stock items that are fast moving and slow selling, as well as items that have proved unsatisfactory and have been returned by customers

Improve Profits. A well-balanced stock will usually lead to greater sales and, thus, fewer markdowns. Good merchandise controls will improve profits by indicating trends and conditions that may affect the balance of stock. Such controls may focus attention on fast- and slow-moving stock items, assist the buyer in reorders, and help keep stocks up to date through sales promotion and advertising.

Minimize Inventory Investment. It is usually desirable to keep the investment in merchandise inventory at the lowest possible level consistent with fulfillment of consumer demand. This also results in a better rate of stockturn. Merchandise controls tell the buyer when it is necessary to reorder merchandise, take markdowns, order new stock items, and eliminate merchandise that has proved unappealing.

Reduce Slow Sellers. Slow-selling merchandise will decrease profits when not handled properly. Therefore, a store manager or buyer continuously seeks feedback information regarding stock turnover from salespeople, department managers, and assistant buyers. Merchandise controls provide accurate information, usually on a daily basis, and facilitate buyer decisions about items that should be marked down, transferred, or returned to vendors.

Reduce the Cost of Selling. Since good merchandise controls provide information about stock turnover, slow-moving merchandise, and popular stock items, the cost of selling may be reduced. Unnecessary markdowns will be eliminated, warehousing and transportation costs reduced, and popular or new items can be moved onto the selling floor into space that might otherwise have been occupied by marked down merchandise. Good controls make selling easier and lead to a well-balanced stock assortment.

Provide Buying Information. For buyers to make accurate decisions regarding the merchandise assortment, they must receive up-to-date selling information. Merchandise control really begins *before* goods are purchased from vendors and manufacturers. Before entering the marketplace, therefore, buyers should be aware of sales trends, customer returns, defective merchandise, popular types and prices of merchandise, current fashion trends, markdowns taken to sell goods, and other information of a similar nature. Good merchandise controls provide information to serve as a guide in making purchasing commitments.

Advantages of merchandise controls

1. Ensure meeting consumer needs, wants, desires
2. Improve profits
3. Minimize inventory investment
4. Reduce slow sellers
5. Reduce the cost of selling
6. Provide buying information

Limitations of merchandise controls

1. Require frequent reviews
2. No substitute for experience
3. Expensive to operate
4. Require follow-up
5. Require thorough understanding

Limitations of Merchandise Controls

Require Frequent Reviews. Since merchandise control systems are set up to provide specific types of information under a given set of circumstances, they should be reviewed frequently. Retailing is always changing; its people and its systems must keep pace. All too often, control systems that provide important merchandise information are continued long past the time when the information they provide becomes obsolete. The merchandise manager, central buyer, or store manager must frequently review the types of merchandise controls in use and to determine if they are effective under new sets of circumstances.

No Substitute for Experience. Merchandise controls should never be used to substitute for experience, knowledge, or decision making. They should be looked upon only as supplementary to management know-how. Whether a buyer deals with staple goods or fashion goods, merchandise information should always be analyzed and interpreted in the light of new situations. A good retail executive will not depend totally on a computer printout, since such information has been supplied indirectly by human beings and is, therefore, subject to inaccuracies.

Expensive to Operate. Merchandise control systems are not only costly to install but also expensive to operate and maintain. Since they need to be revised frequently, additional expense is incurred in retraining personnel to use the new methods. Retailers often hesitate to install newer electronic devices, and then find that their competition is already one jump ahead of them. Other retailers fail to recognize the many benefits of newer control systems. However, the decision as to which type of control system to implement in a business is based upon the finances available and the size and type of the retail operation.

Require Follow-up. Some retail stores, aware that competition is using highly sophisticated control systems, have adopted similar systems, thinking that good control systems would result automatically. However, a good control system exists only when the information received is interpreted and translated into meaningful action. Buyers must learn to accurately interpret information if it is to help them select merchandise assortments that will meet the needs of their customers and, thus, make profits for their stores.

Require Thorough Understanding. For merchandise control systems to operate effectively, merchandise managers, central buyers, assistant buyers, salespeople, and stock personnel—in other words, the entire work force— must thoroughly understand the operating procedures involved in a good merchandise control system. For example, salespeople must properly record returned or damaged merchandise, stock personnel must take accurate counts during inventory periods, and assistant buyers must accurately record merchandise that has been transferred to a branch store or returned to the vendor. All involved in the merchandising activity of the retail store should be made aware of the purposes and objectives of merchandise control systems.

How will the advantages and limitations of merchandise controls affect merchandising activities in:

A small men's wear business?   A specialty chain operation?

A discount department store?   A medium-sized furniture store?

Chapter Summary

Control provides a means to inform top management whether or not established standards are functioning according to plan, and it provides a basis for changes to correct problems that have already occurred. There are three elements important to a good control system: (1) the establishment of control standards, (2) the measurement of performance, and (3) the analysis and correction of deviations from planned standards. The kind and type of control system required by a retail business will depend upon its merchandising policy, the size of the store, and its clientele.

There are certain requirements that are characteristic of any control system. A good control system should (1) call attention to deviations, (2) suggest a means of solving the problem, (3) be accurate and timely, (4) be understood by the members of the organization, and (5) be economical. An important tool used by management in planning, coordinating, and controlling various control systems is the budget, a plan that forecasts specific merchandising activities for a specified period of time.

Merchandise control may be defined as maintenance of a stock of merchandise that is adjusted to the needs of customers and prospective customers. There are two major forms of merchandise control that store management may consider: (1) dollar control and (2) unit control. Dollar control may be defined as the amount of dolalrs at retail prices invested in the merchandise inventory. Dollar control answers the question "How much?" It may be applied to departments, to classifications or to specific price lines. Unit control is an organized method of recording the individual units or pieces of merchandise found in the inventory; it answers the question "What?"

Dollar control and unit control may be operated either through a perpetual inventory system or a periodic inventory system. The perpetual inventory system derives sales information from sales and purchase records that record merchandise on hand in terms of what has been received and what has been sold at regular intervals, such as every day, week, or month. In contrast, the periodic inventory system derives sales information from inventory and purchase data by periodically adding opening inventory and purchases and subtracting the sum of the closing inventory and markdowns. The student should review how dollar control and unit control may be operated through either system.

There are other types of inventory systems used in unit control: visual control, tickler control, warehouse control, want-slip control and the physical inventory. The selection of one or all of these inventory systems depends upon the special needs of the business operation.

The merchandise inventory is the assortment of goods available for sale to the ultimate consumer. Unlike inventories of merchandise carried by most other types of businesses, inventories carried by retail stores have certain differentiating characteristics.

A physical inventory is the actual counting and recording of the amount of merchandise or stock on hand at a specified time together with the cost or retail price of each merchandise item. There are several reasons for taking a physical inventory: (1) to help in the preparation of financial statements; (2) to familiarize personnel with the stock assortment; (3) to aid inventory analysis; (4) to determine stock shortages and overages; (5) sales determination. Some types of retail stores require little advance preparation. However, in a department store or chain operation the procedure for taking a physical inventory is far more complex. The inventory procedure may be broken down into three steps: the times of the inventory, the planning stage, counting, recording, and checking.

Trade Terminology

DIRECTIONS: Briefly explain or discuss each of the following trade terms:

1. Control standards
2. Merchandise control
3. Dollar control
4. Departmental control
5. Classification control
6. Price-line control
7. Unit control
8. Perpetual inventory system
9. Periodic inventory system
10. Tickler file
11. Merchandise inventory
12. Physical inventory
13. Cost method of inventory
14. First-in first-out method (FIFO)
15. Last-in first-out method (LIFO)
16. Book method of inventory
17. Closing book inventory
18. Retail method of inventory
19. Merchandise overage
20. Merchandise shortage

Questions for Discussion and Review

1. What is meant by the statement "A good control system will be built into management's business objectives during the initial planning stage?"

2. What elements should be present in every control system?

3. Discuss how a good control system can accomplish the following: call attention to deviations, be accurate and timely, be economical.

4. Prepare an outline of the steps you would follow when taking a physical inventory. Could this procedure to used in a small retail business? Explain.

5. You have been asked to write a paper on the topic "The use of electronic data processing in merchandise replenishment." What topics would you cover and why?

6. Summarize the essential differences between unit control and dollar control.

7. Under what conditions would you recommend the use of the following inventory reports: daily sales reports; unit control—color/size posting report; exception report; and vendor summary report? Why?

8. At the start of a six-month period a men's shirt department had an inventory of $59,200 at retail. Purchases during the period amounted to $96,400 at retail. Sales for the period were $88,000, and markdowns were $5,000. Find the book inventory.

9. What information must be provided so that you can determine the cost or market value of inventory? What is the retail method of inventory?

10. Define periodic inventory system and perpetual inventory system. What other types of inventory systems may be used in unit control?

11. Why is a knowledge of the average rate of stock shortages necessary to determine actual sales? Illustrate the formula used to determine actual or net sales.

12. What advantages and limitations should the buyer or store manager consider before implementing merchandise control systems?

Case Study—Number Nine

PROBLEMS WITH INVENTORY

As assistant buyer in the children's shoe department, you have been concerned with the problem of too much inventory remaining in stock at the end of the selling season. This situation has resulted in an imbalance in stock assortment, several markdown periods, and an increase in merchandise costs. You have also noticed that, due to faulty vendor deliveries and the lack of adequate follow-up, merchandise has not been received into the department when requested. The buyer has had difficulty in determining how much open-to-buy is available and is unable to meet the steady flow of consumer demand. Your buyer has invited you to attend a meeting with the merchandise manager to discuss the problems with inventory. Develop a list of suggestions you would recommend to help solve the problems. Be prepared to discuss your recommendations in class.

Case Study—Number Ten

STOCK TURN IN A SMALL BUSINESS

As an independent businessman, Jerry Grover felt very strongly about maintaining a competitive yet well-balanced stock assortment. In the first three years of operating his small sporting-goods business, he went through many periods of trial and error while attempting to merchandise the store. He quickly learned the importance of careful and accurate inventory planning and control and was especially concerned with stock turnover. Jerry's business was primarily a discount type of operation; therefore, rapid turnover and low markup were his basic business objectives. He had limited capital and was always concerned with increasing sales volume on the same or smaller stock investment. Often he had to take a short-term loan for additional inventories, particularly during the Christmas season.

Jerry's assistant Bob Meyer was attending college on a part-time basis as a retail-marketing major. Jerry felt that Bob might be of some assistance in the area of good inventory control. One day he expressed to Bob his problems in determining stock turn. He stated that he could not accurately estimate how much merchandise was disposed of or depleted and replaced during certain selling periods. He further stated that in the past he had had to take short-term loans to have enough money to invest in inventory. He felt this was a definite disadvantage, since the cost of the loan was cutting into his profits and, as a discounter, he was working on a low markup to begin with. He asked Bob to make some suggestions regarding the situation.

Bob told Jerry that a retail store may use three methods to compute stock turn. It can determine stock turn on a retail basis, where net sales at retail is divided by the average stock at retail; it can determine stock on a cost basis, where the cost of the goods sold is divided by average cost of stock; or it can determine stock on a physical unit basis, where the number of units sold is divided by the average number of units in stock.

There were other problems in determining the stock turn. Jerry had a problem in determining his average inventory. Bob informed him he could take his actual stock at the beginning of the year and the end of the year, add them, and divide by two. However, as in most stores, 60 percent of the sales occurred during the Christmas season; therefore, the average inventory carried throughout the year would not be accurate and the stock turnover figure too high. Bob suggested that Jerry calculate the inventory at the beginning of the year, during the middle, and at the end. He could sum the three inventories and divide by 3 to determine the average inventory. Or a more accurate method of determining average inventory might be to divide the sum of the stocks on the first of every month, plus the ending stock, by 13 (since he would start out with one month's inventory).

Before Jerry begins to determine the best method of stock turn, what kind of information should be available? When determining average inventory, what method of calculation would you suggest? Do you agree that there are advantages to rapid stock turnover?

Case Study—Number Eleven

THE BEST-MADE PLANS

You have recently been hired to manage The Closet Shop, a specialty store selling linens, towels, bath accessories, and related merchandise. Your previous experience has been with a department store. You feel that The Closet Shop needs to improve its merchandising planning. You have noticed that merchandise is not planned well enough in advance; there is an excess of goods in the bath accessories classification, and not enough merchandise is available in the linen classification. Also, customers have been asking for the season's popular color combinations, and the merchandise assortment of items in these colors is not complete.

From your experience and knowledge of merchandise planning, what course of action would you suggest? Outline a merchandse plan you feel is appropriate for this type of store.

Case Study—Number Twelve

WHITE BEAR— A WHITE ELEPHANT?

The Locker Room is a well-known medium-sized sporting-goods store located in a New England city, where Barbara Blenheim has been the buyer of ski wear for the past five years. Barbara's department has been operating on a very sound basis with respect to profit, volume, inventory turnover, and so forth. The department does an annual volume of approximately $450,000.

For the past five years Ms. Blenheim has conducted an end-of-season promotion on ski wear, which has always met with enormous success. Held in late February, the sale has usually grossed approximately $50,000 for the store each year.

This January, White Bear, a well-known nationally advertised manufacturer of ski clothing and one of Ms. Blenheim's regular suppliers, has announced a reduction in price on all ski wear. White Bear has had a poor selling season due to bad weather and an overloaded inventory. When Barbara Blenheim first became aware of this situation, she realized that the White Bear company would offer the remaining line to her before anyone else in the area. She has been informed that she can have delivery within three days. The total cost of the merchandise will amount to $15,000, less 35 percent special discount. However, Ms. Blenheim is concerned that if she purchases additional merchandise and offers it at a reduced price during the month of January, which is still her peak selling period, it may affect the sale of her complete stock of ski wear, which has already been purchased at the regular prices. Furthermore, she fears that a preseason sale may affect the annual end-of-season sale, which she must offer. Barbara realizes, however, that if she turns down the White Bear offer, it will go to her competition. The advantages of purchasing the reduced line are many. However, there are disadvantages to consider. If you were Barbara Blenheim, how would you handle this situation?

Case Study—Number Thirteen

A FATHER-AND-DAUGHTER BUSINESS

Mr. Stevens has been successfully running his medium-sized children's shoe business for the past twenty years. He decided, however, to pass the business on to his daughter, Elizabeth, who had worked in the store while attending college. His daughter was enthusiastic about taking over her father's business and was eager to institute many changes. For example, she was very concerned about the growth of the children's shoe market and the necessity of broadening the stock assortment to meet consumer demand. To accomplish this, it was necessary to take a closer look at inventory control methods presently in use. Inventory was taken twice a year. The stock assortment was broken down according to price, style, size, and classification, and value was based on the amount of dollars at retail prices. A visual count was taken when "someone had the time," and reorders were placed when the stockroom inventory was depleted. Clerical help was used to tabulate the results of the inventory. Mr. Stevens felt that his method of inventory control was very efficient and resisted the idea of changing an inventory method that had worked well for twenty years. If you were Elizabeth Stevens, how would you convince your father that changes were necessary? Be prepared in class to discuss the changes you would suggest.

Case Study—Number Fourteen

INHERITED
INVENTORY PROBLEMS

Lloyd & Burns, located in a large New England city, has always catered to a well-to-do, conservative clientele. This large women's specialty store does an annual volume of approximately 35 million dollars and prides itself on being a high-quality, personal-service type of retail establishment.

As a conservative business, however, L & B never really enjoyed the reputation of real fashion leadership. The management determined that a number of the store's competitors were using the "boutique approach" in merchandising to add a high-fashion image to their stores. Management decided that Lloyd & Burns would try its hand at this new merchandising approach in an effort to gain higher fashion recognition.

Shortly thereafter, the "Royal Garb Boutique" was opened, with a buyer responsible for purchasing exclusive, high-fashion types of merchandise. The buyer was provided with an assistant, two full-time salespeople, part-time sales help, and stock personnel.

The "Royal Garb Boutique" was a success. Store volume increased as a result of the addition of the boutique, and L & B was gaining an image as a high-fashion store. After three years the buyer was rewarded with a promotion and took over the buying responsibilities of a much larger department, the women's better coat department.

When Gwen Franklin, an assistant buyer in fashion costume jewelry, heard that a buyer's position was available, and in the Royal Garb Boutique, at that, she immediately applied for the position. After several interviews, she was informed that she was to be the new buyer for the boutique. However, Gwen was soon to discover that along with a successful department she was also about to inherit serious inventory problems.

For various reasons, Gwen's predecessor had allowed a large amount of old merchandise to accumulate in the stockroom. The merchandise consisted of expensive blouses, handbags, sweaters, and other accessory items. When Gwen checked the price tickets for the seasonal code, she was amazed to learn that some of the merchandise was more than two years old. She immediately realized that she must take a physical count of all merchandise on hand to determine the condition of the merchandise assortment. She soon discovered that over 25% of her dollar stock was tied up in old or slow-moving merchandise. For some reason, her predecessor had allowed old merchandise to accumulate in stock while new items were being sold.

The Christmas season was rapidly approaching. Gwen realized that almost half of her sales volume would occur between November and January. However, she was overloaded with old and out-of-style goods, a limited open-to-buy, expensive markdowns, and limited storage and selling space. She was in trouble inventorywise, budgetwise, seasonwise. The department's fashion image was in jeopardy.

Outline a plan of activities that Gwen could follow to help her solve her inventory problems. How could she avoid the recurrence of these problems in the future?

Learning Activities

1. Interview the store manager of a variety chain operation; a discount chain; a department store branch. Prepare a list of questions based on the topic "How will the use of EDP improve merchandise replenishment systems?" Develop a list of future computer applications in areas other than merchandising.

2. Interview the manager of a small hardware store; a small variety store. What forms of merchandise control are used by each store? What kinds of problems has each store manager had to deal with when initiating good control procedures?

3. You have been asked to write a term paper on the topic "Why is control an important management activity?" Referring to the list of references that follows, develop an outline of the important points you wish to emphasize.

4. Contact a general-merchandise chain store and interview the store manager on the problems of inventory replenishment. What methods does the store use to communicate control information to its employees? Be prepared to discuss your findings in class.

5. Referring to the reference material listed in "The Retail Student's Reference Library," prepare a paper on the topic "High overhead and its effect on retail profits."

6. Visit three small businesses that deal in different types of merchandise lines, for example, a hardware store, a greeting-card shop, and a jewelry business. Discuss with the owner-manager methods used to determine stockturn for particular selling seasons.

References

THE RETAIL STUDENT'S REFERENCE LIBRARY

Basic Stock Lists, Infants and Children's Wear. New York: NRMA, n.d.

Drew-Bear, R. *Mass Merchandising: Revolution and Evolution.* New York: Fairchild Pub., Inc. n.d.

Ferguson, Frank. *Efficient Drug Store Management.* New York: Fairchild Pub., Inc. n.d.

Mulhern, Helen. *Facts about Department Stores.* New York: NMRA, n.d.

National Cash Register Company. *Register Enforced Automated Control Technique for Total Merchandise Control.* Dayton, Ohio: National Cash Register Co. n.d.

National Retail Merchants Association. Operations Research in Retailing—Case Studies and Electronic Data Processing for Retailers. New York: NRMA, n.d.

Retail Inventory Methods in Practical Operations. New York: NRMA, n.d.

Status of EDP in Retailing. New York: NRMA, n.d.

Taylow, C. G. *Merchandise Assortment Planning.* New York: NRMA, n.d.

Techniques of Fashion Merchandising. Indianapolis: ITT Pub. Co., n.d.

Want Slip Policies and Systems in Department Stores. New York: NRMA, n.d.

REFERENCES

1. Jerry B. Poe, *An Introduction to the American Business Enterprise* (Homewood, Ill.: Richard D. Irwin, Inc., 1972), pp. 158–61.
2. Ibid., pp. 162–64.
3. Delbert J. Duncan and C. F. Phillips, *Retailing Principles and Methods* (Homewood, Ill.: Richard D. Irwin, Inc., 1969), p. 366.
4. Ibid., pp. 371–72.
5. Albert I. Schott and Herbert A. Turetzky, *Retailer's Guide to Merchandise Classification Control* (New York: National Retail Merchants Association, 1969), p. 1.

6. Ibid., p. 55.
7. Bernard Codner, "Retail Management Systems—The Present and the Future," *Retail Control,* April–May 1970, pp. 3–5.
8. Duncan and Philips, *Retailing Principles and Methods,* pp. 382–83.
9. Ibid., p. 385.

SECTION

4

The Buyer's Role in Locating Merchandise Resources: Domestic and Foreign

Photo courtesy of The Merchandise Mart (left) and The Apparel Center (right).

The Resident Buying Office

Performance Objectives

After reading this chapter the student should be able to accomplish the following:

1. Define resident buying office and resident buyer.

2. Trace the development of the resident buying office from the early days of retailing to the present.

3. Outline the two major types of resident buying offices and discuss each.

4. Give the important qualifications that should be considered when selecting a resident buying office.

5. Relate the similarities that exist between the resident buying office and a client store and between the resident buyer and the store buyer.

6. Describe how each type of resident buying office is organized.

7. Evaluate the many and varied services offered by most resident buying offices.

8. Explain the responsibilities of a resident buyer.

The Resident Buying Office

Figure 10–1 Unless there is complete cooperation between the resident buyer and the retail store buyer, the many advantages offered by the resident buyer office may not be realized.

INTRODUCTION

In the previous chapter we were concerned with the control function of management and its application to merchandising. Control is often thought of as the fifth stage in the management process of planning, organizing, staffing, directing, and controlling. However, a good control system will be built into management's business objectives during the initial planning stage. Control provides a way to inform top management if established standards are or are not functioning according to plan. Control also provides a basis for making changes to correct problems that are already present.

There are two major forms of merchandise control, dollar control and unit control, that are regulated by two types of inventory systems, the perpetual inventory system and the periodic inventory system.

In most retail stores, the largest monetary investment is usually in the merchandise inventory. Unlike inventories of merchandise carried by most other types of businesses, inventories carried by retail stores have certain differentiating characteristics. Because the merchandise inventory is so varied, the problems of inventory planning and control become major ones.

In this chapter we are concerned with the kinds of assistance the buyer receives during the actual procurement process, which in turn will help minimize inventory control problems.

Retail buyers, whether of staple goods, fashion apparel, domestics, or hard goods, cannot rely on occasional market trips or visits by manufacturers' representatives alone since such activities may prove to be inadequate, time-consuming, and expensive. Many stores must seek the services of an outside agency called a resident buying office (RBO) that will provide a steady flow of market information on a local as well as on a national and international scope.

How does a store determine which type of resident buying office is suitable and reflects its image? There are a number of factors to consider when selecting an RBO ranging from cost to contractual arrangements to the kind and scope of services offered.

There are two major classifications of RBOs—the independent office and the store-owned office. There are a number of similarities in organization between a resident buying office and the client store. Resident buying offices are organized to save the retail buyer time and money and to provide professional assistance. As the buyer's "right arm" in the market place, the buying office eliminates unnecessary market trips, saves money, and offers a variety of services. A typical well-staffed buying office has four major functions: the merchandising function, which assists the store buyer in obtaining merchandise; the promotion function, which assists the store buying in selling the merchandise; the research function, which assists the store buyer in obtaining up-to-date market information to aid in decision making; and the ancillary function, which offers additional services to the retail buyer.

PART 1—Organization of a Resident Buying Office

AN OUTSIDE AGENCY

A *resident buying office* (RBO) is an agency whose primary responsibility and specialization is coverage of the various trade markets it represents. Those individuals who represent the resident buying office are called resident buyers (Figure 10–1).

A *resident buyer* is a buying specialist who works in the capacity of advisor or assistant to those stores represented by the office and who is responsible for all phases of merchandising and promotion. Resident buying offices, unlike retail stores, are located "in residence," or in the heart of the wholesale district. They become market representatives for the client stores.

A great majority of resident buying offices are located in New York City, since this city is the primary market for fashion apparel, soft goods and related accessories, hard goods, home furnishings, and appliances. Branch offices may also be located in Miami, which serves as a center for stores interested in southern fashion markets, while Los Angeles serves as a center for stores interested in West Coast fashions. Chicago, Rocky Mountain, North Carolina, and Atlanta serve as centers for home furnishings and hard goods. Resident buying offices are also located in the capital cities of Europe, South America and the Far East.

Resident buying offices represent many types of client stores. These stores are usually fairly similar in size and type of trade, but since they are located in different towns and cities, they do not compete with one another. Some offices may represent only large-volume department stores, while other offices represent both large and medium-sized department stores, giving complete coverage of both soft and hard lines. Some offices serve only specialty stores providing a single line of merchandise, such as furs or infants' and children's wear, or even a single department, such as millinery.

Buying offices are of all sizes. Some are literally one-person offices with only a few store accounts, while other offices may revolve around a single individual and yet have several buyers specializing in fashion or soft-goods lines. Still other offices represent several hundred stores and maintain large staffs with separate divisions for various types of goods, for example, men's and boys' wear, housewares, piece goods, and domestics. This concentration gives the retail store access to a team of buyers it could not possibly employ itself.

The resident buying office serves as an important link between stores and manufacturers by offering a variety of services. Buying offices play a major role in store merchandising and distribution. They give the retail-store buyer an opportunity to carry out his or her duties and responsibilities in a particular department with the security of knowing that someone is constantly scanning the principal markets for new merchandise, new resources, and favorable prices.

THE DEVELOPMENT
OF RESIDENT BUYING OFFICES

Resident buying offices first developed during the early days of retailing. The early resident buyer would travel to the central marketplace and purchase goods for a store owner who could not leave the store. The primary objective was the placement of orders.

Resident buying offices have continued to develop for many reasons. First, the small retailer found it was necessary to be represented in the marketplace, especially in the apparel and home-furnishing lines, since he or she was responsible not only for the buying-selling activity but also for the management of the entire retail store. Retailers soon realized that the "I'd-rather-do-it-myself" attitude was depriving them of dollar savings and often found themselves unaware of current customer demands and without popular lines of merchandise.

A second reason for the continued development of resident buying offices was the growth of multitudes of new products and the continuous changes in old products. The retail buyer found it difficult to keep up with new manufacturing techniques, new fibers and fabrics, and modifications of already existing product lines.

A third reason was to obtain assistance and advice in the selection of key resources and to maintain good working relations with these resources. Since retail buyers only visited the marketplace occasionally, it was necessary to provide a representative who would act as an agent between the source of supply and the retail store, ensuring an adequate, reliable communications system.

A fourth reason was to strengthen the trading position and purchasing power of individual stores. A retail store, unlike a chain store, does not have the opportunity to take advantage of volume discounts or private labeling, since it does not have the facility or the demand for the volume necessary for discount purchasing. However, by pooling purchasing power with noncompeting stores, the retail outlet has an opportunity to partake in volume buying or group buying and thus can better meet the competition from large chain-store operations.

In recent years resident buying offices have added a wide variety of services to their original function of placing store orders. They have become merchandising consultants, serving approximately 90 percent of the nation's department and specialty stores, small apparel businesses, and large discount and chain operations.[1]

TYPES OF RESIDENT BUYING OFFICES

How does a store determine which type of resident buying office is suitable and reflects its image? What types of resident buying offices are available?

There are two major classifications of resident buying offices: (1) the independent office, including the salaried office or the merchandise broker, and (2) the store-owned office, including the private buying office, the associated buying office, and the syndicated or chain-owned buying office.

The Classification of Resident Buying Offices

The Independent Office
1. Salaried or fixed-fee office
2. Merchandise broker or commission office

The Store-owned Office
1. Private office
2. Associated office
3. Syndicated or chain-owned office

Independent Buying Office

The *independent buying office* is privately owned and operated, and continuously seeks stores as clients. Some of these independent buying offices represent large department stores, while others represent small apparel shops, specialty stores, home-furnishing stores, and other types of stores that require market representation. The office serves member stores with similar merchandise lines, so that the resident buyer can scout the marketplace for as many as 100 or more member stores carrying similar merchandise. Since noncompeting stores are members of the same resident office, the resident buyer has an opportunity to work with the buyers from each member store to develop private branding, encourage volume buying, and offer a variety of promotional aids. The majority of buying offices fall into this category. An example is Felix Lilienthal and Company.

There are two types of independent buying offices: (1) the salaried or fixed-fee office and (2) the commission or merchandise-broker office.

Salaried or Fixed-Fee Office. The salaried office is paid a fixed fee directly by the client stores it represents. Contractual arrangements are made between the salaried office and the client store. The typical fee ranges from ½ percent to 1 percent of a store's annual sales volume for the past year, payable in equal monthly installments.[2] The relationship of the buying office to the client store is that of a private professional offering service to a client. For example, a department-store buyer of hard goods may seek information and advice regarding new sources of supply, product changes and obsolescence, and special buying problems

Commission or Merchandise-Broker Office. This type of independent office receives its fee directly from the manufacturers or vendors it represents and is found primarily in the fashion apparel trade. The commission is based on the percentage of orders placed in client stores. The merchandise broker receives a commission from the manufacturer or vendor rather than from the client store, and thus is considered a "special type" of resident buyer; however, he or she offers many services similar to those offered by other resident buyers. The fee ranges from 2 to 4 percent of the sale. The merchandise broker usually represents many lines of manufacturers, and thus is often called a manufacturers' representative.

Merchandise brokers have an opportunity to broaden the market to boutiques and other small apparel shops that could not be contacted directly by manufacturers. For example, a manufacturers' representative may call on a small shop to show a line of merchandise, or may display merchandise in local hotel rooms and invite several retailers to view it. In this case, the merchandise is modeled informally, and ideas for display and promotions are also provided. This type of service can be an advantage to the smaller retailer who cannot afford the monthly installments asked by the salaried office. One disadvantage, however, is that the service is confined to the manufacturers and vendors that pay a commission on the orders brought in by the office. The broker is not an employee of the store, not even its agent. There is often conflict of interest between the client store and the manufacturers. The merchandise broker must be careful to give the best service possible to his or her customers to ensure continued business.[3]

The Store-Owned Office

The *store-owned office* is owned by the store or stores that it represents and is organized to provide buying services for them. Very large department and specialty stores are generally represented by their own offices. This type of buying arrangement provides the least conflict of interest. There are three types of store-owned offices: (1) the *private office*, (2) the *associated buying office*, and (3) the *syndicated* or *chain-owned office*.

The Private Office. Some large retail organizations maintain their own private buying offices in major market centers such as New York City. However, due to the large investment involved and the lack of an opportunity to exchange information with noncompeting stores, this type of resident buying office is not very common nowadays. The buyers in these offices perform the same functions as those in the independent office. This enables them to have access to all the services of the large resident buying office and yet to maintain an office for a market representative who is directly responsible to them. Examples of stores owning private buying offices are Neiman-Marcus and Marshall Field, who own offices in New York City. These stores restrict their merchandising activities to their own buying offices.

The Associated Buying Office. Associated buying offices are owned and operated by a group of stores that are its members. They are also called cooperative offices, since their expenses are distributed among the member stores. Fees are based upon the size of each store and the amount of service each requires. Associated offices are more expensive than salaried offices. They must represent all their members and are, therefore, difficult to join and to leave. Since the member stores share similar business interests, they are willing to exchange confidential information and to assist one another in the development of various types of merchandising techniques, promotional buying assists, control and operations, and store management. Associated offices are restricted in choice of membership, as compared to the independent buying office; however, they have the advantage of developing a greater assortment of brand-name merchandise and of operating wholesaling activities that are more difficult to maintain in independent offices. The best-known buying offices are the Associated Merchandising Corporation (AMC), which serves thirty to forty large department stores, and Frederick Atkins, Inc., with some forty to fifty department stores.[4] A buyer who makes a trip to the market, for example, New York City, is accompanied by the office's resident buyer on visits to vendors and manufacturers; the resident buyer arranges fashion shows and provides office space and clerical assistance in the resident buying office. The store buyer who becomes familiar with the services of the store's resident buying office and learns to use its facilities intelligently can make market trips more productive and the entire operation more successful.[5]

The Syndicated or Chain-Owned Office. Syndicated buying offices differ from the associated buying office in that they are divisions of a corporation that owns a chain of department stores. Therefore, most chain stores have central buyers in the stores as well as resident buyers in the principal markets. The syndicated buying office functions in much the same manner as the associated office; however, the syndicated office is better able to maintain a dominant position and can force adoption of its recommendations on stores because of the common ownership. For example, the syndicate office may insist that its stores maintain certain merchandising policies, whereas the associated office may offer suggestions but cannot force a member store to adopt them. Examples of the syndicate buying office are Allied Purchasing Corporation (APC), which serves more than 100 stores and Associated Dry Goods Corporation (ADG). Once central buyers have determined the needs of their individual stores, they will request the resident buyer to go into the marketplace and make the necessary buying arrangements. A major advantage of such an affiliation, even for the central buyer, is the market feedback that is provided. Since central buyers handle large volumes of merchandise, they require fast, accurate information on fashion trends, market conditions, "best sellers," "hot items," and prices. A central buyer may request a resident buyer to place orders, follow up on deliveries, and handle special orders, adjustments, and complaints.

SELECTION OF THE RESIDENT BUYING OFFICE

How does the retail buyer narrow the possibilities and avoid buying offices that do not reflect his or her type of store? The following is a list that should be considered when selecting a resident buying office:[6]

1. What will be the cost of using a resident buying office? Is a minimum monthly fee required?
2. What kind of contract arrangements are required? Are there arrangements for canceling them?
3. What is the extent of the office market coverage? Its fashion knowledge? Its merchandising judgment?
4. What kind of merchandise lines are represented by the resident buying office? Popular-priced merchandise? Promotional merchandise? Higher-priced merchandise? Discount-priced merchandise?
5. Does the office maintain buyers with separate divisions for various types of goods? Or does it specialize in one line of merchandise? Does the resident buying office give full coverage to both hard goods and soft goods?
6. What kind and scope of services are offered by the resident buying office?
7. Do the retail policies of the resident buying office basically agree with yours?
8. Would your type of retail operation be too limited to be serviced properly?
9. Do the executives and staff of the resident buying office provide an atmosphere of work compatibility? What is the size of the staff? What are their abilities?
10. What other clients are represented by the resident buying office? Are most of them similar to your type of retailing operation?

The retail buyer must be careful in the selection of a resident buying office, because this resident office becomes the store's market representative. The buyer should speak frankly with the executives of the buying office and should ask for references, speak to some of the members, get their opinion of the buying office, and discuss its method of operation with them. Also, the buyer should speak with manufacturers and vendors, since they are aware which offices have competent resident buyers and give good reliable service.

ORGANIZATION OF THE RESIDENT BUYING OFFICE

The organization of the resident buying office generally corresponds closely to that of the member or client store or stores. Like the member store, the resident buying office usually has one or more buyers for each classification of merchandise. Depending on the size of the market, however, larger resident offices may have as many as twenty buyers for a particular merchandise line, who cover certain size ranges and price lines intensively.

It is the responsibility of the resident buyer to thoroughly cover the entire market that he or she has been assigned. This requires constant checking and evaluation of vendors and manufacturers, seeking new merchandise resources, and in turn, alerting the client store to changes. The resident buyer must be constantly aware of styles and must be able to meet the needs of all the visiting store buyers. The staff of the resident buying office must keep stores informed of current market trends by using a variety of communications techniques.

Table 10–1 shows the similarities in organization between the resident buying office and a client office.

TABLE 10–1. Similarities in organization between resident buying office and client store.

RESIDENT BUYING OFFICE	CLIENT STORE
Divisional Department Head ⟷	Divisional Merchandise Manager

1. Work closely together, disseminating market information to their staff.
2. Both have the primary function of directing and supervising the activities of their buyers, who report to them. Together they are responsible for organizing and directing divisional meetings.
3. Work with store steering committees in developing group purchases and private brand promotions.
4. Maintain good vendor relationships.

Resident Buyers ⟷	Store Buyers

1. Work closely together in determining current trends, consumer needs, pricing policies, and quality merchandise.
2. Locate new merchandise resources and communicate with store buyers.
3. Maintain sample rooms where, at scheduled hours or by appointment, store buyers may visit the resident office to see lines of merchandise or confer with buyers.

> **The resident buying office and client store have similar structures.**
>
> | Resident buying office | Client store |
> |---|---|
> | Divisional department head | Divisional merchandise manager |
> | Resident buyers | Store buyers |

Independent Buying Office

The independent resident buying office and its member stores enjoy mutual freedom in setting their own merchandise policies. "Across-the-board offices" serve clients who handle both hard goods and soft goods. Their organization is similar to that of their client stores, who also offer "across-the-board" merchandise coverage.

Private Resident Buying Office

As you recall, the private office is owned by and run for a single store. Its organization, therefore, will closely correspond to that of the store that owns and operates it. Merchandise lines represented by the resident buying office will be the same as that represented by the retail store.

Associated Resident Buying Office

Because the associated buying office is owned by several stores, it must organize in such a way that all its members are represented in the formulation of business policies and philosophies. In such offices there is usually a board of directors whose members are executives of the owning stores. The board members determine policy, merchandising techniques, and services, which will in turn benefit all the member stores. The merchandise classification, the scope of merchandise carried, and the price lines offered will depend upon the member stores and their particular interests.

Syndicated or Chain-Owned Buying Office

Since the syndicated buying office is a division of the corporation that owns it, it is organized to serve only the domestic member stores of the corporation. Because it is owned by the stores, it is less flexible in policy formulation than other types of offices and can insist that its rules be followed.

COOPERATION BETWEEN BUYERS IS A MUST

Unless there is complete cooperation between the resident buyer and the retail-store buyer, the many advantages offered by the resident buying office may not be realized. A good, strong working relationship must be developed. The store buyer should take the resident buyer into his or her confidence about business problems, seek the resident buyer's advice, and adopt the suggestions offered.

A typical example of good cooperation between buyers occurs when the store buyer notifies the resident buying office well in advance of plans to visit the market. This will give the resident buyer an opportunity to prepare for the visit by scouting the market for particular store needs, which will save market time for the store buyer. Most resident buying offices require that store buyers make appointments ahead of time to ensure a more productive market trip.

PART 2—Services Offered by the Resident Buying Office

THE BUYER'S "RIGHT ARM"

Resident buying offices are organized to save the retail buyer time and money and to provide professional assistance. As the buyer's "right arm" in the market, the buying office eliminates unnecessary market trips, saves money, and offers a variety of services.[7]

Most resident buyers restrict their activities to the women's and children's apparel trades, although many also offer service in the purchase of men's wear, furs, millinery, and home furnishings, to name but a few. Some resident buying offices are organized to serve only a limited number of stores in a few lines of merchandise, while others are organized to offer a complete line of service encompassing many fields.

A typical well-staffed buying office has four major functions: (1) the merchandising function, (2) the promotion function, (3) the research function, and (4) the ancillary function. Table 10–2 provides a more detailed description of each.

Merchandising Function

The merchandising function assists the store buyer in obtaining merchandise.

TABLE 10–2.   Services offered by the typical resident buying office.

Merchandising Function	Promotion Function
1. Order placement, adjustment, follow-up	1. Providing buyer information
2. Preparation for buyer's visit	2. Promotion of goods
3. Ordering for stores	3. Preparation of advertising
4. Group buying	4. Fashion service
5. Central buying	
6. Private branding	**Ancillary Function**
7. Jobbing service	1. Buying clinics
8. Purchasing	2. Divisional meetings
	3. Foreign service
Research Function	
1. Research and analysis	
2. Management marketing information	

1. Order placement, adjustments, follow-up
   a. Merchandise is ordered from the vendor with the approval of the store buyer.
   b. Adjustments such as returns and cancellations are handled, as well as reorders on successful numbers and special orders. Most store buyers will send copies of their orders and reorders through the resident buyer, since this enables the market representative to keep careful checks.
   c. The resident buyer will follow-up the client's orders to ensure prompt delivery of merchandise.

2. Preparation for the buyer's visit
   a. The best source of merchandise is located in advance, and advice on the most favorable terms of sale and service available is provided.
   b. The resident buyer publishes a notice of the store buyer's arrival in the trade papers in advance and arranges appointments with manufacturer's representatives in the office or in vendors' showrooms (Figure 10–2).
   c. The resident buyer accompanies the store buyer on visits to vendors and manufacturers.
   d. The office provides office facilities for store buyers when they are in the market; this includes telephone service, mail service, a telephone message center, and secretarial help.

3. Ordering for stores
   a. The resident buyer may be called upon to handle "open-to-buy"

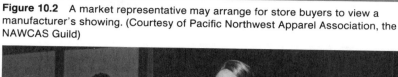

Figure 10.2 A market representative may arrange for store buyers to view a manufacturer's showing. (Courtesy of Pacific Northwest Apparel Association, the NAWCAS Guild)

for the client stores. The store buyer sends in an open order to the resident buyer, which specifies price lines and the amount of money to be spent. However, the choice of the resource and of the type of merchandise is left to the resident buyer's judgment.

b. To do this successfully, the resident buyer must be familiar with the retail store, the type of merchandise it sells, and its particular merchandising problems.

4. Group buying. The resident buying office, because of its many market contacts, is able to arrange for some or all of the member stores to participate in group buying. *Group buying* is a method of buying in which a

number of stores participate to secure better prices, ensure high standards of quality, and obtain goods more readily. For example, the resident buyer will notify its member stores of an opportunity to make a group buy. Store buyers will meet with the resident buyer and discuss the price and quality of the merchandise available, determine consumer needs, consider the manufacturer's specifications, and analyze how the merchandise is best suited to the needs of the individual store. Each store will decide whether or not it wishes to go along with the group; however, it usually is advantageous to do so.

5. Central buying
   a. The resident buying office may organize a form of central buying for certain lines of merchandise, for example, women's sportswear. Figure 4.4 illustrates how a resident buying office will assist the buyer of better misses sportswear purchasing goods.
   b. In central buying, the small independent store is provided with an opportunity to be competitive with large chain operations offering similar merchandise. For example, the resident buyer will send a few pieces of merchandise to each of the member stores. In turn, the stores will report on how the merchandise is selling. The resident buyer, through an efficient system of unit control, can quickly spot trends, facilitate reorders, and determine which pieces of merchandise are not selling.
   c. Under this arrangement the retail store buyer turns over buying authority to the resident office buyer.

6. Private branding
   a. Many resident buying offices have developed private branding programs to assist their member stores to meet competition and provide store individuality.
   b. The resident buyer will work closely with a committee of store buyers who have developed specifications for the product under consideration.
   c. The resident buyer has the responsibility for finding the best resource, having samples made, and communicating any necessary changes (Figure 10–3).
   d. Once the item is approved, the resident buyer will make suggestions for store-advertising and promotion.

7. Jobbing service
   a. Some resident buying offices provide a jobbing service whereby they make purchases, usually of staple items, in their own name and warehouse the merchandise.
   b. The merchandise is then shipped to the client stores on request, or perhaps dropped-shipped directly from the manufacturer to the store.

Figure 10–3 The resident buying office will make arrangements for a store buyer to visit a manufacturer's facilities.

    c. The resident buyer will sell the merchandise to its client stores at a nominal profit. In some cases nonmember stores are permitted to take advantage of this service for a fee.

    d. The jobbing service provides an opportunity for off-season purchases and quantity purchases, the savings from which are passed on to the member stores.

8. Purchasing service

    a. Quantities of goods are purchased by the resident buyer at special price concessions on overstocks or on merchandise lines that have been reduced.

    b. This type of merchandise is usually used by a retail store for special promotion activities.

    c. A great deal of cooperation is required between the resident buyer and the store buyer for the purchasing service to be successful.

Promotion Function

The promotion function assists the store buyer in selling the merchandise by:

1. Providing buyer information
   a. The resident buying office keeps its stores informed of market developments through periodic reports and bulletins.
   b. Reports may forecast fashion trends, styles, colors, and fabrics for the coming season, closeouts and job lots, promotional items and best sellers.
   c. The report may be given orally at meetings held by the resident office for buyers of fashion accessories, men's wear, children's wear, etc., or it may take the form of an attractive booklet that is sent to the stores in advance of the season.

2. Promotion of goods
   a. A buying office may work out arrangements with manufacturers to sell certain styles exclusively to member stores (Figure 10–4).
   b. This merchandise may be used for store promotions, special sale days, or special events.
   c. Since this merchandise was purchased at a lower cost, the goods may be sold at lower prices and thus entice people into the store for the sale. Figure 10–5 is an example of promotion information provided a home-smallwares division in a department store.

3. Preparation of advertising
   a. Promotional departments of the resident buying office will assist their stores in planning and executing promotional events.
   b. The resident buying office will provide suggested advertising calendars, prepare illustrations, write copy, and suggest interior and window displays.
   c. Mailing pieces, Christmas catalogs, and special sale catalogs may be purchased from the resident buying offices at a low price, with the store's name imprinted on them.

4. Fashion service
   a. Most large resident buying offices provide a fashion director and staff to supply merchandise information to soft-goods or fashion-apparel buyers. The information may be presented in the form of a fashion show, usually held during market week, or bulletins devoted to fashion trends, or color and fabric promotions may be planned with cooperating stores.
   b. The resident buying office may offer fashion clinics twice a year

Figure 10–4 A buying office may work out arrangements with manufacturers to sell certain styles exclusively to member stores. (Courtesy of Saks Fifth Avenue, New York, N.Y.)

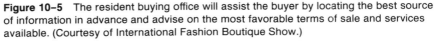

Figure 10–5   The resident buying office will assist the buyer by locating the best source of information in advance and advise on the most favorable terms of sale and services available. (Courtesy of International Fashion Boutique Show.)

to assist buyers in merchandise selection and planning and in store promotions, and to offer suggestions on fashion themes.

Research Function

The research function will assist the store buyer in obtaining up-to-date market information to aid in decision making.

1. Research and analysis
   a. Statistical information concerning economic trends, consumer buying habits, new methods of operation, and changes in market conditions is sent to the member stores to assist them in planning and in selling merchandise.
   b. The resident buying office becomes a clearinghouse of information by continuously collecting data on recent federal legislation, training systems, supplier costs, manufacturer's expenses, markdowns, and other such items of interest to top management.

2. Management information. Research information may be passed on to top management through management seminars that emphasize proper operational procedure and facilitate fast, accurate decision making.

Ancillary Function

The ancillary function offers additional services to the retail buyer, which will vary with the resident buying office:

1. Buying clinics. During the early 1980s, as a result of the fuel shortage, store buyers found it increasingly difficult to travel to the marketplace as often as they would have liked. Resident buying offices offered clinics to discuss more efficient methods of obtaining and selling merchandise. Buying clinics also assist buyers in solving merchandising problems, locating new sources of merchandise, and developing new selling techniques.

2. Divisional meetings. The scheduling of seasonal divisional merchandise meetings is a very important service to merchandisers. During these meetings the market is reviewed for new lines, special offerings, and price concessions.

3. Foreign service
   a. The resident buying office usually has a specialist who provides information on the complexities of buying abroad.
   b. This specialist may have a display of items available from foreign sources. This gives the store buyer the opportunity to actually view and handle particular items of interest.

The services offered by the resident buying office are many and varied, depending on the nature of the buying office and the stores it represents. The major advantage is that time and money may be conserved by the retail buyer. Resident buying offices have the facilities for providing a continuous flow of market information. They have many "ears and eyes" with which to locate new merchandise, new resources, and favorable prices[8] (Figure 10–5).

The services offered by a resident buying office are many and varied. What activities are included in each of the following?

The merchandising activity   The research activity
The promotion activity   The ancillary activity

THE RESPONSIBILITIES
OF THE RESIDENT BUYER

The resident buyer, much like the retail store buyer, has many responsibilities and, therefore, must develop the talent and ability to carry them out. He or she deals with many types of personalities from the member stores and must be able to get along with these people. He or she is not only constantly in touch with store buyers but also with salespeople, vendors, and manufacturers. The resident buyer must have the ability to communicate new ideas, new styles, and new fashion trends, and must possess the ability to conduct merchandising meetings that will generate the enthusiasm and interest of members. This individual usually has had a great deal of experience in the merchandising trade before embarking on a career as a resident buyer.

Chapter Summary

The resident buying office is located in a major trading area and provides highly specialized experts, called resident buyers, who work in the capacity of assistants or advisors to the stores their office represents. A great majority of the resident buying offices are located in New York City, since this city is the primary market for fashion apparel, soft goods, and related accessories, as well as for hard goods, home furnishings, and appliances. Resident buying office branches are also located in Los Angeles, Chicago, Rocky Mountain, North Carolina, and Atlanta. There are two major classifications of resident buying offices. They are the independent office, which includes the salaried office and the merchandise broker, and the store-owned office, which includes the private office, the associate office, and the syndicated or chain-owned office. The student should review Part 1 of this chapter. A retail store buyer must be careful to select an office that will reflect his or her type of store. There are many qualifications that should be considered. The list given in "Selection of the Resident Buying Office" provides information that should be considered when selecting an office.

The organization of resident buying offices usually corresponds closely to that of the member stores. There usually are one or more buyers for each classification of merchandise. The student should review Table 10–1.

The resident buying office provides numerous services to save the store buyer time and money. These services may be classified as follows: merchandising function, promotion function, research function, and ancillary function. The student should review Table 10–2. The resident buyer, like the retail-store buyer, has many responsibilities and must develop the talent and ability to carry out those responsibilities. He or she should have a great deal of retailing experience in a particular area of expertise before embarking on a career as a resident buyer.

Trade Terminology

DIRECTIONS: Briefly explain or discuss each of the following trade terms.

1. Resident buying office
2. Resident buyer
3. Independent buying office
4. Salaried or fixed fee office
5. Commission or merchandise-broker office
6. Store-owned office
7. Private office
8. Associated buying office
9. Syndicated or chain-owned office
10. Group buying

Questions for Discussion and Review

1. Define resident buying office and resident buyer.

2. Why are the majority of resident buying offices located in New York City?

3. In what major trade market/markets would you locate if you were a resident buyer of home furnishings? Of misses' sportswear? Of furniture and furnishings? Of hardware?

4. How does the resident buying office serve as an important communications link between stores and manufacturers?

5. Why did the first resident buying office develop? Why have they continued to be so popular?

6. Explain the differences among the following: private resident buying office; merchandise broker; chain-owned office.

7. Briefly explain the differences in responsibilities between the department-store buyer and the resident buyer; between the central buyer and the resident buyer.

8. Compare the organization of the following: the chain-owned office and the associated office; the salaried office and the commission office.

9. What major types of service are provided by the resident buying office? Select one major service and explain how this service would assist the boutique buyer; the children's wear buyer of a department store; the infants and toddlers' buyer in a discount house.

10. You are considering opening a bath and linen shop. How would you go about finding a suitable resident buying office? What factors would you consider before making a decision?

References

THE RETAIL STUDENT'S REFERENCE LIBRARY

Anderson, Rolph E., Hair, Joseph F., and Bush, Alan J. *Professional Sales Management.* New York: McGraw-Hill Book Co., 1988.

Bedient, John, *Marketing Decision-Making Using Lotus 1-2-3.* Cincinnati: South Western Pub. Co., 1990.

Brightman, Richard W. *Using Computers in an Information Age.* Cincinnati: South Western Pub. Co., 1986.

Cunningham, William H. and Cunningham, Isabella C. M. *Marketing: A Managerial Approach.* Cincinnati: South Western Pub. Co., 1987.

DuBrin, Andrew. *Essentials of Management.* Cincinnati: South Western Pub. Co., 1986.

Harwell, Edward. *Management Development for Discount Stores.* New York: Lebhar-Friedman Inc., 1985.

Hetzel, William. *Computer Information Systems Development: Principles and Case Study.* Cincinnati: South Western Pub. Co., 1985.

Keyes, Ruth. *Essentials of Retailing.* New York: Fairchild Pub. Co., 1985.

Krieger, Murray. *Merchandising Math for Profit: An Executive Handbook.* New York: Fairchild Pub Co., 1985.

Packard, Sidney and Guerreiro, Miriam. *The Buying Game: Fashion Buying and Merchandising.* New York: Fairchild Pub. Co., 1986.

Packard, Sidney. *Strategies and Tactics in Fashion Marketing.* New York: Fairchild Pub., 1986.

Perspectives on Retail Strategic Decision Making. New York: NRMA, 1985.

Productivity in General Merchandise Retailing. New York: NRMA, 1985.

Stamper, Anita A. *Evaluating Apparel Quality.* New York: Fairchild Pub., 1985.

Tepper, Bette K. and Godnick, Newton. *Mathematics for Retail Buying.* New York: Fairchild Pub. Co, Inc. 1985.

REFERENCES

1. Adele C. Elgart, "The Contribution of the Resident Buying Office," in *The Buyer's Manual* (New York: National Retail Merchants Association, 1965), p. 400–1.
2. *How to Select a Resident Buying Office* (Washington, D.C.: U.S. Government Printing Office, n.d.), p. 1.
3. Ibid., p. 2.
4. "Amc's Power on 7th Avenue: Peanuts or High Pressure?" *Women's Wear Daily,* April 27, 1964, pp. 1–18.
5. Elgart, "Contribution of the Resident Buying Office," p. 400.
6. *How to Select a Resident Buying Office,* p. 2.
7. Ibid., p. 3
8. Elgart, "Contribution of the Resident Buying Office," p. 400.

The Resources of Merchandise: Domestic and Foreign

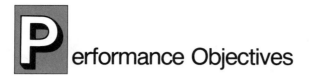

Performance Objectives

After reading this chapter the student should be able to accomplish the following:

1. Discuss how a buyer prepares for the buying trip and plans the market agenda.

2. Identify and define the main sources of merchandise.

3. Discuss five factors that are important when selecting merchandise resources.

4. Become aware of six methods used to contact merchandise resources.

5. Discuss in detail the trade calendar of events.

6. Discuss four major reasons for buying foreign products.

7. Outline problems faced by buyers when purchasing foreign goods.

8. Relate six major methods used by buyers when purchasing foreign goods.

9. Identify major foreign markets in which American buyers are satisfying import needs of consumers.

The Resources of Merchandise: Domestic and Foreign

Figure 11-1 How does the buyer determine who will be a source of supply? The answer to this question as well as to others may be a result of the buyer's experience while working with vendors.

INTRODUCTION

In the previous chapter you learned that retail buyers, whether of staple goods, fashion apparel, domestics or hard goods, cannot rely on occasional market trips or visits by manufacturers' representatives alone, since such activities are often time-consuming. Many stores must seek the services of an outside agency called a resident buying office (RBO), which will provide a steady flow of market information on a local as well as on a national and international scope.

There are two major classifications of RBOs: the independent office and the store-owned office. Resident buying offices are organized to save the retail buyer time and money and to provide professional assistance. As the buyer's "right arm" in the marketplace, the buying office eliminates unnecessary market trips, saves money, and offers a variety of services. A typical well-staffed buying office has four major functions: the merchandising function, which assists the store buyer in obtaining merchandise; the promotion function, which assists the store buyer in selling the merchandise; the research function, which assists the store buyer in obtaining up-to-date market information to aid in decision making; and the ancillary function, which offers additional services to the retail buyer.

In this chapter we are concerned with the buyer's procurement activities in both domestic and foreign market centers. First, however, the buyer must prepare a buying plan that summarizes purchases by classifications, price lines, styles, sizes, and colors. Once the buying plan has been formulated, the buyer will outline the market agenda, which includes a number of important factors, such as number of days in the market, making appointments with the resident buying office, talking to other store buyers, making arrangements to view manufacturers' lines, visiting magazine editors, contacting primary producers, and visiting new merchandise resources.

There are three major sources of supply available: middlemen, manufacturers, and farmers and growers. Certain factors should be considered when selecting merchandise resources.

How does a buyer make buying contacts? He or she may visit local markets, use the resident buying office, use mail and telephone, use catalogs and price lists, be visited by manufacturers' reps, and visit trade market centers. A trade calendar of events is used to provide information regarding the time period when fashion must be in the store as well as when the buyer must be in the market place.

Many retailers have found it profitable to offer their customers merchandise from foreign sources. There are a number of reasons for buying foreign products. However, there are also a number of disadvantages to consider. A number of methods may be used to purchase foreign goods, such as private import wholesalers, foreign exporters or selling houses, purchasing agents or commissionaires, store-owned foreign buying offices, buying trips to foreign markets, and trade fairs. Retail buyers travel all over the world to satisfy the import needs of consumers. A list of major foreign producers is provided in this chapter.

PART 1—Buying in the Domestic Market

PREPARING THE BUYING PLAN

Buying, whether in domestic or foreign markets, requires careful planning before the buying trip is scheduled. Approximately one to two weeks in advance, plans will be summarized regarding purchases by classifications, price lines, styles, sizes, and colors. Plans will be made concerning the merchandise needs of each branch store of a department-store operation, and for individual departments if a small business. (As you recall, the buyer for a chain operation is centrally located in the market; therefore, the need for a special buying trip is eliminated.)

The department-store buyer or the owner-manager will go to the market with a buying plan that will include a list of basic stock items and goods that will tie in to other store offerings, and with money to be used for purchasing new items and special merchandise offerings. The amount of money kept in reserve for specials and new items, however, will depend on the merchandising policies of the store. Often the merchandise manager likes to be kept informed about such matters, since he or she is responsible for coordinating the merchandising offerings as to present stock conditions, past sales, actual sales, expected sales, the open-to-buy in units, and the open-to-buy at retail.

Once the buyer has supplied all the information necessary, the merchandise manager will evaluate the need for a buying trip and offer suggestions and guidance based on his or her own experiences in the trade markets. Thus, the buying plan will meet the needs and wants of store customers and reflect the image of the department and the store (Figure 11–1).

THE MARKET AGENDA

The procedure followed by the buying specialist will depend upon the type and size of the retail operation. The list that follows will outline the market agenda used by most department-store buyers and small business owner-managers.

1. Determine the period of the season for which you are buying. Are you buying for the beginning of the season? Have you returned to the market to replenish the merchandise assortment? Are you seeking special promotion merchandise?

2. Determine the number of days you wish to spend in the market. Usually more time is required if you intend to view a new seasonal line; less time (three to five days) is required if you are seeking fresh styles to liven up the assortment or special promotional goods.

3. Announce your arrival and your wants in advance to your store's resident buying office. If your store belongs to a resident buying office, call the buyer's arrival office and inform personnel of the day and date of your arrival. Contact your resident buyer and inform him or her of your particular interests and merchandising needs.

4. Visit stores in the market center that are selling your particular line of merchandise. These store visits are usually made on the first or second day of the buying trip to provide background information before visiting merchandise resources.

5. Talk to other store buyers who are selling the same or similar lines of merchandise to determine those factors that have led to successful selling.

6. Inform merchandise resources of the day and date of your market visit. Call various merchandise resources you wish to visit so that arrangements may be made to view manufacturers' lines, examine samples, and gain information about best sellers for the coming season.

7. Visit magazine editors to determine the amount and type of cooperative advertising available.

8. Contact primary producers such as fiber, leather, and fabric houses. Primary manufacturers may provide information regarding current fashion trends, popular textures, fabrics, and colors, and successful merchandise resources.

9. Participate actively in buying clinics. If you belong to a resident buying office, buying clinics may be arranged. In these clinics you will have an opportunity to study market trends, economic conditions, and supply conditions, and examine new and innovative patterns of distribution.

10. Discuss current fashion trends with fashion specialists. Manufacturers, resident buying offices, and fashion magazines will provide fashion specialists who will inform you of current trends, popular styles and colors, emerging trends, popular fads, and so forth.

11. Allow time to visit new merchandise resources, as well as the small manufacturers, to seek new items, the unique, and the unusual. In other words, leave no stone unturned while in the market center.

Figure 11–2 An example of a buying plan. A buying plan for the coming season, in this case, back-to-school and fall, will provide information regarding present stock conditions, past sales, actual sales, expected sales, and the open-to-buy at retail. Once the buying plan is formulated, the need for a buying trip to the wholesale market is determined.

Season BACK-TO-SCHOOL	Planned Sales	ADD planned BOM stock	SUBTRACT on hand 7/31	SUBTRACT on order 7/31	OPEN-TO-BUY (in units)	OPEN-TO-BUY (retail)
August	24	48	−16	−0	56	$1,675
September	48	12	− 0	−0	12	359.10
October	12	0	− 0	−0	0	0
November	0	0	− 0	−0	0	0
FALL MERCHANDISE						
August	12	48	− 0	−0	48	$1,438
September	0	12	− 0	−0	12	359.10
October	36	0	− 0	−0	0	0
November	48	36	− 0	−0	36	1,078

It is very important for the buying specialist to do all the necessary planning and paperwork before leaving the retail store to go to the market center. If the buyer works carefully and conscientiously, he or she will arrive in the wholesale market with the information and guidance necessary to ensure a successful, possibly even a prosperous, buying trip. As a result of proper planning, the buyer will focus attention on the business at hand, save time, energy, and money, and be more productive[3] (Figure 11–2).

SELECTING MERCHANDISE RESOURCES

Once the retail buyer has determined what merchandise to buy and what quantities are necessary to meet the anticipated needs of the store's clientele, he or she must locate sources of supply—or merchandise resources, as they are called in the retail trade. There are hundreds of vendors located in many markets, both at home and abroad, and literally hundreds of vendors in a given classification of merchandise. For example, some large-scale retailers and discount houses may stock as many as 50,000 different styles, sizes, or types of merchandise. A small retail store may stock from 5,000 to 7,000 different items. For this reason, buyers, regardless of the size and type of the retail store, must keep constantly aware of sources of supply and must always be appraising new sources for the unusual and the unique. How does the buyer determine who will be the merchandise resources, and whether or not to purchase merchandise from a few vendors or from many vendors? Who will be the key resources?

MAIN MERCHANDISE RESOURCES

Basically, there are three major sources of supply available to the buying specialist. They are: (1) middlemen, (2) manufacturers, and (3) farmers and growers.

The Main Merchandise Resources Available to the Retail Buyer Are:

1. Middlemen
   a. Merchant middlemen
      (1) Service wholesalers
      (2) Limited-function wholesalers
      (3) Rack jobbers
   b. Nonmerchant middlemen
      (1) Brokers
      (2) Commission men
      (3) Selling agents
      (4) Manufacturers' agents (Manufacturers' representatives)
      (5) Auctions
2. Manufacturers
   a. Buying direct
3. Farmers or growers

Middlemen

Broadly speaking, *middlemen* may be defined as individuals or organizations who operate between producers and industrial or ultimate consumers.

A synonym is the term *wholesaler,* who, as you recall from your basic marketing course, purchases goods from manufacturers in relatively large quantities and sells to retail merchants in substantially smaller quantities.[1] Usually, middlemen or wholesalers do not change the physical form of products but merely pass the goods through the distribution system. They may distribute as much as 75 percent of the merchandise handled by the drugstore trade and nearly 90 percent of the goods found in the hardware business. Middlemen may be classified into two broad categories: (1) merchant middlemen and (2) nonmerchant middlemen.

Merchant Middlemen. Merchant middlemen may be defined as wholesalers who take title or assume ownership by taking possession of goods they purchase for resale. Examples are service wholesalers, limited-function wholesalers, and rack jobbers.

Service wholesalers. Service wholesalers, or "regular" wholesalers, assemble merchandise in relatively large quantities and sell it to retailers in substantially smaller quantities. A most important function of service wholesalers is to provide service to the buying specialist. They act as the retailer's buying agent, since they anticipate the needs of buyers, will go into the marketplace to obtain the merchandise, and have goods available when the buyer wants them. Not only does the service wholesaler perform the enormous task of assembling many different items; he or she also provides services such as advertising and promotion, transportation and storage, and the granting of credit (Figure 11–3). This type of wholesaling is especially valuable to the small and medium-sized retail store, since service wholesalers find it to their advantage to provide this type of buying specialist with advertising, transportation, storage, and financing services. For example, the buyer of a small children's wear business may seek a regular or service type of wholesaler because the small business cannot afford the kind of advertising necessary to compete with a local department store and therefore will arrange a cooperative advertising deal with the wholesaler. Or a small retailer may require special credit arrangements to meet the merchandising needs of the back-to-school or Christmas season. Department-store buyers, too, seek services that will enable them to meet the competition of discount houses and general-merchandise chains.

Limited-function wholesalers. Limited-function or "cash-and-carry" wholesalers are merchant middlemen who limit themselves to smaller stocks of fast-moving items and offer no credit or delivery service, thus reducing the cost of the wholesaling. In other words, they do not provide the variety of services offered by service or regular wholesalers. Large chain operations that are able to perform many of the wholesaler's service functions (warehousing, advertising, financing, and so forth) within their own firms will find it more economical to use this type of merchandise resource. For example, a variety-store chain may use a limited-service wholesaler to procure staple goods, store the merchandise in their own warehouse or distribution centers, and ship the merchandise to their various store units as needed. Department stores and small businesses also purchase goods from limited-function wholesalers. Since the cost of wholesaling is reduced, they can offer merchandise at a lower cost and pass the savings on to the department-store buyer or the owner-manager.

    Rack jobbers. *Rack jobbers* (Figure 11–4) are merchant middlemen who are wholesalers of nonfood items and who arrange with independent grocers and chain supermarkets to stock and maintain an assortment of goods on a rack in a particular location in each store. Rack jobbers usually work on a 25 to 33 percent markup, depending on the type of merchandise

Figure 11–3 The service wholesaler performs the enormous task of assembling many different items, in this case, costume jewelry.

Figure 11–4 Rack jobbers provide nonfood items, for example, wearing apparel and hard goods. (Courtesy of Duckwall Stores, Inc., Abilene, Kan.)

and the amount of competition. The rack jobber will select the merchandise and arrange displays when such actions are considered necessary. Rack jobbers have been primarily responsible for the introduction of nonfood items into supermarket chains. Note, for example, the wearing apparel and numerous kinds of housewares found on the shelves in your local supermarket! Even though some large operations such as Acme Markets, Inc., and Mayfair Markets have felt it more economical to take over the function of the rack jobber, many supermarket operators feel that as long as the rack jobbers provide nonfood items that are in demand, continue to provide good service, and meet competitive prices, they will continue to be widely used as merchandise resources. Also, the rack jobber has the ability to scout the markets of wearing apparel and hard goods for interesting and unique types of merchandise; the food merchant does not have the time or the expertise to do this successfully.

Nonmerchant Middlemen. Nonmerchant middlemen may be defined as those middlemen who do not take title or assume ownership by taking possession of goods they purchase for resale. These middlemen usually act in behalf of sellers by negotiating sales and performing other services for their principals. The nonmerchant middleman receives a fee for bringing buyer and seller together. Examples of nonmerchant middlemen are brokers, commission men, selling agents, manufacturer's agents, and auctions.

Brokers. Brokers are nonmerchant middlemen whose primary function is to bring buyers and sellers together. Large food chains will utilize the services of food brokers in grocery specialties, dry goods, fruits and vegetables, and other commodities. Merchandise brokers are also found in resident buying offices. They offer the brokerage service to small retailers interested in purchasing hardware, small appliances, furniture, jewelry, and men's and women's fashion apparel. (Review Chapter 10 on the resident buying office.)

Commission sales. Commission people are nonmerchant middlemen who handle merchandise by displaying the goods for resale in a central marketplace. Commission men also handle grocery specialties, dry goods, and fruits and vegetables. They differ from brokers in that they actually receive the merchandise that they display and sell. Commission men constitute a source of supply for large food retailers; they operate out of the central market, deduct their commissions and other fees from the proceeds of the sale, and remit the balance to their principals.

Selling agents. Selling agents are independent businessmen who take over the entire sales function for their clients by offering advice on styling, extending financial aid, and making collections. Selling agents usually work for small manufacturers of piece goods or fashion apparel or for food specialists who are not large enough to organize their own sales forces. The owner-manager of a small retail outlet is visited by many selling agents, who come to the store and attempt to interest the owner in their merchandise offerings. This type of middleman gives the small retailers the opportunity to see a new line of goods and saves them time, energy, and money by making a trip to the central markets unnecessary. The small retailer is enabled to see merchandise samples and learn how they will tie in to the existing merchandise assortment.

Manufacturers' agents. Manufacturers' agents, also called *manufacturers' representatives,* are nonmerchant middlemen who take over part of their clients' sales activities and have less authority over prices and terms of sale. Manufacturers' agents are also employed by small manufacturers of soft goods and food specialties, but they are restricted to smaller sales territories and for a variety of reasons may sell only part of their clients' lines. They, too, will call on the small business operator. Along with selling agents, they will also visit department-store buyers, specialty-store buyers, and central buyers of discount, variety, and general-merchandise chains.

Auctions. The *auction* is a type of nonmerchant buying, whereby goods are placed on display and sold quickly to the highest bidder. Auctions are an important source of supply for large supermarket retailers who must purchase fruits and vegetables. Since this kind of merchandise is perishable, the auction affords the opportunity of rapid sales and fast delivery. Proceeds from auctions will go to the shipper after commissions and other charges have been deducted. Small food retailers often buy fruits and vegetables from wholesalers who may have used the auction as their source of supply. The small grocer will usually not go directly to the auction, since he cannot afford to buy large amounts of merchandise, nor does he have the outlet to dispose of them. However, he may join with other small grocers and "pool" the buying activity to take advantage of quantity buying and develop buying power in the marketplace. This is the primary method used by the small grocer to meet the competition of the large food chains.

Manufacturers

Manufacturers are a second main merchandise resource used by retail buyers. A *manufacturer* may be defined as an individual or firm who engages in assembling goods for use by the ultimate consumer. Many retailers prefer to purchase their merchandise directly from the manufacturer, since this may save both time and money and often results in better service. Services offered by the manufacturer may include precise and accurate information regarding specific merchandise lines; advice on advertising and promotion; special assistance and sales training once the merchandise arrives in the store; and suggestions on display techniques and materials.

Direct Buying. Buying direct from the manufacturer affords the retailer other advantages. For example, the buyer of fashion apparel gets the merchandise more quickly, since middlemen are eliminated. Direct buying also affords opportunities to large-scale retailers who are seeking goods made according to their own specifications. For example, Sears, Montgomery Ward, and others are responsible for almost 90 percent of the product lines made to their own specifications. Discount houses, drug chains, department stores, and food operations are also buying on this basis. Also, many smaller retailers have joined together in buying pools. For example, hardware retailers, appliance and TV retailers, and fashion shops have grouped together to take advantage of lower net prices and reduced marketing costs.

Farmers and Growers

The farmer or grower is a third merchandise resource and is an important source of supply primarily to those in the food retailing field. Small food retailers often drive to local growers and purchase fruits and vegetables directly. Large chain retailers such as A & P may send out teams of buyers who actually follow the crops northward as they ripen and keep in constant communication with the central headquarters.

FACTORS IN SELECTING
MERCHANDISE RESOURCES

Buyers usually prefer to work with a few key resources rather than with many, since a concentrated source of supply will encourage lower prices and better service. However, the concentration of key resources depends to a great extent on the buying power available, as well as upon the desire of the buyer to broaden market contacts by experimenting with new items and new resources.

The buyer will select resources on the basis of what they will do for the

Figure 11–5 Vanity Fair, Division of VF Corporation, continues to be the only intimate apparel company offering products in all major categories— body fashions, daywear, sleepwear, and loungewear. Vanity Fair has lead the industry in implementing electronic data interchange systems. Bar-coded tags have been in use on all Vanity Fair garments since the mid-1980s. The system enables retailers to transmit point-of-sale information to Vanity Fair, which uses the information to plan for the production and shipment of inventory. (Courtesy of Vanity Fair, Division of VF Corporation, Wyomissing, Pa.)

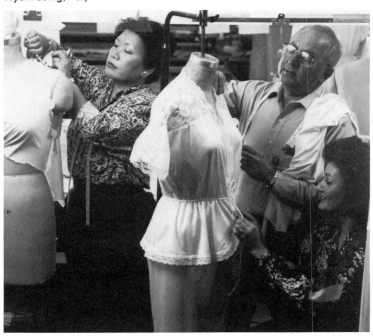

retail firm that he or she represents. Merchandise resources are evaluated on the basis of the amount of goods they supply and the profit potential the merchandise will yield the department and store. Buying specialists will maintain a diary on each vendor, which will contain notes of their dealings with each resource for each selling season (Figure 11–5).

In most cases, a buyer's resources will show a fine record on those points felt to be of importance to the merchandiser. However, a buyer will often feel a need to add new merchandise resources to take advantage of new and different kinds of goods. How is this task accomplished? How does a buying specialist determine when to eliminate certain resources and start afresh with new ones?

There can be several reasons for change. A resource may permit quality standards to fall off; prices may be increased too high for the buyer to maintain a reasonable markup; or the vendor's line may prove unacceptable to a store's merchandising policies. For these and other reasons the buyer may give up a well-established resource and seek new ones. In consultation with merchandise managers and other store buyers, facts and opinions should be carefully weighed and checked. However, once the decision is made, the buying specialist should consider the factors in the list that follows when selecting merchandise resources.

When Selecting Merchandise Resources the Buyer Should Consider the Following:

1. Characteristics of the merchandise assortment
   Quality   Brand   Availability   Price
   Distinctiveness   Styling   Specifications
2. Competition
   Merchandise offering ahead of competition
3. Method of procurement
   Distribution policies   Delivery practices
   Shipping quantities   Vendor dependability
4. Services available
   Display units   Warranty   Trained sales force
   Demonstrations   Repair   Missionary men
5. Pricing and terms of sale
   Market price   EOM   Thirty days
   Market-plus-price   Market-minus-price

MAKING CONTACTS
WITH MERCHANDISE RESOURCES

A retail buyer may make buying contacts in several ways. He or she may (1) visit local markets, (2) use the Resident Buying Office, (3) use mail and telephone, (4) use catalogs and price lists, (5) contacts manufacturers' reps (salespeople), and (6) visit trade market centers.

Visiting Local Markets

If the vendor is located near the retailer, the retailer will take the initiative and visit him. As previously mentioned, the small food retailer will often find it advantageous to seek out local growers of fruits and vegetables and other perishables. Large food retailers will send buyers into local markets to take advantage of an ample supply of goods at the best possible price. Retail buyers may also deal with limited wholesalers; in this case, they will pay cash and take responsibility for transporting the merchandise to the store. This practice is often used by buyers in small apparel businesses, since it affords them the opportunity of getting merchandise ahead of the competition and eliminates some delivery problems.

Resident Buying Offices

As you recall from reading the previous chapter, the resident buyer functions as a merchandise consultant for client stores. Among the many services offered, the resident buyer will arrange for manufacturers' showings, organize fashion shows, scout the marketplace for the best resources, seek the best prices, and utilize those vendors who are most reliable and dependable. Resident buying offices save a great deal of time and energy for member stores and, as a result of the growth and expansion of retail institutions, they have assumed increased importance in the buying-selling activity.

By Mail and Telephone

Staple merchandise is usually kept in stock through mail and telephone orders. The buyer may telephone the order by giving a purchase number and issuing a purchase order shortly thereafter.

Mail and telephone contacts are also used by small retailers for the reordering of fashion merchandise. Or the small retailer may refer to a catalog or price list and send orders to the vendor. The retailers who do this are usually isolated from the buying centers and frequently depend upon catalog descriptions of new goods. This method, however, creates the same difficulty for the buyer that the consumer has when ordering from a catalog. He does not actually see or feel the merchandise and does not have the vendor's formal acceptance or a firm delivery date.

Catalogs and Price Lists

Catalogs and price lists are issued both by manufacturers and wholesalers to provide information concerning their merchandise offerings at the time it is required by the retailer. However, these are used by retail buyers largely for the purchase of fill-in merchandise.

Some vendors will prepare catalogs mainly for use by small retailers located in remote or rural areas. This method of selling has proved successful, since the store does not have to invest in a large inventory and the consumer is willing to wait until the merchandise arrives.

Resident buying offices also prepare catalogs for use by their members. For example, a housewares catalog will describe all the items listed as well as giving the price. Price lists usually have less complete descriptions of the items offered for sale than those appearing in the catalog. Buyers of sewing notions, underwear, small appliances, kitchen utensils, housewares, toys, small leather goods, cleaning aids, closet accessories, laundry and ironing aids, hair goods, beauty supplies—the list is never-ending—will use catalogs and price lists to assist them in merchandise planning.

Manufacturers' Reps (Salespeople)

Using salespeople to call on prospective customers is perhaps the most important activity of vendors. Depending on the stock turnover of certain goods, a salesperson may call on a buyer as often as once each week. This makes the practice of hand-to-mouth buying much easier for the buyer. Or, as in the case of drugs and hardware, the vendor's salesperson may contact their retailers daily by telephone to ensure proper stock maintenance. The manager of a small fashion apparel business will depend upon the manufacturer's salespeople because they will provide an opportunity for obtaining seasonable merchandise and save time, effort, and money. The department-store buyer will also use the services provided by the manufacturer's salespeople.

A disadvantage of this method, however, is the fact that purchasing directly through salespeople does not give the buyer an opportunity to compare the merchandise offerings with those of other manufacturers before placing the order. The advantages of buying directly from salespeople perhaps outweigh this disadvantage. For instance, when salespeople bring in samples, the buyer will show the samples to his salespeople and merchandise manager and seek their opinions. Also, since buying is done on the retailer's home ground, the buyer may more adequately visualize how new lines of merchandise will work into the existing lines. Also, the buyer can usually do a better job of buying, since he or she has more time and can feel more at ease. This method of buying is popular with retail businesses of many types and sizes. As you recall, the rack jobber will visit food markets and small grocers for the primary purpose of checking and maintaining the merchandise inventory.

Visiting Trade Market Centers

Before beginning a discussion on the major trade centers, however, it is important to first talk about the New York "Garment District." The garment district is bounded by Ninth Avenue on the west, the Avenue of the Americas (Sixth Avenue) on the east, 34th Street on the south, and 41st Street on the north. Within the garment district are literally thousands of showrooms displaying various types and price lines of women's and children's apparel, textiles and fabrics, millinery and accessories, handbags, men's and boys wear, notions and trims for the textile industry, lingerie and underwear, and furs and accessories. Industry experts say a buyer on Seventh Avenue can find 150,000 to 200,000 different styles of women's and men's clothing and accessory items. Many showrooms are maintained by New York manufacturers while other showrooms display lines from around the world (Figure 11–6).

New York City is still considered the major fashion apparel market; however, with the proliferation of regional markets throughout the country, many manufacturers and wholesalers are showing their wares at one or more of them. Trade centers or marts offer hundreds of lines—from high fashion to volume merchandise, from hard goods to domestics—and all under one roof. A discussion on various regional marts follows.

Atlanta Apparel Mart. The Atlanta Apparel Mart houses more than 700 showrooms that are divided into sections by merchandise category, such as dresses, sportswear, children's wear, menswear, and accessories. It contains a 3,000 seat theater specifically designed for fashion shows. It serves the 11-state Southeast region.

Chicago Apparel Center. The Chicago mart is a double-towered structure with over 800 showrooms and exhibit halls. It hosts five major women's and children's markets and two men's and boys markets, annually. Over 4,000 lines are available to buyers 52 weeks a year. In addition, the Chicago Apparel Center hosts the National Bridal Show and a women's large-sized show.

Dallas Apparel Mart. The Dallas Apparel Mart has become both an apparel manufacturing center and a domestic fashion center. It is the largest mer-

Figure 11–6 An example of exhibitor information provided by the International Fashion Boutique Show.

chandise complex in the world and is comprised of six buildings on 135 acres and has 7,200,000 square feet of space. The complex includes the World Trade Center, the Trade Mart, Market Hall, the Decorative Center, the Home Furnishings Mart, and the Dallas Apparel Mart. The Dallas Apparel Mart alone has a total capacity of nearly 1,500 showrooms where over 10,000 lines may be exhibited.

California Apparel Mart. With over 2,000 showrooms and approximately 10,000 lines represented, the California Apparel Mart has done much to promote a more sportswear-oriented look or the "California look" in fashion. It is well known for its support of the California garment industry, and as a result, California has become the second largest manufacturing state. It hosts five fashion shows a year and highlights "market weeks," which run as long as two or three months.

Miami International Merchandise Mart. The Miami International Merchandise Mart has established itself in the marketplace for buyers and manufacturers from Central and South America and many of the Carribbean islands. It hosts over 300 showrooms exhibiting giftware, jewelry, apparel, and textiles. It has become a new vehicle for promoting exchange between manufacturers of domestic and Latin American goods.

Retail Buyers Contact Merchandise Resources in the Following Manner:

1. Visit local markets
2. Work with resident buying offices
3. By mail and telephone
4. Through catalogs and price lists
5. Manufacturer reps (salespeople)
6. Visit trade market centers

TRADE CALENDAR OF EVENTS

A trade calendar of events informs the retail buyer of various activities that occur throughout various fashion seasons. The outline that follows (Table 11-1) includes the basic consumer calendar, which as you recall from reading Chapter 6 is important to a retail operation because it provides information

TABLE 11–1.   Trade calendar of events.

Merchandise that Must Be in the Store	*Trade Activities*
JANUARY Cruise and resort wear Sportswear, swimsuits Casual clothing	**JANUARY** Spring ready-to-wear market opens Summer collections are shown to buyers Boutique market opens Sportswear market opens
FEBRUARY Lightweight coats New spring knits Colorful spring suits and dresses	**FEBRUARY** Fall shoe market opens Fall collections are shown Fall knitwear and sweater market opens

MARCH
Fashionable spring coats
Spring suits, dresses, and coordinates
Spring accessories: shoes, millinery,
   handbags and leather goods, belts, hosiery,
   jewelry, scarves, gloves
Spring lingerie and intimate apparel
	MARCH
	Fall men's and boys' market opens
	Junior sportswear market opens
	Boutique market opens

APRIL Presentation of summer colors and fabrics Summer dresses, active sportswear, and accessories Swimwear and beach accessories	**APRIL** Missy sportswear market opens Ski apparel market opens
MAY Transitional cottons, linens Cocktail dresses, long dresses, evening gowns Bridal fashions Summer coordinates	**MAY** Major fall ready-to-wear market opens Dresses, coats, suits, ensembles market opens Fall bridal market opens
JUNE Summer sportswear and accessories Special sports costumes	**JUNE** Couture fall ready-to-wear market opens Fall sportswear market opens

JULY
Fall bridal fashions
Transitional cottons, lightweight woolens
Fall knitwear
Fall ensembles and costumes
Transitional sweaters, jackets, coats
	JULY
	Fall and winter accessories market
	   opens
	Manufacturers' showings: coats,
	   dresses, suits, sportswear

AUGUST Childrenswear, dresses, shoes, accessories Back to school Casual and career clothing Early winter jackets Mediumweight jackets and coats Fall accessories: shoes, handbags, hats, gloves	**AUGUST** Holiday and resort market opens Cruise and resort market opens Spring shoe market opens

TABLE 11–1.   (*Continued*)

Merchandise that Must Be in the Store	*Trade Activities*
SEPTEMBER Fall ready-to-wear; coats, suits, dresses, ensembles, costumes	**SEPTEMBER** Early spring market opens Spring knitwear market opens
OCTOBER Leather and suede accessories, coats, jackets Ski apparel and accessories Medium to heavyweight tweed suits and coats	**OCTOBER** Swimsuit market opens Spring ready-to-wear market opens
NOVEMBER Holiday fashions and accessories Cruise and resort wear and accessories	**NOVEMBER** Spring bridal market opens
DECEMBER Holiday dresses, evening gowns Accessories: jewelry, scarves, handbags, leather accessories, notions, shoes, winter coats, fur coats, dresses, accessories	**DECEMBER** Little activity in the market due to the Christmas season

regarding the time period when fashion must be in the store, as well as a calendar of trade activities that informs the buyer when he or she must be in the market place.

PART 2—Buying in the Foreign Market

WHY PURCHASE FOREIGN MERCHANDISE

Many retailers have found it profitable to offer their customers foreign goods. Carved statues from Africa, chocolate candy from France, ski boots from Austria, cuckoo clocks from Switzerland, lace scarves from Spain, marble tabletops from Italy—all help to provide an assortment that is unusual, competitive, and different. The kind of imported merchandise offered, however, will depend on the merchandising policies of the store, the size of the store, the store's target market, and the amount and kind of competition in the marketplace. There are four major reasons for buying foreign products: (1) they afford an opportunity for larger markup; (2) they provide the unusual and different; (3) they add prestige and leadership; and (4) they help meet direct competition.

An Opportunity for Larger Markup

As a result of competition in the domestic market, retail specialists have had to turn to foreign markets for products that yield a reasonable markup. During the past three decades, however, there have been many fluctuations in the use of foreign markets as a source of supply. For example, years ago few retail stores carried foreign items; thus, the foreign goods selected were often sold for many times their cost. Today, however, this has changed. Many retailers, both large and small, are taking the opportunity to purchase from foreign sources, and as a result, competition has affected the markup price. This has limited the opportunity for a higher than usual markup. A buyer must be careful not to offer imported merchandise at an abnormally high markup, thus running the risk that customers may find the identical merchandise offered elsewhere at a lower price.

Provide the Unusual and Different

A second reason the buyer will balance the assortment with foreign goods is that imported merchandise provides an opportunity to round out the stock. The merchandise is considered to be unusual and different because it cannot be found in domestic markets. For example, the product may involve skilled workmanship or unusual dyes or fabrics or may combine textures and colors that are native to the country of origin. Usually imported merchandise is made by hand; in the United States, products are mass-produced, which restricts product individuality and exclusiveness. Since the buyer is using imported merchandise to round off the stock, he may place small orders with foreign producers and be assured that his orders will be filled.

The buyer may also purchase goods not for resale but to copy and then resell at a lower price. A buyer of women's dresses may attend the couture openings in Rome and purchase dresses ranging from $1,500 to $2,000. The store may have the originals copied and in turn sell the copies for $250. The originals were purchased at a loss; however, the loss will serve its purpose if the copies sell well.

Add Prestige and Leadership

The third reason for adding foreign goods to the assortment is that a store will enhance its image by selling imported merchandise. When the buyer assembles the rare and the unusual, he builds a reputation for leadership. A store may continuously build an image of prestige and leadership by holding storewide promotions of merchandise imported from a single foreign country such as Ireland, Brazil, or Great Britain.

Help Meet Direct Competition

Since there are many foreign resources available, a merchant has an opportunity to provide imported goods that are different from those offered by his competition. The uniqueness in product offerings will help a department store, chain store, small business, or whatever to maintain an image and be readily identified as a distinct type of retail store offering a balanced selection of merchandise.

How Will Foreign Buying Help the Buyer Provide a Balanced Merchandise Assortment?

1. An opportunity for larger markup
2. Providing the unusual and different
3. Adding prestige and leadership
4. Helping meet direct competition

PROBLEMS OF BUYING IN FOREIGN MARKETS

Even though the buyer or small shop owner is afforded a number of advantages by purchasing goods in foreign markets, there are a number of disadvantages to consider, such as (1) delivery problems, (2) variations in quality standards, (3) reorder leadtime, (4) discrepancy of sizes, (5) money allocations, (6) time involved, (7) landed costs, and (8) early selection decisions.

Delivery Problems

Retail buyers are plagued with delivery problems from domestic sources; however, the problem is compounded when great distances are involved as is the case in foreign market purchasing. Delivery delays cannot be predicted or guarded against. Fire, floods, labor strikes, material shortages—all can have a devastating effect on the retail store that is promoting, for example, an oriental import fair, only to have to inform its customers that merchandise is unavailable.

Variations in Quality Standards

Since most imported goods are ordered by sample, catalog description, or illustration, the merchandise ordered may be quite different than anticipated. Faulty workmanship, missing parts or pieces, and careless packaging are also problems associated with American-made goods, but when dealing with resources located great distances, merchandise returns are usually impossible. Foreign resources present even greater risks since a department can be left with merchandise that does not meet with a store's policy objectives regarding image, quality, workmanship, and so forth.

Reorder Leadtime

Unless items offered for sale are used all the time (as is the case in staple types of goods) and reorders allow for long delivery periods, leadtime to guarantee delivery is virtually impossible. The buyer of fashion goods, for example, might have a "hot" item but may not be able to supply enough merchandise for the selling season because delivery time for reorder may take longer than the planned fashion season.

Discrepancy of Sizes

How many times have you tried on a pair of imported jeans that were labeled your size but found they were too tight or too short? Or tried on a shirt that was too long in the sleeve or too loose around the collar? The problem has to do with size variations from country to country. In recent years however buyers—especially those purchasing in significant quantity—have supplied foreign resources with specific sizes and measurements. In this way, retailers have been able to offer the "unique and unusual" and yet still accommodate the American consumer.

Money Allocations

When purchasing from foreign producers, store buyers are expected to make partial payment in advance of shipment. Since capital could be tied up for a long period of time (especially if purchased way in advance of the selling season) retailers must consider the long-term effect when planning budget allowances. In the long run, prepayment of goods in advance of delivery may be an unprofitable arrangement especially for the entrepreneur.

Time Involved

Since many foreign markets are not as convenient geographically as domestic markets, travel abroad usually requires more time and planning. A visit to a local or even regional trade mart may take from a few days to a week while foreign market visits may take from two to three weeks. Retail buyers of smaller retail outlets may find that coverage of foreign markets does not warrant the valuable time away from duties and responsibilities at home.

Landed Costs

A number of costs are involved when purchasing from foreign producers. Aside from the quoted price of the merchandise, merchants need to be aware of other charges, such as delivery charges (air freight, shipping rates), insurance charges, packing charges, storage expenses, commissions, and customs duties. Customs duties may vary according to merchandise and country of origin. For example, the buyer must be aware of U.S. Customs regulations that have granted preferred nations status to many developing countries whereby most items can be imported duty-free to the United States.

Once the buyer determines all the charges involved, *the landed cost,* which is the actual cost of the goods to the buyer, is determined.

Early Selection Decisions

Buyers, especially of fashion merchandise, may have a difficult time in making early selection decisions due to the nature and seasonal life cycle of fashion items. For this reason, it is especially important for the fashion buyer to work closely with his or her store's fashion coordinator as well as the fashion representative from the store's resident buying office. Information regarding color trends, styles, and fabrics is also available in trade papers, such as *Women's Wear Daily,* and from fashion reporting services, for example, RAM reports. You may wish to review trade sources of information in Chapter 5.

PROCESS USED TO PURCHASE FOREIGN GOODS

As previously stated, a retail store will add imported goods to its merchandise assortment to obtain a larger markup, offer the unique and the different, and obtain the prestige often associated with imported merchandise. The following six channels of foreign buying may be used: (1) private import wholesalers; (2) foreign exporters or selling houses; (3) purchasing agents or commissionaires; (4) stored-owned foreign buying offices; (5) buying trips to foreign markets; and (6) import trade fairs.

Private Import Wholesalers

Private import wholesalers serve many sizes and types of retail stores that desire foreign products. Import wholesalers are middlemen who purchase samples of foreign products and in turn offer the goods to retailers through the use of catalogs and salespeople. Even though the goods procured from this type of foreign resource cost more than they would if a direct foreign contact were used, the buyer will find that the private wholesaler is a specialist in a particular merchandise category. Also, he or she will usually assume the risks involved in foreign buying as well as the financial responsibility.

Many small businesses use the private import wholesaler. For example, an owner-manager of a women's speciality shop may receive a catalog from a wholesaler who imports women's sweaters and knit accessories from Italy. The owner-manager may select the goods from the catalog or ask the importer to send a salesperson to the shop. The salesperson will show a wide range of samples of the stocks available and discuss quantity discounts, delivery terms, and methods of payment. When a retailer uses foreign merchandise resources, delivery dates and shipping methods are very important, due to the time and distance involved.

Foreign Exporters or Selling Houses

Foreign exporters are middlemen who export goods from a particular country. Often they will locate in the major market centers, such as New York City, where buying specialists may come to visit them in their showrooms and see samples of the various lines they represent. Depending on the size of the selling house, these foreign exporters may have a special import buying show before particular selling seasons to encourage buyers, especially from specialty stores and department stores, to purchase their goods. Foreign exporters will facilitate foreign buying since they are in a better position to understand market conditions and problems with shipping and supply and may communicate with buying sources almost daily. These exporters will also send catalogs or salespeople to retailers to inform them of the merchandise available for sale.

Purchasing Agents or Commissionaires

Purchasing agent is the title given to the individual who represents a foreign resident buying office under American management, whereas *commissionaire* is the title given to the individual who represents a foreign resident buying office under foreign management. Foreign resident buying offices operate in much the same way as salaried resident buying offices in American cities. These offices assist buying specialists in selecting merchandise for resale. Foreign resident buying offices generally charge a percentage of the net foreign cost of the purchases they make, however the rate of commission will vary according to the type of merchandise being purchased and the nature of the market. Some foreign buying offices also work with New York resident buying offices so that buyers from stores that belong to the buying office in

New York may make use of the services of the commissionaire when abroad. A store may be billed by a commissionaire from the Netherlands, for example.

Store-Owned Foreign Buying Office

A foreign buying office may also be store-owned, that is, owned by a group of noncompeting stores, which will share expenses for the operation and maintenance of the foreign office. For example, the Associated Merchandising Corporation and the Associated Dry Goods Corporation maintain buying offices in London, and the Great Atlantic & Pacific Tea Company (A & P) has buying offices in Colombia and Brazil to purchase coffee beans. The association type of foreign buying office, like the association type of resident buying office, makes possible the exchange of information among member stores, provides ample opportunity for increased buying power for each member store, and gives each store control over the operation of the foreign buying office. Managers of foreign offices will make numerous visits to the stores they represent in this country. During these visits the foreign agent will determine the needs of individual stores and provide a wide assortment of samples for the inspection of various buying specialists. For example, a buyer for a wig department will discuss with the foreign buying specialist the availability of new styles of wigs and hairpieces, the costs of importing the merchandise, shipping and delivery terms, special and promotional goods, and so forth. In turn, the foreign specialist will inform the buyer of how well merchandise is or is not selling in different parts of the country and discuss popular styles and any problems encountered.

Buying Trips to Foreign Markets

Another method of purchasing foreign goods is for buying specialists, particularly chain and department-store buyers, to visit foreign merchandise resources personally. Usually, buyers of high-priced fashion apparel and accessories, giftware, and linens and related domestics will visit foreign markets. For example, a buyer of fashion goods may visit foreign markets late in the winter season and during the spring season to have the merchandise when required. A buyer of linens and domestics may visit foreign resources at least once a year. Today, buyers find it desirable to make direct contact with foreign resources because of the need to style foreign goods to meet the requirements set by American manufacturers.

The foreign buying trip, like the buying trip to domestic markets, requires careful and accurate planning. For example, the buyer of a better dresses department will draw up a foreign purchase plan, on which are listed the assortment of goods according to size, style, color, etc., the quantity to be purchased, the expected costs, terms and methods of shipping, delivery time, discounts available, and terms of sale. Often the buyer will tour several countries, in which case a separate plan should be made out for each resource visited. Once the foreign buying plan is developed, however, the buyer must plan the details of the buying trip—for example, the itinerary to be followed, the date of arrival in each country, the departure time, the hotel accommodations, and so forth. Planning will enable the store to keep in touch with the buyer and allow the foreign buying agent to prepare for the buyer's arrival. It will also ensure that the buyer's time is budgeted properly so that that too much time is not spent with certain resources early in the trip, leaving too little time at the end for the new and unexpected.

As discussed previously, while personal visits to foreign markets provide an opportunity to find the unique and the unusual, there are disadvantages. For example, while the buyer of better dresses is visiting foreign resources, the department tends to suffer. Problems may arise with regard to lost or delayed shipments, slow sellers, inadequacy of sales personnel, customer complaints about inferior goods, and so on.

A major objection to making trips abroad is the expense and time involved. Usually, however, the expense is compensated for by the profit increase resulting from purchasing foreign goods, and time spent may be minimized as the result of air travel.

Another objection is that it is difficult for the buyer to estimate needs. The goods in their foreign setting may possess glamour and excitement, but at home they may be found to be uninteresting or out of place with respect to the rest of the merchandise line. For example, a leather coat may look very luxurious against its native setting, however, when compared to American-made products the coat may look inferior.

Finally, when buyers go to foreign markets, there is a tendency to rush through the buying process, attempting to view as many different lines as possible and perhaps purchasing hastily due to tight buying schedules. Sometimes the time schedule is so tight that the buyer is not able to consult with foreign craftsmen or smaller, less popular resources to find the best in foreign-made goods—goods that will meet the needs and tastes of the American consumer.

Import Trade Fairs

For those American buyers who cannot or do not wish to make buying trips abroad, many foreign producers have organized trade fairs in the United States. Foreign exporters or selling houses will rent space to display and sell merchandise to visiting buyers. For example, the New York Pret held in New York City is one of the largest and most successful trade shows hosting over 1,500 manufacturers showing goods from all over the world. Another example is the International Fashion Boutique Show that is held three times a year at the Jacob K. Javits Convention Center in New York City. This is a wom-

Figure 11–7   The International Fashion Boutique Show is a women's fashion trade show held three times a year. More than 1,800 fashion apparel and accessory manufacturers and suppliers exhibit at the show, which is visited by approximately 30,000 retailers and buyers from across the country and abroad. (Courtesy of International Fashion Boutique Show)

en's fashion trade show, where more than 1,800 fashion apparel and accessory manufacturers and suppliers exhibit, that is visited by approximately 30,000 retailers and buyers from across the country and abroad. Show visitors represent speciality shops, boutiques, department and chain stores, discount and variety stores, and gift stores (see Figure 11–7).

When Will the Buying Specialist Use the Following Foreign Buying Resources:

Private import wholesaler
Foreign exporter or selling house
Purchasing agent or commissionaire
Store-owned foreign buying office
Buying trips to foreign markets
Import trade fairs

THE IMPORT PURCHASE ORDER— ASPECTS AND LEGAL REQUIREMENTS

The import purchase order, like the domestic purchase order discussed in Chapter 13, must be filled out completely and accurately. Several factors require attention when filling out the import purchase order.[3] They are:

(1) Description of merchandise ordered
(2) Textile quota category
(3) Foreign currency exchange
(4) Legal requirements

Description of Merchandise Ordered

The merchandise purchased must be completely described on the order form. For example, if purchasing men's shirts it is important to describe the "shirt" by including the gender of the wearer, generic name of the fiber content, if it is decorated or not, care labeling, country of origin, monetary value, and so forth. A complete description is necessary in order to insure that the appropriate tariff classification and duty rate are applied.

Textile Quota Category

The quota category number must be clearly indicated on the order form especially if the merchandise purchased is covered by a textile quota. This information is usually obtained from the buyer's representative or vendor.

Foreign Currency Exchange

When the order is placed, the buyer must negotiate with the vendor the extent of risk regarding currency rates. For example, if the purchase is being paid in foreign currency then the first rate of exchange must be clearly noted on the order form to protect the buyer from fluctuating rates of exchange. The same is the case if U.S. dollars are used to make purchases. This information must be clearly documented on the order form.

Legal Requirements

Unlike domestic purchases where the manufacturer is held responsible for meeting federal regulations, in import buying the responsibility is wholly that of the retailer—in this case the buyer. The buyer must be fully aware of federal regulations and in turn inform foreign vendors of U.S. trade regulations. As you recall from reading Chapter 2, part 2— Federal Regulations,

Implications for the Retail Buyer, there are a number of federal regulations of which the buyer must be aware. By way of review that are outlined here. However, review Chapter 2 for a more in-depth discussion.

Federal legislation that affects retail buyers in foreign markets:

Product Safety
    Wool Products Labeling Act, 1939
    Fur Products Labeling Act, 1951
    Flammable Fabrics Acts, 1953, amended 1967
    Consumer Products Safety Act, 1972
    Textile Fiber Products Indentification Act, 1958, amended 1965
Consumer Protection
    Magnuson-Moss Warranty-Federal Trade Commission Improvement Act, 1975
Packaging, Labeling, and Advertising
    Fair Packaging and Labeling Act, 1966; amended 1968
    Federal Cigarette Labeling and Advertising Act, 1965
    Food, Drug, and Cosmetic Act, 1938 amended 1976
    Care Labeling of Textile Wearing Apparel, 1972
Unfair Trade Practice Laws
    Federal Trade Commission Act, 1914; amended 1938
    Export Trade Act, 1918
    Lanham Trademark Act, 1946, amended 1962

THE ROLE OF THE CUSTOMS BROKER

In order to speed the clearance of merchandise through customs, the services of a customs broker is required. The customs broker, who is licensed by the Treasury Department, prepares the necessary forms to release the goods, arranges for payments of tariffs, and makes transportation arrangments with shippers and/or local carriers. The customs broker also plays an important role in following up on merchandise until it is safely in the hands of the store buyer.[4]

MAJOR FOREIGN PRODUCERS

Retail buyers travel all over the world to satisfy their merchandise needs. The following list includes the major foreign markets in which American buyers are satisfying the import needs of consumers:

EUROPE AND THE MIDDLE EAST

Austria	Italy
Belgium	Israel
Denmark	Portugal
England	Spain
Finland	Sweden
France	Switzerland
Germany	
Greece	
Holland	

THE FAR EAST

Japan	India
Hong Kong	Philippines
Taiwan	Thailand
Korea	

CENTRAL AND SOUTH AMERICAN

Colombia
Mexico
Brazil
Argentina
Venezuela

OTHER IMPORTANT FOREIGN PRODUCERS

Canada
USSR

Chapter Summary

Buying whether in domestic or foreign markets requires careful planning. Once the buying plan is formulated, a market agenda is determined. The student should review important factors to be included in the market agenda.

Three major sources of supply are available to the retail buyer. The buyer must first determine which major source of supply will best suit the needs of the store or department. Once this decision is made, he must determine who will be the key resources, that is, where buying interests will be concentrated. This concentration on key resources depends to a great extent upon the buying power available, as well as upon the desire of the buyer to broaden market contacts by experimenting with new items and new resources. The buyer must weigh all the selection factors before making a decision as to the choice of merchandise resources.

A buyer may make buying contacts in several ways: visit local markets, use the resident buying office, by mail and telephone, through catalogs and price lists, visits from manufacturers' representatives, and visit trade market centers. The student should review the trade calendar of events which informs the buyer of retailing activities that occur throughout various fashion seasons both in the store and in the trade markets.

Many types of retail institutions have also found it advantageous to purchase goods from foreign resources. Resources may be contacted in much the same way as in the domestic market. For example, a buyer may seek information regarding foreign merchandise resources by contacting the resident buying office. Or foreign resources may send catalogs and price lists to prospective clients. In some cases, foreign offices will send salesmen who will display lines of merchandise and provide samples for their buyers. As a result of competition in the domestic market, retail buyers have turned to imported merchandise because such commodities provide an opportunity for a larger markup, create an atmosphere of the unusual and different, and add an image of prestige and leadership to a retail store. There are also a number of disadvantages to buying foreign merchandise.

A number of methods may be used to purchase foreign goods, such as private import wholesalers, foreign exporters or selling houses, purchasing agents or commissionaires, store-owned foreign buying offices, buying trips to foreign markets, and import trade fairs. The import purchase order must be filled out completely and accurately and a number of factors such as description of merchandise ordered, textile quota category, foreign currency exchange, and legal requirements require attention. The customs broker plays an important role from preparing necessary forms to releasing the goods, to following up on merchandise until it is safely in the hands of the store buyer.

Trade Terminology

DIRECTIONS: Briefly explain or discuss each of the following trade terms:

1. Middlemen
2. Wholesalers
3. Merchant middlemen
4. Service wholesalers
5. Limited-function wholesaler
6. Rack jobbers

7. Nonmerchant middlemen
8. Brokers
9. Commission men
10. Selling agents
11. Manufacturers' agents
12. Auctions
13. Manufacturers
14. Purchasing agent
15. Commissionaire
16. Landed cost

Questions for Discussion and Review

1. Why is it important to prepare a buying plan?

2. What kind(s) of information should be contained in the market agenda?

3. Distinguish between middlemen, manufacturers, and farmers and growers.

4. Why have "marts" or "trade centers" become so popular today?

5. What are regional trade centers? Discuss the various examples provided in this chapter.

6. How do you explain the fact that some retail buyers go to the central market frequently, while others go very little?

7. As a buyer of small leather accessories, you wish to expand your purchases of foreign goods. How would you accomplish this? Explain.

8. Discuss various problems you may encounter when purchasing in foreign market centers.

9. What are the six methods used to make foreign buying contacts?

10. Why is the New York "Garment District" considered a major trade center in fashion apparel?

References

The Retail
Student's Reference Library

Applebaum, W. and Goldberg, R. *Brand Strategy in U.S. Food Marketing.* Boston: Harvard University Press, n.d.

Cahill, Jane. *Can A Small Store Succeed?* New York: Fairchild Pub., Inc., n.d.

Ferguson, F. *Efficient Drug Store Management.* New York: Fairchild Pub., Inc., n.d.

Gold, E. B. *Dynamics of Retailing.* New York: Fairchild Pub., Inc., n.d.

Helfant, S., and Judelle B. *Management Manual for Independent Stores.* New York: NRMA, n.d.

Kelley, P. C. *Variety Stores.* Washington, D.C.: Small Business Administration, n.d.

Lynch, Richard. *Introduction to Marketing.* New York: McGraw-Hill Book Co., 1984.

Mulgern, Helen. *Facts about Department Stores.* New York: NRMA, n.d.

A Retailer Visits the Market. New York: Fairchild Pub., Inc. n.d.

Rice, J. W. *Furniture Retailing.* Washington, D.C.: Small Business Administration, n.d.

Ritter, Dorothy. *Hardware Retailing.* Washington, D.C.: Small Business Administration, n.d.

Robinson, J. W. *Gift and Art Shops.* Washington, D.C.: Small Business Administration, n.d.

Rosenbloom, Bert. *Retail Marketing.* Westminister, Maryland: Random House, 1985.

Schewe, Charles D. *Marketing: Concepts and Applications.* New York: McGraw-Hill Book Co., 1983.

Slom, S. *Profitable Furniture Retailing: For the Home Furnishing Markets.* New York: Fairchild Pub., Inc., n.d.

Stanton, William J. *Fundamentals of Marketing.* New York: McGraw-Hill Book Co., 1987.

Urban, Glen L. and Hauser, John R. *Design and Marketing of New Products.* Englewood Cliffs, N.J.: Prentice Hall Pub. Co., 1985.

References

1. D. J. Ducan and C. F. Phillips, *Retailing Principles and Methods* (Homewood, Ill.: Richard D. Irwin, Inc., 1969), p. 307.

2. *The Buyer's Manual* (New York: National Retail Merchants Association, 1970), p. 75.

3. Ibid., p. 119.

4. Ibid., p. 123.

5. *Fashion Coordination* (New York: ITT Educational Service, Inc., 1969), pp. 12–23.

Services Offered by Merchandise Resources

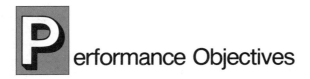

Performance Objectives

After reading this chapter the student should be able to accomplish the following:

1. Classify under major headings services offered by merchandise vendors.

2. Discuss the differences between personal and nonpersonal promotional aids.

3. List and define six selling aids offered by vendors.

4. Discuss the return privilege.

5. Discuss six promotional allowances offered by vendors that reprice.

6. Explain four types of dealer helps and tell how they may be useful in attracting customer attention and interest.

7. Become aware of six types of consumer inducements used by retailers.

Services Offered by Merchandise Resources

Figure 12-1 A type of promotional service from the vendor is free display material. (Courtesy of The Gift Gallery, Havertown, Pa.)

INTRODUCTION

In the previous chapter you learned that the buyer will search both domestic and foreign markets for different types of merchandise. However, the buyer must first prepare a buying plan that will summarize purchases by classifications, price lines, styles, sizes, and colors. Once the buying plan has been formulated, the buyer will outline the market agenda, which includes a number of important factors ranging from making appointments with the resident buying office to making arrangements to view manufacturers' lines to contacting primary producers.

There are three major sources of supply available: middlemen, manufacturers, and farmers and growers.

How does a buyer make contacts in the marketplace? He or she may visit local markets, use the resident buying office, use mail and telephone, use catalogs and price lists, be visited by manufacturers reps, and/or visit trade market centers.

Many retailers have found it profitable to offer their customers merchandise from foreign sources. There are a number of reasons for purchasing foreign products; however, there are also disadvantages to consider. A number of methods may be used to purchase foreign goods, such as private import wholesalers, foreign exporters or selling houses, purchasing agents or commissionaires, store-owned foreign buying offices, buying trips to foreign markets, and trade fairs.

In this chapter we are concerned with services offered by merchandise resources whether domestic or foreign. Services offered may be divided into two types: personal promotional aids that are services that directly affect the selling activity of the buyer and nonpersonal promotional aids that are services that directly influence the buying behavior of the consumer. Examples of personal promotional aides include selling aids, such as demonstrators, finance and credit, return privilege, exclusive distribution, markdown insurance and "on memorandum," and promotional allowances, such as cooperative advertising, preferred selling space, free display material, price decline guarantees, and merchandise deals. Examples of nonpersonal promotional aides are dealer's helps, such as packaging, labeling, and price ticketing and consumer inducements that include premiums, coupons, contests, deals, trading stamps, and sampling.

An important responsibility of all buyers is to solicit every service to which the store is entitled that is available from the merchandise broker, wholesaler, rack jobber, and vendor—whether domestic or foreign. Of course, the services offered to merchants will depend on the type of merchandise resource, the amount and nature of the business conducted between retailer and supplier, and the type of buyer-vendor relationship established. The topic of buyer-vendor relationship will be discussed in detail in Chapter 13.

PART 1—Personal Promotion Aids

SERVICES OFFERED BY MERCHANDISE RESOURCES

When the buyer goes to the marketplace, he or she must be guided by past experience and judgment, as well as the knowledge that most merchandise resources have both the background and the incentive to provide fruitful assistance. An important responsibility of all buyers is to solicit every service to which the store is entitled that is available from the merchandise broker, wholesaler, rack jobber, vendor, whether domestic or foreign. Sometimes a buyer may have to request a particular service, offer suggestions for additional services, or seek improvements on those services already available. Of course, the services offered to merchants will depend on the type of merchandise resource, the amount and nature of the business conducted between retailer and supplier, and the type of buyer-vendor relationship established.

For purposes of study, however, services may be divided into two types. First, *personal promotional aids* are those services that directly affect the selling activity of the buyer; they include selling aids and promotional allowances (Figure 12–1). Second, *nonpersonal promotional aids* are those services that directly influence the buying behavior of the consumer; they include dealers' helps and consumer inducements.

Service Offered By Merchandise Resources

Personal Promotion Aids

1. Selling aids
2. Promotional allowances

Nonpersonal Promotion Aids

1. Dealer's helps
2. Consumer inducements

SELLING AIDS

The following is a list of selling aids offered by merchandise resources. However, it is important to remember that the buyer must determine if the ser-

---

Selling Aids Offered by Merchandise Resources Are:

1. Demonstrators
2. Finance and credit
3. Return privilege
4. Exclusive distribution
5. Markdown insurance
6. On memorandum

vices available are in the buyer's best interests, those of the retail organization, and those of the clientele.

Demonstrators

Assistance from middlemen or manufacturers in connection with personal selling is often welcomed by the retail buyer. In housewares and cosmetics, especially, vendors will often provide their client stores with demonstrators. These individuals will demonstrate the product to salepeople, pointing out product advantages, suggesting selling techniques, and relating pertinent merchandise facts that will help to sell the product. Also, demonstrators may actually demonstrate the item on the floor, showing store customers how to use a particular product to best advantage. In this case, resulting sales may be turned over to regular salespeople, or the demonstrator may actually complete the sale.

Demonstrators are usually used in departments where brand reputation is important. In this case, the department's selling costs are reduced since trained demonstrators are responsible for increasing department sales. However, a retail store must be careful when using demonstrators, especially if they are responsible for completing sales. For example, a customer may come to the department seeking an item, only to be misled by the demonstrator, who is "pushing" a particular brand. The customer may purchase the brand being promoted by the department only to be dissatisfied with the product later.

Usually, when a store decides to use demonstrators, it will place them through its personnel office. The purpose of this procedure is to have it clearly understood that demonstrators are employees of the store and thus subject to the store's merchandising policies and procedures. If this procedure is not followed, it may become difficult to get demonstrators to observe store regulations. The small business, on the other hand, does not use demonstrators, since the cost of their services is not in proportion to the volume of purchases made by the owner-manager. As a result, the small business manager will seek an alternate service from vendors, for example, displays that can help sell merchandise.

Finance and Credit

A second important service offered by many vendors is finance and credit. Most retail buying is accomplished on an open-account basis, with 30 days allowed from date of the invoice until payment. Often a discount is allowed if the bill is paid in a shorter period of time, such as ten days. There are particular terms the student should become familiar with, since this information is necessary in order placement and receiving and in vendor negotiations. These topics will be covered in detail in Chapters 13 and 14.

Return Privilege

The return privilege is a third important service offered by merchandise resources. The vendor in some instances will agree to take back the merchandise if it is not sold within a specified period of time. In this case, the risk of markdown is carried by the vendor. The return privilege may take on two forms: consignment selling, whereby the store acts as an agent for the vendor, and selling with the privilege of return. Unlike consignment selling, sale with return privilege signifies that the title passes to the store buyer when the goods are shipped, yet the vendor will take back the unsold portion of the stock within a specified time period. A contractual agreement is made between vendor and buyer whereby the vendor continues to assume a contractual obligation to take back the unsold portion of the goods.

The return privilege is a device used by most retail stores to shift the risk of selling back to the vendor. Therefore, since the risk of markdown is carried by the vendor or supplier, the buyer's maintained markup is equivalent to the initial markup.

Often consignment selling and sale with return privilege are used by buying specialists as a form of price concession to obtain sales that would not be available otherwise. For example, a department-store buyer may refuse to pay a price of $30 on a dozen items; however, the buyer may agree to the price if he or she need pay only for the merchandise sold at a realistic markup and can have a return privilege contract with the supplier. The vendor may agree to this arrangement if he or she is selling new merchandise or is getting rid of old stock, which may require a large markdown unless sold under these conditions. A disadvantage of this method to the supplier is that it may fostor excessive returns of unsold merchandise, especially if the supplier is not in a position to insist upon the retailer providing adequate advertising and promotional coverage for the product line.

On Memorandum

On memorandum is a term used in connection with a consignment sale or a sale with the return privilege. The specific details of the memorandum will determine its significance. For example, in the fine jewelry trade (in contrast to costume jewelry), it is understood that the title remains with the supplier and that the retail buyer receiving the merchandise is responsible either to sell the merchandise and account for the sales or to return the merchandise to the vendor.[1] Specific details of the memorandum are determined by the buyer and the supplier.

Exclusive Distribution

Vendors may control the distribution of their merchandise by dictating the resale price to the store buyer. You can see how consignment selling was found to be a legal method of achieving this end. The store was an agent, since it did not take title to the merchandise and therefore had to abide by the regulations set by the merchandise resource. It was soon found, however, that few vendors who desired to control retail prices would sell under a resale contract, which is legal in most states. Also, federal law does not allow the merchant to enter into such arrangements if they are considered to be part of a conspiracy with other merchants or suppliers to restrain trade or to monopolize the marketplace.

Markdown Insurance

Markdown insurance is a relatively new form of risk bearing assumed by vendors and is developing particularly in the area of women's fashion apparel. Buyers are requesting that manufacturers guarantee them against markdowns, which are usually necessary late in the season. Store buyers are asking that manufacturers reimburse them for half the amount of markdowns they find necessary to take. Many vendors are resisting such demands, since the general consensus is that such a practice will lead to careless buying and to increases in the cost of distribution.

PROMOTIONAL ALLOWANCES

Often, to ensure maximum cooperation between the buyer and the seller, promotional services, the second type of personal promotional aid, are offered by vendors. Such services may take the form of (1) cooperative advertising, (2) preferred selling space, (3) free display material, (4) unit packaging, (5) price decline guarantees, and (6) merchandise deals.

Promotional Allowances That Reduce Price Offered by Vendors

1. Cooperative advertising
2. Preferred selling space
3. Free display material
4. Price decline guarantees
5. Merchandise deals

Cooperative Advertising

Many consumers are unaware that most retail store advertisements are paid for either in part or wholly by merchandise resources. These resources seek increased cooperation in the sale of their merchandise from retailers at the point of sale. Cooperative advertising is a service offered by suppliers who arrange with retail stores to share advertising expenses. This is a most important promotional tool. Estimates reveal that over $500 million annually is spent on cooperative advertising and that more than 30 percent of the total advertising costs of department stores are supplied by cooperative advertising allowances.[2]

The federal government forbids discrimination in the giving and receiving of advertising. Advertising allowances must be offered to all retailers on proportionately equal terms. Large retail stores will receive the largest cooperative advertising allowances; however, the allowance must have a proportional relationship to the advertising services performed. The federal government further states that the buying specialists for large retail organizations have a greater responsibility than small shop owners to be aware of discrimination.

Most advertising allowances were originally intended for the retailer's newspaper advertising. However, recent trends have been for many retail stores to contract with manufacturers for allowances for radio and television advertising or for magazine space. Also, manufacturers have not only been charged for space in the advertising media, but also for overhead in the store's advertising department.

The advantages of cooperative advertising are many. The retail store is able to meet competition from large chain operations as well as reducing the cost of maintaining its own advertising department. A small store may obtain better copy and art work as a result of the experience of the cooperating advertiser. On the other hand, the cooperating advertiser may be assured adequate and complete advertising that the retail store's budget may not permit. He or she may also pressure the store into selling new products as well as maintaining already existing lines.

There are also disadvantages to cooperative advertising. The store may have a tendency to promote only merchandise that includes an advertising allowance, rather than goods that are of top quality and in demand. Certain lines of merchandise may be given more selling space than they deserve. Also, the type of layout and copy insisted upon by the vendor may not be in keeping with the image of the store or its established standards. A major disadvantage for the manufacturer is that the allowance provided may not be used for advertising by the store, or at least not used effectively. Often advertising allowances are used as price-cutting devices.

Preferred Selling Space

A second type of promotional allowance offered by vendors is preferred selling space. That is to say, the retail buyer will offer preferred selling space to the vendor, and in return will be granted an allowance from the regular price. For example, the merchandise may be given a special window treatment or perhaps will be assigned space near the check-out counter. In many types of stores, especially variety stores and food markets, the value of each display area has been charted; thus, a vendor may be provided with preferred space with the assurance of an increased sales volume. The small business, especially in the hard-goods and drug fields, will take advantage of allowances offered by vendors for preferred selling space. The small business operator will place certain items alongside the cash register, on corner aisles, in the shop window, and in other effective display areas. Usually the merchandise is stable in nature and constitutes convenience items and impulse goods that are readily purchased by customers.

Free Display Material

A third type of promotional service from the vendor is the provision of free display material. Counter exhibits, window displays, elaborate signs, and sometimes "giveaways" are frequently available to the store buyer for the asking. Display material often costs vendors considerable amounts of money; however, they feel that the additional sales produced by it are well worth the expense. The buyer must use such material with caution and restraint, however. A window containing nothing but vendor materials may distract from the image of the store. Display materials offered by merchandise resources are often the results of the creative efforts of advertising agencies and thus do not reflect the image of a particular store. Sometimes the display materials are large and elaborate and the results are impractical, especially for the small retailer.

Price Decline Guarantees

When seasonal merchandise is ordered well in advance, it is often possible to obtain special guarantees against price declines, a fourth type of promotional service from the vendor. For example, if a buyer agrees to purchase merchandise from a vendor in September when seasonally he does not need the good until January, he will be guaranteed protection from a price decline during the time period involved. For example, if the buyer purchases the goods at $7 and the price in January is $6, the vendor will credit or refund the store $1 for each article the buyer has on hand January 1. The vendor will agree to this arrangement to secure orders during the off-season so that he can continue plant operation.

Merchandise Deals

In merchandise deals, a fifth type of promotional service, goods are given free by the vendor if the buyer orders in quantity or performs a promotional service. For example, a buyer for stationery may be offered two dozen pencils free with an order of ten dozen boxes of deluxe writing paper. Merchandise deals are offered by manufacturers to induce buyers to purchase "tie-in" merchandise or some other merchandise made by the manufacturer. Usually, the small business will attempt to secure merchandise deals to stimulate merchandise offerings and thus build sales. For example, the owner-manager of a men's wear shop may purchase fifty units of men's shirts and be offered a deal of one dozen ties to coordinate with the shirts. The shop owner is pleased to get "a little something for nothing," and the vendor is satisfied to have stimulated sales for a line of shirts. Buyers, however, must be careful when accepting such offers, since they must be certain there is a market to sell the goods as well as the merchandise accompanying the items.

Personal Promotional Aids May Include:

I. Vendor's selling aids

Demonstrators	Finance and credit
Return privilege	Exclusive distribution
Markdown insurance	On memorandum

II. Promotional allowances

Advertising allowances	Preferred selling space
Free display material	Price decline guarantees
Merchandise deals	

Review how each will affect the selling activity of buying specialists

---

PART 2—Nonpersonal Promotional Aids

DEALER HELPS

Nonpersonal promotional aids are welcomed by the buyer because they are useful in attracting attention and interest. Since nonpersonal promotional aids are those services that directly influence the buying behavior of the customer, they will be classified as follows: (1) dealer helps and (2) consumer inducements.

> ## Dealer Helps Are a Type of Nonpersonal Promotional Aid
>
> Examples are:
>
> 1. Packaging
> 2. Labeling
> 3. Price ticketing
> 4. Electronic Marking Systems

Packaging

After World War II, improvements in the art of packaging, as well as the trend toward self-service, led retail buyers to recognize that many products take on more value and have more consumer appeal when they appear in well-designed, attractive packages. Also, good packaging can save selling time on the part of the sale personnel. This is especially true in merchandise that in itself has little eye appeal. For example, staple goods such as hardware, tools, auto accessories, kitchen utensils, and stationery are unaffected by fashion seasons. They are not sought for their fashion appeal but for their utilitarian appeal. The vendors then will provide prepackaging to make the

Figure 12–2 Unit packaging offers many advantages to retailers. The buyer is often able to obtain this service at no extra charge, since it will add to the salability of the product.

items more interesting. They usually have the facilities as well as the expertise to do so.

The vendors will also provide unit packaging (Figure 12–2). For example, they will supply tennis balls three to a package or light bulbs two to a package. Since the vendors are first to see changes in unit quantities as well as trends in packaging designs, they are excellent sources of information in this area.

New techniques in packaging have also helped to eliminate problems resulting from shoplifting. For example, small items such as cosmetics and candy are packaged into containers that cannot be easily concealed. Packaging will also protect merchandise from being damaged or soiled. For example, men's shirts and women's blouses are packed in clear cellophane bags. Perishables, such as meats and dairy products, are packaged to provide the consumer with adequate visual inspection as well as easy storage.

Well-designed packaging will attract customer attention and will act as a silent salesperson for the merchandise it contains. The buyer who considers packaging from the point of view of the customer will analyze and study the packaging as well as the contents, considering the following factors:

- Will the package design protect the merchandise while it is in transit, in storage, on the selling floor, and carried home by the customer?
- Will the package design conserve storage space and fit into existing merchandise display fixtures?
- Does the packaging make the merchandise too heavy or bulky to ship or carry?
- Does the packaging provide selling appeal?
- Will the packaging protect the merchandise from pilferage and shoplifting?
- Is the merchandise clearly identified?
- Will the packaging provide an opportunity for the customer to inspect the merchandise?
- Does the package contain required care and labeling information?
- How is the package opened? Is it functional?
- Apart from holding merchandise, what other uses does the packaging serve?

Labeling

Labeling is a nonpersonal selling aid of growing importance today (Figure 12–3). Readying merchandise for resale is an important vendor service, which involves not only packaging but also labeling. In some cases the package may serve as the label; however, products that are not unit packaged,

Figure 12-3 Labeling and ticketing, important vendor services, are types of nonpersonal selling aids growing in popularity today.

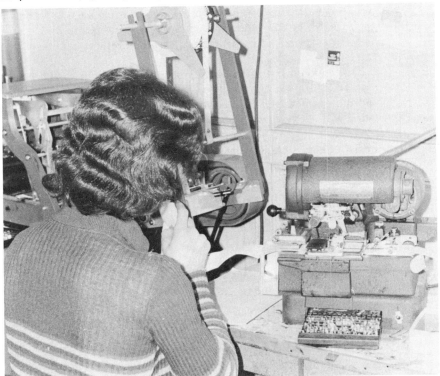

such as clothing, need labels. Labels are usually attached directly to the merchandise; if this is done by the vendor, the label emphasizes the brand name and provides little factual information. However, consumers have demanded product information to assist them in buying, and the federal government has developed trade practice regulations requiring that labels show the fiber content, the percent of fiber used, and instructions for washing and care. (Review the Fair Packaging and Labeling Act, discussed in Chapter 2.) Every buyer should be interested in working with suppliers and the government toward providing consumer protection as well as preventing dissatisfaction, which would foster consumer ill will and thus affect the store's image.

The buyer should carefully study a product presented by a vendor and determine if the printed message contained on the package or on the label contains all necessary information. The buyer must be able to determine the ingredients, fiber content, or whatever in determining merchandise value in relation to cost. If important details are missing or unimportant details are exaggerated, the buyer should call this to the attention of the vendor, and if still in doubt, should consult the store's legal counsel.

For example, in the area of housewares and appliances, the consumer needs to know how much service he or she can expect to derive from a product and what alternatives are available if the product does not perform as expected. The manufacturer and the buyer will provide this information to sell the merchandise. They will spell out the guarantee in words that do not leave them open to unfair and unjust claims for repair, refund, or replacement. The Federal Trade Commission further offers definite recommendations in this area. It states that the guarantee should be a genuine attempt to protect the consumer rather than the manufacturer. The buyer and the manufacturer should check for the following information: the name of the guarantor, products or parts covered by the guarantee, length of the guarantee period, how the customer will secure action if not satisfied, matching of all statements in the guarantee, ease of reading of the guarantee, and the guarantee's location in an obvious place.[3]

Labels, therefore, have two primary functions: (1) they provide salespeople with specific information about the features of the garment, and (2) they assist the customer in making a selection, especially if the retail store carries several quality lines of a particular product.

It is in the best interest of the retail buyer to negotiate for labels that will best satisfy the store's and the client's needs, especially in such matters as size, appearance, type, and amount. The buyer should arrange with the vendor that all merchandise information be included on one label that is attached at a central point. Some vendors may attach three to five labels to each garment; however, this is unsightly and confusing to the customer.

Price Ticketing

To purchase merchandise, the consumer needs specific price information. This information is placed on the merchandise in the form of a label, as just discussed, or on a price ticket, which is either attached directly to the merchandise or placed near the product.

Price tickets are also provided by vendors, which is called preticketing. The Association of General Merchandise Chains has been working on preticketing of merchandise items by suppliers before shipping goods to retailers. This organization has developed a standard reorder ticket that can be inserted in the product's container or bin or attached by a string or pin to a wide variety of items.[4] A preticketing service eliminates heavy costs of ticketing.

Buyers of soft goods and fashion apparel have begun to make demands on the seller by insisting that price tickets include such information as purchase date, department and classification number, manufacturer or vendor number, size, color, season, style number, cost price, and retail price. The buyer insists that this job can best be accomplished by the vendor, who can do the job more cheaply and effectively.

Many kinds of price tickets or tags are used for marking products. Gummed labels and pin tickets, whether machine-attached or hand-attached, are usually the cheapest and fastest forms of ticketing. However, whether to use a label, a string ticket, or a handwritten ticket depends upon the kind of merchandise to be marked. For example, string tags are usually used on clothing; merchandise with a hard surface is usually marked with gummed labels; and pin tickets are used on products that pinholes will not damage.

Not all merchandise needs to be marked, particularly where personal selling is used rather than self-service. For example, low-priced, fast-selling staples are not individually marked. Instead they are sold from containers, shelves, trays, or bins that are marked with the price. In self-service stores, however, each individual item is usually marked. For example, in supermarkets, discount houses, low-margin retail stores and variety stores, individual items are marked so that neither the customer nor the cashier performing the check-out process will have problems in attempting to determine the correct price.

Electronic Marking Systems

As stated earlier, most large chain, department, speciality, and food stores use a checkout system that expedites the input of various data (vendor, style, color, size, etc.) into the company's existing computerized (point of sale) system. The system uses an optical scanning device to read computerized tickets by passing a "wand" over digits or product codes.

There are two vendor electronic marking systems: (1) the optical character recognition–font A (OCR–A) system and (2) the universal product code (UPC) bar coding system.

The optical character recognition–font A (OCR–A) system is human readable and wand readable and is used by those primarily in the business of selling general merchandise.

The universal product code (UPC) bar coding system is wand readable and is used by those primarily in the grocery business. It identifies both the product and the manufacturer.

In the late 1980s, however, Federated Department Stores, Inc. and Allied Stores Corporation—the largest operator of traditional department stores in the country—endorsed the UPC bar coding system as the standard for all vendor marking. All Federated Divisions (A&S, Bloomingdale's, Burdines, Lazarus, Rich's, and Goldsmith's) and Allied Divisions (Bon Marche,

Jordan Marsh, Maas Bros, and Stern's) were committed to a rapid conversion to UPC, which would ultimately lead to faster merchandise processing, faster determination of reorder quantities, and improved operating efficiencies.

CONSUMER INDUCEMENTS

Not only do manufacturers provide selling assistance to retail buyers to influence a consumer purchase, but they will also attempt to influence the consumer directly. For example, the vendor will provide certain inducements to influence the consumer to buy a certain brand of televison, a particular flavor of toothpaste, a certain size of soap powder. Such attempts on the part of the manufacturer may interfere with normal business activities; therefore, they require cooperation between the vendor and the retail buyer.

The following examples of consumer inducement may be used: (1) premiums, (2) coupons, (3) contests, (4) deals, (5) trading stamps, and (6) sampling.

Consumer Inducements Offered by Vendors

1. Premiums
2. Coupons
3. Contests
4. Deals
5. Trading stamps
6. Sampling

Premiums

A *premium* may be defined as an article of value or "gift" that can be obtained by the consumer for a nominal price after the advertised item has been purchased. The consumer may be required to tear off the label or box top and send it to the manufacturer with a small sum of money. A method often used by cosmetic companies is to offer, for example, a beauty face cream for $1.50 with a minimum $6.00 purchase.

The premium is a common selling device used by vendors. The retailer usually has no hand in the advertising or promotion, since the manufacturer will advertise the merchandise nationally. However, the store may be forced to warehouse and distribute the premium as well as the advertised merchandise. The Robinson-Patman Act prohibits the use of premiums as a form of price discrimination among competing retailers. It also prohibits deceptive advertising that calls a premium "free" if the cost of the article is included in the purchase price of the article sold in connection with it.

An example of a common type of premium is a two-for-one sale in a dress shop, whereby the customer will purchase one dress at the regular price to obtain a second dress at a drastically reduced rate. This is a very popular method of selling today. A gasoline station may offer free glassware with each full tank of gasoline; a supermarket may offer an opportunity to purchase a place setting of china or silverware at a reduced price with each $25 order; or a small variety store may offer fingernail polish with a 1¢ sales allowance whereby the customer will purchase two bottles of nail polish for the price of one bottle plus 1¢.

Coupons

The *coupon* is an award granted by the manufacturer or vendor for purchasing his product. Usually the objective of the manufacturer is to grant the consumer an indirect price cut that will help make the merchandise a leader in that particular market. The consumer may receive a coupon through house-to-house distribution, by mail, by cutting it out of the newspaper, at the store, or in the packaged product (Figure 12–4). The coupon usually has a value stated in cents and may be used instead of cash in the purchase of particular branded products. The retailer is expected to accept coupons instead of cash and in turn to hand them in to the vendor for redemption. The vendor will usually grant the retailer a small commission for handling coupons and for waiting for the money.

Sometimes the coupon is a device used by vendors to force the buyer to carry merchandise that is not already in stock. For example, a can of coffee may contain a coupon worth 25¢; however, the coupon may have to be redeemed for a product not carried by the store. If enough customers return to the store seeking the article, the retailer may decide to stock it.

Contests

A third device used by vendors is the consumer contest. The *contest* usually offers expensive prizes and may require that the consumer present evidence of purchase to qualify. It many also require the customer to elaborate upon the advantages of the product and its value in relation to competition. The store buyer is often required to provide entry blanks and information. Sometimes the store's sales personnel may also receive a prize along with the winning contestant. Some stores may stage contests and offer a variety of prizes. For example, a department store may offer a sewing course and then offer a prize to the participant who sews the best garment, as well as to those who take second and third place. Usually, those who enter the contest will pur-

Figure 12–4 An example of coupons that have been sent through the mail and distributed in the store (restaurant). (Courtesy of Dante's Inferno, Philadelphia, Pa.)

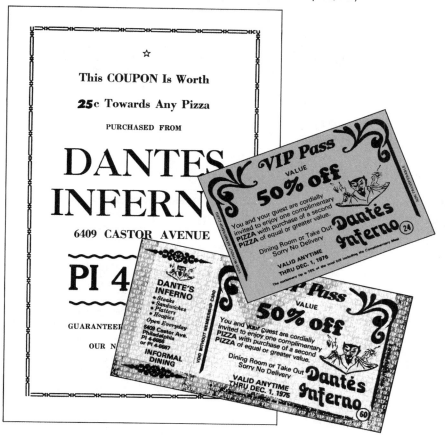

chase the material and sewing notions from the store's piece goods department. Or a store may offer contests in cooking, painting, woodworking, table setting, and so forth. Participants in these contest, too, will usually purchase the required materials or tools from the store offering the contest.

Deals

A *deal* may best be defined as a temporary special retail price offered to store customers. For example, the vendor may band two items together; instead of selling one article for 39¢, the store may sell "two for 66¢." This offers an obvious advantage to the store's clientele; however, the buyer makes a lower profit. Also, merchandise that is not banded together will not sell until the deal is over.

Trading Stamps

Trading stamps are given to a consumer with each purchase of merchandise. The number of stamps received is based upon the cost of the merchandise. For example, a consumer may receive 10 trading stamps if the article costs $1.

Technically speaking, trading stamps are not offered by vendors; however they definitely influence the consumers as they decide on their purchases (Figure 12–5). Trading-stamp companies such as S & H Green

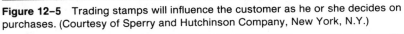

Figure 12–5 Trading stamps will influence the customer as he or she decides on purchases. (Courtesy of Sperry and Hutchinson Company, New York, N.Y.)

Stamps, Blue Chip, Top Value, Plaid Stamps, and Gold Bond sell stamps to retail stores and provide the premium merchandise for which the stamps are redeemed. The premium merchandise may be distributed through cooperating stores or through stamp redemption centers where the merchandise is on display.

Trading stamps became a popular customer inducement during the 1950s and even more so during the 1960s. They were commonplace in supermarkets, gasoline stations, drugstores, discount houses, and even in garden and supply centers. Customers accepted them wholeheartedly, and stores found them to be builders of repeat patronage.

During the early 1980s, however, trading stamps declined as a popular customer inducement. Since retail stores had to pay for the stamps, their cost was included in the retailer's markup price. As a result of competition, fuel shortages, and supply conditions in general, customers sought lower prices. As a result, many retail stores gave up trading stamps to lower the price of their merchandise. For example, one retail merchant's ad read, "No More Stamps or Other Gimmicks—Only Quality Merchandise and Lower Prices."

It is important that the buyer become acquainted with vendor policy regarding such activity. No action should be taken without first considering the interests of the store and the customers and his or her duties and obligations as a buyer.

Trading stamps offer many advantages to retail buyers. They are not offered by vendors or manufacturers but by companies dealing specifically with this type of consumer protection. The trading-stamp inducement plan has been found to be especially suited to convenience goods, those goods which consumers expect to have readily available in a handy location. However, retailers who handle shopping goods, those products for which a consumer will accept no substitutes, have not been convinced of the advantages of the trading stamp plan.

Sampling

Sampling is a frequently used method of reaching customers directly, especially in food markets, cosmetic counters in retail stores, and drugstores. For example, a food merchant will offer free samples of cheese, meat products, candy, or a new type of gourmet food. The customer is given an opportunity to taste and smell the food and as a result may purchase the item. Cosmetic departments will offer lipstick, cologne, perfume, nail polish, and so forth to give the shopper an opportunity to try the product. Samples are found in many merchandise areas and often help customers to decide on a purchase. The sample may be given out in the store or may be sent through the mail to potential customers.

Nonpersonal Promotional Aids Will Directly Influence the Buying Behavior of the Retail Customer. They May Be Classified As:

I. Dealer helps   II. Consumer inducements

Packaging   Premiums   Deals
Labeling   Coupons   Trading stamps
Price ticketing   Contests   Sampling

Review how each will affect the selling activity of buying specialists.

Chapter Summary

Personal promotional aids are those services offered by vendors that will directly affect the selling activity of the buyer. Such services may take the form of vendor's selling aids—the use of demonstrators, the availability of finance and credit, a return privilege, controlled distribution, markdown insurance, and memorandum buying. Promotional allowances are also offered to the retail buyer. Such allowances are used to ensure maximum cooperation between the buyer and the seller. They may take the form of cooperative advertising, preferred selling space, free display material, price decline guarantees, and merchandise deals.

The buyer may negotiate for price adjustments through specific credit arrangements. Whatever method is used, the buyer must be certain that such buying techniques are in his or her best interest, that of the retail store and, of course, that of the customers.

Nonpersonal promotional aids are welcomed by the buyer, since they are useful in attracting customer attention and interest. They may be classified as (1) dealer helps and (2) consumer inducements. Dealer helps may come in the form of packaging, labeling, and price ticketing.

Packaging may add value and attractiveness to a product. Good packaging may help minimize problems with shoplifting, protect merchandise from being damaged or soiled, and provide easy storage for retailer and consumer alike.

Labeling is a nonpersonal selling aid of growing importance. Labels have two primary functions: (1) they provide salespeople with specific information about the features of the garment, and (2) they assist the customer in making a selection, especially if the retail store carries several quality lines of a particular product.

Not only is the consumer provided information through the use of labeling but also by price ticketing. Price tickets may be attached directly to the product or placed near the merchandise. The many types available include gummed labels, pin tickets, string tickets, and many variations. Not all merchandise needs to be marked, particularly where personal selling is used. On the other hand, self-service requires that each individual item be marked, since this will assist the cashier in performing his or her job at the check-out counter.

Not only do vendors provide selling assistance to retail buyers, but they will also attempt to influence the consumer directly. Consumer inducements may include (1) premiums, (2) coupons, (3) contests, (4) deals, (5) trading stamps, and (6) sampling. Such devices as premiums, coupons, contests, and deals place a degree of pressure on the retail buyer to stock the merchandise offered in substantial quantity.

Trade Terminology

DIRECTIONS: Briefly explain or discuss each of the following trade terms:

1. Personal promotional aids
2. Nonpersonal promotional aids
3. On memorandum
4. Premium

5. Coupon
6. Contest
7. Deal
8. Trading stamps

Questions for Discussion and Review

1. What questions should the buyer ask when considering the types of services offered by merchandise resources?

2. Under what major classifications may vendor services to the buyer be analyzed?

3. What types of retail stores gain the most by offering trading stamps? Why?

4. What methods are used by merchandise resources to extend credit to buyers?

5. What is cooperative advertising? Cite five examples from your local newspaper.

6. Other than advertising allowances, what forms of promotional allowances are offered by merchandise resources?

7. From the customer's point of view, what are the advantages and disadvantages of a store's using demonstrators provided by suppliers?

8. Name six kinds of inducements used by vendors to influence the consumer directly. Select three examples from your local newspaper. Explain how each is used by the retail store to increase customer traffic.

9. What is the difference between buying on consignment and buying with a return privilege?

10. What is floor planning? What types of retail stores favor the floor-planning method?

References

THE RETAIL STUDENT'S REFERENCE LIBRARY

Basic Stock Lists, Infants' and Children's Wear. New York: NRMA, n.d.

The Buyer's Manual. New York: NRMA, n.d.

Children's Wear Merchandiser. New York: NRMA, n.d.

China and Glassware Merchandiser. New York: NRMA, n.d.

Cohen, Richard L. *The Foootwear Industry.* New York: Fairchild Pub., Inc., n.d.

The Complete Dictionary of Buying and Merchandising. New York: NRMA, n.d.

Creative Men's Wear Retailing. New York: Fairchild Pub., Inc., n.d.

Essentials of Merchandising. Albany: State University of New York Press, n.d.

The Fashion Buyer's Job. New York: NRMA n.d.

Ferguson, F. *Efficient Drug Store Management.* New York: NRMA, n.d.

Gillespie, Karen. *Apparel and Accessories for Women, Misses, and Children.* Washington, D.C.: U.S. Government Printing Office, n.d.

Logan, W. B. and Moon, H. M. *Facts about Merchandising.* Englewood Cliffs, N.J.: Prentice Hall Inc. n.d.

The Management of Fashion Merchandising—A Symposium. New York: NRMA, n.d.

Manual for Reducing Transportation Costs. New York: NRMA, n.d.

Merchandise Assortment Planning. New York: NRMA, n.d.

A Retailer Visits the Market. New York: Fairchild Pub., Inc. n.d.

Taylor, C. G. *Merchandise Assortment Planning.* New York: NRMA, n.d.

REFERENCES

1. J. W. Wingate and J. S. Freidlander, *The Management of Retail Buying* (Englewood Cliffs, N.J.: Prentice-Hall Inc., 1963), p. 319.
2. Donald L. Belden, *The Role of the Buyer in Mass Merchandising* (New York: Chain Store Publishing Corporation, 1971), p. 191.
3. Belden, *Role of the Buyer,* p. 189.
4. Ibid., p. 89.

Developing Good Buyer-Vendor Relations

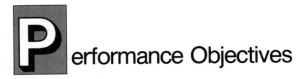

Performance Objectives

After reading this chapter, the student should be able to accomplish the following:

1. Explain five activities important to the negotiation process.

2. Discuss various buying methods used.

3. Define four kinds of discounts and allowances available to the buyer from the vendor.

4. Become aware of two important factors a buyer must consider when determining transportation and storage.

5. Discuss four terms used in transportation (FOB).

6. Learn the importance of the buyer's order form, the necessity of properly filling out the order form, and the legal responsibilities involved.

7. List seven kinds of orders that may be placed by a buyer.

8. Discuss guidelines a buyer should observe when negotiating with a vendor.

9. Understand the circumstances that dictate when a buyer may return merchandise to a vendor.

10. List five trade practices that must be observed by vendors and buyers when writing and accepting an order.

11. Discuss ten practices that may cause friction between vendors and buyers.

12. Become aware of the policies that should be established to ensure the development of good buyer-vendor relations.

Developing Good
Buyer-Vendor Relations

Figure 13-1 At Vanity Fair divisions such as Red Kap, service is more than the delivery of apparel. It means having the systems in place to predict as accurately as possible the products a customer will need and to produce them so that they are ready when needed. Red Kap is augmenting its strength in inventory management through a commitment to the latest computer-based systems. (Courtesy of Red Kap, division of VF Corporation, Wyomissing, Pa.)

INTRODUCTION

In the previous chapter you read that merchandise resources, whether domestic or foreign, offer a number of services to retailers. Services may be divided into two types: personal promotional aids, which are services that directly affect the selling activity of the buyer, and nonpersonal promotional aids, which are services that directly influence the buying behavior of the consumer. Examples of personal promotional aides include selling aids and promotional allowances. Examples of nonpersonal promotional aides include dealer's helps and consumer inducements.

An important responsibility of all buyers is to solicit every service to which the store is entitled. Of course, the services offered to merchants will depend on the type of merchandise resource, the amount and nature of the business conducted between retailer and supplier, and the type of buyer-vendor relationship established.

In this chapter we are concerned with how good buyer-vendor relations are established. The negotiation process is the bargaining activity that occurs between the buyer and the seller over certain goods and services. There are a number of activities involved in the negotiation process, which includes buying authority, securing discounts and allowances, arranging transportation and storage, establishing the terms of sale, and seeking price guarantees.

Sound buying practices between buyer and vendor should be followed in the procurement of goods and include numerous methods of buying, such as regular buying, buying job lots, buying irregulars and second, advance buying, promotional buying, special order buying, buying manufacturers' brands, private label buying, and buying designer labels.

Once the buyer determines the merchandise assortment and negotiates the terms and conditions of sale, he or she is ready to go on to the next step, that is, to fill out the order form. The order form, then, becomes a most important document, since it contains all details of the business transaction. Certain information should be contained on the front of the buyer's order form. Furthermore, there are a number of different kinds of orders that may be placed by the buying specialist ranging from placing regular orders to advance orders to back orders to blanket orders, to name a few.

There are a number of guidelines the buyer should observe when negotiating with vendors, and it goes without saying that the vendor or manufacturer has certain obligations to the buyer. Certain trade practices must be observed by vendor and buyer alike. Activities such as returns and adjustments, order cancellations, shipping problems, special ordering, and so forth, should be discussed by all parties concerned to avoid friction between vendor and retail buyer.

PART 1—The Buyer's Responsibility to the Vendor

EARLY ENCOUNTERS

During the early days of retailing the store buyer often had difficulties in determining what he or she would or would not purchase for resale. Manufacturers had not yet fully developed the complete lines of merchandise they carry today. A buyer would purchase one item at a time or purchase closeouts or lots. Highly competitive bargaining over single units of merchandise was not uncommon. It was soon realized, however, that such chaotic conditions could not continue if retail distribution in the United States were to prosper and meet the demands of an ever-increasing population.

Eventually, a teamwork approach to buyer-vendor relations was developed. This led to a modification of trade practices that allowed both buyer and vendor the freedom of creativity and expression, yet ensured fair play for both (Figure 13–1).

THE NEGOTIATION PROCESS

The *negotiation process* involves the mutual discussion and agreement between the retail buyer and the merchandise resources to terms of various business transactions. It is the bargaining activity that occurs between the buyer and the seller over certain goods and services. As you recall, the seller may be a manufacturer, a wholesaler, a vendor, or a manufacturer's representative.

The size of the retail institution will greatly influence both the purchasing potential of the buyer and the willingness of the vendor to grant concessions. For example, a buyer from a small women's apparel shop would have less influence in the negotiation process for more than 2 percent cash discount than would a buyer of women's apparel in a department store.

The negotiation process provides an opportunity for the buyer to implement a most important store objective profit maximization. A variety of activities involved in the process will help the buyer meet this objective. Chief among the negotiating activities are: (1) buying authority, (2) securing discounts and allowances, (3) arranging transportation and storage, (4) establishing the terms of sale, and (5) seeking price guarantees.

Chief Activities Involved in the Negotiation Process

1. Buying authority
2. Securing discounts and allowances
3. Arranging transportation and storage
4. Establishing the terms of sale
5. Seeking price guarantees

Buying Authority

When the buyer is employed by the retail store, he or she is given the authority to act on behalf of that store as a duly authorized agent and will represent the firm in dealings with merchandise resources. However, a buyer for curtains and draperies cannot place orders for sporting equipment or for towels and linens, but can only purchase for the department for which hired.

The authority delegated to the buyer by the retail firm is important to the negotiation process. The merchandise resource is aware that contracts placed and signed by the buyer and merchandise manager are valid and will be honored by the retail firm involved.

As the representative or agent of the retail store, the buyer has certain responsibilities, which are listed as follows:

1. To be loyal and act in good faith in the best interest of the retail organization.
2. To act in person—that is, the buyer must do the purchasing himself—unless permitted to appoint another individual to act on his or her behalf.
3. To work with reasonable care, effort, and skill.
4. To follow all lawful instructions, that is, to abide by any special instructions that require a countersignature.
5. To render an accounting for all merchandise belonging to the retail organization and for all activities performed in the store's behalf.
6. To give the retail organization an account of all purchases made and money spent.
7. To turn over all profits received and to make no personal profit.

Securing Discounts and Allowances

A second activity involved in the negotiation process is securing discounts and allowances. A *discount* or *allowance* may be defined as any reduction in the list or quoted price given to the retailer by the merchandise resource.

Discounts and Allowances Available to the Retail Buyer from Merchandise Resources

1. Quantity discounts
2. Seasonal discounts
3. Trade discounts
4. Cash discounts

There are four kinds of discounts and allowances available to the retail buyer. They are (1) quantity discount, (2) seasonal discount, (3) trade discount, and (4) cash discount. The formulas used to calculate each of the following will be discussed in Chapter 14, Pricing Merchandise for Profit.

Quantity Discount. May be defined as a reduction from list price given to buyers purchasing in unusually large quantities. It may be stated in terms of a percentage reduction or in the form of free goods. For example, a manufacturer of women's hosiery may offer a "1 dozen free with 10 dozen purchased" deal or a 15 percent discount for purchasing 10 dozen stockings. Manufacturers often use quantity discount to encourage the retailer not only to purchase from them but to purchase larger quantities. The buyer must be careful not to be misled by such attractive offerings, since this may lead to overbuying.

Seasonal Discount. May be defined as a reduction in list price granted to the retail buyer for purchasing goods during the off-season. Certain kinds of goods are in demand only at particular times of the year. For example, ski clothing is in demand during the winter and bathing suits during the summer. Vendors will offer discounts to retailers to encourage them to order as well as accept delivery of goods during the off-season. As a result, vendors can continue a minimum production schedule while the buyer assumes the added expense of warehousing the goods until the season arrives. The retailer, however, is compensated for additional warehousing expenses and added investment cost by the price reduction that has been granted by the vendor. Seasonal discounts may run as high as 10 or 20 percent. To take advantage of these discounts, the buyer must anticipate requirements far in advance. Along with the price advantage, the merchandise is likely to be more carefully checked, packed, and delivered. It may also be more carefully made.

Trade Discount. May be defined as a reduction in price granted to a certain category or trade of customer to cover the costs of a particular trading function. The trade discount is granted in addition to a quantity discount. Trade discount is usually not a form of price concession but a method of quoting prices based on list prices. For example, in some trades it is an accepted practice for a manufacturer to quote a list price that may approximate the actual retail price. The retail buyer may then be granted a trade discount of 50 percent off the list price. The discount is high enough to cover the buyer's markup for expenses, risk, and profit. However, some manufacturers distort the list price. In this case, the retailer will offer the merchandise at a price far below the list price and still make an adequate markup. For example, a clock may be listed at $90.00 but be sold to a buyer for $32.50. The buyer than resells the clock at $69.95 but advertise it as a "gigantic bargain."

Cash Discount. May be defined as a reduction in price granted to the retail buyer if the buyer pays within a specified period of time. The time period is usually expressed as a certain number of days after the invoice date. Take, for example, cash discount terms of 2/10 net 30. The buyer may take a cash discount of 2 percent by paying within ten days after the invoice date. The cash discount is taken after all other discounts are deducted. For example, the buyer deducts the trade, quantity, and/or seasonal discount before deducting the cash discount. This type of discount is often granted by merchandise resources to encourage the buyer to pay bills within a specified time period. As a result, the supplier is enabled to invest the money and in turn take advantage of discounts offered by merchandise resources.

Arranging Transportation and Storage

Arranging transportation and storage is a third important negotiating activity. When considering such arrangements, the buyer should ask himself or herself two important questions: (1) Who is to pay for the cost of transportation? (2) Who is to own the merchandise and be responsible for it while it is en route?

Important Factors When Determining Transportation and Storage

1. Who is to pay for the cost of transportation?
   The buyer? The vendor?
2. Who is to own the merchandise and be responsible for it while it is en route?
   The buyer? The vendor?

Transportation terms offered by the vendor may take any one of the following forms: (1) FOB factory, (2) FOB destination, (3) FOB shipping point, (4) FOB destination, charges reversed, (5) FOB factory, freight prepaid.

FOB (Free on board) Factory. This agreement states that the buyer will pay all transportation costs and will own the goods from the moment they are shipped.

FOB Destination. This agreement states that the seller is to pay all transportation costs and is to own the merchandise until it arrives at the retail store.

FOB Shipping Point. In this agreement the seller pays any crating necessary for sending the goods to the place at which they are to be turned over to a transportation company.

FOB Destination, Charges Reversed. Such an agreement means that the seller will own the goods until they get into the retail store; however, the buyer agrees to pay the transportation charges.

FOB Destination, Freight Prepaid. This agreement means the goods are to become the possession of the buyer as soon as they are shipped; however, the seller will pay freight charges.

In addition to determining the form of FOB, the retail buyer must determine the method of shipment. The main methods are railroad freight, railway express, motor freight, parcel post, air express, air freight, and truck-rail. The truck-rail method is a combination whereby merchandise is loaded into a trailer and hauled by truck to a railroad siding, where the entire trailer is lifted onto a flatcar. Once the goods arrive at the destination, the trailer is removed and transported by truck to the warehouse or directly to the store.

Time and cost are two important elements the buyer must consider when determining methods of transportation and storage. For example, a buyer of larger quantities of staple goods may achieve lower unit rates by concentrating his purchases and by using less expensive methods of shipment. However, if the merchandise is needed quickly, as is often the case with fashion goods, faster methods of transportation are generally used.

How Will the Terms of Transportation Assist the Buyer During the Negotiation Activity?

FOB factory
FOB destination
FOB shipping point
FOB destination, charges reversed
FOB destination, freight prepaid

Establishing the Terms of Sale

The fourth important activity in the negotiation process is the establishment of the terms of sale. As was mentioned in the previous chapter, the terms of sale are often offered to the retail buyer in the form of vendor services. The student should become familiar with the following terms since this information is necessary in order placement and receiving and in vendor negotiations.

Advanced Dating. In the case of advanced dating, the invoice is dated from a specified future date, not from the designated invoice date. For example, the invoice covering a shipment of towels made on October 15 may have terms of 2/10 net 30 as of December 1. This arrangement will give the buyer until January 1 to pay the bill. This technique will provide a store that is inadequately financed with an opportunity to sell merchandise before paying for it.

Anticipation. An extra discount is taken for paying an invoice in advance of the cash discount date. This is usually done by those store buyers who have ready cash available. The buyer will deduct interest, usually at the rate of 6 percent a year, for the number of days of prepayment.

Cash Discount. A reduction in price is allowed by the vendor for prompt payment. The common practice is to allow the buyer 10 days from the invoice date. For example, if the goods are shipped on August 5, with terms of 2/10 net 30, the invoice must be paid on August 15 to earn a discount of 2 percent. The entire amount is due on September 4.

COD Dating. Cash on delivery terms state that merchandise may be sold for cash on delivery. However, nearly all retail stores have achieved a credit rating that permits them to buy on credit.

Consignment. Merchandise sold on consignment does not become the property of the buyer, but remains the property of the seller. Unsold goods are returned to the vendor.

Dating. This refers to the length of time the seller will extend credit to the store buyer. For example, the vendor may state net 30 or net 60, which signifies that the bill must be paid within thirty days or sixty days of the invoice date.

EOM. End of month states that the time for payment is calculated from the end of the month in which the invoice is dated and the merchandise shipped, and not from the invoice date. For example, if dresses are shipped on May 5, they do not have to be paid for until a specified number of days after May 31. In ready-to-wear EOM is a typical term.

Extra Dating. The buyer is given a specified number of extra days in which to pay the bill and to earn the discount. For example, instead of 30 days, the buyer may be granted 60 extra days, giving a total of 90 days, or 120 days, giving a total of 150 days. Additional days may also be extended to enable a buyer to earn a discount, for example, 2/10–90 extra.

If the goods are shipped on September 10, with terms of 2/10 net 90, the invoice must be paid on September 20 to earn a discount of 2 percent. The entire amount is due on December 8.

Floor Plan. The vendor will turn an assortment of merchandise over to the store buyer, who in return signs a trust receipt. The title will remain with the vendor, and the store buyer agrees to make payment as he makes sales. This finance plan is commonly used to finance stocks of expensive merchandise such as major appliances. If payments are made to the retail store on credit sales, this will include turning over the customer paper to the seller or his agent which may be a bank or finance company.

Proximo Dating. This is a common credit term, a synonym for EOM dating.

Regular Dating. This means that the length of time for which the vendor will extend credit is calculated from the date of the invoice. For example, "net 30" signifies that the billed amount is due within 30 days of the invoice date.

Postdating. This is also referred to as advanced dating.

ROG. This term is commonly granted to retailers who are some distance from the market. Receipt of goods means that the date of payment is based on the date the goods are received by the store, rather than the date of shipment or the invoice date.

Loading the Invoice. This term describes a practice used by retailers whereby the amount of the retailer's invoice is increased to permit a larger cash discount than is normally available at the supplier's going rate. Thus, the department or store will increase the amount of the invoice received from the supplier by a certain percentage and charge the department the increased or loaded price. For example, a supplier will send a store a bill (invoice) for the amount of $200 with a 2 percent discount if the bill is paid within 10 days (2 percent net 30). However, the store has a standard policy that requires an 8 percent discount for bills paid within 10 days. The store will take the usual 2 percent discount, or $4, from the invoice cost of $200, which leaves an adjusted invoice of $196 ($200 − $4). To achieve the 8 percent discount, the store will load the invoice cost of $196 by dividing it by 92 percent (100% − 8%), which gives a loaded invoice price of $213, or 8 percent of $213 gives an invoice cost of $196.

Seeking Price Guarantees

As you recall from reading Chapter 12, Services Offered by Merchandise Resources, seeking price guarantees is a necessary activity to the negotiation process. The retail buyer may seek a guarantee from the vendor to protect him or her against possible future price fluctuations. For example, a buyer may ask for a seasonal discount along with a price guarantee. The vendor may be willing to make concessions to obtain early orders from buyers. The price guarantee is fairly common for seasonal merchandise because the vendor is eager to encourage the buyer to place early orders. Or the vendor may use the price guarantee along with the quantity discount to encourage buyers of staple goods to place especially large orders.

METHODS OF BUYING

Sound buying practices between buyer and vendor should be followed in the procurement of goods, domestic and foreign, by the numerous methods of buying available. These methods are: (1) regular buying, (2) buying job lots, (3) buying irregulars and seconds, (4) advance buying, (5) promotional buying, (6) special-order buying, (7) buying manufacturer's brands, (8) private label (specification) buying, and, (9) buying designer labels.

A Buying Specialist May Use the Following Buying Methods

1. Regular buying
2. Buying job lots
3. Buying irregulars and seconds
4. Advance buying
5. Promotional buying
6. Special-order buying
7. Buying manufacturers' brands
8. Private label (specification) buying
9. Buying designer labels

Regular Buying

Regular buying, or buying goods at regular retail prices, is the method used by most buyers of fashion merchandise and staple goods. The buyer is assured of a normal delivery period of from two to four weeks, the usual discount of 2/10 net 30, extra dating whereby the buyer is given a specified number of extra days to pay the bill, a return privilege, and so forth. (Terms used in finance and credit will be discussed in detail in the next chapter.) The buyer will order goods he or she thinks will sell and then place reorders as soon as possible to keep an adequate supply of merchandise in stock at all times. For example, the fashion buyer of men's shirts will draw as much information as possible from salesmen who come to the store, from the representative in the market center (the resident buyer), and from personal visits to manufacturers.

The buyer of staple goods will also use the regular buying method when purchasing goods. However, most staple products or never-out goods may, with some seasonal variations, be purchased mechanically or automatically through the store's computer system. Once the buyer determines the composition of the merchandise assortment, the quantity, and the price range, adequate stock will be planned to minimize inventory "outs." As you recall from Chapter 9, the amount to be purchased at any one time depends on sales estimates for the coming season, the quantity of goods on hand and on order, and the desired stock at the end of the selling season.

In some types of retail stores, for example, discount houses, there is a temptation to operate with minimum inventory and hand-to-mouth buying. As a result, a smaller investment is required, and money is available to broaden the merchandise assortment and add new lines of goods. The disadvantage of buying in this way is that unexpectedly large sales or slow deliveries may lead to the store's being out of stock, so that customers will shop elsewhere. On the other hand, a surplus of stock may result from the desire to take advantage of quantity discounts or special buys and lead to high markdowns and slow selling of goods. The quantity of goods on hand can be determined by stock reports. Usually, a stock count is required immediately prior to reordering to determine how much is needed.

The regular buying method requires the buying specialist of fashion goods and staple items to determine the maximum or total amount of goods on order and on hand. As you recall from an earlier discussion the following formula may be used when ordering fashion goods or staple items:

$$\text{Maximum} = (\text{Reorder Period} + \text{Delivery Period})\ \text{Rate of Sales} + \text{Reserve}$$

$$M = (RP + DP) \times S + R$$

or

$$\text{Maximum} + (\text{Lead Time})\ \text{Rate of Sales} + \text{Reserve}$$

$$M + (LT)\ S + R$$

Buying Job Lots

A *job lot* may be defined as an assortment of merchandise the vendor has been unable to sell at regular prices and is now offering at a reduced price per item. The buyer will not buy job lots unless the price is low enough to ensure that the entire lot will sell at a satisfactory markup.

Since the lot is an assortment of vendor leftovers of various styles, sizes, and colors, the buyer must be careful in determining how these items will fit into existing stock. For example, a department-store buyer of curtains and drapery accessories will purchase job lots for a special January clearance sale. The assortment may consist of limited color selections, out-of-season patterns and prints, extra wide panels, and limited styles and sizes. This assortment of leftovers will round out the end-of-season stock to make an interesting offering for bargain-hunting customers.

Many retail buyers will use the job-lot method of buying. The small business owner, the discounter, the specialty-store buyer, the chain buyer—all will shop the various trade markets seeking specials to pass on to their customers. However, the buyers must be certain the job lots they select will not lead to increased markdowns, lower the store's image of quality merchandise offerings, or detract from already existing lines of goods. He or she must not be talked into making purchases that will lead to lost sales. Often a buyer may purchase things he or she does not like to round out the assortment according to size, color, price, or whatever. It would be very unwise for a buyer to purchase only those goods that appealed to personal likes or dislikes. A good merchandiser will develop an awareness of what to look for and be quick to distinguish what customers' tastes are for both regular goods and special buys.

Buying Irregulars and Seconds

An *irregular* may be defined as an item that contains an imperfection or repair not visible to the naked eye. A *second* may be defined as an item that contains a more obvious damage or repair. This definition may also be applied to "thirds." Manufacturers will often have merchandise left over at the end of the selling season. To rid themselves of unwanted goods, they offer these items to buyers at reduced prices. Manufacturers may inform retail buyers of their offerings through trade-paper advertisements, by word of mouth, or through market representatives. Many buyers will purchase these substandard units, since very often the performance or durability of the product remains unimpaired. The saving is passed on to the customer. Also, the values achieved are often greater than those of perfect goods that have been manufactured at a lower quality. However, some buyers will not purchase irregulars and seconds, since they feel their quality image may be damaged, while others will offer only limited amounts.

When shopping, you may notice that a special tag or ticket is affixed to a garment or product informing you that the item is an irregular or second; depending on the imperfection or the repair, the merchant will adjust the price accordingly. Perhaps you will find knit dresses or knit trousers that contain tiny pulls or snags. If the imperfection is hardly noticeable, you will purchase the item and take advantage of the lower price offering.

A vendor will offer irregulars and seconds at reduced prices to deplete his own stocks as well as to provide special buys to store merchants. However, the buyer must be certain that goods purchased will meet the demand flow, coordinate with assortments offered in his or her own as well as in other departments, and continue to maintain merchandising policies set forth by top store management. The buyer must consider the risks involved in offering imperfect goods at the end of the season, the markup, and the kind and amount of pulling power possessed by such items.

Advance Buying

Advance buying is used primarily by buyers of staple goods. It permits the buyer to place orders in advance of the selling season; as an incentive, the buyer is offered a discount by the vendor. The buyer may in turn pass the savings on to customers; or, if the merchandise must be warehoused, the savings will be used to pay part of the cost of warehousing.

Advance buying ensures adequate delivery and a steady flow of merchandise. For example, the store manager of a variety chain is usually assured of a steady flow of goods because the central buyer has ordered merchandise in advance of the season. Since staple goods are "never out" and are always needed by store customers, the risk of purchasing in advance and placing goods in a warehouse is minimized. The central buyer may also arrange to have certain goods delivered to store units at various times to avoid having to handle all the merchandise at one time. The Christmas season is a good example. The central buyer may arrange with manufacturers to have Christmas-tree ornaments shipped either directly to individual store units during September, October, and November, or to have them sent directly to a distribution center, from which store managers may request them as they are needed.

The fashion buyer will also use advance buying. However, the buyer must be certain that the merchandise will not become out of style while it is in the warehouse. For example, a buyer of ladies' robes may wish to place advance orders to ensure a balanced stock of goods throughout a particular selling season, for example, Mother's Day. Usually, advance orders will be placed for already proved styles, classic lines, or basic types of soft goods. Fashion apparel buyers will place advance orders for special sales promotions, the Christmas season, the spring season, or whenever large amounts of goods are required.

Promotional Buying

Stores are always featuring special events and general sales promotions, and buyers are continuously seeking special purchases. If the store is having a pre-Easter Sale, the buyer will seek merchandise of a lower price that will appeal to customers interested in purchasing goods for the spring season, for example, children's shoes, women's spring coats, or paint and garden supplies. The buyer must be careful in calculating the amount of merchandise required for the sale. Previous sales records may provide some information;

however, the buyer must also rely on previous experience with regular-line merchandise and personal knowledge of the consumer market. For example, a store may be having an Oriental promotion, and the buying specialists may be required to seek resources offering appropriate goods to feature during the event. A buyer of fashion goods may offer women's blouses with Oriental designs on silk fabric; a buyer of men's better sportswear may feature quilted jackets with mandarin collars; a buyer of loungewear and pajamas may offer two-piece silk pajamas, while a buyer of giftware may offer various imports that carry the Oriental influence.

Special-Order Buying

A store may offer an individualized service whereby customers may order special merchandise. In this case, the buyer must "special order," that is, place orders with the vendor indicating a particular color, size, or style. Since this service *(special-order buying)* takes time in order placement, checking, and receiving, as well as additional costs from the vendor, it is primarily used by full-service stores. Also, stores offering limited selections in color, size, and style may use this method of buying and make almost as many sales as those offering larger merchandise selections. The overall savings in small inventories will often more than compensate for the extra cost charged by the vendor.

A small business will use this buying method to provide a special service to persons who are good steady customers. This is one method a small business may use to meet competition. Department stores and specialty shops, especially those dealing in men's and women's fashion apparel, will also special order for certain customers. For example, a men's wear buyer may place an order for a customer who wants a suit in size 44 extra long. Or a buyer in the women's better suit department may special order a smaller size jacket rather than break up a suit ensemble. Special orders may be placed by the buyer of handbags and leather goods whereby a monogramming and initialing service is made available, thus, something unique and interesting has been added to an otherwise ordinary merchandise assortment.

The buying specialist will soon learn that selecting merchandise to implement the buying plan is basically a process of elimination. The "perfect item," the "best seller," the "sure winner" is not likely simply to declare itself the season's best seller. More often the buyer must seek it out and discover it from among the many items that are almost right. Before purchasing goods for resale, the buyer, department manager, or store manager must have a clear image of what is wanted and needed by the store's clientele. The purchaser must work within the guidelines set forth by the store's merchandising team and follow established procedures.

Buying Manufacturers' Brands

Many retailers, from large scale businesses to small business operators, purchase manufacturers' branded merchandise. There are a number of advantages:

1. Successful manufacturers' brands have an established reputation so customers will be attracted to a store carrying the brand.
2. Branded manufacturers will oftentimes share advertising costs (cooperative advertising).
3. Since manufacturers' brands are usually well known, a store's selling expenses (displays, advertising, sales help) are minimized.
4. A store may reorder branded merchandise more frequently (thereby reducing inventory costs) since manufacturers of branded goods usually carry large inventories.
5. Manufacturers' branded goods are produced by specialists in a particular merchandise area therefore quality control may be maintained.
6. Manufacturers' branded goods add prestige to a store's merchandise mix since they are advertised nationally and have an established reputation.

Recently, however, one advantage—price maintenance—has become a disadvantage in the purchasing of branded merchandise. Today, it is no longer the policy for manufacturers of branded merchandise to maintain the price of goods sold to retailers to the end of a selling season. Oftentimes, you will see branded merchandise (with labels affixed) sold in off-price outlets as well as in manufacturers' factory outlets. As a result department and specialty store buyers are facing competition for the same goods from discounters, factory outlets, and off-price retailers. Therefore, markdowns may occur frequently, sometimes early in the selling season.

Private-Label (Specification) Buying

Private-label buying or specification buying is a request by a store's merchandising team *for minor changes in a product that has already been produced, or it may include specifications for production from raw materials to final package.*

Today many stores urge their buyers to do private label buying instead of using national-branded items. There are a number of advantages:

1. Private-label buying enables the stores to offer merchandise that is different from that offered by its competition and often of better

quality at prices considerably lower than those asked for comparable national brands.

2. Customers benefit from this type of buying because they are provided a merchandise assortment that is distinctive and unique.

3. Since private-label merchandise is controlled by the retailer, price cutting, style changes, and poor quality control are eliminated.

4. If the retailer is also the manufacturer, it has the additional advantage of adding manufacturers' profits to normal selling profits.

5. A store carrying private brands cannot be comparison shopped by customers.

6. The customer following that is built up by the private brand belongs to the store and not to the manufacturer.

A number of activities must occur in order for a retailer to introduce private labels and make customers aware of private-label lines:

1. The store must embark on an extensive advertising campaign using various advertising media, window displays, visual merchandising, giveaways, demonstrations, fashion shows, and so forth.

2. Sales training classes must be provided to inform personnel of product features, advantages, and uniqueness.

3. Private-label merchandise can be compared to national brands through promotional advertising highlighting its price, product characteristics, and differences.

4. A separate division or department should be establihsed within the store's organizational structure to promote private-label development.

How then does a retailer decide the source of supply for private-label merchandise?

There are a number of methods a retailer can use to procure private-label merchandise.

1. The retailer may make arrangements with a well-known manufacturer to produce goods (with minor changes) and affix the store's private label. This is advantageous for the retailer since he or she may assess quality and performance based on past experience and consumer satisfaction.

2. Some retailers may purchase private-label merchandise from manufacturers who produce exclusively for private-label retailers. An example is Mitchell Paige who has worked successfully with such major retailers as Marshall Field, Garfinckel's, Saks, and Sakowitz.

3. A store may elect to offer private-label goods developed by its resident buying office. Even though the private label is not exclusive to that particular store, it does make possible the purchase of merchandise that will be distributed solely to noncompeting member stores. An example is Frederick Atkins Resident Buying Office, which distributes its private label in men's and women's apparel under the Jonathan Stewart label. Independent Retailers Syndicate, a resident buying office with more than 200 members stores, offers 21 brands under its own labels.

4. A store may decide to produce its own merchandise, which is sold under the store's name. For example, Marshall Field manufactures giftware and apparel and Edison Bros. manufactures shoes for its own stores, such as Bakers, Chandlers, and Burt's Shoes.

Figure 13–2 Large-scale retailers have embarked on labeling programs that will bring them merchandise exclusivity and instant customer recognition. For example, K mart has introduced a fashion apparel line from actress Jacquelin Smith. (Courtesy of Ladies Apparel Department, November, 1988, K mart Corporation, Troy, Mich.)

On the other hand, the small business buyer may have to join with other small businesses and form buying pools to encourage a manufacturer to "tool up" or make minor changes in a product. The small business may have a more difficult time locating a manufacturer, since it does not have the buying power, that is, it does not have the ability to buy in large quantities as do chain operations or department stores. For this reason, you will usually not find a small business offering goods under its own private label.

Buying Designer Labels

Large scale retailers will embark on labeling programs that will bring them merchandise exclusivity and instant customer recognition. For example, J. C. Penney decided to deemphasize its hard goods offerings and increase its selection of soft goods. In its determination to expand its role in the fashion market, J. C. Penney announced a licensing agreement with the fashion designer Halston, a recipient of four Coty Awards, which in turn gave birth to Halston III, an exclusive designer label carried only by J. C. Penney. Sears has followed with the introduction of a sportswear line by model, Cheryl Tiegs and K Mart with a fashion apparel line from actress Jacqueline Smith (Figure 13–2).

Review the Buying Methods Discussed

1. Regular buying
2. Buying job lots
3. Buying irregulars and seconds
4. Advance buying
5. Promotional buying
6. Special-order buying
7. Special manufacturers' brands
8. Private label (specification) buying
9. Buying designer labels

How Will Each Method Be Used by the Following Buying Specialists?

The total buyer in a department store
A buyer of boys' wear in a discount house
A children's wear buyer in a small business
The housewares buyer in a department store

PLACING THE ORDER

Once the buyer determines the merchandise assortment and negotiates the terms and conditions of sale, he or she is ready to go on to the next step, that is, to fill out the buyer's order form.

In the past, the sales contract was relatively simple and the negotiations were relatively uninvolved. However, with increased sales activity, more and more care was taken to assure the buyer that merchandise ordered would be received in good condition and according to the prearranged specifications.

A buyer may order merchandise by telephone or in person. Such an agreement is legally binding up to an amount of $50 in most states. However, since many retail buyers are acting as agents of stores and oral orders may prove uncertain and unreliable, it is a practical necessity for retail stores to place written orders.

The order form, then, becomes a most important document, since it contains all details of the business transaction. Although every retail store has its own order form, they all basically contain the same information. Both the front and the back of the order form constitute a legal contract. The following information should be contained on the front of the buyer's order form:

> Name and address of the retail organization
> The order number
> The date
> Department or store ordering the merchandise
> Delivery date
> Cancellation date
> Terms and dating
> Method of transportation
> FOB point
> Place of delivery
> Complete description of the merchandise: style, quantity, color, unit
>   price, total price
> Authorized signatures

The back of the order form usually contains stipulations concerning arrangements whereby the vendor is legally held responsible when he accepts the order from the buyer. The *Basic Trade Provisions* formulated by the National Retail Merchants Association appear on the reverse side of most buyer order forms. These provisions and the information contained on the front of the order form constitute a legal contract when signed by the

Figure 13-3   Basic trade provisions. *Source:* National Retail Merchants Association.

BASIC TRADE PROVISIONS

Adopted by the NRMA for inclusion in an order form, specifically or by reference.

1. It is mutually agreed and understood that all the terms and conditions set forth on this Order are satisfactory unless the Seller notifies Purchaser to the contrary, before shipment is made, within 15 days from the date of this order.

2. Purchaser may not cancel this Order for any reason before date for completion of delivery; cancellation after date for completion of delivery shall be effective only upon Purchaser's written notice to Seller, but shall not be effective with respect to any shipments made by the Seller within three (3) working days after receipt of such notice.

3. No returns of merchandise shall be made except for defects therein, or for non-conformity with some material provision of this Order. Where defects are discoverable upon reasonable inspection, or where non-conformity is claimed, such returns shall be made within five (5) working days after the receipt of goods affected. The Purchaser shall send the Seller a separate written notice, setting forth the nature of the defects or non-conformity claimed, prior to or simultaneously with the return. Seller may replace such returned merchandise, provided such replacement is made within five days after the last permissible delivery date.

4. In the event of the material interruption of the business of either the Seller or Purchaser by reason of fire, war, Act of God, governmental action, or strikes which materially affect the performance of this contract, the party so affected may cancel the order for such merchandise as has not been delivered, upon notice to the other party, notwithstanding any other provisions herein.

5. In the event that the Seller should be unable to manufacture, or determine not to manufacture, any style contained in this Order, he shall immediately notify the Purchaser to that effect and thereupon the Seller shall not be liable for non-delivery of such merchandise. Purchaser shall, however, accept delivery and pay for all other merchandise.

6. Seller shall have the right, from time to time, on any unfilled portion of this contract, to limit any credit to be extended hereunder or to require payment before delivery.

7. Any controversy or claim rising out of or relating to any of the provisions of this Order shall be settled by arbitration in accordance with the rules of the American Arbitration Association. For any purpose relating to this arbitration clause or an award rendered hereunder, the Purchaser and Seller consent to the jurisdiction of the Courts of the State in which the Seller has his principal place of business, and any legal process or paper may be served outside of such State by registered mail, or by personal service, provided that a reasonable time for appearance is allowed. Purchaser and Seller further consent that service in accordance herewith shall be sufficient to confer upon the Court jurisdiction in personam over the Purchaser and Seller.

8. No modification of the terms of this agreement shall be effective unless stated in writing, and no waiver by either party of any default shall be deemed a waiver of any subsequent default.

store's authorized agent, the buyer, and accepted by the seller. (See Figure 13-3.)

The buyer is also concerned with other details such as the method of invoicing, method of packaging, and the method of labeling for distribution to branch stores, other units of the company, or various departments within the store. This information is also specified on the front and back of the buyer's order form (see Figure 13-4).

Kinds of Orders

There are seven kinds of orders that may be placed by the buying specialist. They are listed as follows:

1. Regular orders. Regular stock orders are placed by the buyer directly with the vendor. They give complete specifications regarding time, amount, and shipment.

2. Reorders. These are orders for goods previously purchased.
3. Open orders. These are orders placed by the resident buying office whereby the resident buyer fills in the name of the vendor believed to be best suited to fill the merchandise requirements of the store.
4. Advance orders. These are regular orders that are placed in advance of immediate need.
5. Special orders. These are orders placed by the buyer for merchandise units to meet the needs of an individual customer or a few customers.
6. Back orders. These are order placed by the buyer for shipments or parts of shipments that were not filled on time by the vendor.
7. Blanket orders. These are orders placed by the buyer for merchandise for all or part of a season. The order does not indicate details such as shipping, dates, size, finish, color, etc. The buyer will place a requisition against these orders as the merchandise is needed.

Since the order form is a legal agreement between the retail firm and the merchandise resource, it is important for the buyer to fill it out carefully. When writing orders the buyer should observe the following rules:

Figure 13–4   An example of a buyer's order form used by a women's specialty shop.

STYLE	QUAN.	DESCRIPTION	CLR.	INSERT SIZES HERE					COST		RETAIL		TOTAL RET.	
1506	5	Navy Blue - Trim J. S.	06	10	12	14	16	18	14	99	29	95	149	75
1586	10	Pant Suit - Terry Tou	03	10	12	14	16	18	18	95	32	95	329	50
1701	6	Tops — V-Neck	01	S	M	L			5	95	9	95	59	70
1840	18	Jeans - Trim	04	12	14				9	95	18	-	324	-

DEPT. 62

Hecker's
Portland, Oregon 97200

PURCHASE ORDER NO. **17411**

TERMS _2/10 Net 30_

DATE ___3_ / _18_ / 19 **90**

TO _TRIM LINE_

ADDRESS _1401 BROADWAY, NEW YORK CITY_

SHIP VIA _U.P.S._

SHIP AS READY BY _4_ , _30_ , **90** OR CANCEL ___

MERCHANDISE MANAGERS APPROVAL BY _Francis McNeil_

1. Use the order form provided by the retail store.
2. If an oral order has been placed, confirm it immediately by filling out an order form.
3. It is usually best if the buyer writes out his or her own order form; however, some retail buyers will permit the manufacturer's representative to do so.
4. Always check the order carefully before signing it.
5. Write out specifications and directions carefully and precisely.
6. Put all agreements or any special arrangements in writing.

By observing pre-established rules concerning the writing of the order form, the buyer will facilitate the follow-up procedure. Follow-up is usually the task of the assistant buyer or department head. Order forms written legibly and accurately will enable the assistant to communicate better with vendors regarding merchandise shipments, terms of sale, and order specifications.[1]

Some Hints for Retail Buyers

Whether a new buyer or "an old pro," there are guidelines the buyer should observe when negotiating with vendors. They are listed in Table 13–1.[2]

Don't Be Unreasonable

The buyer should not expect unreasonable concessions from the vendor or manufacturer. For example, a buyer who takes advantage of a vendor by returning merchandise when he or she has no legal right to do so will only encourage the ill will of the vendor, who may eventually ignore the buyer when specials or job lots are available. However, certain circumstances may dictate when merchandise may be returned to the vendor. Once the buyer has taken title to the goods, they should not be returned unless:

1. The merchandise received fails to meet the sample specifications.
2. The merchandise arrives too early or too late in terms of the promised date.
3. Merchandise quantity, style, or color is not as ordered.
4. The terms of sale on the invoice differ from those agreed upon during the negotiation process.

To avoid the tendency on the part of some buyers to take advantage of vendors and manufacturers, many large retail stores require that cancellations of orders and merchandise returns be approved by the merchandise manager. The vendor should not suffer because a retail buyer used poor judgment in buying.

TABLE 13–1. Some hints to the retail buyer.

Do's	*Don'ts*
1. Notify the resident buying office when you will be in the market. The resident buyer will help you determine the market's best sellers before you buy.	1. Seek unreasonable concessions from vendors.
	2. Avoid playing the "bluff" game.
	3. Pretend to be a "know it all." Ask the vendor for help.
2. Seek the opinion of others. Consult with your merchandise manager, other buyers, salespeople and assistants as well as merchandise resources.	4. Try to redesign the manufacturer's merchandise. Suggest detail changes which will help both you and the manufacturer to sell the goods.
3. Study all merchandise units carefully and critically. Consider fabric quality, performance, texture, and construction. Ask questions.	5. Unfairly cancel merchandise.
	6. Accept personal favors and thus become obligated.
4. Look for goods which will become fast moving items and provide a steady re-order business.	7. Try and pass your buying "mistakes" on to the vendor.
5. Carefully check past sales records before determining quantity and price.	8. Put in unfair damage or shortage claims.
6. Visit all manufacturers before making a final decision.	
7. Fill out the order form at home where you can think clearly and away from pressure.	
8. When purchasing bargains, be sure the merchandise will be suitable to the entire line.	

PART 2—The Vendor's Responsibility to the Buyer

THE CONDUCT OF THE VENDOR

It goes without saying that the vendor or manufacturer has certain obligations to the buyer. For example, the vendor has the responsibility of offering the same *opportunities* for price concessions to small retailers as he does to buyers for large retail operations. This, however, does not mean that vendors must offer the same *prices* to all buyers. Lower prices and concessions must be based on the specific quantities ordered, as well as the conditions of the terms of sale. Any buyer, therefore, placing orders for specified quantities and conditions of purchase is entitled to similar concessions on proportionately equal terms.

The vendor has the responsibility of fair play when dealing with the buyer. A vendor should not "ship short," that is, the specified amount of merchandise should be shipped. He or she should not ship unordered merchandise or include extra goods in the hope that the buyer will accept and pay for the whole shipment. A vendor who continually engages in this type of activity not only breaks the contractual agreement but also soon develops a reputation among store buyers for being unreliable and lacking good business conduct.

LEGAL ASPECTS
OF THE BUYER'S ORDER

It is important to remember that, *once the vendor accepts the order, the contract has been made.* Vendors who offer merchandise for sale and who accept orders from retail buyers complete the cycle that forms the legal contract. A *legal contract* may be defined as an order that has been properly filled out, signed, and accepted by the vendor. Since the buyer's order is an agreement containing a promise enforceable by law, the laws of contract require that the buyer and the vendor observe the trade practices listed in Table 13–2 when writing and accepting the order.[3]

TABLE 13–2. Trade practices that must be observed by the vendor and the buyer.

1. The order must be established for a lawful purpose
   The sale of merchandise
2. The order is made by competent parties
   Both parties must be over 21 years of age, sane, competent, and not enemies.
3. Contains an offer and an acceptance
   The buyer offered money in payment and the offer was accepted by the vendor.
4. Entails a consideration
   The buyer promises to give up money. The vendor promises to give up goods; or, a payment is actually made.
5. There is a meeting of the minds
   Both the buyer and the vendor agree that the order is reasonable and acceptable.

It is important to remember that both the buyer and the vendor must follow established trade practices and customs, since their observance will affect legal decisions regarding the validity of the order. The buyer must be aware of and understand his legal rights, and the actions of both parties must be governed by the principles of good business conduct and fair dealing.

CAUSES OF FRICTION BETWEEN VENDORS AND BUYERS

The following is a list of practices that may cause friction between vendors and buyers.[4]

Causes of Friction Between Vendors and Buyers

1. Returns and adjustments
2. Cancellations
3. Shipping problems
4. Special order and minimum orders
5. Selling competitors and exclusives
6. Fashion piracy
7. Advancing seasons
8. Substitutions
9. Failure to follow instructions

Returns and Adjustments

Some retail buyers may return unsold merchandise at the end of the season for credit without the consent of the vendor, and when they have no legal right to do so. For example, the merchandise may have been damaged by rough handling in the store, or it may have been returned by customers to the store for a refund. Some buyers may return goods that are slightly soiled and expect the vendor to replace them. The buyer is not legally justified in making such returns unless he and the vendor have agreed in writing that such goods may be returned and will be accepted for credit.

Vendors may agree to take back merchandise, particularly if the retail store is a good customer. On the other hand, some vendors may refuse to accept legitimate returns or to make adjustments when they themselves are responsible or at fault. Such practices will cause friction and lead to poor vendor-buyer relations. If objectionable practices become excessive, the buyer may seek another vendor, or the vendor may drop the buyer's account.

Cancellations

A cancellation policy should be agreed upon between vendors and buying specialists. The following list is representative of conditions under which orders may be cancelled:

1. When merchandise is not shipped by the final due date specified on the buyer's order form
2. When the vendor or manufacturer receives a cancellation notice from the buyer
3. When the vendor changes merchandise specifications or other conditions of the order
4. When there is mutual agreement between the vendor and the buyer regarding merchandise cancellations
5. When the merchandise manager's approval is obtained

Figure 13–5 is an example of an order cancellation used by a department store to notify a vendor that the style numbers on the orders listed are cancelled.

Shipping Problems

Early, late, or split shipments can cause friction between vendors and buyers. If, for example, the buyer has limited storage space, it may be impossible to accept merchandise before the time designated on the order. Also, early shipments require earlier payment unless the vendor or manufacturer provides for extra dating. If a buyer does not want an early shipment of goods, this should be stated in writing on the order form: for example, "Do not deliver before October 1."

Late shipments also cause problems for buyers. They may find themselves with an inadequate assortment of merchandise, which may cause their customers to shop elsewhere. Or the buyer may be "stuck" with out-of-season goods. A telephone call or a letter from a vendor explaining the situation would help the buyer plan more effectively and eliminate costly markdowns.

Split shipments often are an unusual hardship for the vendor as well as the buyer. A manufacturer or a vendor who is not able to fill an entire order as specified may make a partial shipment on the designated delivery date with a notation that the remainder will be shipped at a later date. However, when the unfilled portion arrives, the buyer may refuse to accept the

Figure 13–5 An example of an order cancellation. (Courtesy of John Wanamaker Department Store, Philadelphia, Pa.)

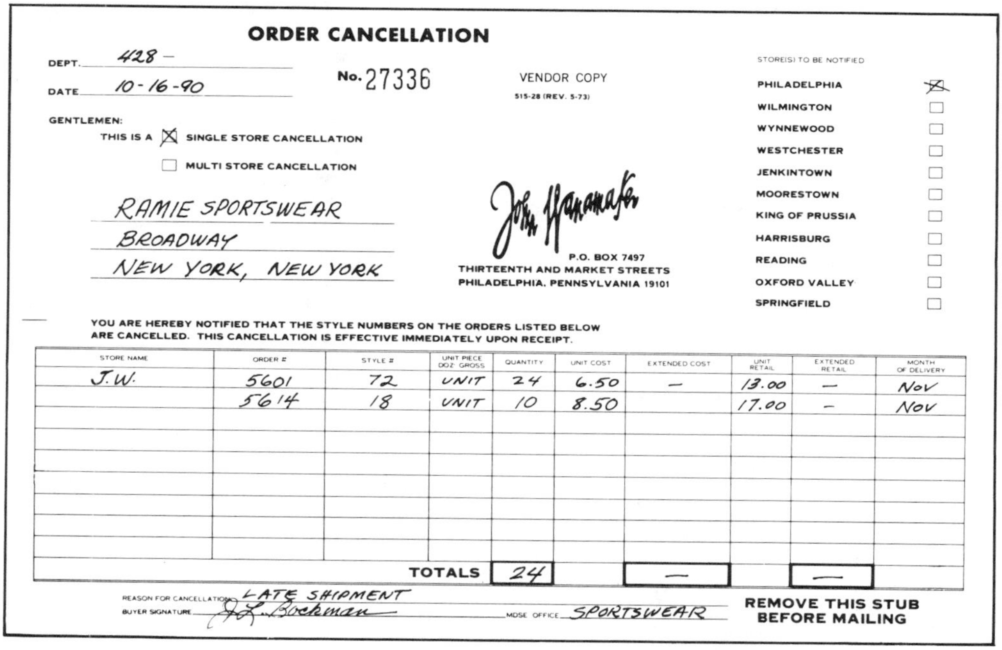

ORDER CANCELLATION

DEPT. 428 –

DATE 10-16-90

No. 27336

VENDOR COPY

515-28 (REV. 5-73)

GENTLEMEN:

THIS IS A ☒ SINGLE STORE CANCELLATION

☐ MULTI STORE CANCELLATION

RAMIE SPORTSWEAR
BROADWAY
NEW YORK, NEW YORK

John Wanamaker
P.O. BOX 7497
THIRTEENTH AND MARKET STREETS
PHILADELPHIA, PENNSYLVANIA 19101

STORE(S) TO BE NOTIFIED

PHILADELPHIA ☒
WILMINGTON ☐
WYNNEWOOD ☐
WESTCHESTER ☐
JENKINTOWN ☐
MOORESTOWN ☐
KING OF PRUSSIA ☐
HARRISBURG ☐
READING ☐
OXFORD VALLEY ☐
SPRINGFIELD ☐

YOU ARE HEREBY NOTIFIED THAT THE STYLE NUMBERS ON THE ORDERS LISTED BELOW ARE CANCELLED. THIS CANCELLATION IS EFFECTIVE IMMEDIATELY UPON RECEIPT.

STORE NAME	ORDER #	STYLE #	UNIT PIECE DOZ. GROSS	QUANTITY	UNIT COST	EXTENDED COST	UNIT RETAIL	EXTENDED RETAIL	MONTH OF DELIVERY
J.W.	5601	72	UNIT	24	6.50	—	13.00	—	NOV
	5614	18	UNIT	10	8.50		17.00	–	NOV
TOTALS				24		—		—	

REASON FOR CANCELLATION LATE SHIPMENT

BUYER SIGNATURE J.L. Bockman

MDSE. OFFICE SPORTSWEAR

REMOVE THIS STUB BEFORE MAILING

merchandise, even though he or she has not previously notified the vendor of intention to reject the goods.

Special Orders and Minimum Orders

A retail buyer may wish to place special orders with a vendor, especially if the buyer carries a limited stock of merchandise. Special orders enable buyers to provide for individual needs of customers while eliminating the necessity for carrying a large assortment of goods. On the other hand, special orders are costly for manufacturers to handle; therefore, they dislike working on them. To discourage special orders, a manufacturer may charge an extra handling fee, which retailers object to rather strongly.

Some buyers use the "hand-to-mouth principle" when ordering merchandise, whereby they buy in small quantities those goods they can sell within a short period of time; therefore, some manufacturers charge extra for minimum orders. This practice also causes friction between vendors and

Figure 13–6 An example of a special order form.

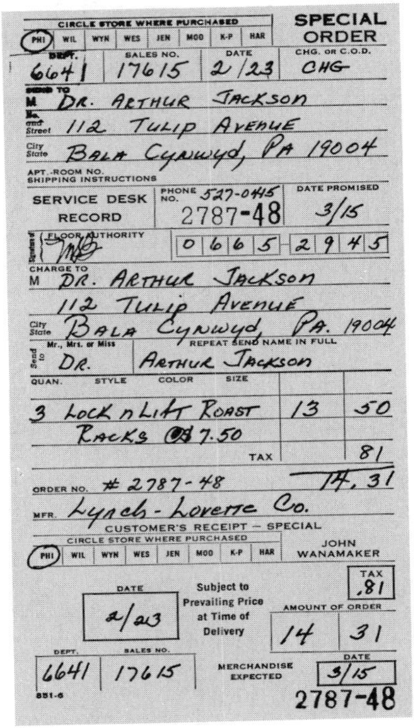
CIRCLE STORE WHERE PURCHASED
PHI | WIL | WYN | WES | JEN | MOO | K-P | HAR
SPECIAL ORDER

DEPT.	SALES NO.	DATE	CHG. OR C.O.D.
6641	17615	2/23	CHG

SEND TO
M DR. ARTHUR JACKSON
No. and Street 112 TULIP AVENUE
City State BALA CYNWYD, PA 19004
APT.-ROOM NO.
SHIPPING INSTRUCTIONS
SERVICE DESK RECORD
PHONE NO. 527-0415
2787-48
DATE PROMISED 3/15
FLOOR AUTHORITY
0665-2945
CHARGE TO
M DR. ARTHUR JACKSON
112 TULIP AVENUE
City State BALA CYNWYD, PA. 19004
Send to Mr., Mrs. or Miss DR.
REPEAT SEND NAME IN FULL ARTHUR JACKSON

QUAN. STYLE COLOR SIZE		
3 LOCK N LIFT ROAST RACKS @ 7.50	13	50
TAX		81
	14.	31

ORDER NO. # 2787-48
MFR. Lynch-Lovette Co.
CUSTOMER'S RECEIPT — SPECIAL
CIRCLE STORE WHERE PURCHASED
PHI | WIL | WYN | WES | JEN | MOO | K-P | HAR
JOHN WANAMAKER
TAX .81
DATE 2/23
Subject to Prevailing Price at Time of Delivery
AMOUNT OF ORDER 14 31
DEPT. 6641
SALES NO. 17615
MERCHANDISE EXPECTED DATE 3/15
851-6
2787-48

buyers. Figure 13–6 is an example of a special order placed by a salesperson, which in turn will be forwarded to the vendor by the buyer.

Selling Competitors and Exclusives

For the most part, a manufacturer will not sell special lines of merchandise to buyers from retail stores that are in direct competition with one another. However, to increase volume, a manufacturer may sell identical merchandise to those traditionally not associated with the selling of such goods. For example, a manufacturer of women's stockings may sell his product to a manufacturer of soap or detergent to be available in return for the coupon attached to the box of soap. Some retail buyers may see this as a threat to product sales. Buyers may seek to have agreements established preventing the selling of identical goods in such nontraditional ways to more than one company.

Exclusive agreements may be arranged between vendors and buyers. The purpose of an exclusive agreement is primarily to protect the buyer from having the same goods offered for sale to his competition. Also, such an agreement will ensure the vendor of full coverage of his lines in a store that will best merchandise his product.

Fashion Piracy

Fashion piracy is a matter of concern among vendors themselves. However, occasionally a retail buyer will copy a vendor's sample or hold out a sample and seek another manufacturer to reproduce the article. Buyers and vendors must establish policies prohibiting such practices.

Advancing Seasons

Competition has promoted the practice of advancing seasons, whereby both vendors and buyers cut prices before a season is over and while an active consumer demand still exists. Usually, the next season's line is promoted before the period of normal consumer demand. Often, however, such premature markdowns cause unnecessary losses to both vendors and buyers. Individual vendors or buyers may find it to their immediate advantage to act ahead of the competition. However, there is a need for a general but flexible agreement between vendors and buyers as to the proper time to institute seasonal clearance and offer new seasonal merchandise.

Substitutions

Often a vendor will have to send the buyer substitutes for the original merchandise offered. For example, in the fashion goods trade a manufacturer is frequently unable to obtain unlimited quantities of certain fabrics or color combinations. When the manufacturer receives a reorder, he fills it with merchandise that follows as closely as possible the original merchandise specifications. The manufacturer should notify the buyer of the substitution and get permission to ship the merchandise; however, the rush of business and the desire of buyers to receive merchandise, even though it is different from the shipment ordered, makes this difficult.

Failure to Follow Instructions

Finally, friction between vendors and buyers is caused by failure to follow instructions. For example, a vendor may add greatly to the cost of transportation by failing to follow shipping instructions. This has led retail stores to compare shipments with shipping instructions and charge back to the vendor the added cost caused by failure to follow the instructions provided. The vendor must remember that additional shipping charges will increase the cost of goods, thus lowering the buyer's profit.

ESTABLISHING GOOD VENDOR-BUYER RELATIONS

Needless to say, vendors and buyers can supply long lists of complaints against each other. However, most problems arise because some vendors and some buyers are thoughtless about their responsibilities. The vendor and the buyer must remember that each is responsible for actively promoting and protecting a company's image. Problems and complaints that reflect on the image of the vendor's or the buyer's company will eventually prove costly and lead to a serious loss of business. It is important to both parties that mutual confidence and respect become more evident than distrust or disrespect. Each must effectively communicate with the other, respect the other's business policies, and attempt to understand the other's potentials and problems. Both should work together in mutual agreement and understanding.

The following policies should be considered to ensure the establishment and maintenance of good vendor-buyer relations.[5]

1. Be as loyal to a good vendor as he is expected to be to the buyer.
2. Never discontinue business without sufficient cause and only when mutual discussions and criticisms have failed to produce desired results.
3. Be fair and honest when considering one another's offerings.
4. Make all commitments definite and precise.
5. Do not partake in commercial bribery, that is, accept or offer gifts, rewards, and commissions.
6. Continuously improve trade relations through education, self-regulation and government regulation.
7. Represent the best interest of the company at all times.
8. Do not take unfair advantage of one another.
9. Become thoroughly knowledgeable of the merchandise line you represent.
10. Work hard to establish and maintain a good working relationship.

Chapter Summary

The activities that occur during the negotiation process are very important to buyer and vendor alike. The buyer has the responsibility of ethically representing his retail organization to the vendor, securing discounts and allowances, arranging transportation and storage, establishing the terms of sale, and seeking price guarantees. This interchange between buyer and vendor occurs before the order is written and signed.

There are several kinds of orders that may be placed by the buyer. They are: (1) regular orders, (2) reorders, (3) open orders, (4) advance orders, (5) special orders, (6) back orders, and (7) blanket orders.

The order form is a most important document, since it contains all details of the business transaction. Because it is a legal agreement between the retail firm and the merchandise resource, it is important for the buyer to fill it out carefully. By observing the rules concerning the writing of the order form, the buyer will facilitate the follow-up procedure and assist in establishing communications between the store and the vendor.

Retail buyers should not expect unreasonable concessions during the negotiation process. They must observe certain guidelines or "do's and don'ts" when dealing with vendors and manufacturers.

Vendors have certain obligations to retail buyers. Once the vendor accepts an order from the buying specialist, a legal contract has been made. Since the buyer's order is an agreement containing a promise enforceable by law, the laws of contract require that the vendor and the buyer observe specific trade practices when writing and accepting the order.

Although the vendor and the buyer must follow established trade practices, problems may arise that may cause friction between them. Causes of friction are: (1) returns and adjustments, (2) cancellations, (3) shipping problems, (4) special orders and minimum orders, (5) selling competitors and exclusives, (6) fashion piracy, (7) advancing seasons, (8) substitutions, and (9) failure to follow instructions.

Most problems arise because some buyers and some vendors are thoughtless about their responsibilities. It is important for each to remember that he or she carries the good name and reputation of the company in all dealings. Problems and complaints that reflect on the image of the vendor or the buyer will eventually prove costly and lead to a serious loss of business. Both the vendor and the buyer should establish policies that will ensure the establishment and maintenance of good vendor-buyer relations.

Trade Terminology

DIRECTIONS: Briefly explain or discuss each of the following trade terms:

1. Private-label (specification) buying
2. Negotiation process
3. Discount or allowance
4. Quantity discount
5. Seasonal discount
6. Trade discount

7. Cash discount
8. FOB factory
9. FOB destination
10. FOB shipping point
11. FOB destination, charges reversed

12. FOB destination, freight prepaid
13. Legal contract
14. Job lot
15. Irregular
16. Second
17. Advance buying

Questions for Discussion and Review

1. What is the negotiation process? Name five activities involved and explain the importance of each.

2. Discuss the seasonal discount from the point of view of (1) the retail buyer, (2) the vendor, and (3) the consumer.

3. As the retail firm's representative, the buyer has certain responsibilities. Name five of these, and explain how each is important in developing good buyer-vendor relations.

4. Why is the buyer's order considered to be a most important document?

5. What kind of information is usually found on the order form?

6. What is meant by the statement, "Once the vendor accepts the order, the contract has been made?"

7. What rules and recommendations should the buyer observe when filling out the order?

8. What kinds of orders may be placed by the buying specialist?

9. Referring to "Some Hints for Retail Buyers," what guidelines would you suggest to help the new buyer when negotiating with the vendor?

10. What trade practices should be observed by the vendor and the buyer when writing and accepting the order?

11. What are some important causes of friction between vendors and buyers?

12. Consider each of the ten policies that should be followed by vendors and buyers. What suggestions can you offer to improve upon these policies?

Case Study Number Fifteen

SIVARD'S, INC.

Sivard's, Inc. is a full-line department-store chain containing five department-store units. It is located in the southeastern part of the United States; top management operates from the main store in West Palm Beach, Florida. The organization has always been under the control of its original founders, the Sivard family. Store policies over the years have been rather conservative, and sales are beginning to decline. After a complete analysis of the buying system, it was recommended by retail specialists that Sivard's affiliate with other stores to organize a type of private buying office or form its own separate buying office. It was also recommended that Sivard's join a large resident buying office to take complete advantage of merchandise offerings in both the hard-goods and fashion-goods lines.

The board of directors have met for several months. They are convinced that they must use some type of resident buying affiliation if they are to provide a merchandise assortment that will increase sales and profits. However, they have not been able to reach a decision as to which type of resident buying office they need.

Keeping in mind that Sivard's is still controlled by a very conservative management team, what course of action would you suggest? Develop a list of alternatives. After considering all alternatives, which type of structure would you recommend? Why?

Case Study Number Sixteen

MR. PHILLIPS
AND LAURIE JACKSON

Paul Phillips was the costume-jewelry buyer for Bryant's department store, which was located in a large New England city. He ran a large department in the main store and its ten branches. In fact, Bryant's was now in the process of opening its eleventh branch store.

One afternoon the resident buyer for costume jewelry, Laurie Jackson, called to inform Mr. Phillips that Dalmer Jewelry Company, one of Mr. Phillips' principal resources, was offering a new line of jewelry for $1.98 retail. She felt that this line would be excellent for the store's forthcoming pre-Christmas promotion and advised Mr. Phillips to come to the market to view it. She emphasized that Mr. Phillips should "grab hold" of the opportunity to be one of the first in the area to handle the line.

As usual, Mr. Phillips was very involved in his daily activities, and now even more so with the opening of a new branch store; however, he felt that this advice should be followed up. Laurie Jackson and he had a very good working relationship, and he had a great deal of confidence in her ability to select merchandise that met the taste and price range of Bryant's customers. Therefore, he instructed Miss Jackson to take another look at the line and, if she was still impressed with it, to place an order.

She later called Mr. Phillips to inform him that the order was placed and also provided information regarding delivery date, discounts, display fixtures, and the opportunity for a cooperative advertising arrangement.

Three weeks later the merchandise arrived from Dalmer Jewelry Company. When Mr. Phillips saw it, he was horrified. He was shocked that such junk had been ordered and immediately told his assistant to return the merchandise to the jewelry company. When Laurie Jackson was informed of this action, she argued with Mr. Phillips, insisting that the merchandise had excellent sales potential, especially if it was advertised and displayed properly. She also argued that to return the merchandise was a breach of contract and would seriously jeopardize future business dealings with the jewelry company.

If you were the resident buyer, how would you handle this situation?

Case Study Number Seventeen

GOING TO
THE MARKET

A buyer for a men's shoe department in a small department store decided that he could increase sales volume by assessing new but related lines of merchandise. Since he did not use the services of a resident buying office, he had to make his own market contacts by visiting shoe manufacturers in the central market and by seeing sales representatives as they came to the store. He soon realized, however, that locating new merchandise resources was no easy task. He found that going to the market was very time-consuming and that his departmental duties and responsibilities began to suffer. Also, he was interested not only in adding new items but also imported goods.

Be prepared in class to discuss what advice you would offer the shoe buyer to help him locate new merchandise resources. How would he locate foreign merchandise resources?

Case Study Number Eighteen

THE BETTER OF TWO

Monroe's is a large department store located in the Northwest. Mike Jackson, the buyer of men's sweaters, was asked to make a special purchase of seventy dozen sweaters for a forthcoming storewide pre-Christmas sale. After the four-day sale, all merchandise that was not sold would be marked up to its original value. For this reason, Mike Jackson was directed by his merchandise manager not to purchase seconds, irregulars, odd prices and colors, etc. He was further instructed to maintain an initial markup of 45 percent on all special purchases, if possible.

After visiting several manufacturers, Mike Jackson determined that he had two suppliers from which to select his goods. The first supplier was one with whom he had been doing business with over the past year and with whose line he was familiar. This manufacturer, however, had a limited selection of styles, which he would offer at a special price. The buyer would have the option of selecting suitable colors and sizes, but style selection was limited and did not include best sellers. The cost price of the goods, however, would enable the buyer to maintain his initial markup goal of 45 percent.

The second merchandise resource was a manufacturer with whom Mike Jackson had not done business previously. Since the manufacturer was very anxious to secure Monroe's account, Mike Jackson was offered a one-time special price on seventy dozen sweaters. He was also given the opportunity of selecting the sizes, styles, and colors required from the manufacturer's complete line. However, the special price offered would only allow him to obtain an initial markup of 37 percent.

In your opinion, which supplier would offer Mike Jackson the best opportunity to obtain his merchandise goal?

Case Study Number Nineteen

TOO MANY SUPPLIERS?

You have been promoted to the position of furniture buyer in a rather large department. After working there for only a few weeks, you realize that a large number of sales representatives are interested in seeing you. When you check back through the department's invoices, you notice that orders have been sent to as many as forty different manufacturers. You check with the assistant buyer and learn that the previous buyer's policy was to order from as many different sources as possible. The previous buyer argued that this policy enabled the store to offer a wide choice of merchandise. Your predecessor also felt that if merchandise ran short, it was always possible to find a supplier. Will you follow the same buying policy in selecting vendors? Be prepared in class to explain your answer.

Case Study Number Twenty

IS CAPE COD ALL WET?

Cape Cod is the manufacturer of Ship Side Rainwear, which is sold by a number of specialty shops and exclusive sporting-goods stores along the New England coast. The rainwear retails for about $125, and most of the full rain suits sell for $250. The product has long been recognized as a leader in the marketplace for quality, style, and prestige.

Cape Cod advertises in the leading boating magazines and various fashion periodicals. To promote the Cape Cod name and label further, the company participates in major boat shows and other sporting activities.

In recent years, however, it has become evident that more and more stores are removing the Cape Cod label and replacing it with their own labels. Jim Walker, president of the Cape Cod manufacturing company, is disturbed by this. He believes that, if the stores are permitted to continue this practice, Cape Cod rainwear will lose its prestige and status in the marketplace, which will lead to a decrease in sales. At a meeting with his sales representatives, it is decided that to protect the Cape Cod label, the company will have to adopt a policy that obliges store accounts to feature and promote the label.

What methods may be used to stimulate an interest in the Cape Cod label?

Learning Activities

1. Select a leading retail department store in your local shopping area. Make an appointment with a buyer of staple goods to discuss the various methods of buying and how they are used by a buyer of staple goods. Interview the buyer of fashion merchandise. Discuss the various methods of buying fashion goods. Compare and evaluate your findings.

2. Select a small retail business in your local shopping area. Make an appointment with the store manager to discuss various methods of buying. Determine how they are used by the entrepreneur during the buying process.

3. Interview a buyer of fashion goods in a department store. Discuss the importance of understanding the Basic Trade Provisions as formulated by the National Retail Merchants Association. Cite specific examples.

4. Interview the store manager of a variety chain operation; a specialty chain; a department-store branch. Prepare a list of questions based on the topic "the kind of vendor services available to encourage customers to buy." How will the services available differ with each store? How will they be similar?

5. Interview the owner-manager of a hardware store; a specialty shop. What forms of dealer helps are used by each store? What kinds of problems has each store manager had to deal with when seeking dealer helps?

6. You have been asked to write a term paper on the topic "Does the small retailer get the same advantages from vendors as the large store?" Referring to the books listed in The Retail Student's Reference Library, develop an outline of the important points you wish to emphasize.

References

THE RETAIL
STUDENT'S REFERENCE LIBRARY

Directory of Retail Software. New York: NRMA, n.d.
Drew-Bear, R. *Mass Merchandising: Revolution and Evolution.* New York: Fairchild Pub., Inc. n.d.
Gold. E. B. *Dynamics of Retailing.* New York: Fairchild Pub., Inc. n.d.
How to Select an Advanced Communications System. New York: NRMA, n.d.
OCR-A Cost Benefit Study. New York: NRMA, n.d.
OCR-A Implementation Handbook. New York: NRMA, n.d.
OCR-A The Key to Productivity and Profit. New York: NRMA, n.d.
OCR-A Users Guide. New York: NRMA, n.d.
Profitable Merchandising of Men's Clothing. New York: NRMA, n.d.
A Retailer's Guide to Controlling Communications Expenses. New York: NRMA, n.d.
Rising Telecommunications Costs: Sources and Solutions. New York: NRMA, n.d.
Taylor, C. G. *Merchandise Assortment Planning.* New York, NRMA, n.d.
Techniques of Fashion Merchandising. Indianapolis: ITT Pub. Co., n.d.
To Multiply A Buyer. New York: NRMA, n.d.
Walker, H. S. and Mendelson, N. J. *Children's Wear Merchandiser.* New York: NRMA n.d.

REFERENCES

1. J. W. Wingate and Joseph S. Friedlander, *The Management of Retail Buying* (Englewood Cliffs, N.J.: Prentice-Hall, Inc., 1963), pp. 334–337.
2. Donald L. Belden, *The Role of the Buyer in Mass Merchandising* (New York: Chain Store Publishing Corporation, 1971), pp. 22–23.
3. Karen R. Gillespie and Joseph C. Hecht, *Retail Business Management* (Hightstown: McGraw-Hill Book Company, 1970), p. 178.
4. Wingate and Friedlander, *Management of Retail Buying,* pp. 348–351.
5. Belden, *Role of the Buyer,* pp. 22–24.

SECTION

The Buyer's Role in Preparing Merchandise for Sale

Pricing Merchandise for Profit

14

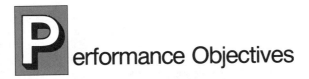

Performance Objectives

After reading this chapter, the student should be able to accomplish the following:

1. Recall three techniques used by a buyer to develop a thorough knowledge of prices.

2. Prepare a list of sources used by buyers to obtain price information.

3. Define wholesale price and retail price.

4. Discuss three important elements included in the wholesale price.

5. List five kinds of discounts offered to a retail buyer by merchandise resources.

6. Explain quantity discount, seasonal discount, cash discount, and series discount.

7. Identify three major factors to consider when determining the retail price.

8. Define markup and markdown.

9. Write the markup formula and the markdown formula.

10. Identify three major price laws that have been passed to protect both the retailer and the consumer.

Pricing Merchandise for Profit

Figure 14–1 Before buying specialists can begin price negotiations, they must accumulate a vast amount of price information. One source of price information is the merchandise offerings in their own departments. (Photograph by Steve Hawkins)

INTRODUCTION

In the previous chapter you read of the importance of establish good buyer-vendor relations. The negotiation process is the bargaining activity that occurs between the buyer and the seller over certain goods and services. There are a number of activities involved in the negotiation process. Furthermore, sound buying practices between buyer and vendor should be followed in the procurement of goods, whether domestic or foreign. There are many buying methods that can be used.

Once the buyer determines the merchandise assortment and negotiates the terms and conditions of sale, he or she is ready to fill out the order form. The order form is a most important document since it contains all details of the business transaction. Certain information should be contained on the front of the buyer's order form. There are a number of different kinds of orders including regular orders, advance orders, back orders, and blanket orders, to name a few.

There are guidelines the buyer should observe when negotiating with vendors, and the vendor or manufacturer has certain obligations to the buyer as well.

In this chapter, we are concerned with how merchandise is priced for profit. How does a retail buyer develop a thorough knowledge of prices? Three techniques may be used: price guessing, price memorization, and price buildup.

Price neogiation is a very important responsibility of the buyer and includes negotiating the wholesale price and the retail price. There are three elements included in the wholesale price: wholesale or quoted price, wholesale discounts, and transportation and shipping costs.

Not only is the retail buyer responsible for determining the wholesale price, but he or she is also responsible for determining the retail price. There are three major groups of factors the buying specialist should consider when determining the retail price. First, there are certain internal factors, such as pricing objectives of the retail firm, the cost of goods sold, and business expenses. Second, there are a number of external factors, such as market price, market-plus price, market-minus price, and competition.

Third, there are other important factors, such as the markup formula, price linings, one-price and varying-price policy, prestige pricing, odd pricing, leader pricing, and markdowns.

There are also legal aspects of pricing. The laws passed by Congress that affect business are wide-ranging and often complex. The government influences business through anti-price discrimination laws, unfair trade practice laws, and fair trade laws.

PART 1—Determining the Wholesale Price

OBTAINING THE
BEST POSSIBLE VALUE

As you recall from earlier chapters, two very important responsibilites of the retail buyer are to obtain a profit for the store and to serve the needs and wants of the store's customers. To accomplish these two tasks, the buying specialist must obtain the best values possible when negotiating with merchandise resources. This means familiarizing himself or herself with the price offerings of various merchandise resources who carry the particular line of goods wanted.

The capable buyer, as a result of past experience, will know when he or she is paying too much for merchandise. Upon close inspection, the buyer will be able to approximate the cost price, or the price to be paid to the vendor, as well as estimating the retail price, or the price the goods will be sold for in the retail store. How does the buyer develop this thorough knowledge of prices? (See Figure 14–1.)

A THOROUGH KNOWLEDGE OF PRICES

The following three techniques are used by all types of buyers to assist them in developing a thorough knowledge of prices. They are: (1) price guessing, (2) price memorization, and (3) price buildup.

Price Guessing

Before the buyers begin price negotiations with merchandise resources, they accumulate a vast amount of price information. The sources of price information are too numerous to list completely, but they may include conversations with vendors and manufacturers' representatives, examination of merchandise in his or her own department (see Figure 14–1) and of similar merchandise offered by the competition, trade journals, catalogs and price lists, and conversations with others in the trade. As a result of accumulating price information, buyers develop a remarkable skill in price guessing and are able to place prices upon merchandise wherever it is to be seen, in retail stores, manufacturers' showrooms, o: as sample displayed by salespeople. Sources of price information used by buyers are:

1. Merchandise offerings in the buyer's own store
2. Merchandise offerings of competitors
3. Trade journals
4. Catalogs and price lists
5. Conversations

What other sources of price information are available?

Price Memorization

Once the buyers learn the cost prices offered by vendors and the retail prices of similar goods offered in retail stores, they memorize them. Buyers also remember price changes as reported by trade journals or vendors. They have the ability to build up a storehouse of memorized prices based upon careful and close concentration on price information and close attention to price changes in the marketplace.

Price Buildup

A third technique used by buyers in developing a thorough knowledge of prices is the ability to estimate manufacturers' expenses. If the buyers can estimate the cost of materials used in the manufacturing of the product and the manufacturer's operating expenses, they are better able to evaluate the fairness of the manufacturer's quoted price. Using this method, the buyer may determine whether or not the vendor or manufacturer is attempting to make too much profit. Or, if the goods offered are priced too low, there is a possibility that the merchandise is of poor quality or workmanship, or that the finished product may not be a good seller.

How Will the Following Techniques Help the Buyer Develop a Thorough Knowledge of Prices?

Price Guessing
The buyer is enabled to place prices upon merchandise wherever and whenever seen.
Price Memorization
The buyer will remember prices seen in the marketplace and price changes as reported by trade journals and vendors.
Price Buildup
The buyer will estimate the manufacturer's cost of materials and operating expenses to determine the fairness of the manufacturer's quoted price.

ELEMENTS IN THE WHOLESALE PRICE

Wholesale price may be defined as the price paid for goods purchased from merchandise resources, for example, vendors, manufacturers, or suppliers. Since price negotiation is a very important responsibility of the buyer, he or she must be aware of three elements that are included in the wholesale price. They are: (1) wholesale or quoted price, (2) wholesale discounts, and (3) transportation and shipping costs.

Wholesale or Quoted Price

While most buying is done at the wholesale price or quoted price, the capable buyer is always attempting to secure the lowest price possible. A successful buyer is usually a skilled trader. If it seems that the vendor's price is too high, that the value of the purchase does not equal the quality, that production costs are unfair, that the season indicates a lower price, or that there are unusual conditions of sale, the buyer will negotiate with the vendor or manufacturer for a price concession. However, a smart buyer will be careful not to press for rock-bottom prices unless such a bid can be justified. A buyer who habitually makes unsupported demands on merchandise resources will develop a reputation throughout the trade. Sellers will find considerable satisfaction in quoting higher than normal prices to this buyer, whose job will become unnecessarily difficult. Generally, a buyer will enter the marketplace intent on purchasing the right goods at the right time and at the right amount, rather than on saving a few dollars on the purchase price. The store buyer will have ample opportunity to obtain price concessions when buying *special merchandise,* that is, goods offered not for quality appeal but for price appeal.

Wholesale Discounts

There are five kinds of discounts offered a retail buyer by merchandise resources. They are: (1) trade discounts, (2) quantity discounts, (3) seasonal discounts, (4) cash discounts, and (5) series discounts. As you recall from reading Chapter 13, Developing Good Buyer-Vendor Relations, discounts are offered to buyers in the form of vendor aids. In this chapter we will discuss how discounts are formulated:

Five Kinds of Discounts Offered by Merchandise Resources to Retail Buyers Are:

1. Trade discounts or functional discounts
   A reduction in price given to certain trade customers to cover costs involved in performing particular trade functions
2. Quantity discounts
   A discount offered to retail buyers to encourage large-quantity purchases
3. Seasonal discounts
   A reduction in wholesale price granted to buyers to encourage off-season buying
4. Cash discounts

> A reduction in price given to a retail buyer when a cash payment
> is made within a certain date specified on the invoice
> 5. Series discounts or chain discounts
> A series of discounts granted to the buyer to stimulate a greater
> volume of business

Trade discount. It is important to remember that trade discounts are usually not considered a form of price concession but rather a method of quoting prices based on list prices. For example, a manufacturer may list prices in a catalog that are often suggested retail prices or "offering prices." A retailer may be granted a trade discount perhaps 25 percent off the list price. Also, a manufacturer may use the trade discount as a method of changing the prices of all the merchandise in his line. For example, the manufacturer's catalog may lists as many as 1,000 items. Rather than reprinting the catalog with new prices, the manufacturer will send a notice to buyers informing them that the former 25 percent trade discount is changed to 25 percent and 10 percent, thus the buyer is granted an additional 10 percent discount. Or, if merchandise prices need to be increased, the vendor may issue new price lists informing the trade of a reduction in discount.

A supplier may sell to service wholesalers, drop-shipment wholesalers (wholesalers who ship directly to retail stores), chain-store buyers, resident buyers, and small independent retailers, and may offer a 50 percent trade discount to all wholesalers, chain buyers, and resident buyers; 40 percent to drop-shipment wholesalers; and 25 percent to the small independents. The trade discount bears no relationship to the amount of goods purchased at any given time period. It may be given in addition to other discounts, for example, the quantity discount.[1]

The trade discount offered to buyers will vary for a number of reasons. First, the vendor's cost of selling to a small independent retailer as opposed to a chain-store buyer may vary significantly. It is less costly for a vendor to sell 5,000 units of his product to a single chain buyer than it is to sell the same quantity to 300 small independent retailers. Second, variations in trade discounts may differ as a result of the buyer's operating costs. By way of illustration, the cost of selling to wholesalers and discount buyers may be the same. However, the wholesaler may have lower operating costs as compared to the discount buyer, who must ship and warehouse the merchandise throughout a region or territory.

According to the Robinson-Patman Act and other regulations, trade discounts appear to be justified if they actually represent a savings to suppliers. From a legal standpoint, trade discounts which are offered to all in a business category are legal; otherwise, legal problems arise.

Trade discounts may be computed as follows:

A vendor may offer a 50% trade discount to chain-store buyers, wholesalers, and resident buyers.
Thus:

List Price Per Unit (suggested retail price)	$50.00
Less 50% (trade discount)	− 25.00
(50% of $50.00 = $25.00)	$25.00

A vendor may offer a 40% trade discount to drop-shipment wholesalers.
Thus:

List Price Per Unit (suggested retail price)	$50.00
Less 40% (trade discount)	− 20.00
(40% of $50.00 = $20.00)	$30.00

A vendor may offer a 25% trade discount to small independent retailers.
Thus:

List Price Per Unit (suggested retail price)	$50.00
Less 25% (trade discount)	− 12.50
(25% of $50.00 = $12.50)	$37.50

A vendor may offer a 25% trade discount and an additional 10% trade discount to buyers.
Thus:

List Price Per Unit (suggested retail price)	$50.00
Less 25% (trade discount)	− 12.50
	37.50
Less 10% (additional trade discount)	− 3.75
	$33.75

Quantity Discount. The quantity discount is offered by vendors to encourage retail buyers to make large quantity purchases. For example, a buyer who agrees to purchase 500 units of merchandise instead of 300 units may be given a 10 percent reduction in the wholesale price. However, the buyer must be aware that quantity discounts may lead to overbuying and hence must carefully weigh the advantages and disadvantages of quantity purchases and be certain that the additional units of merchandise will make a profit for the department and thus for the store.

According to the Robinson-Patman Act, the same quantity discounts must be given to all retailing specialists buying the same amount of merchandise of "like grade and quality." Problems have arisen however on the meaning of "like grade and quality." Furthermore, the discount should be consistent with the amount of savings resulting from a large quantity order. Also, both the supplier and the retail buyer can be charged with price discrimination if the size of the quantity discount is greater than the vendor's savings. Also, if a large retailer puts pressure on a vendor to agree to a price which discriminates against other retailers, the retailer may be held accountable under the law.

A quantity discount may be computed as follows:

A vendor may offer a 10% quantity discount if the buyer purchases 500 units of stock instead of 300 units.

Thus:

Wholesale Price	$500.00
Less 10% (quantity discount)	− 50.00
(10% of $500.00 = $50.00)	$450.00

As you recall, a quantity discount may also be stated in the form of "free" merchandise given to the buying specialist. For example, a wholesaler of gourmet food may offer a 1-case-free-with-15-cases-purchased deal for food buyers who wish to make purchases for the Christmas season.

Seasonal Discount. The seasonal discount is a percentage reduction in wholesale price or list price granted by suppliers to buyers to encourage off-season buying. Since many kinds of staple merchandise are in demand only during particular seasons throughout the year—for example, air conditioners, skiing equipment, Christmas ornaments, and bathing suits—vendors will offer discounts to encourage buyers to anticipate their needs in advance of the season. Vendors find it good business to offer seasonal discounts because off-season orders enable them to stabilize production activities on a year-round basis, rather than being swamped with orders during particular seasons. Also, the buyer may gain not only a price concession, but also goods manufactured during the off-season months, which are more carefully produced, marked, and packaged. However, once again the buyer must carefully anticipate needs because, if the merchandise does not sell, there is the problem of storage and warehousing expenses as well as the problem of merchandise becoming out of style. A seasonal discount may range from 10 percent to 40 percent, depending on the type of retail store and the nature of the goods.

Once again, federal law requires the supplier to give the same seasonal discount to all retail firms in a particular business category.

Seasonal discounts may be computed as follows:

A vendor may offer a 40% seasonal discount to a toy buyer to encourage the buyer to place orders and to accept delivery in June rather than wait until August.
Thus:

List Price	$175.00
Less 40% (seasonal discount)	− 70.00
(40% of $175.00 = $70.00) $	$105.00

A vendor may offer a 30% seasonal discount to a buyer of lawn supplies to encourage the buyer to place orders and to accept delivery in December rather than wait until February.
Thus:

List Price	$85.00
Less 30% (seasonal discount)	− 25.50
(30% of $85.00 = $25.50)	$59.50

A vendor may offer a 10% seasonal discount to a buyer of children's shoes to encourage the buyer to place orders and accept delivery in March rather than waiting until June.
Thus:

List Price	$15.00
Less 10% (seasonal discount)	− 1.50
(10% of $15.00 = $1.50)	$13.50

Cash Discount. A cash discount is a reduction in price given by a vendor to a retailer when a cash payment is made within a certain time period specified on the invoice. For example, 2/10 net 30 will allow the buyer a 2 percent discount if he pays the bill promptly. It must be remembered, however, that often a period of several days from the date of the invoice elapses before the merchandise is received. The cash discount may still be granted because payment need be made only within the stated period of the terms of sale. Cash discounts are taken after trade discounts, quantity discounts, and seasonal discounts.

There are other forms of cash discount. For example, a vendor may send an invoice (bill) with terms of 2/10 net 30 extra, whereby the 2 percent cash discount is extended for a thirty-day period in addition to the ten-day period, which gives a total of forty days from the invoice date. Or a vendor may send an invoice (bill) with terms of 2/10 EOM, whereby the 2 percent cash discount period runs for ten days following the end of the month (EOM) in which the goods were purchased. If, for example, a purchase was made on

September 1 with terms of 2/10 EOM, the 2 percent discount could be taken any time through October 10.

Cash discounts may be computed as follows:

A vendor may send an invoice (bill) with terms of 2/10 net 30. Thus:

Amount of Invoice	$250.00
2/10 net 30	− 5.00
(2% cash discount if paid within ten days)	$245.00
(2% of $250.00 = $5.00)	

However, if payment is not made within the ten days, it is customary for the buyer to wait twenty days longer and pay the total invoice price at that time, thus the terms are usually stated on the invoice as 2/10 net 30.

A vendor may send an invoice (bill) with terms of 2/10 net 30 extra. Thus:

Amount of Invoice	$250.00
2/10 net 30 extra	− 5.00
(2% cash discount is extended for a thirty-day period, in addition to ten days, which gives a total of forty days)	$245.00

A vendor may send an invoice (bill) with terms of 2/10 EOM. Thus:

Amount of Invoice	$250.00
2/10 EOM	− 5.00
(2% cash discount period runs for ten days following the end of the month [EOM] in which goods were purchased)	$245.00

Series Discount. A *series discount* or *chain discount* may be defined as a combination of discounts granted by the merchandise resource to the retail buyer. Extra discounts are granted to secure the business of a particular retail store or to stimulate a greater volume of business. It is important to remember that in taking a series discount, the discount is taken from the cost price and then on from the preceding price. For example, if the series discount is 10/30/20 percent, these are *not* added together to equal 60 percent.

A series discount may be computed as follows:

A vendor may offer a series discount of 10 percent, 30 percent, 20 percent.
Thus:

List Price	$50.00
Less 10% (trade discount)	5.00
Cost Price	$45.00
Less 30% (extra trade discount)	13.50
	$31.50
Less 20% (quantity discount)	6.30
Net Price	$25.20

Transportation and Shipping Costs

As you recall from reading Chapter 13, Developing Good Buyer-Vendor Relations, the method of transportation as well as the method of shipping will also affect the cost of goods purchased from merchandise resources. Usually, the vendor or manufacturer will quote the selling price of goods (wholesale price) at the point of production. Or the buyer may purchase goods from a middleman, a warehouse, or a limited-function wholesaler. In most instances, the buyer will pay the entire cost of transportation and will also assume responsibility for damage and all other costs while the merchandise is en route to the retail store.

Review the Elements Included in the Wholesale Price.

1. Wholesale or quoted price
   A capable buyer is able to secure the lowest price possible.
2. Wholesale discounts
   Discounts will enable the buyer an opportunity for a reduction in goods.
3. Transportation and shipping costs
   The buyer must determine who is going to pay for transportation and shipping.

Why are the elements of the wholesale price important?

PART 2—Determining the Retail Price

AN IMPORTANT
SELECTION FACTOR

Not only is the retail buyer responsible for determining the wholesale price or cost price of merchandise; he or she is also responsible for determining the retail price. The *retail price* may be defined as the first price at retail that is placed on merchandise by the retailer regardless of later sales or other special event prices. The retail price of an item becomes an important factor during the consumer selection process. If the retail price is too high, the consumer may not purchase the item because he or she "cannot afford it" or can

Figure 14–2   The retail buyer will learn through experience that customers are interested in merchandise that sells at a particular price.

purchase the merchandise elsewhere for a lower price. If the product is priced too low, the consumer may become suspicious of product quality (Figure 14–2).

IMPORTANT FACTORS TO CONSIDER

There are three major groups of factors the buying specialist should consider when determining the retail price. First, there are certain internal factors, such as pricing objectives of the retail firm, the cost of goods sold, and business expenses. Second, there are a number of external factors, such as market price, market-plus price, market-minus price, and competition. Third, there are other important factors such as the markup formula, price linings, one-price and varying-price policy, prestige pricing, odd pricing, leader pricing, and markdown. Each will be explained in detail in the following pages.

Internal Factors

The buyer should give consideration to internal factors that may affect pricing decisions. Important internal factors are:

Pricing Objectives. The pricing policies of the retail business should be carefully considered, since an effective pricing policy is directly related to the overall objectives of the retail organization. Top management will usually determine pricing objectives, which in turn are communicated to the buyer or store manager. With pricing objectives in mind, a good retailer attempts to maximize profits on a long-term basis, although not necessarily to maximize profits on every item sold. For example, a boy's denim jacket may cost the buyer $4.50 and may be sold at retail for $6.00, a markup of 33⅓ percent. However, a cotton suede jacket costing the buyer $10.00 may be sold at retail for $14.00, a markup of 40 percent. Better-quality merchandise, less competition, and greater consumer demand may make the higher markup necessary. A buyer considering long-term objectives must realize that profit maximization depends on a variety of factors, including those that follow.

Cost of Goods Sold. The retail buyer must consider the price paid for merchandise when establishing the retail price. For example, a vendor may sell a certain type of sweater for $4.95 to two retailers in the same trading area, yet one of these retailers may sell the sweater at a higher markup. Both, however, will build the retail price from the cost of the merchandise ($4.95), using the cost price as a base when determining the retail price. As you recall from reading Part 1 of this chapter, all elements of the wholesale or cost price should be considered when determining the retail price, such as discounts and transportation and shipping costs.

Business Expenses. The buyer must also consider various business expenses when determining the retail price. You will recall that fixed costs are costs that usually remain constant and do not vary with the rate of sales. Examples of fixed costs are rent, utilities, taxes, and insurance. The buyer must also consider variable costs, which are costs that vary or change with the sales volume. Examples of variable costs may include commissions paid to salespeople or salaries paid to salespeople and stockpeople, clerks, and other supportive personnel.

External Factors

The buyer should give consideration to external factors that may affect pricing decisions. Important external factors are:

Market Price. The *market price* is the price established by consumers and competition alike. It is "whatever price the traffic will bear." A merchant will work on a particular markup percent, for example, 50%, 100%, or 300% (which is determined by the types of goods sold, amount of risk involved, and cost of operation), and must consider whether or not the cost of goods offered by the vendor will make it possible to meet the department's profit potential and maintain the store's markup policy.

Market-Plus Price. *Market-plus price* means that the vendor will ask a higher market price on the basis of the special and distinctive characteristics of the merchandise offerings. Usually buyers of boutique goods, specialty-store buyers, and buyers of better-priced merchandise will deal with such vendors. A higher markup percent is maintained by buyers who seek distinctive goods.

Market-Minus Price. *Market-minus price* refers to a vendor's policy of "underselling" by offering less service and less palatable products. Buyers who purchase goods from such vendors are usually seeking discount merchandise for the middle- to lower-income consumer.

Some vendors will maintain a steady price policy throughout the season (market price), offering clearances only toward the end of the season (market-minus price). Or some vendors will offer special price inducements at frequent intervals throughout the season.

In regards to terms of sale, the small retailer, particularly, is looking for merchandise resources who will grant end-of-month (EOM), thirty days, or longer. However, the buyer may decide that long terms may mean the loss of substantial discounts and perhaps lessen the opportunity for vendor assists.

Competition. The retail buyer must give consideration to the price of the same or similar items offered by the competition. Most stores will attempt to meet competitive prices; however, some retail stores, due to high overhead and other expenses, are forced to charge a higher price. To compensate for the higher markup, the store will offer additional services such as free delivery, a variety of credit arrangements, and a flexible return policy. If, however, the price of the merchandise has been predetermined by the manufacturer, the retailer and his competition have very little to do with the pricing.

Other Factors

Markup Formula. You will recall that the amount a retail buyer adds to the wholesale or cost price in determining the retail price is called a markup. The markup equation may be written as follows:

$$\text{Retail Price} = \text{Cost Price} + \text{Markup}$$
$$\$5 = \$4 + \$1$$

Markup may be expressed as the difference between the cost price and the retail price. The markup equation may also be written as follows:

$$\text{Markup} = \text{Retail Price} - \text{Cost Price}$$
$$\$1 = \$5 - \$4$$

Markup may be used to determine the cost price; the cost price equals the retail price minus the markup price. The equation may be written as follows:

$$\text{Cost Price} = \text{Retail Price} - \text{Markup}$$
$$\$4 = \$5 - \$1$$

To provide an easy working tool, markup is usually expressed as a percent. Markup percent can be figured as a percent of the retail price or of the cost price. Since the retail method of inventory is prevalent in large stores, the markup percent figured on the retail price is most common; the cost method of calculating is considered relatively old-fashioned. The markup equation as expressed in percent may be written as follows:

$$\frac{\text{Markup \%}}{\text{Retail Price}} = \frac{\text{Markup}}{\text{Retail Price}} = \frac{\$1.00}{\$5.00} = 20\% \text{ of retail price}$$

$$\frac{\text{Markup \%}}{\text{Cost Price}} = \frac{\text{Markup}}{\text{Cost Price}} = \frac{\$1.00}{\$4.00} = 25\% \text{ of cost price}$$

In merchandising, the markup percent is calculated as a percent of the retail price because all operating costs and profit or loss are determined as a percentage of net sales. The student will notice that the markup percent of retail price is less than the markup percent of cost price. This is often considered an advantage, since customers associate a high markup with a high profit. It is also important to remember that most of the markup reflects store overhead and expenses.

An additional factor, not part of the formula, is needed to solve markup problems. This factor is known as the *cost percent,* which is found by deducting the markup percent from the retail percent (100%). Since cost price plus markup equals retail dollars, the cost percent plus the markup percent equals the retail percent, which is also 100%. Therefore, given a markup percent of 45, and knowing that the retail percent is 100, we find that the cost percent is 55.

1. Given: Cost price $300   Retail price $500
   Find: Markup %

$$\text{Markup Percent} = \frac{\text{Retail Price} - \text{Cost Price}}{\text{Retail Price}}$$

$$= \frac{\$500 - \$300}{\$500} = \frac{\$200}{\$500}$$

$$= 40\%$$

2. Given: Cost Price $325   Markup % 35
   Find: Retail Price (remember: cost % = 100% − Markup %)

$$\text{Retail Price} = \frac{\text{Cost Price}}{\text{Cost \%}}$$

$$= \frac{\$325}{65\%}$$

$$= \$500$$

3. Given: Retail price $325   Markup % 35
   Find: Cost price

$$\text{Cost Price} = (100\% - \text{Markup \%})\,\text{Retail Price}$$

$$= (100\% - 35\%)\,\$325$$

$$= \$211.25$$

4. Given: Retail price $500   Cost price $300
   Find: Cost %

$$\text{Cost \%} = \frac{\text{Cost Price}}{\text{Retail Price}}$$

$$= \frac{\$300}{\$500}$$

$$= 60\%$$

Price Lining. *Price lining* is a common pricing practice used by many retail buyers whereby the buyer does not attempt to price merchandise at all possible prices but predetermines the retail price at which an assortment of merchandise will be carried.

For example, a store buyer will create a stock assortment by considering the price lines to be carried and the depth of the merchandise assortment offered at various price ranges. The number of price lines depends on the consumer income bracket the buyer wishes to attract as well as the types of goods offered for sale. Price lines may cover a variety of styles, sizes, and fabrics, which will appeal to customers in a particular income bracket.

Price range refers to the spread of the price line carried from the lowest to the highest price carried (for example, $5 to $35). *Price zone* refers to a series of price lines that are likely to appeal to one group of customers. When more than two price lines are inventoried, a price zone situation exists. Thus, price zones can be referred to as:[2]

Promotional	Low Price Zone	For Example, $5.00
Mass Volume	Medium Price Zone	For Example, $10, $25, $35
Prestige	High Price Zone	For Example, $40, $50, $60

Price lining offers the buyer a number of advantages when attempting to price merchandise for resale. Advantages of price lining are listed in the chart that follows.[3]

1. It facilitates selling by simplifying customer choice during the selection process.
2. A wide assortment of goods may be offered at popular-selling price lines.
3. Buying becomes simplified, since the range of wholesale costs is limited.
4. It results in a favorable turnover and decreased markdowns, and reduces size of stock.
5. Stock control is simplified.
6. Marking costs are decreased.

One-Price–Varying-Price Policy. This method of pricing is used by many retailers. Under the *one-price policy,* the same price is charged to all consumers who purchase merchandise in the same quantities under similar circumstances. A major advantage of the one-price policy is that consumer "bargaining" is eliminated. Also, the one-price policy does not foster preferential treatment of one consumer over another. In contrast to the one-price policy, the buyer may follow a *varying-price policy* whereby a consumer seeking to purchase merchandise at a lower price will bargain with the retailer until an agreement has been reached. For example, if a buyer is anxious to make a sale, he may allow the consumer to find some fault with the merchandise and mark down the price of the item to compensate for the fault.

Prestige Pricing, Odd Pricing, Leader Pricing. In *prestige pricing,* a high-price policy is followed for particular kinds of merchandise that appeal to the prestige- or status-minded consumer. Stores that have a high-fashion image or carry status-type merchandise follow this method of pricing. *Odd pricing* is a psychological method of pricing. Instead of pricing an item at $1, the price is set at 99¢. The use of an odd number creates the illusion of a lower price and often increases sales. *Leader pricing* involves the offering of a well-known brand of merchandise at a special low price. The primary objective of this method is to attract consumers into a store in the hope that they will purchase additional merchandise as well as higher-priced goods. If a well-known brand of merchandise is offered at a price below the buyer's cost, the merchandise is termed a *loss leader.*

Markdowns. As stated earlier, a reduction in price from the original retail price is called a *markdown.* Here is an example of the markdown equation:

Original Retail Price	$5.00
— Markdown Price	−$4.00
Dollar Markdown	$1.00

Markdown is the difference between the original retail price and the markdown price. The markdown percent equation may be expressed as in the following example:

$$\text{Markdown \%} = \frac{\text{Dollar Markdown}}{\text{Markdown Price}} = \frac{\$1.00}{\$4.00} = 25\%$$

Markdowns are expressed as a percentage of net sales, not as a percentage of original retail price.

The buyer will use a markdown as a method for stimulating sales and cleaning out remaining slow-moving merchandise. However, the markdown percent must be carefully determined to appeal to the consumer. For example, a blouse marked down to $9.00 from $10.00 (10% markdown) may have little sales appeal, whereas if the same blouse were marked down to $5.00 (50% markdown), the consumer would think of it as "a real bargain."

Review the following:

When determining the retail price, the buyer should consider:
Internal factors

1. Pricing objectives of the firm
2. The cost of goods sold
3. Business expenses

External factors

1. Market price
2. Market-plus price
3. Market-minus price
4. Competition

Other factors

1. Markup formula
2. Price linings
3. One-price–varying-price policy
4. Prestige pricing, odd pricing, leader pricing
5. Markdowns

How will this information assist the buying specialist when determining the retail price?

LEGAL
ASPECTS OF PRICING

As you recall from Chapter 2, the major purpose of government regulation of business is to promote the public welfare, benefit the economy as a whole, and protect the small business enterprise. The laws passed by Congress that affect business are wide-ranging and often complex. Also, each state in which a business operates has laws regulating business conduct. The objective of this section will be to discuss the impact of government's influence on retail businesses through: (1) price discrimination laws, (2) unfair trade practice laws, and (3) fair trade laws.

The Government Influences Business Through

Price discrimination laws
Unfair trade practice laws
Fair trade laws

Price Discrimination Laws

In 1914, the Clayton Act was passed, which outlawed price discrimination, exclusive and tying contracts, intercorporate stockholdings, and interlocking directorates. It is quite specific in forbidding certain practices. The principal provisions of the Clayton Act include:[4]

1. Section 2, which makes it unlawful for sellers to discriminate in price among different purchasers of commodities either directly or indirectly, and among different purchasers of commodities of like grade, quality, or quantity, whether the commodities are sold for use, resale, or consumption.

2. Section 3, which prohibits sellers from making tying contracts that prevent purchasers from dealing with the seller's competition, on the condition that the purchaser shall not deal in the commodity of a competitor.

3. Section 7 prohibits any corporation from acquiring shares of stock or assets of a competing corporation where the effect may be substantial to lessen competition or tend to create a monopoly.

4. Section 8 disallows interlocking boards of directors in competing corporations, except banks, banking associations, common carriers, and trust companies where one has capital accounts of $1 million or more.

In 1936, the Robinson-Patman Act revised Section 2 of the Clayton Act, which dealt with price discrimination. This act was written to make the price-discrimination provisions of the Clayton Act more flexible, as well as giving increased protection to smaller retailers. The Robinson-Patman Act forbade a vendor selling in interstate trade to give a lower price to one buyer than to another under the following circumstances.[5]

1. If the commodities offered to the buyers are of the same grade and quality.
2. If the sale of goods at unreasonably low prices would substantially lower competition, tend to create a monopoly or injure or destroy competition with a vendor or buyer or the customers of either.

3. If a broker's commission, which is, in effect, a reduction in price when an independent broker is not employed, is paid.
4. If advertising and promotional allowances are given on purchases made by large-volume retailers that are not available on "proportionally equal terms" to smaller competitive retailers.

Unfair Trade Practice Laws

In 1890, Congress passed the Sherman Antitrust Act in order that business organizations might operate in a free-enterprise economy without restraint of trade from other firms. Many smaller businesses and stockholders had been injured by the abusive and aggressive practices of larger businesses, which led to monopolistic and collusive practices in restraint of trade.

In 1914, Congress passed the Federal Trade Commission Act to strengthen the Sherman Antitrust Act. A federal agency called the Federal Trade Commission (FTC) was organized to police the antitrust laws. The powers of the commission dealt with Section 5 of the Act, which declared unfair or deceptive methods of competition unlawful. Other duties of the FTC included investigation of alleged restraint of trade and of discriminatory practices or other attempts at unfair competition, as well as the enforcement of acts forbidding such practices. In 1938, the Wheeler-Lee Act amended Section 5 of the Federal Trade Commission Act.

Fair Trade Laws

Small businesses had been active in securing protective legislation at the state level. By 1937, most states had followed California's lead and passed fair trade legislation. These laws permitted manufacturers or distributors of branded products in open competition to sign a contract with the retailer establishing the minimum retail price for which the merchandise would be sold to the consumer. These fair trade laws, however, were applicable only in intrastate commerce. The Miller-Tydings Act, which was passed in 1937 as an amendment to the Sherman Act, legalized the practice in interstate commerce (where manufacturers and retailers or wholesalers were in different states).

In 1952, Congress passed the McGuire Act, which permitted states to include nonsigner clauses in their resale price maintenance laws. The nonsigner clause states that all retailers in a state are bound by resale price agreements as long as one retailer in the state agrees to sign the contract.

Today, fair trade laws are not popular with consumers or retailers because such laws do not provide the retailer with an opportunity to meet competitive prices or changes in consumer demand. A number of large manufacturers have abandoned fair trade pricing policies. However, certain products, such as cosmetics and drugs, are still subject to resale price maintenance laws in some states.

Chapter Summary

There are three techniques a buyer may use in developing a thorough knowledge of prices: (1) price guessing, (2) price memorization, and (3) price buildup. The wholesale price may be defined as the price paid for goods purchased from merchandise resources such as vendors or manufacturers. Since price negotiation is a very important responsibility of the retail buyer, he or she must be aware of three elements that are included in the wholesale price: (1) the wholesale or quoted price, (2) wholesale discounts, and (3) transportation and shipping costs.

The major purpose of government regulation of business is to promote the public welfare, benefit the economy as a whole, and protect the small business enterprise. The government has had an influence on retail businesses through price discrimination laws such as the Clayton Act and the Robinson-Patman Act; through unfair trade practice laws such as the Sherman Antitrust Act, the Federal Trade Commission Act, and the Wheeler Act; and through fair trade laws such as the Miller-Tydings Act and the McGuire Act.

Not only is the buyer responsible for determining the wholesale or cost price of merchandise; he or she is also responsible for determining the retail price. There are three major factors that the buyer should consider when determining the price of goods for resale. First, there are certain internal factors such as pricing objectives of the business, the cost of goods sold, and business expenses; second, there are external factors such as market price, market-plus price, market-minus price, and competition; and third, other important factors are the markup formula, price lining, one-price and varying-price policy, prestige pricing, odd pricing, leader pricing, and markdowns.

The student should remember that pricing policies of a retail business can vary widely. The techniques presented in this chapter, however, are basic approaches used by most retailers when determining retail price.

Trade Terminology

DIRECTIONS: Briefly explain or discuss each of the following trade terms:

1. Wholesale price
2. Special merchandise
3. Series discount or chain discount

4. Retail price
5. Market price
6. Market-minus price
7. Market-plus price
8. Cost percent
9. Price lining
10. Price range

11. Price zone
12. One-price policy
13. Varying-price policy
14. Prestige pricing
15. Odd pricing
16. Leader pricing
17. Loss leader

Questions for Discussion and Review

1. Explain three techniques that may be used by a retail buyer in developing a thorough knowledge of pricing.

2. There are several sources of price information available to the retail buyer. Other than those mentioned, name five sources that a buyer may consult when determining the best price.

3. Discuss three important elements that must be included when determining the wholesale price.

4. Define quantity discount, series discount, and trade discount.

5. How can transportation and shipping costs increase the cost of goods sold?

6. Define price lining, varying-price policy, and leader pricing.

7. What is a markdown? A dollar markdown? Calculate the markdown percent when the dollar markdown is $1 and the markdown price is $5.

8. What is a markup? Calculate the markup percent when the markup is $5, the cost price is $25, and the retail price is $9. Why do retailers calculate the markup percent as a percent of the retail price?

9. Briefly outline the major provisions of the Robinson-Patman Act.

10. Explain the important factors a buyer should consider when determining the retail price.

References

THE RETAIL STUDENT'S REFERENCE LIBRARY

Basic Trade Provisions. New York: NRMA, n.d.

The Buyer's Manual. New York: NRMA, n.d.

Children's Wear Merchandiser. New York: NRMA, n.d.

China and Glassware Merchandiser. New York: NRMA, n.d.

The Complete Dictionary of Buying and Merchandising. New York: NRMA, n.d.

The Fashion Buyer's Job. New York: NRMA, n.d.

The Independent Store Policy Manual. New York: NRMA, n.d.

Lewis, R. D. and Lewis, J. N. *What Every Retailer Should Know about the Law.* New York: Fairchild Publications, Inc., n.d.

The Management of Fashion Merchandising—A Symposium. New York: NRMA, n.d.

Merchandise Assortment Planning. New York: NRMA, n.d.

Merchandise Control and Budgeting. New York: NRMA, n.d.

Practical Merchandising Math for Everyday Use. New York: NRMA, n.d.

Stocking, Jessie. *Fundamentals of Buying.* Kent, Ohio: Kent State University, n.d.

314 Ways to Run a Better More Profitable Store. New York: NRMA, n.d.

To Multiply a Buyer. New York: NRMA, n.d.

Visual Merchandising Principles and Practices. Bronx, New York: Educational Pub., n.d.

Watson, Donald S. *Price Theory and Its Uses.* Boston: Houghton Mifflin Co., n.d.

Weiss, E.B. *The Decline of the Store Buyer.* New York: Doyle, Dane, Berbeck, Inc., n.d.

Wingate, Isabel. *Buying for Retail Stores.* Washington, D.C.: U.S. Government Printing Office, n.d.

REFERENCES

1. D. J. Duncan and C. F. Phillips, *Retailing Principles and Methods* (Homewood, Ill.: Richard D. Irwin, Inc., 1970), pp. 343–344.
2. *Retail Mathematics Manual* (Philadelphia: Strawbridge & Clothier Department Store, 1970), pp. 37–40.
3. Ibid.
4. *The Clayton Act,* 1914, Federal Trade Commission, Washington, D.C.
5. *The Robinson-Patman Act,* 1936, Federal Trade Commission, Washington, D.C.

The Buyer and the Selling Process

15

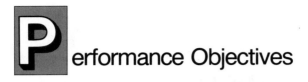

Performance Objectives

After reading this chapter, the student should be able to accomplish the following:

1. List nonpersonal selling devices that may be used by a buyer to communicate with customers indirectly.

2. Define advertising, sales promotion, and publicity.

3. Discuss several reasons why a retail buyer will advertise.

4. Define promotional advertising, institutional advertising, and combination advertising.

5. Outline the psychological steps that must be followed when planning advertising, and list six steps that should be followed when planning an advertising campaign.

6. Identify four activities included in sales promotion.

7. Define personal selling, and discuss three types of retail personal selling.

8. Outline the activities performed by a buyer when managing sales personnel, and explain the duties and responsibilities of sales personnel.

9. Discuss six steps that should be followed during the selling process.

10. Outline the importance of different management techniques, and identify problems encountered by new sales personnel.

The Buyer and the Selling Process

Figure 15–1 To influence customers to take a desired action, the buyer must be able to send messages, in this case through a store advertisement, that contain a proper balance of information and persuasion.

Introduction

The preceding chapter discussed pricing merchandise for profit. However, how does a retail buyer develop a thorough knowledge of prices? Three techniques are used: price guessing, price memorization, and price buildup.

Price negotiation, which includes negotiating the wholesale price and the retail price, is a very important responsibility of the buyer. Elements to consider when negotiating the wholesale price are: (1) wholesale or quoted price, (2) wholesale discounts, and (3) transportation and shipping costs.

There are three major groups of factors the buying specialist should consider when determining the retail price. First, there are internal factors, such as pricing objectives of the retail firm, the cost of goods sold, and business expenses. Second, there are external factors, such as market price, market-plus price, market-minus price, and competition. Third, there are other important factors, such as the markup formula, price linings, one-price and varying-price policy, prestige pricing, odd pricing, leader pricing, and markdowns.

There are legal aspects of pricing. The laws passed by Congress that affect business are wide-ranging and often complex. The government influences business through price discrimination laws, unfair trade practice laws, and fair trade laws.

In this chapter we are concerned with the buyer's role in the selling process.

To influence customers to take a desired action—that is to purchase goods—the buyer must be able to send messages that contain a proper balance of information and persuasion. Customers need to know what specials are available, what styles are in season, the location of the store, and so on. The buyer, therefore, will use nonpersonal selling methods to communicate with customers indirectly. Information about a store is communicated through nonpersonal selling devices, such as advertising, sales promotion, publicity, word of mouth, and packaging.

Retail personal selling is still a very important aspect of retailing, especially during healthy economic periods when customers tire of the impersonality of self-service and turn toward full-service stores.

The consumer who enters a store, other than a self-service establishment, expects to be greeted by sales people. A good salesperson, should have a proper attitude toward selling and possess the art and skill of modern selling techniques. As you recall from reading previous chapters, many retail buyers also have the responsibility of guiding and directing the sales staff. Certain activities are performed when managing sales personnel and include: (1) sales force planning, (2) recruitment and selection, (3) induction and training, (4) scheduling, (5) compensation, and (6) supervision.

During the induction and training process, the buyer must instruct new sales personnel on various duties and responsibilities ranging from department standards and routines to handling complaints to developing good selling techniques.

In most large retail stores, the most popular management technique used to reach salespeople is the department meeting. The advantages of department meetings are many. Salespeople can exchange views, meet new people, and have personal contact with the buyer and the assistant. Some objections to holding department meetings are that they become too routine, lack good planning and organization, and do not always include the entire staff.

Most buyers will develop a variety of successful management techniques as they attempt to instruct their salespeople.

PART 1—Advertising and Sales Promotion

THE IMPORTANCE OF EFFECTIVE COMMUNICATION

The retail buyer will make every effort to offer a combination of goods and services that will appeal to potential customers. However, for the customer to become aware of such offerings, the store executive must develop methods of sending messages or communicating with his or her trading area. The buyers must relate price, products, service, and store image in such a way that customers will be motivated to purchase goods from a particular store or department.

To influence customers to take a desired action, the buyer must be able to send messages that contain a proper balance of information and persuasion (Figure 15–1). Customers need to know what specials are available, what styles are in season, the location of the store, what the store hours are, the features of particular products, and so on.

Since effective communication will stimulate and create demand, buying specialists must be aware of those activities that are used in the communication process.

THE ROLE OF NONPERSONAL SELLING

Nonpersonal selling is a method of communicating with customers indirectly. Information about a store is communicated through nonpersonal selling devices such as advertising, sales promotion, publicity, word of mouth, and packaging. Since many types of nonpersonal selling devices are used by store buyers in various combinations, each will be discussed in detail.

Advertising

Advertising may be defined as a set of activities that involves the presentation of a mass message, called an advertisement, about a product, a service, or an idea; and the message is paid for by an identified sponsor.[1] According

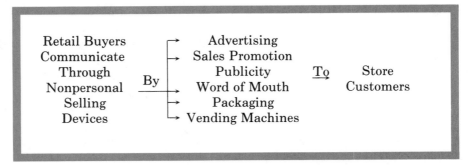

to the American Marketing Association, advertising may be defined as "any paid form of nonpersonal presentation and promotion of ideas, goods, or services by an identified sponsor."[2]

Since a store spends the greatest portion of its promotion budget on advertising, a buyer has the responsibility for planning advertising that will reach a large number of people. Primarily, advertising is used by the buyer to: (1) bring customers into the store; (2) motivate them to make purchases; and (3) build good will for the retail store. *It is important to remember that the prime objective of advertising is to attract potential customers to the store.* There are other reasons why buying specialists, department managers, or store managers will use this method to communicate with the trading area. The following list is representative of why retailers advertise.

1. To attract customers to the store
2. To motivate customers to make purchases
3. To build good will for the store
4. To introduce new products, fashions, and services
5. To stimulate and create demand for products and services
6. To build a favorable store image
7. To show new applications of a product
8. To develop a list of potential customers
9. To assist the salesperson through preselling
10. To increase mail and telephone orders
11. To maintain store name, trademark, or product before the public
12. To keep customers satisfied with previous purchases

THE MAIN TYPES OF RETAIL ADVERTISING

For purposes of study, there are three types of retail advertising: (1) promotional advertising, (2) institutional advertising, and (3) a combination of promotional and institutional advertising.

Promotional Advertising

Promotional advertising may be defined as direct-action advertising. The primary objective is to bring customers into the store to purchase specific items of merchandise. This is the most popular type of advertising used by buying specialists and may take any one of the following three forms:

1. Regular-price advertising. Merchandise is offered at regular prices; however, consumer appeal is based on the product's characteristics and desirability.
2. Sale-price advertising. Merchandise is offered at a sale price or as a special. Consumer appeal is based on the opportunity to save.
3. Clearance-sale advertising. Merchandise is offered at a lower price; however, the prime objective is to move out slow-moving inventory,

Figure 15–2 An example of promotional advertising. (Courtesy of Clover Division of Strawbridge Clothier, Philadelphia, Pa.)

broken and odd assortments, obsolete goods, and irregulars and seconds.

In this type of advertising one or more items are featured by regular, sale, or special prices with the primary objective that of increasing store traffic, since the merchandise offered is available only for a limited time period. The increase in store traffic will usually boost the sales of advertised goods (see Figure 15-2).

For example, a ladies' wear factory outlet may advertise merchandise that has been left over from a previous season with consumer appeal based on the opportunity to save while selecting from "fantastic" bargains. Or a discount house will advertise special discounts on seasonal merchandise.

Institutional Advertising

Institutional advertising may be defined as indirect-action advertising. The primary objective is to create good will for the store, build confidence in its merchandise and services, and establish customer loyalty. There are two forms of institutional advertising.

Prestige Advertising. This type of institutional advertising aims to attract present and prospective customers by the store's ability to offer the latest styles, designs, and materials, as well as maintaining past traditions. Figure 15-3 illustrates examples of prestige advertising.

Service Advertising. This type of institutional advertising seeks to attract present and prospective customers by calling attention to the store's various services and facilities, which make it a desirable place to shop. In service advertising no merchandise is advertised, no special sale is mentioned, and no attempt is made to build immediate customer traffic. However, this type of advertisement is attempting to build good will for the store by showing that it has a pleasant atmosphere, offers a variety of services, and is concerned about the welfare of its customers (see Figure 15-4).

A Combination of Promotional and Institutional Advertising

Combination retail advertising is a method whereby institutional and promotional approaches are blended together in the same advertisement. For example, merchandise in competing stores is often so similar that merchandise advertising in itself is not enough to draw customers to that particular store. By blending the prestige characteristics of the store in the advertisement, the product is made to take on the characteristics of the store, thus making it appear different from that carried by its competition.

Figure 15–3 Examples of prestige advertising from various departments in a well-known jewelry store. (Courtesy of Bailey Banks & Biddle, Philadelphia, Pa.)

New York we love you

You're the skyline of our hopes and dreams,
the City of Lights
that quicken our life.
We love you
City of the World
City of our Hearts.

From all of us at

> ### Under What Circumstances Will the Retail Buyer Use the Following Types of Advertising?
>
> | Promotional Advertising | Institutional Advertising | Combination Advertising |
> |---|---|---|
> | Regular price
Sale price
Clearance sale | Prestige
Service | Promotional and Institutional |

THE PSYCHOLOGICAL ASPECTS OF ADVERTISING

As you learned in Chapter 5, psychological studies of the emotions and drives of people have greatly influenced the use of advertising as an effective communications device. Such studies suggest that people may act on three levels: (1) on the conscious level, where people know why they perform certain acts; (2) on the subconscious level, where people know why they perform certain acts but do not admit the real reason for their actions; and, (3) on the unconscious level, where individuals act in a certain way but do not know the reason. A review of Chapter 6 will further suggest that appeals to emotional drives are more effective than those aimed at reason.

Since the buyers are responsible for assisting in the planning and promotion of advertisements for their departments or the store as a whole, they must also be aware of certain psychological steps that every advertisement must contain: (1) attracting attention; (2) developing interest; (3) creating desire; (4) securing action. The student will note that these psychological steps are also applicable to personal selling, which will be discussed in Part 2 of this chapter.

Attracting Attention

For the advertisement to meet its objective, that is, to bring customers into the store to purchase merchandise, it must attract the attention of the customer. For example, the use of illustrations, vivid use of colors, unusual lettering, bold print, or unusual or decorative spacing are just some of the techniques that may be used to attract the attention of the customer (Figure 15–5). Psychological studies have also shown that attention must be secured before a message can be communicated to the customer.

Figure 15–4 An example of an institutional advertisement. (Courtesy of Lord & Taylor, New York, N.Y.)

Figure 15-5　Bold print and unusual or decorative spacing are just some of the techniques used in advertisements to attract the attention of store customers. (Courtesy of George Jacobs, Philadelphia, Pa.)

Developing Interest

Once the customer's attention is attracted by the advertisement, interest must be aroused. Since people are usually interested in matters that relate to themselves, merchandise that fulfills their needs and wants will interest them. Thus, the advertisment should relate products to the needs of customers for them to develop an interest. Also, merchandise descriptions should be simply written, in nontechnical language.

Creating Desire

Desire for particular products is created by appealing to both emotional and rational desires. As you recall from reading Chapter 6, people may buy from such motives as hunger, security, pride, attracting the opposite sex, and a desire for comfort, economy, and dependability, to name but a few. The type of goods being advertised and the kind of customers to be reached will determine which buying motive are used to create a desire or need for the product.

For example, Figure 15–2 seeks to create a desire for the particular items advertised through the appeal to reason. If the reader of the advertisement is interested in savings, she will hurry in and purchase the blouses that are being offered at "super savings." Also, an advertisement may inform the reader that the items are offered for a limited time only and after that time there will be "no rainchecks." Thus, the ads will appeal to budget-conscious customers who are seeking bargains and who desire to get the most for their money.

Securing Action

The desired action should result if all the preparatory steps have been carefully followed. The action may involve a visit to the store, a mail order, a telephone call, or the filling out of a coupon. The customer must take some kind of desired action if merchandise is to be sold. For example, in the type of advertisement illustrated in Figure 15–2, customers are encouraged to hurry in to make their purchases, since no coupon or mail order is provided.

PLANNING ADVERTISING FOR YOUR DEPARTMENT OR STORE

If you own your own business, you will have the responsibility of planning advertising for the entire store. If the budget permits, you may seek the services of an advertising agency; however, usually you will have to plan the store's ads, and perhaps seek the advice and assistance of your employees throughout the planning process. One of the advantages of working for a large retail business such as a department store, a discount house, a general-merchandise chain, or a specialty store, is that you have a well-trained group of professionals to assist you in planning advertising for your particular department. It is important, however, for you to understand how advertising plans are developed so that you may constructively contribute to the overall planning process. Thus, whether you are the owner-manager of a small retail business or a buying specialist for one or more departments, consideration should be given to the following six steps when planning an advertising campaign: (1) setting specific objectives; (2) identifying a theme; (3) establishing a budget; (4) selecting merchandise to promote; (5) selecting the media; and (6) preparing the advertisement.

Setting Specific Objectives

Those individuals usually responsible for planning advertising in a large retail operation are the sales promotion manager, the fashion copywriter, the fashion illustrator, the fashion coordinator, and the display manager. These promotion executives will determine advertising objectives for the store as a whole. Advertising objectives may be based on a long-term plan (yearly objectives) or on a short-term basis (daily or weekly objectives). Objectives must determine *who* will be the target market and *what* is to be accomplished.

The promotion team will review last year's sales promotion efforts and lay out a program based on this year's suggested objectives. Once the plan has been approved by top store executives, programs are developed for each department individually. These plans may be based on three-month or six-month periods, depending upon the store's advertising policy. At this point the buyer may be requested to submit a tentative schedule of what he or she would like to promote. Later, as the season progresses, the merchandise

---

Consideration Should Be Given to the Following When Planning an Ad Campaign:

1. Setting specific objectives
2. Identifying a theme
3. Establishing a budget
4. Selecting merchandise to promote
5. Selecting the media
6. Preparing the advertisement

---

manager and the promotion division will develop a plan for each department to ensure that overall coordinated promotional efforts are maintained.

The buyer will develop a preliminary outline of the promotions he or she would like to have during particular selling seasons. The outline will include a review of the previous year's sales promotion activities, the costs involved, and the results of previous promotions. Also, suppliers will run sales promotion activities; thus, the buyer must consider the department's immediate goals as well as those of the division and the store as a whole.

Identifying a Theme

The second step when planning an advertising campaign is to identify a theme. The *advertising theme* will determine *how* the objectives can be accomplished. It will describe the benefits the consumer will receive by purchasing the advertised product and by shopping in a particular store. For example, a buying theme may read, "Inflation Fighters—Prices Good through Sunday, April 13th—Shop As Late As 10 P.M."

The advertising theme used by individual departments or the store as a whole will depend upon the merchandising policies of the store, the target market, the kinds of merchandise to be advertised, and the store's overall promotional objectives. For example, a fashion department will use a number of promotional approaches that best suit the needs of its customers. Emphasis may be on trends, prestige, feelings of security or insecurity, and so forth. The fashion theme may use fashion shows, clinics (for example, teen-age model and charm clinics), special cosmetic demonstrations, designer fashion shows, or the opportunity to meet an important author, celebrity, or rock star. For some fashion departments, the advertising theme may emphasize the availability of certain styles at moderte or budget prices.

The buyer of hard goods will also use a variety of advertising themes geared to the needs of the customers. For example, the buyer of hardware and paints may use "Fix Up, Paint Up, and Clean Up" as an ad theme during the spring of the year. A buyer of furniture may use "Dress Up Your Living Room for the Holidays" as an incentive to encourage consumer spending. Or the home-appliances buyer may use "Beat the Heat and Save" as an ad theme for selling air conditioners before the selling season begins.

Establishing a Budget

The third important step when planning an advertising campaign is to prepare a budget. Since advertising is usually the second or third largest expense, next to payroll and overhead, it must be planned with the utmost care. As you recall from previous readings, certain monies have already been allotted to each department for the cost of its advertising. The buyer will be consulted during the initial planning stages, and thus should be aware of the following four steps in planning the advertising budget:

1. Analyzing last year's sales figures as well as the figures of the previous selling season and setting a realistic sales goal.
2. Referring to past years' advertising budgets to determine how much advertising will be necessary to meet departmental sales goals as well as those of the store as a whole.

3. Determining the sales contribution of each department and deciding what merchandise lines to promote.
4. Planning advertising expenditure based on a month-to-month and then a day-to-day schedule. Special consideration should be given to heavy-selling seasons such as Christmas; special promotions such as inventory clearance sales; special events such as Washington's birthday; and night openings such as those that occur from Thanksgiving to Christmas.

The buyer must have a general idea of costs to make tentative promotional plans for the department, evaluate cooperative advertising offers, and estimate expected advertising costs in return for various kinds of tie-in promotions. Store management will usually allot a percentage of planned sales to each department when planning the advertising budget. The cost of advertising is based on storewide considerations and the merchandising objectives of the individual departments.

Selecting Merchandise to Promote

The fourth step to consider when planning the advertising campaign is selecting the right merchandise. The buyer and the advertising department will work together in determining which goods will be selected for promotion. They must decide what goods will appeal to the most customers. *Selecting the "right" products to advertise is a single most important factor in store promotion.* The buyer must be aware that all merchandise in the store can-

TABLE 15–1.   Selecting the right products to advertise.

Merchandise that *Should* be Advertised	Merchandise that *Should Not* be Advertised
1. Fast-selling, popular items that are in demand	1. Old and obsolete goods
2. New fashion items	2. Limited-quantity merchandise
3. New and unusual merchandise	3. Merchandise that cannot be quickly reordered
4. Exclusive and distinctive goods	4. Goods not in stock when the advertisement appears
5. Special-occasion merchandise	5. Goods previously advertised and still in stock
6. Merchandise with distinct price appeal	6. Merchandise that has not been promoted to salespeople
7. Convenience goods	7. Merchandise that does not meet store standards of price and quality
8. Private or store brands	
9. National brands	
10. Related lines of merchandise	

not be advertised, since this would mean an increase in advertising expenses without a proportional sales increase. The buyer must select representative items that will bring the largest number of people to his department and create the most good will. The list in Table 15-1 is representative of those goods that should be considered for store promotion, as well as of those items that should not be given promotional consideration.

When a buyer is requested to provide information to the advertising division for planned advertising, the following procedure should be carried out:

1. Selecting the merchandise to be featured. The selection will be based on the factors previously discussed.
2. Filling out the appropriate forms sent to the buyer by the ad department. As Figure 15-6 illustrates, the buyer should supply factual information about the merchandise, including price, size, material, and color range. Information regarding special features such as how the article is to be worn, its fashion importance, its brand name or designer, fabric care, type of occasion for which it is to be worn, and whatever else the customer needs to know, should also be supplied. The buyer of hard goods should also supply complete information about the merchandise to be promoted.

The buyer should also brief salespeople about the promotional activities of the department. It is important to build enthusiasm about the merchandise and, in turn, get that enthusiasm across to the sales staff. The buyer, store manager, or department manager should inform salespeople of:

1. Merchandise to be advertised, when it is to be advertised, and where—for example, store windows, displays, the media.
2. Special features of the merchandise that should be emphasized by salespersons.
3. The fashion message used to promote the goods.
4. When and where the promotion will occur—at what dates and in what store units, departments, or branches.
5. How other department merchandising activities will tie in.
6. How storewide promotional activities will relate to this promotion.
7. Important features or fashion emphasis to point out to customers.
8. Anticipated questions regarding the merchandise advertised.
9. Customer reactions to merchandise advertised.
10. Reactions of sales personnel to the merchandise promoted.

Most buyers realize that feedback received from sales personnel on a department's advertising promotion is vitally important. Feedback will help the buyer determine how effective promotional efforts have been. Also, the

Dept. No.	Indicate by "X"		Newspaper Preferred
Amount Involved in Promotion:	Special Purchase		Inquirer
	Reduced Price		
	Clearance		Bulletin
2-Day Sales Expected:	Regular Stock at Usual Price		
	Size of ad requested		Space Cost:
Ad to appear _____Day of Wk._____	Number of Illustrations		Old New
_____ Month Date			

Description of Merchandise to be Advertised

Price, Size, Material, Color Range: _____

Special Features: _____

Window Requested   _____   I hereby certify that all the above

Posters   _____   statements are true and that every

Direct Mail   _____   fact which vitally affects the truth

Other   _____   of this advertisement has been

included.

3 copies of this form must be okayed by Merchandise Manager and Comparison Office.

_____
Buyer

_____
Date

Then

Original stays in Advertising Dept.

OK   _____
Mdse. Mgr.

_____
Date

Duplicate stays in Comparison Office

_____
Date

Triplicate stays in Buyer's Office

OK   _____
Comp. Off.

_____
Date

Received by:

_____
Adv. Dept.   Date

This Sheet, together with a sample of the merchandise, is due in the Advertising Department _____ days in advance.

TABLE 15–2.   Media used to carry messages to the public.

Television	Handbills
Radio	Billboards
Newspapers	Signs
Magazines	Exhibits
Direct mail	Posters
Announcements	Leaflets
Pamphlets	Package inserts
Displays	

buyer will post copies of the advertisement in the department, send copies to the branches or store units, make certain that merchandise is in stock or on the floor when required, possibly arrange for salespeople to wear the advertised items while working, and constantly check sales results as the promotion is in progress.

Selecting the Media

The fifth step to consider when planning the advertising campaign is selecting the media. The media selected for carrying the advertising message to the public are usually determined by the advertising department. The choice of which medium to use depends on: (1) what is to be advertised; (2) the trading area of the store; (3) the medium used by competition; (4) the particular selling season; (5) the type of customers to be reached; and (6) the amount of money available.

Usually the best advertising a retail store can have is "word-of-mouth" advertising. This is not a type of medium because the store does not pay for time or space. However, it is very instrumental in building prestige and good will for the store.

The list in Table 15–2 is self-explanatory and is representative of various types of media used to advertise merchandise.

A small business will usually advertise in local newspapers, since its customers are drawn from the immediate trade area. Also, this is less expensive than advertising in the large metropolitan newspapers. On the other hand, the large chain operation will advertise in metropolitan newspapers

Figure 15–6   An example of a form sent by the advertising department to the buyer. The buyer is required to supply all factual information. (Courtesy of John Wanamaker Department Store, Philadelphia, Pa.)

on a daily and weekend basis, as well as nationally. Department stores may advertise on local television stations as well as in the newspapers, especially on the weekends. Department stores will also use leaflets and pamphlets, which may be inserted in billings sent to charge-account customers. As you can see, retailers will use a variety of advertising media, depending on their sales promotion objectives and the amount of money available for advertising.

Preparing the Advertisement

The last step to consider when planning the advertising campaign is the actual preparation of the ad. Even though this is the responsibility of the advertising department and its staff of capable professionals, the following information will help the buyer better understand the total advertising procedure. There are five major parts of an advertisement. Each will be discussed as follows:

1. *The Headline.* The *headline* in an advertisement must attract the attention of the public, it must arouse interest, and it must lead the reader to read the entire ad. Popular headlines are: "Last Sales Day before Christmas," "Spring Clearance Sale," "Gigantic Inventory Reductions," "Founder's Day Sale," "Fire Sale," "Warehouse Sale," "Liquidation Sale," and so forth.

2. *The Illustration.* The *illustration* or picture will attract attention to the whole advertisement as well as developing the reader's interest in the product. The illustration may show women's nylon jackets with special features such as front zipper closings, fur-lined hoods, tie belts, and fancy top-stitching. Or the illustration may show portable AM/FM radios and describe special features such as carrying case, antenna, pocket size, regular size, or whatever.

3. *The Copy.* The *copy* constitutes the language of the ad. Using dialog in advertising provides detailed information about the product and helps the consumer see a need for the product, which in turn leads to the appropriate action. Usually, the buyer is consulted when writing the copy to make sure that all required and correct information is used. For example, the copy for the women's nylon coats may read: "The perfect winter jackets. They'll keep you warm all winter without adding a lot of weight. A fantastic buy at our regular price. At 30% off, these jackets are the buy of the season. Sizes 10 to 18. Winter's coming, hurry!" Or the advertisement for the AM/FM portable radios may read: "Pocket radio with telescopic whip FM antenna. AFC, carry strap. Great Father's Day gift, hurry while they last!"

4. *The Layout.* The *layout* is the arrangement of the ad. Layout should be so arranged as to lead the eye of the reader in regular sequence to the other parts of the advertisement. This will take the reader through the psychological steps of developing interest, creating desire, and securing action.

5. *The Signature Plate.* The store's *signature plate* is usually the emblem, trademark, symbol, or distinctive print that immediately identifies the store to the public. The signature plate is usually placed near the top or bottom of the advertisement, and close to the store name is the address of the store, the location of branch stores, and the store's slogan.

Review the Following:

The headline
The illustration
The copy
The layout
The signature plate

How will a knowledge of the major parts of an advertisement help the buying specialist understand the total advertising procedure?

ETHICS IN ADVERTISING

Advertising has been primarily responsible for increased mass production, lower prices, and higher standards of living. It has been considered as an educational tool used to inform the public about the great variety of goods and services available to them so they may make intelligent buying decisions. However, when advertising to the public, the buyer has the responsiblity for giving information that is true and will not prove misleading.

The Federal Trade Commission (FTC) has been primarily responsible for controlling deceptive advertising practices in interstate commerce. The Commission is particularly responsible for retail businesses that sell across state lines and for the advertising of products that come under the Federal Textile Products Identification Act. Stores must disclose, in advertisements and on signs, the names of the generic fibers from which the advertised products are made, and textile fibers must be stated in order of their weight in the item. The Federal Trade Commission is also responsible for the advertising ethics of television. One rule is that substitutions may not be used simply to give a visual effect on the screen; for example, shaving cream may not be used as whipped cream. The Federal Communications Commission (FCC) is responsible for putting pressure on television stations not to accept deceptive advertisements for broadcasting.

Review How the Following Information Will Assist the Buyer When Planning Advertising for a Particular Department or the Store as a Whole:

1. The primary objective of advertising
2. Reasons why retail buyers will advertise
3. Main types of retail advertising
4. Psychological aspects of advertising
5. Six steps involved in planning an ad

SALES PROMOTION—A TYPE OF NONPERSONAL SELLING

Sales promotion is the second type of nonpersonal selling used by all types of buying specialists to sell merchandise. *Sales promotion* may be defined as any promotional activity other than advertising, publicity, and personal selling that attracts the public to a retail store to stimulate purchasing and make a profit for the store. Thus, sales promotion will include the following types of activities: (1) display and (2) special events.

Display

A good merchandise presentation or display will reinforce a store's advertising campaign. Display is considered an important selling device because it provides a visual presentation of what is available for sale and will assist customers in making buying decisions (Figure 15–7). A buyer may use two types of display: (1) the window display, and (2) the interior display. Usually, the store's display or promotion department will decorate store windows to promote a price, a merchandising theme, a product line, or a store image. In a small business, the owner-manager or the assistant will decorate store windows. Regardless of who does the work, window displays are designed to attract attention and draw people into the store. Once the customer comes into the store or department, interior displays should be designed to encourage customers to try the products sold by that particular department.

Since the importance of the first impression cannot be overlooked, the buyer or department manager must carefully plan merchandise presentations. For example, the department-store buyer will give careful consideration to the type of customer who comes to the department, since the customer may or may not be similar to those served in other departments throughout the store. The buyer, especially a buyer for a specialty department such as a bridal shop, a boutique, a women's large-size or half-size department, or a teen department, should present merchandise displays that emphasize the unique qualities of the merchandise available for sale. A

Figure 15–7 Display is considered an important selling device because it provides a visual presentation of what is available for sale. Good displays will assist customers in making buying decisions.

buyer for a small business should develop a merchandise presentation that projects the store's overall image as well as the self-image of those who patronize a particular department.

A buyer of fashion goods in particular has a responsibility for providing merchandise displays that will invite customers into the department and thus stimulate sales. For example, a good display will help the customer visualize herself wearing the fashion look that is being promoted during a particular fashion season. The buyer for a boutique-type department may wish to emphasize a new fabric or color. Thus, many displays, especially at the entrance to the department, will feature the new color or fabric in a variety of applications. Or the boutique buyer may feature a certain style that he or she feels will be popular throughout the season.

The buyer of staple goods will also use merchandise displays to encourage consumer spending. For example, the buyer of stereo equipment may emphasize price and quality throughout various display presentations; a toy buyer may present movable displays, for example, a display of an electric train set that features the interesting characteristics of the product. A buyer of sewing notions may display buttons, threads, patches, and pins and needles on the counter to provide ease of selection and perhaps encourage impulse buying.

The responsibility for good merchandise displays rest with the buyer in a department-store operation; a department manager in a branch operation; a store manager in a chain store; and the owner-manager in a small business. Since good merchandise presentation is one of the least expensive yet most powerful forms of selling available, the time and energy spent on displays that communicate with store customers are very important.

Special Events

Special events will be used by many buying specialists to promote good will and increase customer traffic. The nature and extent of the special event depends on the kind of retail store, the size of the trading area, and the

---

Review the Following Types of Sales Promotion Activities

Display
Special events

How will each type of sales promotion activity attract customers to the store?

nature of the competition. Special events may include fashion shows, historic events, ethnic promotions, or civic events.

PUBLICITY, WORD OF MOUTH, PACKAGING

Publicity is a third type of nonpersonal selling used by merchants. *Publicity* may be defined as the presentation of goods or services in a nonpersonal way both outside and within the retail establishment. Most publicity is paid for by the store, although some is free. For example, a small business may receive "free" publicity when it supports the local basketball or baseball team by providing uniforms. A department store will receive publicity when it presents a fashion show to senior citizens; a variety store will receive publicity when it provides toys and games for a children's Christmas party.

Word of mouth, the fourth type of nonpersonal selling, is primarily responsible for building store image and good will. If consumers are satisfied with their purchases, they will tell their friends and neighbors. If they are dissatisfied, they will also communicate this feeling to others. Word of mouth, even though not directly paid for by the store, is a valuable store promotion activity.

Packaging is the fifth type of promotional device. In recent years more attention has been given to product packaging by manufacturers and by retailers. Today, well-designed packaging is important both to stores where display must carry a major part of the sales task and to retail stores that rely primarily on sales help. Well-designed packaging offers many advantages to the buyer. Good packaging will attract customer attention, stimulate interest in the product, protect the merchandise, make the product available

---

Nonpersonal Selling Is a Method of Communicating with Customers Indirectly

Review the following types of nonpersonal selling devices. How are they used by the buying specialist?

Advertising
Sales promotion
Publicity
Word of mouth
Packaging

in proper quantity and size, reflect the use of the product, and make displays more attractive and effective.

| PART 2—Retail Personal Selling |

THE IMPORTANCE OF PERSONAL SELLING

The consumer who enters a store, other than a self-service establishment, expects to be greeted by salespeople. Since sales personnel have direct contact with customers, they are very important to the retail business. A good salesperson, therefore, should have a proper attitude toward selling and possess the art and skill of modern selling techniques. The salesperson must know the merchandise thoroughly, know the store's selling system to avoid errors, and be aware of the store's merchandising policies and objectives. He or she must be aware of the needs and wants of the customers and be able to communicate to them the merchandise assortment provided by the store. Personal selling is still used by many retail establishments, especially department stores and specialty shops, since direct contact with store customers proves to be a most effective merchandising technique.

During the last few years, however, the importance of the retail salesperson has been diminishing. Many retail stores have turned to self-service in an effort to cut selling costs; others have been virtually forced to it because of increasing competition and difficulty in keeping good sales help. Discount houses and vending machines, in particular, have thrived in the absence of sales help. However, during healthy economic periods, customers tire of the impersonality of self-service and turn toward full-service stores.

THE TYPES OF PERSONAL SELLING

Personal selling, broadly defined, includes wholesale selling or contact selling, since the seller usually contacts the customer, and retail selling, where the customer usually approaches the retail store. There are three types of retail personal selling: (1) house-to-house selling, (2) mail and telephone selling, and (3) over-the-counter selling. A discussion of each follows.

House-to-House Selling

House-to-house selling is still a very popular type of retail personal selling (Figure 15–8). A salesperson representing a store or a company will person-

Figure 15–8 House-to-house selling is still a popular type of retail personal selling. A salesperson representing a company—in this example, Avon—will personally call at the home of one of the customers. (Courtesy of Avon Products, Incorporated, New York, N.Y.)

ally call on customers at their homes. The business organization may hold periodic sales drives, give demonstrations, or send representatives who offer advice on interior decorating or provide some other service. As you recall from Chapter 1, house-to-house selling is used primarily to sell staple items that offer convenience and comfort to customers.

Mail and Telephone Selling

Mail and telephone selling is also very popular. For example a department store or a general-merchandise chain will advertise that mail and telephone orders will be accepted for special advertised products and will provide a special department to answer telephone calls and receive mail orders. Once the orders are received, information is sent to the particular departments involved, and sales personnel will make certain that customers receive their merchandise. Mail and telephone selling is especially popular during the Christmas season. Most major retailers will print special catalogs for the Christmas season to induce customers to make purchases.

Over-the-Counter Selling

Over-the-counter selling takes place in most retail stores, unless they are self-service operations, and is performed by salespeople. Unlike retail order taking, where the salesperson does not assist the customer during the decision-making process, over-the-counter selling will help the consumer reach a decision regarding the merchandise. Since over-the-counter selling is so important to the successful and profitable operation of the retail store, the remaining sections of this chapter will be devoted to this topic. However, by way of review, you will recall that the selling activity is a responsibility of the department-store buyer and the small business owner-manager, since the buying-selling activity is a combined responsibility. In the chain operation, you will recall, the selling responsibility is primarily that of the store manager and his staff, with the buying activity performed by central buyers.

MANAGING RETAIL SALESPEOPLE

Regardless of the type and size of the retail operation, the responsibility for guiding and directing the sales staff is an important one. Whether the buyer specialist is managing a small business, or a department store, he or she has certain tasks to perform to ensure that personal selling is successful. The following activities are performed when managing sales personnel: (1) sales force planning, (2) recruitment and selection, (3) induction and training, (4) scheduling, (5) compensation, and (6) supervision.

The Role of the Buying Specialist in Sales Management

1. Sales force planning
2. Recruitment and selection
3. Induction and training
4. Scheduling
5. Compensation
6. Supervision

Sales Force Planning

When planning the sales force, consideration should be given to store image, the type of clientele the store must cater to, store policies and practices, and the type of department. Attention should also be given to the characteristics of salespeople and how they will match against the characteristics of the store's customers. For example, if the department caters to prejunior and junior sizes, it would be unwise to employ salespeople who cannot relate to the youth market. Or if the department sells sporting goods and equipment, and the salesperson does not play various sports or is not interested in sporting activities, selling attempts would prove unsuccessful and lead to a loss of sales.

Sales force planning will also include the budgeting of salespeople required on a full-time basis as well as on a part-time basis. For example, the sales force may be increased during particular seasons, such as Christmas, Easter, and special sales promotion periods such as Valentine's Day, Father's Day, or Mother's Day. Additional part-time help may be required during the evening hours or on weekends, since full-time people are not available.

Recruitment and Selection

The buying specialist will usually work with the store's personnel office when recruiting and selecting the sales staff. He or she will send a requisition to the personnel director in charge of sales, and, in turn, potential candidates will be sent to the buyer or department head to be interviewed. The selection process may consist of a brief interview or may be more complex, consisting of several interviews with various store executives, psychological testing, and a physical examination. The buyer is usually interested in the candidate's past work experience, educational background, merchandising attitude, ability to get along with people, and the ability to lead as well as follow orders. Figure 15–9 is an example of an employee rating form that measures characteristics important in retail selling.

Induction and Training

If the retail store has its own training division, new employees will be introduced formally into the organization. They will be provided with useful and accurate information about the retail store, the policies that will affect them, and the services that may be provided for their benefit. Besides the induction program, the employee may be subject to specific training that will relate to the job he is assuming. Specific job training will provide information on successful selling techniques, operation of the cash register, wrapping and packaging merchandise, telephone sales, team selling, and customer relations. Once the new employee has completed the training program, he is sent to a particular department, where he will receive additional training or on-the-job training. Here, the new salesperson is usually assigned a sponsor who will give special instructions on the specific operations of the department. Figure 15–10 is an example of the kind of information given new employees.

Figure 15–9 An example of an employee rating form.

Name	Dept.	Emp. No.	Salary	Last Increase	Amount	Tenure Date	Position	Store
Annual Follow-Up		Rated By		Date		Interviewed By		Date
Increase	New Salary		Effective Date	Approved By	Date	Personnel Dept. Approval		Date

	Excellent	Very Good	Good	Average	Unsatisfactory
I. PERSONAL CHARACTERISTICS					
1. Self control-maintains poise under pressure.	☐	☐	☐	☐	☐
2. Analytical mind-disects problems, sets correct priorities.	☐	☐	☐	☐	☐
3. Creativeness-has imagination. Produces new ideas.	☐	☐	☐	☐	☐
4. Initiative-self starting.	☐	☐	☐	☐	☐
5. Motivation and drive-has goals, enthusiasm and sence of urgency.	☐	☐	☐	☐	☐
II. MANAGEMENT ABILITIES					
1. Administration-organizes work and delegates intelligently.	☐	☐	☐	☐	☐
2. Control-knows status of activities under his supervision.	☐	☐	☐	☐	☐
3. Planning-develops programs for future events.	☐	☐	☐	☐	☐
4. Communication-effectively and concisely conveys his thoughts to people at all levels.	☐	☐	☐	☐	☐
5. Leadership-motivates subordinates. Receives a high degree of cooperation.	☐	☐	☐	☐	☐
6. Executive attitude-makes decisions promptly, objectively and accepts responsibility for his decisions.	☐	☐	☐	☐	☐

Figure 15–10 An example of the kind of information provided by the store's personnel department to new employees. (Courtesy of John Wanamaker Department Store, Philadelphia, Pa.)

Scheduling

Before scheduling additional sales help, it is important to be certain that the level of service, which presumably grows as more salespeople are hired, is not less than the costs resulting from salespeople's wages. Systematic scheduling requires that certain factors be considered, such as the amount of customer traffic during particular store hours, the amount of time a salesperson spends performing particular tasks, the department sales volume, the average number of transactions per salesperson, and consumer spending patterns. When arranging work schedules, the buyer, department head, or store manager should consider employee preferences regarding hours of work, days off, and vacation periods.

Compensation

The compensation is the salary paid to salespeople and is determined by store policy. According to retailers and other observers, however, a basic cause of personal selling problems is the relatively low pay. As a result, the supply of applicants is reduced. Often those who become sales employees do so only until they find a higher-paying position, while others who will accept a sales position are often poorly motivated. To help offset this problem, some retail stores offer incentive programs for the purpose of improving the quality of retail selling. Incentive programs may take the form of contests, commissions, bonuses, and special employee shopping days.

Supervision

As a supervisor, the buying specialist should give frequent encouragement and praise as well as constructive criticism to the sales staff. Sales employees should be informed of department standards, and be given the proper supervision to avoid problems on the selling floor. The following section will discuss in detail the duties and responsibilities of sales personnel as instructed by the buyer and other store executives.

DUTIES AND RESPONSIBILITIES OF SALES PERSONNEL

During the induction and training process, the buyer has the responsibility for instructing new sales personnel on the following: (1) department standards and routines, (2) housekeeping duties, (3) display techniques, (4) stock control methods, (5) assisting customers, (6) handling complaints, (7) preventing waste and losses, pilferage and shoplifting, and (8) developing good selling techniques.

The Buyer Should Instruct New Sales Personnel on:

1. Department standards and routines
2. Housekeeping duties
3. Display techniques
4. Stock control methods
5. Assisting customers
6. Handling complaints
7. Preventing waste and losses: pilferage and shoplifting
8. Developing good selling techniques

Department Standards and Routines

The buyer, assistant buyer, or department head will provide the new sales employee with information regarding department standards. For example, the proper dress regulation that will reflect the image of the store and that of the department will be emphasized, as well as the importance of the "right" retail attitude. The buying specialist will assist the new recruit in learning and understanding store routines such as the check-in procedure when he or she arrives on the job and when he or she takes lunch period, and department routines regarding break time, shopping privileges, and the store's lay-away system. Since well-motivated salespeople will sell effectively, it is important to give them the facts about the department as a whole, the merchandise offered for sale, and the store's overall merchandising policies. As a fashion buyer, you will soon learn there is no better way to sell fashion goods than through well-motivated, well-trained, and well-informed sales personnel. Needless to say, the same applies to the buyer of hard goods. Through well-informed sales personnel, the buyer of patio furniture, for example, will get the selling message through to customers, and in return the buyer will get customer reactions to the merchandise offered for sale.

All salespeople, whether new on the job or old-timers, need constant training and motivation. A wise buyer will recognize good performers and continuously encourage and assist them on the job.

Housekeeping Duties

Sales personnel must also be informed of their responsibilities regarding maintenance and general housekeeping duties. The salesperson is usually responsible for keeping merchandise properly organized, neat, and attractive. A sloppy and disorganized merchandise presentation will lead to confusion for customer and salesperson alike and thus minimize department efficiency. A primary responsibility of a buyer specialist, therefore, is to teach salespeople about the presentation of the merchandise assortment and what benefits it will bring to the store's customers. For example, if you run a fashion department, you will point out to the salesperson what merchandise will coordinate with goods offered in other departments. However, fashion goods must be presented in an orderly, neat manner if the customer is to interpret the fashion message properly. For example, salespeople should be instructed on how to fold merchandise, refill empty cases or bins, check that each item is in its proper location, report any sizes, styles, prices, or colors that are running low, and so forth. The buyer may instruct the assistant or department head to show salespeople how to organize packaged merchandise samples. Also, senior salespeople may be instructed by the store manager or buyer to teach new, part-time, or temporary salespeople about department housekeeping duties and routines.

Display Techniques

As you learned in Part 1 of this chapter, displays are used to promote and sell merchandise. The new salesperson should know something about color, texture, line, and design. Displays should be attractive enough to draw customer attention and should create a desire on the part of the customer to purchase the product. The salesperson should be aware that good displays should be kept fresh and clean and changed frequently. A display may show goods used in a particular way or coordinated with related lines of merchandise. The buyer of men's better-priced shirts may arrange merchandise displays that present, for example, goods with a high markup, items that invite the purchase of related items, classic styles, or new merchandise. The buyer should communicate the fashion message to salespeople so they may relate the information to store customers. Also, if the display becomes soiled or damaged, the salesperson may arrange a new merchandise presentation that will continue to emphasize the fashion message.

Stock Control Methods

Sales personnel are very instrumental in assisting the buyer or store manager in stock control methods. Usually, a salesperson is assigned a portion of stock and is responsible for the counting and control of the stock, both in the stockroom and on the selling floor. The salesperson will let the buyer or the assistant know when merchandise is ready for reorder and how much reserve stock is available by taking daily or weekly inventories. The salesperson is also provided with a list of slow-selling merchandise and is asked to report on the amount of merchandise on hand and the price for which the merchandise is selling.

Assisting Customers

Assisting and directing customers is a most important responsibility of the salesperson. Often, the consumer will enter the retail establishment without knowing exactly where to go to purchase specific items. The salesperson should be courteous, attentive, and patient when directing customers. A salesperson who does not know where a particular item may be found should volunteer to find someone who does. Nothing is more annoying to a customer than to be directed from one department to the next, only to realize that the merchandise sought is not carried by the store.

Personal customer attention is a service provided by special stores, most small businesses, and department stores. Specialty shops, especially those catering to the middle and upper income levels, will emphasize personal selling by offering fewer merchandise displays, since they require sales personnel to show the merchandise personally to customers and assist them in making purchases.

Handling Complaints

Many times the salesperson is required to handle complaints and adjustments. This calls for a great deal of patience and tact. The salesperson should become familiar with the products he or she sells to know how to make merchandise adjustments. He must develop an understanding of consumer problems if he is to make a satisfactory adjustment and continue to maintain good customer relations.

Many retailers have discovered, however, that salespeople need assistance in handling consumer complaints. Thus, many stores will instruct their sales personnel to send customers to the service manager or adjustment counter. As a result, salespeople can go about their job of selling, customers are taken care of more efficiently and effectively, and the store continues to have happy, well-satisfied customers.

Preventing Waste and Losses: Pilferage and Shoplifting

Good salespeople will help prevent waste and losses and thus keep store expenses down. The salesperson can prevent waste and loss by keeping goods clean, handling merchandise carefully, avoiding overselling that may lead to complaints and returns, and being careful not to damage fixtures, merchandise, and store property.

As you recall, when there is a discrepancy between book inventory figures and physical inventory figures and the physical inventory is less than the book inventory, there is a stock shortage. Salespeople can further assist the retailer in controlling stock shortages by carefully receiving and checking merchandise when it enters the department, properly recording any broken or missing items, and carefully weighing and measuring merchandise.

However, pilferage (employee theft) and shoplifting (consumer theft) still continue to be the leading cause of merchandise waste and loss. Today there is increased attention to both problems. According to one report, shoplifting is growing at the rate of 20 percent a year, with stock shortages estimated at $4.5 billion a year. For some retail stores, especially self-service operations, inventory losses are as high as 3 or 4 percent of sales.[3] It is also believed that employee dishonesty may be a bigger source of inventory shrinkage than many realize. For example, one report suggests that employee dishonesty accounts for about 70 percent of inventory shortages, shoplifting 15 percent, and bookkeeping errors approximately 15 percent.[4]

Some factors that contribute to both pilferage and shoplifting are poor inventory controls, inadequate shipping and receiving procedures, and poor display techniques. To remedy these problems, many stores have: (1) employed the services of security guards; (2) improved lighting in stockrooms and shipping areas; and (3) placed alarms in stairways, entrances and exits, and throughout various departments.

Developing Good Selling Techniques

Salespeople should also be taught selling techniques that will assist them when waiting on store customers (Figure 15–11).

Selling Techniques That Should Be Learned by the Salesperson

1. Approaching and greeting the customer
2. Determining customer needs and wants
3. Effectively presenting the merchandise
4. Answering objections
5. Closing the sale
6. Maintaining customer good will

Approaching and Greeting the Customer. The salesperson should prepare himself or herself and the department surroundings before the customer enters the store. He or she should have a neat appearance, be knowledgeable about stock, be aware of department and store advertising, provide appealing merchandise displays, and learn the name, background, and interests of specific customers. Once the customer enters the store, the salesperson should approach and greet the shopper with confidence and a friendly and sincere desire to be of service. It is important that the customer be welcomed with a pleasant greeting and be made to feel appreciated by the salesperson and the retail store. If this is accomplished properly, the sales transaction is off to a good start. Often, however, salespeople gather in groups to converse and as a result neglect, if not ignore, the customer. Those in charge must correct this situation by proper instruction and supervision.

Determining Customer Needs and Wants. The second step in the selling process is determining customer needs and wants. After the customer has been properly greeted, his or her needs and wants should be defined. This task is usually easy for staple items, since they are asked for by brand name; however, fashion merchandise is more difficult. The salesperson must carefully size up the customer through a few well-phrased questions relating to

Figure 15-11 A knowledge of good selling techniques will assist the salesperson when waiting on store customers.

customer needs. The salesperson will receive valuable guides from the customer's dress, manner, and reaction to the merchandise displayed. By eliminating as quickly as possible those articles that do not meet the customer's needs, the salesperson may then concentrate on those that prove interesting. Salespersons must be careful not to judge customer interests and purchasing power by their own tastes and desires. Such a mistake will only irritate and annoy the customer and lead to a loss in sales if not a loss in good will.

Effectively Presenting the Merchandise. Once the customer's needs are known, the salesperson is ready for the third step in the selling process, that of effectively presenting the merchandise for sale. The following five points should be considered when presenting merchandise:

1. Knowledge of the location of goods in the department or in the stockroom.
2. Wise selection of merchandise.
3. Displaying the merchandise properly.

4. Pointing out the important characteristics or selling points of the item.
5. Developing skill and confidence when making a sales presentation.

Answering Objections. Answering objections is the most difficult step in the selling process. There are two types of objections that a salesperson will experience: (1) genuine objections based on sincere reasons for failure to purchase, and (2) excuses designed to conceal the real reason for failure to take action. Genuine objections are usually easier to answer because they are based on definite obstacles, whereby excuses may not in all cases genuinely reflect the opinions of the customer. Therefore, they provide no logical basis to which the salesperson may react. There are certain general rules that may prove helpful to a salesperson when attempting to answer objections:

1. Anticipate objections and incorporate them into the presentation.
2. Never argue with a customer, since this will only aggravate and annoy both parties concerned. Customers are valuable to a store, and it is best not to prove a point only to lose a potential shopper.
3. Understand customers' objections by not condescending to them or belittling their questions,
4. Tactfully and confidently handle customer objections.
5. Encourage the customer to raise genuine questions.
6. Avoid mentioning competition and their merchandise. If the customer mentions them, then speak of them briefly and courteously.

Closing the Sale. If objections have been properly handled and adequately answered, closing the sale, the fifth step in the selling process, will occur without particular attention being given to it by the customer. Often, however, the salesperson does not close the sale. The salesperson, especially a new one, may make one or more of the following mistakes when closing the sale:

1. Hurrying the customer in making a decision.
2. Failing to assist the customer during merchandise selection.
3. Not answering objections, real or otherwise, confidently and intelligently.
4. Emphasizing unimportant and irrelevant selling points.
5. Being too confident a salesperson.
6. Using high-pressure techniques to force action.
7. Assuming the customer is aware of all product characteristics.
8. Acting discourteously or disappointed when customers fail to purchase.

Maintaining Customer Good Will. The last step in the selling process is to maintain customer good will after the sale is made. The customer will remember a store that employs courteous and friendly salespeople who are genuinely interested in the customers. Even if no sale has been made, the customer should be made to feel at home and feel that his or her interest was appreciated. Such an approach on the part of salespeople will make friends for the store and for themselves as well as increase store patronage and continue to maintain good will.

GOOD MANAGEMENT TECHNIQUES: COMMUNICATING WITH SALESPEOPLE; THE DEPARTMENT MEETING

Regardless of the size and type of retail operation, the buying specialist or manager should develop management techniques that will guide and direct sales personnel. For example, a department-store buyer may send informal memos to salespeople telling them of a forthcoming store promotion, new items that have been added to the merchandise assortment, fashion trends, special events, or whatever. Also, the buyer will contact the department or group manager in each branch store and send out similar kinds of information. Or the buyer may contact senior sales personnel and ask them to instruct new and part-time salespeople on stock conditions, sales promotions, advertising specials, and so forth. A central buyer, for example, a buyer for a women's discount chain, may send fashion clippings, publications, news bulletins, or samples to store managers and ask each to communicate items of importance to individual department supervisors or managers. The supervisors or managers, in turn, may post the information on bulletin boards and hold informal meetings before the store opens to discuss new arrivals, slow sellers, or "hot" items. The buyer for a boutique or specialty shop may hold special fashion seminars; permit sales personnel to view the lines of manufacturers' representatives who visit the department or store, to view films, or to listen to tapes; and provide demonstrators to show salespeople how to use certain products. The small business owner may post fashion photos, newspaper clippings, store ads, and other pertinent information on a bulletin board. Since the business is small, it is usually easier for the owner-manager to brief salespeople continuously on changes in merchandise offerings, special sales, new merchandising policies, the activities of competition, and so forth.

In most large stores, however, the most popular management technique used to reach salespeople is the department meeting. Department meetings are usually held once a week. The advantages are many. Salespeople are provided an opportunity to exchange views; meet new people, especially part-timers and temporary full-time help; and have personal contact with the buyer and the assistant, and the department manager, store manager, or store owner, depending on the nature of the organization.

Some objections to holding department meetings are that they may become too routine, lack good planning and organization, do not always include the entire staff, and become dull and uninteresting. Thus, when planning interesting and informative department meetings, you as a buyer should consider the following activities:

1. Determine the purpose or objective of the meeting. What points are you trying to get across? New style trends? New fibers? New packaging methods?
2. Determine how you will introduce the subject matter and how you will arouse interest. For example, if a new style trend is predicted for the coming season, you may introduce the topic by describing various events that have fostered its development.
3. Determine how you will develop your presentation. For example, you may wish to show fashion photos, slides, or a movie to illustrate your discussion of new fashion trends.
4. Determine how you will summarize the meeting. Once you have completed the presentation, you may wish to provide salespeople with illustrated leaflets that describe how the new fashion trend will be worn and accessorized.
5. Determine how you will follow up on your meeting to ensure that your message got across. You may observe sales personnel to determine whether or not they understood the message you were trying to convey; you may check sales figures for increases; or you may hold another meeting and retrain to secure the proper action.

Most buyers will develop a variety of management techniques that they have found to be successful when attempting to get messages across to salespeople. The buyer, or manager, or whoever, soon realizes that no one management technique can carry every message or reach all salespeople.[5]

PROBLEMS ON
THE SELLING FLOOR

Due to lack of confidence and lack of experience in selling and in getting along with others, the new salesperson (and sometimes the sales veteran) may encounter many difficulties when working on the selling floor. It should be recognized that salespeople may have problems in communicating with other salespeople, the assistant buyer, the sponsor, the department manager, or the buyer. The salesperson often has problems not because of lack of product knowledge or of selling ability, but because he or she has not adopted the right retail attitude. A salesperson who feels self-conscious and insecure may try to give the impression that he or she is superior; thus, a poor attitude may develop. This may also happen if one is overconfident about one's ability. A poor attitude may lead to a personality that antagonizes others and to irresponsibility toward department housekeeping duties; it may create customer ill will and lead to problems with co-workers. For example, a new salesperson may take advantage of fellow workers by waiting on customers out of turn or "grabbing" customers. Such a practice will cause much friction among salespeople and often will drive customers away. Store executives must be aware of these and other problems on the selling floor, such as shoplifting and pilferage, return sales, arguments, tardiness, and absenteeism.

Problems on the Selling Floor Usually Result from:

Poor retail attitude	Arguments
Shoplifting and pilferage	Tardiness
Return sales	Absenteeism

What methods can be used to help minimize problems on the selling floor?

The buyer and the assistant buyer have the responsibility of providing the direction and leadership as well as the kind of selling atmosphere that leads to effective selling. When this is accomplished, customers will be pleased with their shopping surroundings, and salespeople will become congenial in their working relationships with one another.

Chapter Summary

The buyer and other store executives must be able to communicate with or send messages to customers to make them aware of store offerings. Nonpersonal selling is a method of communicating with customers indirectly and includes such promotional devices as advertising, sales promotion, publicity, word of mouth, packaging, and vending machines.

The buyer will advertise for many reasons; however, the prime objective is to attract potential customers to the store. There are three types of retail advertising: promotional advertising, institutional advertising, and a combination of both. Psychological studies of the emotions and drives of people have greatly influenced the use of advertising. Such studies suggest that people may act on three levels. There are four psychological steps that every advertisement must contain: (1) attracting attention, (2) developing interest, (3) creating desire, and (4) securing action. The student will note that these psychological steps are also applicable in personal selling. There are six steps the buyer should follow when planning advertising: (1) setting specific objectives, (2) identifying a theme, (3) establishing a budget, (4) selecting merchandise to promote, (5) selecting the media, and (6) preparing the advertisement. When preparing the advertisement, the buyer will work with the advertising department, which consists of copywriters and artists. The advertisement uses five major parts: headline, illustration, copy, layout, and signature plate. The buyer should practice good ethics in advertising. The Federal Trade Commission (FTC) has been primarily responsible for controlling deceptive advertising practices in interstate commerce.

Sales promotion, the second type of promotional device, may be defined as any promotional activity other than advertising, publicity, and personal selling that attracts the public to a retail store to stimulate purchasing and thus makes a profit for the store. The student should review the following sales promotion activities: (1) display and (2) special events. Publicity, word of mouth, and packaging, are also effective sales promotion activities.

Personal selling, broadly defined, includes wholesale selling or contact selling, since the seller usually contacts the customer, and retail selling, where the customer usually approaches the store. There are three types of retail personal selling: (1) house-to-house selling, (2) mail and telephone selling, and (3) over-the-counter selling. The buyer performs certain activities when managing sales personnel. Such activities include planning of the sales force, recruitment and selection of the sales staff, induction and training, scheduling, compensation, and supervision. Sales personnel have many duties and responsibilities to perform when working in a retail store. Responsibilities include learning department standards and routines, keeping the department maintained and organized, keeping displays fresh and clean and changed frequently, following department stock control procedures, assisting and directing customers, handling complaints, preventing waste and losses, and developing good selling techniques. There are certain well-defined selling techniques that should be learned by the salesperson. They are (1) approaching and greeting the customer, (2) determining the customer's needs and wants, (3) effectively presenting the merchandise, (4) answering objections, (5) closing the sale, and (6) maintaining customer good will.

The buying expert will develop and use different management techniques when reaching salespeople. The most popular of these is the department meeting. As a result of inexperience and a lack of confidence, the new salesperson may encounter many difficulties when working on the selling floor. The buyer and the assistant buyer have the responsibility of providing the direction and leadership as well as the kind of selling atmosphere that leads to effective selling.

Trade Terminology

DIRECTIONS: Briefly explain or discuss each of the following trade terms:

1. Nonpersonal selling
2. Advertising
3. Promotional advertising
4. Institutional advertising
5. Combination retail advertising
6. Advertising theme
7. Headline
8. Illustration
9. Copy
10 Layout
11. Signature plate
12. Sales promotion
13. Publicity
14. Personal selling

Questions for Discussion and Review

1. What is the primary objective of retail advertising? Retail buyers will advertise for many reasons. List five and explain why each is important.

2. How does institutional advertising differ from the promotional type? Which type is used most by the retail buyer? Why?

3. Scan the local newspaper and select examples of the following: prestige advertising, sale price advertising, and service advertising. How do they differ?

4. There are certain psychological steps that must be followed when planning advertising. What are they? Select an advertisement from the local newspaper and determine whether or not the advertisement employed each of the psychological steps named.

5. Once the buyer becomes familiar with the types of retail advertising and its important psychological implications, he or she is ready to plan. What six steps should the buyer follow when planning an advertising campaign? Explain.

6. In your opinion, what is the most popular medium used to carry messages to the public? Cite specific examples.

7. Interview the advertising manager of your local TV station. Determine how an advertising program is developed using the TV medium. Also,

include a discussion of the rules and regulations set forth by the Federal Communication Commission (FCC) and its role in preventing deceptive advertising.

8. What is meant by the term "sales promotion"? Select three examples of sales promotion activities and relate how each will stimulate purchasing and help make a profit for the store.

9. Interview the display director of a traditional department store and of a discount house. How will display techniques differ? How will they be similar? Explain.

10. Define personal selling. Do you consider the role of the salesperson important to the operation of a discount house? A specialty store? A variety store?

11. Review the special forms of sales promotion that have been used in your community. What have been the results of these efforts?

12. What management techniques are used by buyers to reach salespeople? What steps are followed when setting up a department meeting?

13. Discuss the salesperson's responsibility for effective personal selling. What is the obligation of the buyer and the assistant buyer in connection with this activity?

14. Many problems are encountered by the new salesperson in beginning a sales career. Review those listed in this chapter. What other problems would you add to the list? Why?

Case Study Number Twenty-One

MRS. WEED AND HER COMPANION

You have been working six months as a salesperson in the Early American department of a leading furniture specialty store. The previous day you showed Mrs. Weed and a companion a dining-room set. You recall the frustration you felt when you attempted to point out specific features of the furniture only to be contradicted by Mrs. Weed's highly critical companion. Throughout the sales presentation, Mrs. Weed heeded her companion's opinion and, as a result, she left without making a buying decision. She did state, however, that she would return the following day to make her final decision. Today, as you see Mrs. Weed coming toward your department, you shudder slightly when you see Mrs. Weed's friend trailing her. Once again you prepare yourself for a no-sale meeting. What assumptions would you make about the fact that the customer is returning for a second time? Be prepared in class to discuss how you could close the sale this time.

Case Study Number Twenty-Two

PROBLEMS
WITH COMPETITION

O'Brien's was a well-established medium-sized department store located in a Midwestern city. The store would not be considered a discount house; however, some of its high-fashion merchandise was sold at cut-rate or discount prices. O'Brien's felt this pricing policy permitted it to draw customers from several income brackets as well as providing an opportunity to sell staple goods at a full markup. One of the fashion items discounted by O'Brien's was the Lucky Lucy handbag. Since O'Brien's did an excellent job of advertising, it became the top merchandiser for the Lucky Lucy manufacturing company.

Harriet MacMillan was the buyer of handbags and leather accessories at Albright's department store, located in the same city. She had handled Lucky Lucy merchandise for the past five years and had always merchandised the goods successfully. She had always expressed a great deal of confidence in Lucky Lucy handbags and had gone so far as to tell the saleswomen in her department that there was not a better handbag manufacturer in the country. Harriet had been selling the handbags at full price and had lately found that sales were falling off. When she investigated the problem, she discovered that O'Brien's was discounting the handbags up to 30%. Harriet was aware that most of Albright's customers did not shop at O'Brien's; however, she did feel that O'Brien's heavy advertising campaign had directly contributed to a loss of sales in her department.

Harriet decided to call Lucky Lucy's sales representative and attempt to persuade the company not to sell to O'Brien's at such a low price, or at least to have Lucky Lucy talk to O'Brien's about selling the merchandise at list price. When Harriet spoke to the sales representative, she was informed that O'Brien's was at present Lucky Lucy's biggest customer. She was also told that perhaps Albright's should lower its price to meet competition, or that perhaps she should increase her purchases to take advantage of quantity discounts.

If you were Harriet MacMillan, how would you handle this situation?

Case Study Number Twenty-Three

SPECIAL BUYS

As the sportswear buyer for a men's specialty store, you are aware that turtleneck sweaters priced at $19.95 have sold extremely well during the months of December and January. Meanwhile, the vendor has offered you a special buy on the same turtleneck sweater in an assortment of sizes and colors. If you purchase the sweaters, you must decide whether you will sell the goods at the same price as before and make even a higher markup, or sell the sweaters for less and include them in the special promotion sale that is to be held the last week of February. How would you price the merchandise? Why? What problems could you encounter by purchasing season merchandise towards the end of the season? Be prepared to explain your answers in class.

Case Study Number Twenty-Four

THE OLD-TIMER AND THE NEW RECRUIT

Ed Long was a recent college graduate who joined the executive training program of Hopkins Department Store. Part of Ed's job consisted of working in the area of men's suits for a three-month period to learn sales floor supervision. Ed worked on a salary basis and was expected to make sales on a noncommission basis.

Richard Smith was a salesman in the men's suits department and had worked at Hopkins for the past twenty years. He worked on a commission basis and over the years had made an adequate salary, enough to support himself, his wife, and two children. Mr. Smith's success as a salesman could be attributed to his positive attitude towards his job and his ability as a salesman. He had many old customers who would ask for him when they came to the department.

Troubles began, however, when Mr. Smith discovered that Ed Long was handling customers who previously had been buying from him. After all, Ed was very young, very enthusiastic, and had a good sales personality. Mr. Smith was getting older and was starting to lose the "old sales spark" that had successfully carried him along for many years.

Mr. Smith complained to the department manager that, since Ed was an executive trainee and worked on a straight salary, he should not be placed in a sales-commission department. He also stated that Ed was impulsive, discourteous, and greedy—that he was out only to make a name for himself at the expense of the regular sales help.

When the department manager discussed the situation with Ed, Ed told him that the sales staff (especially Mr. Smith) were envious of his position and of his ability to succeed in merchandising. Ed further stated that he was confused about how he was supposed to get sales experience when people were complaining about his waiting on customers. The department manager informed Ed that he was to continue working as he had been but to attempt to consider the needs of the full-times sales staff. The manager reminded Ed that he was also responsible for teaching and training salespeople and for providing a pleasant work environment.

As a result of this conversation, Ed decided to stay in the background and let Mr. Smith take over. However, after several weeks the department manager noted that Ed had undergone a change in attitude and was definitely losing interest in his job. In fact, Ed finally informed the manager that he was losing his enthusiasm for merchandising and was very uncertain about his responsibilities.

If you were Ed's department manager, how would you remedy this situation?

Learning Activities

1. Interview the display manager of a department store, a boutique, and a men's specialty shop. Prepare a list of questions based on the topic "How do you plan in-store displays and window displays for the coming season?" Are there similarities in the methods used in each type of store? How do they differ?

2. Prepare a paper on the topic "Why is a knowledge of salesmanship important to the retail buyer?" Refer to The Retail Student's Reference Library for selected references.

3. Select five types of media that may be used by a small business, a department store, and a variety chain operation to advertise their products. What kind of advertising (promotional, institutional, or combination) is

used by each? Why do you suppose the retailers use these particular media to advertise their merchandise?

4. Prepare a paper on the topic "How does the retailer price for profit?" Refer to The Retail Student's Reference Library for selected references.

5. Interview the store manager of a small grocery business and a supermarket chain. Select ten items sold by each business. Find out how each business manager determines the markup price of the various items you have selected. What kinds of expenses are incurred by each? What are the risks?

6. Select five types of businesses in your local area, for example, a department store, a variety chain, a boutique, a shoe store, and a women's specialty shop or a men's specialty store. Interview the department manager or assistant buyer and determine the price policy used by each type of store. For example, find out whether the store uses prestige pricing, odd pricing, loss leaders, a one-price policy, or a varying-price policy. Attempt to determine the reasons for the stores' using various methods of pricing.

References

THE RETAIL STUDENT'S REFERENCE LIBRARY

Annual Christmas Planning and Idea Workbook. New York: NRMA, n.d.

Bernstein, Jack. *Selling Space.* New York: Adweek, n.d.

Direct Mail Advertising and Selling for Retailers. New York: NRMA, n.d.

Feinman, J. P., Blashek, R. D., and McCabe, R. J. *Sweepstakes, Prize Promotions, Games and Contests.* New York: Adweek, n.d.

Futrell, Charles. *Fundamentals of Selling.* Homewood, Ill.: Richard D. Irwin Pub. Co., 1988.

How to Be a Retail Advertising Pro. New York: NRMA, n.d.

How to Design Effective Store Advertising. New York: NRMA, n.d.

Increasing Retail Sales Via the Telephone. New York: NRMA, n.d.

Marketing, Sales Promotion, Advertising Planbook. New York: NRMA, n.d.

Pederson, L., Wright M., and Weitz, B. L. *Selling: Principles and Methods.* Homewood, Illinois: Richard D. Irwin Pub. Co., 1988.

Reilly, Tom. *V.A.S.T.: Value Added Selling Techniques.* New York: Adweek, n.d.

Rust, Roland T. *Advertising Media Models: A Practical Guide.* New York: Adweek, n.d.

Sayers, Dorothy L. *Murder Must Advertise.* New York: Adweek, n.d.

Seltz, David. *How to Conduct Successful Sales Contests and Incentive Programs.* New York: Adweek, n.d.

Sissors, Jack and Surmanek, Jim. *Advertising Media Planning.* 2nd ed. New York: Adweek, n.d.

The Specialty Store and Its Advertising. New York: NRMA, n.d.

Television Promotions for Retailers. New York: NRMA, n.d.

Visual Merchandising. New York: NRMA, n.d.

REFERENCES

1. D. J. Duncan and C. F. Phillips, *Retailing Principles and Methods* (Homewood, Ill.: Richard D. Irwin, Inc., 1970), pp. 519–520.
2. *Journal of Marketing,* October 1948, p. 205.
3. "Stores Find It's Not Easy to Stop Thieves—Pros or Amateurs," *Wall Street Journal,* October 11, 1971, pp. 1–15.
4. "Leary's High Pay Position at A & S Hailed as Pace Setter," *Women's Wear Daily,* September 8, 1970, p. 6.
5. Beatrice Judelle, *The Fashion Buyer's Job* (New York: National Retail Merchants Association, 1971), pp. 38–39.

Appendix A

GLOSSARY OF TRADE TERMS
USED IN MERCHANDISE BUYING

advanced dating the invoice is dated from a specified future date, not from the designated invoice date.

advertising a set of activities that involves the presentation of a mass message about a product, a service, or an idea; the message is paid for by an identified sponsor.

advertising theme benefits the consumer will receive by purchasing the advertised product and by shopping in a particular store.

allowance a term used synonymously with *discount.*

anticipation an extra discount is given for paying an invoice in advance of the cash discount date.

assistant buyer an individual who has been selected for his or her managerial potential and is capable of assuming the managerial functions of the department in the absence of the buyer.

associated office a resident buying office owned and operated by a group of stores that controls it.

assortment breadth characteristic of an inventory assortment offering a large number of different categories or classifications but not a large stock of any one style.

assortment depth characteristic of an inventory assortment offering limited versions of proved popular styles.

auction a type of nonmerchant buying whereby goods are placed on display and sold quickly to the highest bidder.

automatic open-to-buy a plan whereby a predetermined portion of funds is allotted to the central buyer after the coming months' purchases have been planned, with the balance allotted to the store manager.

balanced assortment an inventory assortment using both assortment breadth and depth.

billing record a term used synonymously with *purchase journal.*

book method of inventory the record of stock that should be on hand in view of what has been purchased and what has been sold. The record of what should be left is called the *closing book inventory.*

bottom-up planning planning for a specific department, whether it be located in one store or in many selling units.

boutique a French word that means "shop"; usually used for a women's fashionable specialty shop or department.

broker nonmerchant middleman whose primary function is to bring buyers and sellers together.

business objective the goals toward which the management activities of the business establishment are directed.

business policies guidelines providing management with a frame of reference for decision making that is consistent with planned objectives.

buying the purchase of consumer goods in relatively large or wholesale quantities for subsequent resale in smaller (retail) lots to the ultimate consumer.

buying committee   a three- to eight-person committee that acts in behalf of a single buyer and assists in decision-making policies regarding the procurement of specific merchandise categories.

capital budget   a plan for the investment of assets that will last longer than a year. It contains a list of future investment projects, with a justification for each proposal listed next to each item on the list.

cash budget   an estimate of the retail business' cash receipts and cash disbursements for a specified period of time.

cash discount   a reduction in list price is allowed by the vendor for prompt payment. The common practice is to allow the retail buyer 10 days from the invoice date.

cash on delivery (COD) dating   cash on delivery terms state that merchandise may be sold with the agreement that cash will be paid when the merchandise is delivered.

central buying   the centralization of all buying activities from a central headquarters that is located in the market center and in which the authority and responsibility for the selection and purchase of merchandise is limited to buyers of particular merchandise categories.

central merchandise plan   a form of central buying whereby the central buying authority assumes complete responsibility for the merchandise plan, for the buying of the assortment of goods, pricing, warehousing, and distribution to the many store units.

chain discount   a term used synonymously with *series discount.*

chain store   an organization with two or more centrally owned and managed outlets that operate on the same plane of distribution and handle same or similar lines of merchandise.

chain-owned office   a term used synonymously with *syndicated office.*

classic styles   those styles that remain in good taste over a long period of time.

classification   the subdividing by the buyer of each general line of merchandise into subdivisions.

classification control   refers to the use of dollar control based upon classifications of related types of merchandise within individual departments.

classification merchandising   a term used synonymously with *classification control.*

combination retail advertising   a method whereby institutional promotional approaches are blended together in the same advertising.

commissionaire   the title given to the individual who represents a foreign resident buying office under foreign management

commission men   nonmerchant middlemen who handle merchandise by displaying the goods for resale in a central marketplace.

commission office   this type of independent office receives its remuneration directly from the manufacturer or vendor it represents and is found primarily in the fashion apparel trade

comparison shopping bureau   a special bureau whose objective is to shop competing stores and determine if the competition is selling the same merchandise at the same price and quality or merchandise of inferior quality at a lower price.

consignment   merchandise sold on consignment does not become the property of the buyer but instead remains the property of the seller.

consumer buying behavior   a decision-making process whereby individuals or groups of people react in a particular manner to various situations involving the planning and purchasing of goods and/or services.

contest   a competition offering expensive prizes; usually requires that the consumer presents evidence of purchase to qualify.

control standards   represent a business firm's objectives and goals.

convenience goods those goods consumers expect to have readily available at a convenient location.

copy constitutes the language of the ad.

cost method of inventory goods are recorded at cost price, and the ending inventory values are determined by actually counting the merchandise in stock and recording values at cost prices.

cost of goods sold amount of money paid for merchandise sold during a particular period covered by the profit-and-loss statement.

coupon an award granted by the manufacturer or vendor for purchasing his product. May be used to purchase an item at a lower price.

dating the length of time the seller will extend credit to the store buyer.

deal a temporary special retail price offered to store customers.

department store large retailing institutions that carry a wide variety of merchandise lines with a reasonably good selection within each line.

department-store buying a term used synonymously with *local buying.*

departmental control refers to the use of dollar control on a departmental basis.

departmentalized specialty store a departmentalized retail store that concentrates its merchandise offerings in one broad category such as fashion apparel or home furnishings.

departmentalizing organizing different activities and functions into departments or compartments, with individuals assigned to each department to see that the various activities and functions are carried out.

detail the design lines that are held within a silhouette.

discount any reduction in the list or quoted price given to the retailer by the merchandise resource.

discount department store a departmentalized retail store that offers hard goods and major appliances along with fashion apparel and soft goods, but at discount or cut-rate prices.

disposable personal income (DPI) the income persons have available for saving or spending, and the most useful measure of income for retailers. Disposable personal income may be determined by subtracting personal taxes from personal income.

diversifications allows retailers to become active in businesses outside their particular trade.

dollar control the amount of dollars at retail prices that is invested in the merchandise inventory.

economic buying motive a term used synonymously with *rational buying motive.*

emergency goods goods purchased by consumers when a severe need arises.

emotional buying motive involves little logical thought. Such buying decisions come from feelings rather than from thinking or rationalizing.

employee discount a reduction from the retail price granted to store employees.

end of month (EOM) end of month states that the time for payment is calculated from the end of the month in which the invoice is dated and the merchandise shipped, and not from the invoice date.

extra dating the buyer is given a specified number of extra days in which to pay the bill and to earn the discount.

fad a minor fashion that has been adopted by a group of people for a short period of time. A fad is usually taken up with exaggerated zeal and quickly abandoned.

fashion a distinctive method of expression that has been accepted and adopted by a number of people at a given time in a particular consumer market.

fashion coordinator an individual who is responsible for promoting the sale of fashion merchandise throughout the entire store.

fashion cycle fashion goes through a series of six stages to complete a life cycle. The stages are: rise, acceptance or rejection, consumer popularization, mass-production, decline in popularity, and abandonment of the fashion.

fashion department a department that sells feminine outer apparel and accessories.

fashion goods new merchandise that appeals to consumers for a short period of time and has a relatively short life cycle.

fashion trend the direction in which a style or fashion is moving.

first-in-first-out method (FIFO) under the FIFO method of inventory evaluation, larger profits result during periods of rising prices because higher values are placed on ending inventories than on the merchandise on hand at the beginning of the year.

fixed-fee office a term used synonymously with *salaried office.*

floor plan the vendor turns an assortment of merchandise over to the store buyer, who in return signs a trust receipt. The title will remain with the vendor, and the store buyer agrees to make payment as he makes sales.

free on board (FOB) destination an agreement in which the seller is to pay all transportation costs and is to own the merchandise until it arrives at the retail store.

free on board (FOB) destination, charges reversed the seller will own the goods until they get into the retail store; however, the buyer agrees to pay the transportation charges.

free on board (FOB) destination, freight prepaid goods are to become the possession of the buyer as soon as they are shipped; however, the seller will pay freight charges.

free on board (FOB) factory an agreement that the buyer will pay all transportation costs and will own the goods from the moment they are shipped.

free on board (FOB) shipping point an agreement that the seller pays any crating necessary to the place at which the goods are to be turned over to a transportation company.

functional departmentalization activities of a similar nature are grouped together in the same department.

general-merchandise chain offers merchandise in the soft goods and fashion apparel lines, as well as in the hard goods or staple goods area.

geographical departmentalization activities are departmentalized on a territorial or geographical basis.

good taste implies a knowledge of the proper use of materials, of design, and of color.

gross margin the amount of profit before operating costs are deducted.

gross national product (GNP) represents the total output of goods and services produced in a year.

group buying a method of buying in which a number of stores participate to secure a better price, ensure high standards of quality, and obtain goods more readily.

hand-to-mouth buying the practice of limiting orders to immediate needs and ordering goods for immediate delivery rather than well in advance.

haute couture refers to an expensive original style created by a French fashion designer or manufacturer in limited editions for a group of people considered leaders of fashion.

headline the line of an advertisement that must attract the attention of the public, arouse interest, and lead the reader into reading the entire ad.

heterogeneous staples a group of staple goods that are alike but are not identical.

high fashion high-priced fashion goods, usually created by a famous designer in limited editions and bought by an elite group of consumers who are the first to accept the new style.

homogeneous staples   a group of staple goods that are identical, that is, they are all of the same size, color, fabric, and style.

illustration   an illustration or picture will attract attention to the whole advertisement and develop the reader's interest in the product.

impulse goods   goods purchased by consumers on impulse, that is, with little logical thought.

income   is measured in money and is derived from producing and selling goods or services in the marketplace.

income statement   a term used synonymously with *profit-and-loss statement.*

independent buying office   a privately owned and operated resident buying office that continuously seeks stores as clients.

initial markup   also called the *mark-on* or *original markup,* this is the difference between the cost price and the retail price of goods.

institutional advertising   indirect-action advertising whose primary objectives are to create good will for the store, build confidence in its merchandise and services, and establish customer loyalty.

irregular   an item that contains an imperfection or repair not obviously visible to the naked eye.

job lot   an assortment of merchandise the vendor has been unable to sell at regular prices and is now offering at a reduced price per item.

journal   a term used synonymously with *trade paper.*

landed cost   actual cost of the goods to the buyer and may include charges (aside from the quoted price), such as delivery charge, insurance charges, packing charges, storage expenses, commissions, and customs duties.

last-in-first-out method (LIFO)   the LIFO method assumes that those goods purchased recently are sold first.

layout   the arrangement of the ad.

leader pricing   the offering of a well-known brand of merchandise at a special low price.

legal contract   an order that has been properly filled out, signed, and accepted by the vendor.

life cycle   a series of stages of marital status and child raising through which most people move in the course of their lives.

limited-function wholesalers   also called "cash-and-carry" wholesalers. Merchant middlemen who limit themselves to smaller stock of fast-moving items and offer no credit or delivery service, thus reducing the cost of wholesaling.

loading the invoice   a practice whereby the amount of the retailer's invoice is increased (loaded) to permit a larger cash discount than is normally available at the supplier's going rate.

local buying   a method of buying that is accomplished by a retail specialist who works out of the main store and procures the necessary merchandise for the main store and its various branches and twigs.

loss leader   occurs when a well-known brand of merchandise is offered at a price below the buyer's cost.

maintained markup   the difference betweem the cost price and the final retail price.

manufacturer   an individual or firm who engages in the assembling or "putting together" of goods for use by the ultimate consumer.

manufacturers' agents   nonmerchant middlemen who take over part of their client's sales activities and have less authority over prices and terms of sale.

manufacturers' representatives   a term used synonymously with *manufacturers' agents.*

markdown   a reduction in price from the original retail price.

markdown percent   the difference between the net dollar markdown and original retail price divided by net sales.

marketing   the performance of business activities that direct the flow of goods and services from producer to consumer or user. Marketing may also be defined as human activity directed at satisfying needs and wants through exchange processes.

marketing channel of distribution   the sequence of marketing specialists or activities involved in bringing a product from the producer to the ultimate consumer.

mark-on   a term used synonymously with *initial markup.*

markup   the difference between the cost price and the retail price of an item.

markup percent   the difference between the retail price and the cost price divided by the retail price.

mass fashion   a style or design that is mass-produced at a moderate price and is widely accepted by the majority of consumers.

membership group   a composition of people that the individual looks to when formulating concepts, beliefs, opinions, and attitudes. Reference groups may be organized according to age, sex, religion, ethnic membership, occupation, income, life-style, or likes and dislikes.

merchandise broker   a term used synonymously with *commission office.*

merchandise budget   a budget planned by the buyer (local or central) along with other store executives. It is a plan that forecasts specific merchandising activities for a department or store for a specified period of time.

merchandise control   the maintenance of a stock of merchandise that is adjusted to the needs of consumers and prospective consumers.

merchandise inventory   merchandise that is available for sale to the ultimate consumer.

merchandise manager   the individual usually found at the head of the merchandising division.

merchandise overage   occurs when the physical inventory is more than the book inventory.

merchandise quality   the best or finest material available, or superior to that of lesser quality or standards.

merchandise scrambling   the overlapping of one or more lines of different types of merchandise in a given type of retail store.

merchandise shortage   occurs when the physical inventory is smaller than the book inventory.

merchandising   the planning and supervision involved in marketing a particular merchandise or service at the places, times, and prices, and in the quantities that will best serve to realize the marketing objectives of the business.

merchant middlemen   wholesalers who take title or assume ownership by taking possession of goods they purchase for resale.

merger   occurs between similar types of retailers. By merging, retailers attempt to maximize their resources thereby gaining a competitive advantage.

middlemen   individuals or organizations who operate between producers and industrial or ultimate consumers.

model stock   the desired assortment of stock broken down according to predictable factors such as classification, price, material, color, and size, based on consumer demand.

national income (NI)   the sum of the total amount earned by employees, proprietors' income, corporate profits, rental income, and net interest for a given year.

negotiation process   involves the mutual discussion of, and agreement between the retail buyer and the merchandise resources to, terms of various business transactions.

net profit   may be determined by deducting operating expenses from gross margin.

net sales the difference between gross sales (all the sales that were made) and customer adjustments or returns.

never-out goods a term used synonymously with *staple goods.*

new item an item that introduces certain new and different characteristics not yet available in merchandise of a similar type.

nonmerchant middlemen middlemen who do not take title or assume ownership by taking possession of goods they purchase for resale.

nonpersonal promotional aids those services that will directly influence the buying behavior of the consumer; includes dealer's helps and consumer inducements.

nonpersonal selling a method of communicating with customers indirectly.

nonstore retailing a retailing transaction that may occur without the customer's actually visiting the store.

odd pricing a psychological method of pricing. Instead of pricing an item at $1.00, the price is set at 99¢.

one-price policy the same price is charged to all consumers who purchase merchandise in the same quantities under similar circumstances.

one-stop concept boasts of providing all the merchandise needed under one roof.

on memorandum a term used in connection with a consignment sale or a sale with the return privilege.

operating expenses these may be classified as *direct expenses* (those paid out directly for the benefit of the department) and *indirect expenses* (those that serve the whole store).

operating profit that part of the gross margin that remains after operating expenses have been deducted.

operating statement a term used synonymously with *profit-and-loss statement.*

operations budget a forecast of expected sales along with expected costs for a specified time period.

original markup a term used synonymously with *initial markup.*

patronage motives may be emotional or rational; explain why a consumer purchases products or services from one retail store rather than another.

periodic inventory system a method of inventory that derives sales from inventory and purchase data by adding opening inventory and purchases and subtracting the sum of the closing inventory and markdowns, periodically or at certain intervals.

perpetual inventory system a system where sales information is derived from sales and purchase records that record merchandise on hand in view of what has been received and what has been sold at regular intervals such as every day, week, or month.

personal income (PI) may be calculated by first subtracting from national income the undistributed corporate profits, taxes on profits, and social security taxes, then adding all transfer payments (payments unrelated to current production, such as Social Security benefits and pensions).

personal promotional aids those services that will directly affect the selling activity of the buyer; include vendor's selling aids and promotional allowances.

personal selling includes wholesale selling or contact selling, since the seller usually contacts the customer, and retail selling, where the customer usually approaches the retail store.

physical inventory the actual counting and recording of the merchandise or stock on hand at a specified time, together with the cost or retail price of each item.

physical inventory system a figure for net sales is obtained by adding the former physical inventory to the purchases received from vendors and subtracting the ending physical inventory.

postdating a term used synonymously with *advanced dating.*

premium an article of value or "gift" that can be obtained by the consumer for a nominal price after the consumer purchases the advertised item.

prestige pricing a high-price policy is followed for particular kinds of merchandise that appeal to the prestige- or status-minded consumer.

price agreement plan a form of central buying whereby a central buyer will work with vendors and manufacturers and agree on the retail price, color, size, style, and assortment of staple types of merchandise as well as on the terms of shipping.

price-line control refers to the use of dollar control based upon a single retail price.

price lining method the buyer does not attempt to price merchandise at all possible prices but predetermines the retail price at which an assortment of merchandise will be carried.

price range the spread of price line from the lowest to the highest price carried, for example, $5 to $25.

price zone a series of price lines that are likely to appeal to one group of customers.

private-label buying (or specification buying) a request by a store's merchandising team for minor changes in a product that has already been produced, or it may include specifications for production from raw materials to final package.

private resident buying office some large retail organizations maintain their own private buying offices in major market centers such as New York City.

procedures the necessary steps that must be followed to implement a given policy. A *rule* is a statement that must be obeyed; a *guide* is a statement that recommends an action be taken and is not necessarily mandatory.

product line a broad category of products having reasonably similar characteristics and similar end uses.

product-line departmentalization organizing a business enterprise according to the various types and kinds of merchandise that it sells.

product mix all the products and services offered for sale.

profit-and-loss statement a summary of the transactions conducted by a business during a specific period of time such as one month, six months, or a year, which shows the relationship that has prevailed for the period among amount of sales, cost of goods sold, and expenses.

promotional advertising direct-action advertising, whereby the primary objective is to bring customers into the store to purchase specific items of merchandise.

proximo a term used synonymously for end of month (EOM).

publicity communication to the public about goods or services in a nonpersonal way both outside and within the retail establishment.

purchase journal a record that contains invoices providing information on department transfers, vendor returns, short shipments, damages, lost merchandise, and other claims.

purchasing agent the title given to the individual who represents a foreign resident buying office under United States management.

quantity discount a reduction from price given to buyers purchasing in unusually large quantities.

rack jobbers middlemen who are wholesalers of nonfood items and who arrange with independent grocers and chain supermarkets to stock and maintain an assortment of goods on a rack in a particular location in each store.

rational buying motive involves ability to reason or learn and to make the most effective use of limited resources.

receipt of goods (ROG) means that the date of payment is based on the date the goods are received by the store rather than the date of shipment or invoice date.

reference group a term used synonymously with *membership group.*

regular dating the length of time the vendor will extend credit, calculated from the date of the invoice.

resident buyer a buying specialist who works in the capacity of advisor or assistant to those stores that the resident buying office represents and who is responsible for all phases of merchandising and promotion.

resident buying office an outside agency whose primary responsibility and specialization is coverage of the various trade markets it represents. (See *resident buyer.*)

retail buyer the key individual within the retail institution; responsible for providing merchandise that will meet the needs of the consumers.

retail consumer an individual who attempts to satisfy physical and psychological needs and wants through the use of goods and services.

retailer a merchant whose primary business is selling goods or services directly to the ultimate consumer.

retailing the summation of all activities involved in the sale of goods or services directly to the ultimate consumer for personal, nonbusiness use.

retail institution (or store) the place where the actual retailing activity or exchange takes place.

retail method of inventory a combination of the cost method of inventory with the book method of inventory at retail prices.

retail price the first price at retail, which is placed on merchandise by the retailer regardless of later sales or other special event prices; the cost price of an item plus the markup.

retail reduction the allowance for the difference between the original retail value of merchandise and the actual final sales value of the merchandise; consists of three major factors; merchandise shortages and overages, employee discounts and discounts for other special groups, and markdowns.

salaried office the salaried office is paid a fixed fee directly from the client store it represents.

sales promotion any promotional activity other than advertising, publicity, and personal selling that attracts the public to a retail store, stimulates purchasing, and makes a profit for the store.

seasonal discount a reduction in list price granted to the retail buyer for purchasing goods during the off-season.

seasonal goods merchandise that is in demand only at certain times of the year or for particular seasons of the year.

second an item that contains obvious damage or repair.

selling agents nonmerchant middlemen who are independent businessmen and take over the entire sales function for their clients by offering advice on styling, extending financial aid, and making collections.

series discount a series of discounts granted by the merchandise resource to the retail buyer.

service wholesalers also called "regular" wholesalers. They assemble merchandise in relatively large quantities and sell it to retailers in substantially smaller quantities.

shopping goods those products for which a consumer will accept no substitute and about which the consumer does not have a thorough product knowledge.

signature plate the emblem, trademark, symbol, or distinctive print that immediately identifies the store to the public.

silhouette the overall shape or contour of a costume; the basic ingredient, which changes slightly with each new season.

social classes groups of people who share the same income bracket and the same goals and attitudes toward life.

special merchandise   goods offered not for their quality appeal but instead for their price appeal.

specialty goods   products for which the consumer will usually accept only a well-known brand and of which the consumer has full knowledge.

specialty store   a retail store that concentrates its merchandise offerings in one broad category, such as fashion apparel or home furnishings.

specification buying (or private label buying)   a request by a store's merchandising team for minor changes in a product that has already been produced or it may include specifications for production from raw materials to final package.

speculative buying   the decision to purchase goods based on an expected rise or fall in price level.

staple goods   goods that should always be in stock, since they are demanded by consumers year in and year out.

store-owned office   a resident buying office that is owned by the store or stores it represents and is organized to provide buying services for those stores.

style   the characteristic that makes one fashion different from another.

style-out technique   a method used to detect trends in customer preferences.

syndicated office   a syndicated resident buying office; differs from the associated buying office in that it is a division of a corporation that owns a chain of department stores.

tickler file   a system that serves as a reminder and is arranged to bring items to timely attention.

top-down planning   the planning of general, overall sales activity based on economic trends, environmental conditions, and changes in store policies.

trade discount   a reduction in price granted to a certain category or trade of customer to cover the costs of a particular trading function.

trade paper   a publication containing information that is of importance and interest to people dealing with a specific trade or line.

trading stamps   stamps given to a consumer with each purchase, which can eventually be exchanged for merchandise.

traditional department store   a retail store that employes 25 or more people and is engaged in selling merchandise in the areas of home furnishings, fashion apparel, and linens and dry goods.

twig store   representative of one line of merchandise or one price line carried by a main store. It is usually found in or near a major shopping center.

unit control   an organized method of recording the individual units or pieces of merchandise found in the inventory.

varying-price policy   policy whereby a consumer seeking to purchase merchandise at a lower price will bargain with the retailer until an agreement has been reached.

warehouse and requisition plan   a form of central buying whereby the central buyer arranges for the initial stock assortment and has it shipped to the individual stores.

wholesale price   the price paid for goods purchased from merchandise resources, for example, vendors, manufacturers, or suppliers.

wholesalers   a term used synonymously with *middlemen.*

Appendix B

MERCHANDISE MATHEMATICAL FORMULAS
USED BY BUYING SPECIALISTS AND THEIR ASSISTANTS

sales = opening inventory + purchases − closing inventory and markdowns

actual or net sales = derived sales ÷ (100% + shortage percentage)

indirect expenses = department expenses − cost of goods sold − direct expenses

net sales = gross sales − customer adjustments and returns

cost of goods sold = opening inventory + purchase costs + cost of shipping

gross cost of goods sold = opening inventory + purchase costs + shipping costs − closing inventory (cost value)

net cost of goods sold = opening inventory + purchase costs + shipping costs
= cost of goods sold − closing inventory
= gross cost of goods sold − cash discounts

gross margin = net sales − net cost of goods sold

net profit = gross margin − operating expenses

beginning of the month (BOM) stock = planned sales for the month + (average stock at retail − average monthly sales)

the percentage − variation (or deviation) method:

beginning of the month (BOM) stock = average $\dfrac{\text{yearly sales}}{\text{turnover}}$

$\times \left[\left(1 + \frac{1}{2}\, \dfrac{\text{sales for month}}{\text{average monthly sales}} \right) \right].$

weeks supply method = 52 weeks ÷ desired stock turn

stock-sales ratio method:

beginning of the month (BOM) stock = planned monthly sales volume × planned BOM stock-sales ratio

stock-sales ratio = $\dfrac{\text{beginning stock}}{\text{sales}}$

stock turn, retail basis = $\dfrac{\text{net sales}}{\text{average stock at retail price}}$

stock turn, cost basis = $\dfrac{\text{cost of goods sold}}{\text{average cost of stock}}$

stock turn, unit basis = $\dfrac{\text{number of units sold}}{\text{average number of units in stock}}$

average inventory = $\dfrac{\text{sum of all inventories in a period}}{\text{number of inventories}}$

merchandise shortage = book inventory − physical inventory

merchandise overage = physical inventory − book inventory

employee discount percent = $\dfrac{\text{employee discounts for month}}{\text{net sales}}$

markdown = original retail price − markdown price

markdown percent $= \dfrac{\text{net dollar markdown}}{\text{net sales}}$

markup percent at retail $= \dfrac{\text{markup}}{\text{retail price}}$

maintained markup $=$ cost price $-$ final retail price

net profit $=$ gross margin $-$ total operating expenses

planned purchases $=$ planned sales $+$ planned reductions
                 $+$ planned end of month stock
                $=$ total need for month
                $-$ beginning-of-the-month (BOM) stock

open-to-buy $=$ planned purchases $-$ merchandise on order

maximum (total amount of staple goods to be on order and on hand) $=$ (reorder period $+$ delivery period) rate of sales $+$ reserve

OR

maximum $=$ (lead time) rate of sales $+$ reserve

unit open-to-buy $=$ maximum $-$ (on-hand orders $+$ outstanding orders)

99–100% protection against reserve depletion:
     reserve $= 2.3 \times \sqrt{\text{(lead time)}}$ sales

when 95% protection is <u>adequate to</u> maintain a maximum reserve level:
     reserve $= 1.6 \times \sqrt{\text{(lead time)}}$ sales

maximum or total amount of fashion goods and home furnishings to be on order and on hand:
     maximum $=$ reorder period $+$ delivery period $\times$ rate of sales $+$ reserve

OR

     maximum $=$ lead time $\times$ rate of sales $+$ reserve

trade discount $=$ list price per unit $\times$ suggested retail price $-$ trade discount

quantity discount $=$ wholesale price $-$ quantity discount

seasonal discount $=$ list price $-$ seasonal discount

cash discount $=$ amount of invoice $-$ terms

series discount $=$ list price $-$ trade discount $-$ extra trade discount $-$ quantity discount

retail price $=$ cost price $+$ markup

markup $=$ retail price $-$ cost price

cost price $=$ retail price $-$ markup

markup percent $= \dfrac{\text{retail price} - \text{cost price}}{\text{retail price}}$

retail price $= \dfrac{\text{cost price}}{\text{cost percent (100\% } - \text{ markup \%)}}$

cost price $=$ (100% $-$ markup %) retail price

cost percent $= \dfrac{\text{cost price}}{\text{retail price}}$

Appendix C

SELECTED FIRMS SEEKING QUALIFIED PEOPLE FOR MERCHANDISING POSITIONS

Abraham & Straus
420 Fulton Street
Brooklyn, N.Y. 11201

Abrahams Dept. Store
P.O. Box 221–Laurel St.
Conway, S.C. 29526

Abrams Inc.
4740 No. Lincoln Ave.
Chicago, Ill. 60625

Albertson's
1623 Washington
Boise, Idaho 83726

Alexander's
Lexington Avenue at 59th Street
New York, N.Y. 10022

B. Altman & Co.
361 5th Avenue
New York, N.Y. 10016

Ames
2418 Main St.
Rocky Hill, Conn. 06067

Annes Dept. Store
4810 No. Milwaukee Ave.
Chicago, Ill. 60630

Elizabeth Arden Inc.
691 Fifth Ave.
New York, N.Y. 10022

Associate Merchandising Corp.
1440 Broadway
New York, N.Y. 10018

Atlantic Dept. Stores
111 8th Ave.
New York, N.Y. 10011

Babbitt Bros. Trading Co.
East Aspen and North San Francisco
 Streets
Flagstaff, Ariz. 86001

Baskin Clothing Co.
835 No. Michigan Ave.
Chicago, Ill. 60605

Belk-Lindsey
3950 Britton Plaza
Tampa, Fla. 33611

Henri Bendel, Inc.
10 West 57th St.
New York, N.Y. 10019

Bon Marche Stores, Inc.
Seattle, Wash. 98101

Bonwit Teller
721 5th Ave.
New York, N.Y. 10022

Brittany Ltd.
29 South LaSalle St.
Chicago, Ill. 60603

Broadway Department Stores
3880 North Mission Road
Los Angeles, Calif. 90031

Lane Bryant, Inc.
1501 Broadway
New York, N.Y. 10036

Bullock's
Seventh and Hill Sts.
Los Angeles, Calif. 90055

Capwell's
20th and Broadway
Oakland, Calif. 94612

Carson Pirie Scott & Co.
1 South State Street
Chicago, Ill. 60603

Carter, Hawley Hale Stores
550 South Flower St.
Los Angeles, Calif. 90071

Cherry & Webb Co.
789 Waterman Ave.
East Providence, R.I. 02914

City Stores
500 5th Ave.
New York, N.Y. 10036

S. Cohen & Co.
245–55 Locust St.
Columbia, Pa. 17512

M. M. Cohn
510 Main St.
Little Rock, Ark. 72203

Colonial Stores
2251 North Sylvan Road
Atlanta, Ga. 30344

Cook United
16501 Rockside Road
Maple Heights, Ohio 44137

Davison's Co.
180 Peachtree Street, Northwest
Atlanta, Ga. 30303

Dayton Hudson Corp.
777 Nicollet Mall
Minneapolis, Minn. 55402

Deb Shops
1101 Hawthorne Lane
Charlotte, N.C. 28205

De Mar's Inc.
6101 West Cermak Rd.
Cicero, Ill. 60650

Denver Dry Goods Co.
16th and California Streets
Denver, Colo. 80218

Emporium
835 Market Street
San Francisco, Calif. 90031

Samuel Evans & Co.
107 Main St.
Berlin, N.H. 03570

Marshall Field's
111 No. State St.
Chicago, Ill. 60690

Filene's
426 Washington St.
Boston, Mass. 02101

Fine's
Box 8819
15 West Broughton St.
Savannah, Ga. 31402

L. Fish Furniture
4242 West 42nd Pl.
Chicago, Ill. 60632

Foley's
1110 Main Street
Houston, Tex. 77001

G. Fox & Co.
960 Main Street
Hartford, Conn. 06115

Fries & Schuele Co.
W. 25th St. at Lorain Ave.
Cleveland, Ohio 44113

Gatley's
36 S. State Street
Chicago, Ill. 60603

Garfunckel's
1629 K Street, N.W.
Washington, D.C. 20004

Genesco
1117th Avenue, North
Nashville, Tenn. 37202

Giant Good, Inc.
6900 Sheriff Road
Landover, Md. 20013

Gimbel's New York
33rd and Broadway
New York, N.Y. 10001

Glamour Shops Inc.
404 So. Main St.
Burlington, N.C. 27215

Garden Merchantile Co.
P.O. Box 831
Durango, Colo. 81301

Grand Union
100 Broadway
Elmwood Park, N.J. 07407

Great Atlantic and Pacific Tea Co.
2 Paragon Drive
Montvale, N.J. 07645

Haber & Co.
1226 F Street, N.W.
Washington, D.C. 20004

Hecht Co.
7th and F Street
Washington, D.C. 20004

Hess Apparel
205 West Main St.
Salisbury, Md. 21801

Higgin Botham Bros. & Co.
Comanche, Tex. 76442

Highbee
100 Public Square
Cleveland, Ohio 44113

J. F. Hink & Son
2224 Shattuck Avenue
Berkeley, Calif. 95704

The Home Store of Roseland
11800–16 So. Michigan
Chicago, Ill. 60628

I. Magnin & Co.
Union Square
San Francisco, Calif. 94108

Georg Jensen, Inc.
601 Madison Ave.
New York, N.Y. 10022

Jewel Companies, Inc.
O'Hara Plaza
5725 East River Road
Chicago, Ill. 60631

Johnson Hill's Inc.
300 Third St.
Wausau, Wis. 54401

Jordan Marsh Co.
38 Chauncy Street
Boston, Mass. 02107

Just Pants Co.
1034 Bonaventure Dr.
Elk Grove Village, Ill. 60007

Karoll's
1408 S. Clinton St.
Chicago, Ill. 60607

K-Mart
7373 West Side Avenue
North Bergen, N.J. 07047

Kinney Shoe Corp., Apparel Div.
233 Broadway
New York, N.Y. 10007

Korby's Department Store
3400 E. Speedway
Tucson, Ariz. 85716

Kroger Co.
1014 Vine St.
Cincinnati, Ohio 45201

M. H. Lamston Inc.
212 Fifth Ave.
New York, N.Y. 10010

F. R. Lazurus & Co.
High & Town Streets
Columbus, Ohio 43216

Leath Furniture Co.
7111 No. Lincoln Ave.
Chicago, Ill. 60646

Lerner Shops
460 West 33rd Streets
New York, N.Y. 10001

Lord & Taylor
424 Fifth Avenue
New York, N.Y. 10018

Maas Brothers
P. O. Box 311
Tampa, Fla. 33601

R. H. Macy
New York, N.Y. 10001

Marlene's
1761 National Avenue
Hayward, Calif. 94545

McDonald's
McDonald's Plaza
2111 Enco Drive
Oak Brook, Ill. 60521

Merchantile Stores Co., Inc.
128 West 31st Street
New York, N. Y. 10001

Meystel's
1222 So. Wabash Ave.
Chicago, Ill. 60605

Morrisons Inc.
P.O. Box 2608
Mobile, Ala. 36625

G. C. Murphy Co.
531 Fifth Avenue
McKeesport, Pa. 15132

Myerson Stores, Inc.
P.O. Box 2429
Tuscon, Ariz. 85702

Nathan's Inc.
203–205 E. Lafayette St.
Jackson, Tenn. 38301

Neiman-Marcus
Main and Ervay Streets
Dallas, Tex. 75201

Nerland's Home Furnishings
Anchorage, Alaska 99501

Ohrbach's
5 West 34th Street
New York, N.Y. 10001

Dennis O'Shea, Inc.
Laconia Mall
Laconia, N.H. 03246

Palais Royal
Box 35167
726 Maryland Plaza Mall
Houston, Tex. 77035

C. D. Peacock, Inc.
101 So. State St.
Chicago, Ill. 60603

J. C. Penney Co.
1301 Avenue of the Americas
New York, N.Y. 10010

Pomeroy's Inc.
4th & Market Sts.
Harrisburg, Pa. 17105

D. M. Read, Inc.
1050 Broad Street
Bridgeport, Conn. 06602

Reiter's Inc.
2460 George St.
Chicago, Ill. 60618

Rich's
45 Broad Street
Atlanta, Ga. 30302

E. P. Roe Stores, Inc.
1220 W. 6th St.
Cleveland, Ohio 44113

Ruby's Apparel Shop
149 North York St.
Elmhurst, Ill. 60126

Roland's Inc.
111–117 W. Jefferson St.
Bloomington, Ill. 61701

Safeway Stores
4th and Jackson Streets
Oakland, Calif. 94660

Saks Fifth Avenue
611 Fifth Ave.
New York, N.Y. 10022

Sears Roebuck and Co.
Sears Tower
Chicago, Ill. 60684

Southland Corp.
2828 North Haskell Avenue
Dallas, Tex. 75204

Joseph Spiess Co.
35–52 Fountain Square Plaza
Elgin, Ill. 60120

Stern Brothers
Route 4—Bergen Mall
Paramus, N.J. 07652

Stone & Thomas
1030 Main St.
Wheeling, W.Va. 26003

Strawbridge & Clotheir
8th and Market Streets
Philadelphia, Pa. 19105

Super Stores, Inc.
P.O. Box 333
1310 Telegraph Road
Chicasaw, Ala. 36611

The Thornton Co.
Federal & Raleigh Sts.
Bluefield, W.Va. 24701

Thrifty Drug Stores Co., Inc.
5051 Rodeo Road
Los Angeles, Calif. 90016

The Trading Union, Inc.
P.O. Box 489
Petersburg, Alaska 99833

Ups 'N Down Stores
461 8th Avenue
New York, N.Y. 10001

Waldbaum's
Hemlock Street and Boulevard Avenue
Central Islip, N.Y. 11772

Walgreen
300 Wilmot Road
Deerfield, Ill. 60015

John Wanamaker
13th and Market Streets
Philadelphia, Pa. 19101

Ward's Dept. Stores
15 S. Main St.
Hanover, N.H. 03755

Winn-Dixie Stores, Inc.
Box B
Jacksonville, Fla. 32203

Woodward & Lothrop
11th and F Streets
Washington, D.C. 20013

F. W. Woolworth
233 Broadway
New York, N.Y. 10007

Young Department Store
1614 Broadway
Mattoon, Ill. 61938

Zayre
Speen Street
Framingham, Mass. 01701

Appendix D

SBA PUBLICATIONS

Free Management Assistance Publications

MAs (Management Aids) and **SMAs (Small Marketers Aids)** recommend methods and techniques for handling management problems and business operations. Usually **MAs** are aimed at manufacturing businesses and **SMAs** at retail and service businesses. Both, however, have information that is useful to owner-managers of any business.

SBBs (Small Business Bibliographies) list key reference sources for many business management topics. These sources include books, pamphlets, and trade associations' data.

MAs

170. The ABC's of Borrowing
178. Effective Industrial Advertising for Small Plants
186. Checklist for Developing a Training Program
187. Using Census Data in Small Plant Marketing
189. Should You Make or Buy Components?
190. Measuring Sales Force Performance
191. Delegating Work and Responsibility
192. Profile Your Customers to Expand Industrial Sales
193. What is the Best Selling Price?
195. Setting Pay for Your Management Jobs
197. Pointers on Preparing an Employee Handbook
200. Is the Independent Sales Agent for You?
201. Locating or Relocating Your Business
203. Are Your Products and Channels Producing Sales
205. Pointers on Using Temporary-Help Services
206. Keep Pointed Toward Profit
207. Pointers on Scheduling Production
208. Problems in Managing a Family-Owned Business

209. Preventing Employee Pilferage
212. The Equipment Replacement Decision
214. The Metric System and Small Business
216. Finding a New Product for Your Company
217. Reducing Air Pollution in Industry
218. Business Plan for Small Manufacturers
219. Solid Waste Management in Industry
220. Basic Budgets for Profit Planning
221. Business Plan for Small Construction Firms
222. Business Life Insurance
223. Incorporating a Small Business
224. Association Services for Small Business·
225. Management Checklist for a Family Business
226. Pricing for Small Manufacturers
229. Cash Flow in a Small Plant
230. Selling Products on Consignment
231. Selecting the Legal Structure for Your Business
232. Credit and Collections
233. Planning and Goal Setting for Small Business
234. Attacking Business Decision Problems With Breakeven Analysis

235. A Venture Capital Primer for Small Business
236. Tips on Getting More for Your Marketing Dollar
237. Market Overseas With U.S. Government Help
239. Techniques of Time Management
240. Introduction to Patents
241. Setting Up a Pay System
242. Fixing Production Mistakes
243. Setting Up A Quality Control System

244. Product Safety Checklist
245. Exhibiting at Trade Shows
246. Developing New Accounts
247. Negotiating International Sales Contracts
248. Can You Make Money with Your Ideas or Invention?
249. Should You Lease or Buy Equipment?
250. Can You Use a Minicomputer?
5.008. Managing Employee Benefits

SMAs

71. Checklist for Going Into Business
119. Preventing Retail Theft
123. Stock Control for Small Stores
126. Accounting Services for Small Service Firms
129. Reducing Shoplifting Losses
130. Anaylze Your Records to Reduce Cost
133. Can You Afford Delivery Service?
134. Preventing Burglary and Robbery Loss
135. Arbitration: Peace-Maker in Small Business
137. Outwitting Bad Check Passers
140. Profit By Your Wholesalers' Services
142. Steps in Meeting Your Tax Obligations
143. Factors in Considering a Shopping Center Location
144. Getting the Facts for Income Tax Reporting
146. Budgeting in a Small Service Firm
147. Sound Cash Management and Borrowing
148. Insurance Checklist for Small Business
149. Computers for Small Business— Service Bureau or Time Sharing?
150. Business Plan for Retailers
151. Preventing Embezzlement

152. Using a Traffic Study To Select a Retail Site
153. Business Plan for Small Service Firms
154. Using Census Data to Select a Store Site
155. Keeping Records in Small Business
156. Marketing Checklist for Small Retailers
157. Efficient Lighting for Small Stores
158. A Pricing Checklist for Small Retailers
159. Improving Personal Selling in Small Retail Stores
160. Advertising Guidelines for Small Retail Firms
161. Signs and Your Business
162. Staffing Your Store
163. Public Relations for Small Business
164. Plan Your Advertising Budget
165. Checklist for Public Watching
166. Simple Breakeven Analysis for Small Stores
167. Learning About Your Market
168. Store Location: "Little Things" Mean a Lot
169. Do You Know the Results of Your Advertising?
170. Thinking About Going into Business?

SBBS

1. Handicrafts
2. Home Businesses
3. Selling by Mail Order
9. Marketing Research Procedures
10. Retailing
12. Statistics and Maps for National Market Analysis
13. National Directories for Use in Marketing

15. Recordkeeping Systems—Small Store and Service Trade
18. Basic Library Reference Sources
20. Advertising—Retail Store
29. National Mailing-List Houses
31. Retail Credit and Collections
37. Buying for Retail Stores
55. Wholesaling
64. Photographic Dealers and Studios

___ 67. Manufacturers' Sales
       Representative
___ 72. Personnel Management
___ 75. Inventory Management
___ 79. Small Store Planning and Design
___ 80. Data Processing for Small
       Businesses

___ 85. Purchasing for Owners of Small
       Plants
___ 86. Training for Small Business
___ 87. Financial Management
___ 88. Manufacturing Management
___ 89. Marketing for Small Business
___ 90. New Product Development

To get copies of the listed publications, check the titles you want, fill in your name and address, and mail this order form to:

U.S. Small Business Administration
P.O. Box 15434
Fort Worth, Texas 76119

or call toll free 800-433-7212 (Texas only call 800-792-8901).

Notice: *Five* (5) copy limit per publication requested. Requests for *more than five* (5) copies of a publication must be sent to the SBA District Office nearest you. Please give the reason you need more than five (5) copies.

Name _____

(Please Print or Type)

Street _____

City/State/Zip _____

Appendix E

SELECTED MANUFACTURERS OF MEN'S, WOMEN'S, CHILDREN'S AND INFANTS' WEAR SEEKING QUALIFIED MERCHANDISING GRADUATES

I. APPEL CORPORATION
136 Madison Ave., 11th Flr.
New York, NY 10016
Tel.: 212-685-3900
Mfr. Robes, Gowns & Underwear

BARBIZON CORP.
475 Fifth Ave.
New York, NY 10017
Tel.: 212-684-5720
Sleepwear, Daywear, Loungewear,
   Childrenswear

BAYLY CORPORATION
5500 So. Valencia Way
Englewood, CO 80111
Mailing Address: P.O. Box 5148
Denver, CO 80217
Tel.: 303-773-3850
Mfr. & Mkt. Jeans & Sportwear

BOBBIE BROOKS, INCORPORATED
(Sub. of Pubco Corp.)
3830 Kelley Ave.
Cleveland, OH 44144
Tel.: 216-881-5300
Mfr. of Womens Coats & Outerwear

BON JOUR INTERNATIONAL LTD.
1411 Broadway
New York, NY 10018
Tel.: 212-398-1000
Garment Mfr.: Bon Jour Sportwear, Jeans,
   Pants, Activewear Shirts & Accessories

BRIDAL ORIGINALS, INC.
1700 St. Louis Rd.
Collinsville, IL 62234
Mailing Address: P.O. Box 749
Collinsville, IL 62234
Tel.: 618-345-4499
Bridal Gowns, Bridesmaids Dresses,
   Mother Of The Bride Dresses & Formals

CALVIN KLEIN INDUSTRIES, INC.
1400 Broadway
New York, NY 10018
Tel.: 212-575-0800
Calvin Klein Jeans

CATALINA
(Div. Kayser-Roth Corp.)
6040 Bandini Blvd.
Los Angeles, CA 90040
Tel.: 213-726-1262
Catalina Swimsuits & Sportswear

COLE OF CALIFORNIA
(Sub. of Kayser-Roth)
2615 Fruitland Ave.
Los Angeles, CA 90058
Tel.: 213-587-3111
Cole of California Swim Suits and
   Sportswear for Misses, Cole Swim Suits
   For Jrs.

COUNTRY MISS, INC.
(Sub. of Hartmarx)
1407 Broadway, 15th Floor
New York, NY 10018
Tel.: 212-921-1313
Women's Apparel: Coordinated Sportswear,
   Dresses, Separates, Suits, Coats

CUPID FOUNDATIONS, INC.
200 Madison Ave.
New York, NY 10016
Tel.: 212-686-6224
Ladies' Foundations

H. H. CUTLER COMPANY
120 Ionia Ave., S. W.
Grand Rapids, MI 49503
Mailing Address: P.O. Box 2488
Grand Rapids, MI 49501
Tel.: 616-459-9101
Infants & Children's Wearing Apparel

DAMON CREATIONS, INC.
16 E. 34th St.
New York, NY 10016
Tel.: 212-683-2465
Men's Shirts, Neckwear, Sportswear,
   Sweaters

DANSKIN, INC.
(Sub. of Esmark Apparel, Inc.)
111 W. 40th Ave.
New York, NY 10018

Tel.: 212-764-4630
Bras, Panties, Leotards, Tights, Hosiery, Childrens' Wear, Accessories

FLORIAN FASHIONS, INC.
4515 Superior
Cleveland, OH 44103
Tel.: 216-431-1800
Jerrie Lune Misses Dresses, Mynette Ladies' Half-Size Dresses & Kevin Stuart-Petites, Jessica Sportswear

FORMFIT ROGERS
(Div. of I. Appel Corporation)
136 Madison Ave.
New York, NY 10016
Tel.: 212-685-3900
Ladies' Intimate Apparel: Bras, Girdle, Foundationwear, Daywear, Leisurewear Loungewear

THE FOUKE CO.
8100 White Horse Rd.
Greenville, SC 29611
Tel.: 803-246-3210
Processors of Fur & Tanners of Exotic Leathers

GARAN, INCORPORATED
350 5th Ave.
New York, NY 10118
Tel.: 212-563-2000
Garanimals Color Related Sportswear for Infant, Toddlers, Boys & Girls; Men's, Boys & Girls Knitted & Woven Sport Shirts, Slacks & Jeans

GELFO MFG. CO., INC.
(Sub. of Athlone Industries, Inc.)
650 Cantiague Rd.
Jericho, NY 11753
Tel.: 516-333-9800
Swimwear

GLAMOURISE FOUNDATIONS, INC.
135 Madison Ave.
New York, NY 10016
Tel.: 212-684-5023
Glamorise Bras, Girdles & All in Ones

GODDESS BRA COMPANY
143 Albany St.
Cambridge, MA 02139
Tel.: 617-569-3000
Goddess Bras, Revelation Bras

GUESS, INC.
123 E. 35th St.
Los Angeles, CA 90011
Tel.: 213-235-7700
Mfr. Junior Outerwear

HANES PRINTABLES, INC.
(Oper. Unit of Hanes Group)
3334 Healy Dr.
P.O. Box 15901
Winston-Salem, NC 27103
Tel.: 919-744-2600
Mfr. Printable T-Shirts

HEALTH-TEX
1411 Broadway
New York, NY 10018
Tel.: 212-840-0333
Infant & Children's Wear, Swimwear, Boyswear

INDERA MILLS CO.
400 S. Marshall St.
Winston-Salem, NC 27102
Mailing Address: P.O. Box 3119
Winston-Salem, NC 27104
Tel.: 919-723-7311
Coldpruf Thermal Underwear, Snuggies, Vests: TopStyle Tops, Shirts

JANTZEN, INC.
(Sub. of VF Corp.)
411 N.E. 19th Ave.
Portland, OR 97232
Mailing Address: P.O. Box 3001
Portland, OR 97208
Tel.: 503-238-5000
Mfr. Misses & Jr's Spectator & Active Sportswear & Swimwear, Men's Sportswear, Swimwear & Sweaters

JONATHAN LOGAN
(Div. of United Merchants & Manufacturers, Inc.)
1407 Broadway
New York, NY 10018
Tel.: 212-930-3900
Junior & Missy Dresses, Sportswear

JONES APPAREL GROUP, INC.
One Connecticut Ave.
Norwich, CT 06360
Tel.: 203-889-3801
Shorts, Suits, Pants, Skirts, Coats

R & M KAUFMANN
(Div. of Russ Togs, Inc.)
1601 E. Mountain St.
Aurora, IL 60507
Tel.: 312-898-6700
Vicky Vaughn Junior Dresses, Toni Todd Dresses, Toni Petite Dresses, Lady Laura Dresses, Sprouts, Possibilities Sportswear

SAM LANDORF & CO., INC.
1333 Broadway
New York, NY 10018

Tel.: 212-244-3077
Children's Dresses

LESLIE FAY COMPANIES
1400 Broadway
New York, NY 10018
Tel.: 212-221-4000
Mfr. Ladies' & Men's Apparel

THE MI DESIGNER GROUP
(Div. of Manhattan Industries, Inc.)
1407 Broadway
New York, NY 10018
Tel.: 212-221-1212
Mfr. of Misses & Women's Blouses, Tops,
    Skirts, Bottoms & Designer Sportswear

MALOUF COMPANY, INC.
944 S. Lamar
Dallas, TX 75202
Tel.: 214-565-0126
Mfr. Women's Dresses, Sportswear,
    Blouses & Shirts

MARISA CHRISTINA INC.
1410 Broadway
New York, NY 10018
Tel.: 212-221-5770
Importers of Ladies Sweaters; Marisa
    Christina & Sonia Rykiel Knits

MARY JANE CO.
5510 Cleon Ave.
North Hollywood, CA 91609
Mailing Address: P.O. Box 736
No. Hollywood, CA 91609
Tel: 213-877-7166
Mary Jane; Underfashions & Sleepwear

PALM BEACH INC., WOMEN'S WEAR
    GROUP
c/o Evan Picone
1411 Broadway
New York, NY 10018
Tel.: 212-536-9500
Women's Sportswear, Dresses, Coats, Suits
    & Pantyhose

PANDORA SPORTSWEAR, INC.
(Sub. of Wingspread Corp.)
P.O. Box 5240
Manchester, NH 03108
Tel.: 603-668-4800
Junior & Missy Sweaters & Sportswear

PAT FASHIONS INDUSTRIES, INC.
1370 Broadway
New York, NY 10018
Tel.: 212-695-3510
Importers & Mfrs. of Sportwear

PRISCILLA OF BOSTON, INC.
40 Cambridge
Charlestown, MA 02129
Tel.: 617-242-2677
Priscilla of Boston Wedding Gowns,
    Bridesmaid Dresses, Teeny by Priscilla

ABE SCHRADER CORP.
530 Seventh Ave.
New York, NY 10018
Tel.: 212-840-7733
Designs, Mfrs. & Sells Ladies Ready-To-
    Wear; Abe Schrader, Schrader Sport
    Petite, Schrader Sport Dresses &
    Separates, Schrader Custom Casuals

SEATTLE PACIFIC INDUSTRIES, INC.
1844 Westlake Ave. North
Seattle, WA 98109
Mailing Address: P.O. Box 58710
Seattle, WA 98188
Tel.: 206-282-8889
Mfr., Designer & Wholesaler of Clothing

SEIBLE & STERN CORP.
112 W. 34th St.
New York, NY 10001
Tel.: 212-563-0326
Children's Dresses

SERGIO VALENTE APPAREL, INC.
498 7th Ave.
New York, NY 10018
Tel.: 212-239-4440
Jeans & Sportswear for Men, Women,
    Children

VF CORPORATION
1047 N. Park Rd.
Wyomissing, PA 19610
Mailing Address: P. O. Box 54
Reading, PA 19603
Tel.: 215-378-1151
Apparel Mfg. Cos.

WHITE STAG MANUFACTURING CO.
(Sub. of Warnaco Inc.)
5100 S.E. Harney Dr.
Portland, OR 97206
Tel.: 503-777-1711
White Stag Sportswear for Women; Ski
    Wear for Men & Boys, Women & Girls;
    Warm-Ups For Men & Women

JACK WINTER, INC.
8100 N. Teutonia Ave.
Milwaukee, WI 53209
Tel.: 414-357-4840
Missy Sportswear

Index